COMMEMORATING IRELAND

COMMEMORATING IRELAND

History, Politics, Culture

Editor

Eberhard Bort

University of Edinburgh

IRISH ACADEMIC PRESS
DUBLIN • PORTLAND, OR

First published in 2004 by
IRISH ACADEMIC PRESS
44 Northumberland Road, Dublin 4, Ireland

and in the United States of America by
IRISH ACADEMIC PRESS
c/o ISBS, 920 NE 58th Avenue, Suite 300
Portland, OR 97213-3786

Website: www.iap.ie

British Library Cataloguing in Publication Data

A catalogue record of this book is
available from the British Library.

ISBN 0-7165-2768-5 (cloth)
0-7165-2796-0

Library of Congress Cataloging-in-Publication Data

A catalog record of this book is
available from the Library of Congress.

Typeset in 11/12.5pt Times New Roman by Irish Academic Press
Printed by Beta Print Ltd. Dublin

Contents

II

Illustrations

Acknowledgements

Thanks are due to the University of Edinburgh for hosting the Commemorating Ireland conference. The conference and this publication were made possible by the generous financial support of the Justin Arbuthnott Fund for Anglo-Irish Understanding, itself an act of commemoration (Justin Arbuthnott was a young student at Edinburgh University when he drowned in 1989 off the Donegal coast. The fund was instigated by his family as a memorial to him, providing support for research and academic contacts with the aim of improving relations between Scotland, the UK and Ireland). We are, finally, very grateful to Linda Longmore, Jonathan Manley and Irish Academic Press for their patient faith in the project.

Foreword

DANIEL MULHALL

When Eberhard Bort asked me to contribute a foreword to this volume, I was delighted to oblige. It is based on papers delivered at a conference held at the University of Edinburgh. This event took place in September 1998 which, as it happens, was when I came to Scotland to take up my post as Ireland's first Consul General here.

When embarking on a fresh diplomatic assignment, there is always a steep, but fascinating, learning curve to be scaled. It is necessary to come to terms with a country in which one is destined to spend a considerable slice of time. Different countries pose different challenges – political, economic, cultural, linguistic and climatic. For an Irishman in Scotland it is a case of savouring the many similarities while noting the important differences. There are many ways in which to approach this 'getting to know you' process. For me, the key to understanding any country is to be found in an exploration of its history. From the outset, I was conscious of the depth of Scotland's historical connection with Ireland, although this was not something I had dwelt upon unduly in my own study of Irish history. I have since given considerable thought to the intriguing parallels, the telling differences, and the continuous interaction between the two countries.[1]

I arrived in Scotland against the background of the Good Friday Agreement and the advent of Scottish devolution, and saw it as my mission to encourage and promote Irish–Scottish links as a 'dimension of wider British–Irish relations'.[2] This entailed building on, and reinforcing, the many existing Celtic connections, while adding new strands to an ancient relationship at a time of hope and expectation in both countries. One of the things that impressed me was the extent to which scholarly contact between Ireland and Scotland was evidently flourishing. I quickly became aware of the substantial interest in Irish studies within Scottish universities, and of the work being done by the Irish–Scottish Academic

Initiative (with the participation of Trinity College Dublin, The Queen's University, Belfast and the Universities of Strathclyde and Aberdeen) in developing a productive scholarly network. When inaugurating the Research Institute of Irish and Scottish Studies in Aberdeen on 30 November 1999, President McAleese welcomed this parallel flowering of Irish and Scottish studies. The President pointed out that

> these developments are no academic accident. They echo what's happening in the relationship between our two neighbouring societies. They reflect a desire to know more about each other, to point the benign light of scholarship at the past misunderstandings that have come between us and compli-cated our relations.

There is indeed great scope for comparison. Scotland and Ireland are near neighbours, alike in size and population. Our Celtic languages and cultures have many unmistakable affinities. Both countries have been deeply affected by their proximity to a far more populous society. Our respective histories have been much concerned with the working out of that variegated relationship, in the Irish case through a sustained push for national independence and, since 1922, a struggle to shake off the frailties of economic dependence.

Commemoration became an important theme in Ireland during the latter part of the 1990s. At a time of conspicuous economic achievement, the anniversaries of the Great Famine and the United Irishmen's Rising of 1798 provided an opportunity to reflect on some central aspects of our national experience. This urge to commemorate has sometimes been derided by those who suspect that it is motivated by contemporary political considerations as opposed to a genuine urge to understand the past for its own sake. Every commemoration is probably something of a child of its time. At the end of the nineteenth century, the events of 1798 were seen as a Catholic rebellion against religious oppression, whereas by the 1990s the pluralist nature of the Rising (the men and women of Down and Antrim as well as 'The Boys of Wexford') had been brought more fully into focus. This broadening of perspective and deepening of analysis, to encompass Scullabogue as well as Boolavogue, seems to me to be a desirable process. It helps to unearth complex realities buried under simplified images weathered by the passing of time. If historical commemoration succeeds in resurrecting lost details and reshaping, even temporarily, public perceptions of past events, it represents a worthwhile exercise.

The theme of commemoration has cropped up periodically during my time in Scotland. The Columba Initiative, which has been successful in promoting links between the Irish Gaeltacht and Scotland's Gaelic-speaking communities, was an important by-product of the 1400th anniversary commemoration of the death of St Columba (or Columcille as we know him in Ireland). This event from our overlapping past inspired a visit to Scotland by President Robinson in 1997 during which the Initiative was launched. Supported by the two governments, it has resulted in the restoration of links between two kindred linguistic communities which past religious and political upheavals had sundered.

In 1999, I was approached by Joe Wiggins from the Isle of Islay who was attempting to erect a monument to commemorate a forgotten Irish maritime disaster. On 24 April 1847, a wooden brig, the *Exmouth*, set sail from Derry carrying some 250 passengers and crew. Bound for Quebec, it ran into a dreadful storm which raged for days resulting in the hapless vessel being dashed on the rocks at Islay. Just three crew members survived while 108 bodies were retrieved from the sea and buried on the beach at Sanaigmore. Joe Wiggins was determined that these misfortunate people should not rest forever in unmarked graves. In June 2000, I had the honour of unveiling a fine Celtic cairn in the presence of a great great granddaughter of one of the victims, Sara McCaffrey of Creeslough in County Donegal. I was struck by the organisers' genuine urge to commemorate a disaster with which none of them had any personal family connection. The *Exmouth* monument has a contemporary purpose in that the organisers hope it will serve to reconnect their island with the northern counties of Ireland which are visible from Islay on a clear day.

The evening of 20 June 2001 provided one of the highlights of my time in Scotland when several thousand people turned out at Carfin for the inauguration by the Taoiseach, Bertie Ahern, of a Scottish memorial to the Great Famine. In Ireland, our commemoration of the Famine entailed grappling with what was probably the most traumatic event in Irish history. Although it inevitably had a powerful and lasting effect on Irish society, the Famine never captivated our national imagination in the way that other aspects of our past had done. The novelist, Colm Tóibín, has made the point that

> neither Yeats nor Lady Gregory wrote plays or poems about the Famine. It was not part of the Ireland they sought to celebrate or lament or dream into being.[3]

It was probably only in the 1990s, when the post-Famine tradition of emigration was finally petering out under the influence of rising levels of national prosperity, that we could have dealt properly with something as highly-charged as the Great Hunger. The commemoration coincided with a period of hope in the evolution of the Northern Ireland peace process. As the Taoiseach observed when he spoke at Carfin,

our national famine commemoration also played its part in the building of a new relationship between Britain and Ireland founded on a
recognition of past difficulties and a determination to resolve the
remaining problems through dialogue and in a spirit of reconciliation.

The absence of a Famine memorial in Scotland had puzzled me, especially as Scotland became home to large numbers of Famine immigrants
and their descendants. It was suggested to me that many people of Irish
descent felt that their community's contribution to the evolution of modern Scotland was not always appreciated. I even heard comments about
the desirability of 'keeping the head below the parapet'. Such inhibitions
flew in the face of the fact that the Irish were

> the main immigrant group of modern times, vastly outnumbering the
> Italians, Jews and Lithuanians … and the Asians who settled in the
> second half of this [i.e. the 20th] century.[4]

I viewed the Carfin memorial as an important recognition of a significant
historical reality – the contribution made to the evolution of modern
Scotland by the large number of people of Irish descent who came here
from the 1840s onwards. The presence in Carfin of Scotland's First
Minister, Henry McLeish, the Secretary of State, Helen Liddell, and the
Secretary of State for Northern Ireland, Dr John Reid, together with representatives of the country's political, civic, business and religious life,
served as a handsome tribute to the hundreds of thousands of Irish immigrants who crossed the Irish Sea in times of tribulation. As the former
moderator of the General Assembly of the Church of Scotland, the very
Revd Andrew McLellan, acknowledged in a moving speech at Carfin,
these Irish immigrants were often made to feel unwelcome in nineteenth
and early twentieth-century Scotland. However, their legacy, in the form
of a substantial community of Irish descent in modern Scotland, contributes an important strand to the developing tapestry of Irish–Scottish
relations.

July 2003

Commemorating Ireland: towards an inclusive culture of commemoration? An introduction

EBERHARD BORT

If we lose our memory, we lose ourselves.

Ivan Klima

History, despite its wrenching pain,
Cannot be unlived, but if faced
With courage need not be lived again.

Maya Angelou

This is the age of the anniversary. We seem to be in a constant state of commemoration, celebrating the good, the bad, the indifferent – and that which is better forgotten.

Sunday Herald, 7 January 2001

Setting the scene

This is not yet another book on '98 or on the Famine, contributing to the already existing shelf-load of publications commemorating the bicentenary of the one,[1] and the 150th anniversary of the other.[2] Many of these have, in the case of 1798, added regional perspectives[3] and valuable insights into previously neglected groups like women, who had been all but written out of history;[4] through personal papers and letters,[5] others have highlighted the effect of the Famine in specific regions of Ireland[6] and on emigration and the establishment of a sizeable Irish diaspora.[7] The present volume, by contrast, is not so much a book *of* commemoration as it is *about* commemoration.

The title of this book is ambiguous, and intentionally so. On the one hand, there are echoes of 'Writing Ireland', 'Visualizing Ireland', or '(Re)-Inventing Ireland'[8] – indicating an active process, "the construction of 'Irishness'",[9] if you like, shaping our perception of what Ireland is and how it has become what it is. On the other hand, there is an element of glancing back. Only what is gone, what is in the past, can be commemorated. Ireland, having undergone rapid and profound changes in the past decades, often conjures up feelings of nostalgia, of an older Ireland having been lost in the 'filthy modern tide'.

At the very historical moment when Ireland – the 'poor old woman' – metamorphoses into the 'Celtic Tiger', shedding its image of 'living in the past' and showing signs of buoyant confidence, exporting its culture to the world, from music, plays and poetry to pubs and 'Riverdance', this seems to coincide with an increased need to re-examine the past, a greater need for reassurance and orientation, but also the urge and ability to address 'unfinished business' – a talking cure, debunking myths and coming to terms with an often distorted image of the past; telling the full story so that it can be laid to rest, not to be forgotten, but perhaps to enable forgiveness. Commemoration can be unfinished business – as, for example, in the case of 'Justice for the Forgotten', formed in 1996 to represent the relatives of the victims of the Dublin–Monaghan bombings of 1974 and their demand for a full inquiry.[10]

Commemorations may serve competing goals – to pay tribute to the dead, to console the bereaved, and to incorporate mourners' individual memories into a larger political discourse.[11] Thus, public commemoration seems to have multiple functions, ranging from being a benchmark for the measuring of progress (where are we ten years after the fall of the Wall or twenty-five years after the Portuguese revolution?) and for comparing aspirations with achievements, to being an active motor in a process, an instrument in the steering of social and cultural developments.

Commemorations – the annual repetition of commemorating events and dates as well as grand anniversaries, the work of museums and folk parks as well as major exhibitions and retrospectives – can be seen as part of what Michael Billig calls 'banal nationalism',[12] uniting society by creating common images, thus providing social and cultural glue, collective reassurance, shared beliefs, coherence and identity.[13] The nation as an 'imagined community'[14] becomes, in Anthony Smith's words, 'the constant renewal and retelling of our tale by each generation of our descendants.'[15] A people, one might quip, that commemorates together sticks together. 'People construct community symbolically,' as the social anthropologist Anthony Cohen put it, 'making it a resource and repository of meaning, and a referent of their identity.'[16] Beveridge and Turnbull add that 'if a national culture is to remain alive, its history too must live in some distinctive way and must be perceived as integral to the lives of those who share it. This,' they conclude, 'helps to define their sense of collective identity, gives them their confidence, lets them know where they are.'[17] The aim is not to argue for a single, unified view of history and the past, but to create the space for diversity, a 'complex theatre of memory', as the sociologist David McCrone has called it in the case of Scotland.[18] Changes in the ways we commemorate reflect changes in politics, culture and society, and the way diverse commemorations are allowed to take place is a benchmark of inclusive social diversity.

Thus, if commemoration operates like a mirror, but also as a defining factor, of society, it is interesting to examine what is being commemorated and how, individually and collectively, privately and publicly. There is also the question, particularly in the case of public, official commemorations, of who decides what is commemorated, how and for what purpose. Memory and commemoration have become part of a shift towards cultural history.[19] John Bodnar argues that historical consciousness through commemoration (monuments, public events, parades, etc.) does not necessarily preserve the past but rather addresses serious political matters of the present.[20] Joseph Ruane and Jennifer Todd argue strongly against Northern Ireland being perceived as 'a place apart', but they single it out as 'unusual':

> All modern societies tell and retell their pasts; their cultures are pervaded with myths about past defeats and victories, the ways of life of previous generations and the origins of the society, its distinctive cultures, its national customs and institutions and its present inequalities. These myths are embedded in the popular culture; many are publicly and ritually celebrated on a regular basis. ... Northern Ireland is unusual in that so many of its myths stress conflict and division. Elsewhere the dominant myths stress harmony and integration. ... Myths of past conflict and division offer explanations and justifications for present conflict; they are not indulged in for their own sake.'[21]

Commemorations can be an unwanted burden, a hollow ritual, an ironic distancing of the past,[22] or a liberating celebration. Commemorations can be convenient or inconvenient. The Famine commemorations, with their potential of stirring up old grieveances,[23] seemed to be perceived, at least initially, as belonging to the latter category – particularly for the political establishment; the '98 commemoration in its attempts at inclusiveness – Protestant, Catholic and Dissenter – seemed to fit neatly into the context of the peace process and the Belfast Agreement. After all,

> 1798 was a time of savagery and mayhem as well as idealism. During the Famine commemorations historians were criticised for ignoring the trauma of its million victims; now we're being asked to ignore the 30,000 dead of the 1798 rebellion and to focus instead on the ideals of the United Irishmen. It's hard to avoid the conclusion that the dead of 1798 are politically inconvenient, because they raise the question

of the responsibility of Irish Republicans, whereas the dead of the
Famine brought the failures of the British into focus.[24]

Yet, in his preface to the present volume, Dan Mulhall contends that, as
they unfolded, both the Famine and the '98 commemorations had a positive effect. 'Remembering history too much or in the wrong sort of way
could rub salt in the wounds of the present', the Presbyterian Revd Walter
Forde had warned at the Wexford Bridge service in honour of the dead of
'98. He elaborated his theme further in a letter to the *Irish Times*:
'Commemorations should be healing, bonding experiences and should
help us to focus on contemporary challenges.'[25]

George Schöpflin has pointed out the 'religious dimension' of commemoration, in providing society with the 'moral framework into which
to place its experiences.'[26] Speaking about small nations in Central Europe,
his deliberations strike a note with possible resonances for Ireland:

> Small nations, small in population not in prestige or renown or
> achievement, cannot afford the kind of complacency that large ones
> make their own. They are driven by a particular imperative, the
> imperative of cultural reproduction, of recognition, of gaining the
> approbation of the world for their existence as communities of moral
> worth, that their culture must survive precisely because it is a repos-
> itory of moral values, one that is unique, a way of narrating how
> people should live, when they should laugh and cry, when they
> should shudder and rejoice, and how in the widest sense they should
> know good from evil, clean from polluted.[27]

If this sounds very prescriptive, Schöpflin clarifies:

> Shared morality does not mean a perfect conformity of views, ideas
> and hopes. But this is where commemoration is vital. It creates soli-
> darity, but does not impose consensus, or even compliance. It leaves
> us our individuality and thus our dignity as individual bearers of
> moral values.[28]

And he adds, again with applicable value for, in particular, Northern
Ireland: 'If we have the confidence in ourselves, in our values, then the
commemorations of others need not be seen as offensive.'[29]

The age of commemoration

The trigger for this publication – and the conference at the University of
Edinburgh which it is based on – was the year of 1998 and the commemorations that dominated most of that year: over 800 events were

listed for the bicentenary of 'The Year of the French' alone;[30] add to that
the 150 years since the Great Famine, the Young Ireland Uprising of
1848; add the impact of 1898, the centenary commemorations of 'the '98'
(playing their part in paving the way to Dublin 1916 and subsequent
events); and other historic dates coming into the framework, like the 1918
Sinn Féin landslide victory; the 1948 Republic of Ireland Act; Craigavon
Bridge on 5 October 1968 (often seen as the 'official' beginning of the
'Troubles'); and Sunningdale 1973 finding its – it is to be hoped more
successful – successor in the Belfast (Good Friday) Agreement twenty-
five years later.

Casting the net slightly beyond the year of '98, we find that 1997 was
the 25th anniversary of Bloody Sunday, with all its implications of a revision of the Widgery Report and the demand for a British apology; and the
75th of the Civil War – the 'original' 'Troubles' – as well as of the birth
of the Irish state;[31] since 1995, there have been the Famine commemorations, culminating in just such an apology by British Prime Minister Tony
Blair. But are apologies the proper way to deal with the past? And what
are their implications for the present? There was no apology for the crime
of slavery forthcoming at the Durban conference of 2001, as it was
thought that it would lead to massive reparation payments.[32] In 1996, the
Battle of the Somme was the focus of commemorations, highlighting the
difficulties Tony Canavan outlines in this volume of how to commemorate the two World Wars in Ireland – North and South. The turn of the
century marked the bi-centenary of the Union with Great Britain.[33] The
year 2001 saw the 20th anniversary of the hunger strikes in the Maze and
the 400th anniversary of the Battle of Kinsale. A man very much preoccupied with his posthumous commemoration – 'Whilst the man dies, his
memory lives' – was the focus of attention in 2003. Robert Emmet's
bicentenary may attempt to put an answer to the question of whether the
time has come to write his epitaph at long last. And the assessment may
well be linked with an examination of the thirty years since Ireland joined
the European Community in 1973.

Beyond Ireland, there were the commemorations/celebrations in
France of the bicentenary of the 1789 revolution, causing considerable
rethinking on national history and national identity. Since the 1960s,
France has questioned the myth of *résistance*, and the 50th and 60th
anniversaries of the defeat of France, in 1990 and 2000 respectively, have
added to the re-examination of Vichy France.[34] The European revolutions
of 1848 – Paris, Vienna, Frankfurt, Berlin – had their first major commemoration in Germany (in post-war 1948 the Germans were otherwise
preoccupied; 1898 was overshadowed by Bismarck's death).[35] Fifty years
after the end of the Second World War in 1945, there was ample opportunity to assess the course of Europe in the second half of the twentieth

century. One of the curiosities of this period was certainly the 40th anniversary of the GDR in September 1989 – a bizarre celebration a mere two months before the Berlin Wall came down and Eastern communism crumbled. In 1999 and 2000, there was much retrospection on achieve-ments (and unfulfilled expectations) since the demise of the GDR and German unification. Since the fall of the Berlin Wall in 1989, Germany has marked the anniversary of the building of the Wall on 13 August 1961 with commemorations for the 960 people who were killed trying to cross into the West over the Wall or across the border between East and West Germany.

A fierce debate has been going on for more than ten years in Germany on how the Holocaust should be commemorated – through a new central monument in Berlin, the capital, where that disaster of humanity was planned; or on the sites of the concentration camps themselves, decen-trally, where the genocide was actually executed?[36] And who is to be commemorated? The victims – the Jews on their own, or other victims like gypsies or homosexuals as well? Or the perpetrators?[37] After all, it is, as Salomon Korn has argued, much easier to engage with a victim's mon-ument than with a memorial that focuses on the perpetrators of, say, the Holocaust.[38] Similar questions have been raised in the USA about the Vietnam Veterans' War Memorial.[39] Lyn Spillman has reflected on the imaginative creation and re-creation of national identities, based on observations of centenary and bicentenary celebrations in the USA and in Australia, and has analysed the role cultural production plays in the process of nation-forming and in the expression of nationhood.[40]

Thirty years on, Prague 1968 evoked an interesting commemorative response, particularly in the light of subsequent events: Gorbachev's glasnost and perestroika, and the reforms and revolutions of 1989/90. The student rebellions of Berkeley, Paris and Berlin in 1968 also triggered a spate of reassessments, commemorating the 'swinging sixties', the 'summer of love' and, more seriously, trying to trace the fate of the '68 generation and the impact of their ideas, as they 'marched through the institutions' (to become government ministers like Joschka Fischer) or descended, in the 1970s and '80s, into terrorism (like Ulrike Meinhof).

Our conference on, mainly, Irish commemoration, convened on 11 September 1998, exactly a year after the momentous Scottish referendum which paved the way for Scotland's first Parliament in nearly 300 years. It was also the 25th anniversary of General Pinochet's military putsch in Chile, in which its democratically elected president, Salvador Allende, was killed. But, of course, in future this particular date will be associated, first and foremost, with the heinous terrorist attack on the World Trade Centre in New York in 2001.

Irish commemorations in a comparative perspective

The contributions to this volume mostly concentrate, as the title of the conference suggests, on aspects of commemoration – history, politics, culture – in Ireland. In addition to comparing different aspects of commemoration within Ireland, we have tried, I think successfully, to broaden the scope, and have chapters which add an international comparative dimension to the discourse – a dimension particularly needed to broaden the often insular and introspective debates in Ireland (and, for that matter, Britain or 'these isles').[41]

Peter Collins of the Cultural Traditions Group in Belfast gives a history of '98 commemorations, focusing on the centenary, the curious 1938 (!) commemoration, 1948, and up to 1998, charting the changes in the way 1798 has been commemorated – contrasting 1898 (which was a rallying point for the Irish Republican Brotherhood (IRB) and other nationalist/republican groups, with far-reaching consequences for 1916 and beyond), and 1998 (against the backdrop of the Belfast Agreement and in the context of more inclusive approaches to history and commemoration). UCD historian Mary Daly concentrates on the Famine commemorations since 1996 (which segued or 'developed' into the '98 commemorations, sometimes with the same organisers at the helm). Questions concerning the similarities and differences between these two main commemorative events touch upon the issue of what is being commemorated, and how, and for what purpose. When Mary McAleese became President in 1997, one of her first decisions concerned the question of whether or not to wear a poppy during a Remembrance Day service on Armistice Day. Tony Canavan, a member of the editorial board of *History Ireland*, addresses the difficult commemorations of the two World Wars, the clash of symbols, the different perspectives of North and South, Nationalist and Unionist, and tentative ways in which the gulf is being bridged.[42]

On the Orange Order's Drumcree commemorative marches, Fintan O'Toole has recently commented:

> The deep significance of the Drumcree parade, that it commemorates the Battle of the Somme in 1916, is itself evidence of the changing meaning of the parade. Before the First World War, it meant one thing: afterwards, it meant something else.
>
> During that war, moreover, the order cancelled the annual parades because, as the Portadown headquarters put it, 'our celebrations should be modified to suit the circumstances of the time'. If that motto were to be adopted now, it would have at least as much historical sanction as the current insistence on carrying on regardless.
>
> The Orange festivities, in any event, have always been a moveable feast.[43]

Edinburgh-based historian Owen Dudley Edwards takes a broad look at history, legend and myth, addressing the central question of control over memory, and leading his discourse towards a perplexingly simple solution to the problem of Drumcree. He argues that Drumcree is in fact a commemoration of the Bann (1641) rather than the Boyne (1690), commemorating a defeat rather than a triumph – which, he contends, ought to be reflected in its commemoration. Furthermore, if it is a commemoration of 1690, then the Catholic priests should be taken aboard, as the pope at that time was among the supporters of King Billy!

Paul Arthur of the University of Ulster, one of Northern Ireland's leading political scientists, looks at the nexus of memory and forgiveness – does post-Troubles Northern Ireland need a Commission for Truth and Reconciliation?[44]

Fintan O'Toole reminded us in the *Irish Times* that the defeat of the 1798 rising was 'also a terrible blow to the democrats of Scotland and England'.[45] With a nod to the hosting country of our conference, Ray Burnett of the Dicúil Foundation on Benbecula opens the set of international comparisons, relating the Scottish radical tradition from the United Scotsmen to James Connolly to its Irish counterparts and influences. Christopher Harvie, Professor of British and Irish Studies at Tübingen University, looks at nineteenth-century Ireland in a comparative European context, beginning and ending with Shaw's *John Bull's Other Island*, using the figures of Thomas Carlyle (and his influential work on the French Revolution), and the church-building Cardinal Cullen as his focal points.

Arguably, 1798 in Ireland would not have happened without the French Revolution of 1789. Malcolm Anderson, Emeritus Professor of Political Sciences at the University of Edinburgh, takes the bicentenary of the French Revolution and the Baptism of Clovis as two defining French experiences of 1990s' commemoration, analysing the different approaches, controversies, and agendas involved in the commemorations.[46] The distinguished journalist and author Neal Ascherson uses his experience and knowledge of Central and Eastern Europe to look at modes of commemoration in different historical periods, finding a link between the stages of nation-building and nationalism and the centralisation of memory/commemoration, ending on a comparison involving the (non-centralised) commemoration of the Scottish Covenanters.

The poet and literature professor Gerald Dawe (TCD) takes up Ascherson's example of the covenant, yet offers a more private and literary exploration of personal history, taking as his angle the Ulster Covenant of 1912, the involvement of his own ancestors and how the memory of it was (or indeed was not) handed down through the generations, an engagement which has found expression in some of his poems over the past few years. Christopher Murray, Professor of Anglo-Irish Literature (UCD), critic and historian of Irish theatre, concentrates on Sean O'Casey's development from *The Plough and the Stars* (1926), and his critical–satirical approach to Irish historical events – subverting the myth-making commemorations of 1916–1922 – to his more visionary, myth-making plays about the future.

It should not surprise that there is a strong relationship between the question of commemoration and the theatre. Drama is the most public form of literature and, particularly in Ireland, history and identity have been the themes of a string of impressive plays, from the Literary Revival through the twentieth century, to the present day. Furthermore, the art of theatre shares its roots with modern commemoration in ritual and pageant. Aideen Howard, dramaturg at the Abbey and Peacock theatres, rounds off the volume with a close reading of Frank McGuinness's memory play, *Observe the Sons of Ulster Marching Towards the Somme*, discussing the role of drama, and particularly the National Theatre, in the commemorative process.

Talking cures

The past decade or so has seen the emergence of a series of plays which, like *Observe the Sons of Ulster Marching Towards the Somme*, can be seen as 'talking cures' – telling the story, finishing the story, to clear oneself, to free oneself of the trappings of one's biography, one's past, in order to get on with one's life. This personal level, it can be assumed, functions as a mirror for contemporary politics and the historical predicament of Ireland. The strong Irish storytelling tradition is thus combined with a psychoanalytical diagnosis of post-colonial trauma which must be overcome in an emancipatory way. Plays as diverse as Tom Murphy's *Bailegangaire* (1985), Bernard Farrell's *The Last Apache Reunion* (1993), Frank McGuinness's *Baglady* (1985), Ivy Bannister's *Lift Me Up and Pour Me Out* (1994) and Geraldine Aron's *The Donahue Sisters* (1990) – even, in an ironically inverted way, Stewart Parker's *Pentecost* (1987) - belong into this category. Elements of loss are matched with a firm focus on the future and its acceptance, insecure and problematic as it may be.[47] 'This is not the sense of loss that creates nostalgia, of which there is hardly a trace,' observed Fintan O'Toole of Dermot Bolger's *The Holy Ground* (1990) and *In High Germany* (1990), 'but the sense of loss that creates a hole that must be filled.'[48]

What Fintan O'Toole said of Tom Murphy's play *The House* (premiered at the Abbey in April 2000), holds for most of these plays as well:

> In *The House*, the return to the 1950s is not a nostalgic trip down
> memory lane, but a voyage to the roots of a deep unsettlement. *The
> House* is, in fact, the precise opposite of nostalgia: a vision of the past
> that, instead of releasing us from the present, confronts us with the
> forces that shaped it.[49]

A particular, ritualistic, way of recalling past events is the evocative
roll-call. The roll-call of casualties or victims – Gerry Adams's incanta-
tion of the hunger strikers' names at the April 2000 Ard Fheis of Sinn
Féin – can be a rallying call;[50] but, as Frank McGuinness has shown in
Carthaginians (1988), roll-calls can also be acts of exorcism, part of a
healing ceremony. Which brings us back to both the relationships
between individual and collective memory, and forgiving and forgetting.

Memory and forgetting

'To remember everything is a form of madness',[51] hedge-schoolmaster
Hugh O'Donnell warns his son Owen in Brian Friel's *Translations*
(1980). The play is about the renewal of images of the past, of identity as
a process, not the past as an event preserved in aspic, or, as Hugh would
put it, 'fossilized'. For Hugh 'it is not the literal past, the "facts" of history, that shape us, but images of the past embodied in language'. He
remembers 1798 as 'a miraculous matching of hope and past and present
and possibility'[52] a time, as Seamus Heaney famously put it in *The Cure
at Troy* (1990), where 'hope and history rhyme[d]'.[53]
    There needs to be a dialectic relationship between individual and col-
lective memory, making the present the dynamic interface between past
and future, experience and expectation. If that dynamic and dialectic
breaks down, the past is prone to colonise the present and future, limiting
options and possibilities. Arguably, we have seen such an instance in the
stand-off about Drumcree where, as Patsy McGarry put it in 1998,
'memory imprisons the living'.[54]
    Remembering is an active, creative process, and while the events, the
'facts' of history, cannot be changed, their interpretation is subject to
revision; the images we have of the past can – perhaps must – change.[55]
Memory is a selective process, and selection is a form of 'active forgetting'.[56] Paul Ricoeur has linked this to history-writing; by constructing a
narrative, selection takes place, which in turn makes it possible to revisit
the evidence and apply different perspectives. In Brian Friel's *Making
History* (1988), Lombard's historical–biographical narrative overrules
O'Neill's insistence on 'the facts' in favour of a gripping story, a 'heroic
history', around which Irish identity could be shaped. This kind of active

forgetting is myth-making, and is often undertaken 'Lest we forget'. Ricoeur argues, instead, for a 'rational use of forgetting'. For him, a particular form of 'active forgetting' is forgiving which, when taken seriously, remains the privilege of the victim, and liberates the recipient from the necessity of being obsessed by deeds perpetrated in the past. It is not the deed itself that is 'actively' forgotten, but the guilt that paralyses the mind and the ability to deal creatively with concepts of the future.[57]

Memory and identity

Memory and identity are inextricably linked. 'Nations are destroyed by first robbing them of their memory. Their books are destroyed, their learning, their history. And then someone else writes different books, gives them a different kind of learning and invents a different history.'[58] Ivan Klíma, after quoting his compatriot Milan Kundera, continues:

> Memory is not expressed only through a dutiful recording of a certain experience; it is, rather, a responsibility that flows from an awareness of a continuity with everything that went before, with all those who came before, that is, a responsibility for what must not be forgotten if we are to avoid ending up in a vacuum.[59]

So, what is the contribution of commemoration in the reinterpreting and reaffirming of Ireland's changing identity? Is it divisive or uniting? Is it an assertion of sectarian culture or a transcending of it: exclusive or inclusive? Is commemoration used as a tool to sharpen our awareness of the past and its impact on the present? Is commemoration part of the disease or part of the cure? Do we strike the right balance between actively remembering and actively forgetting to liberate ourselves from the past, as talking cures may help to overcome traumatic experiences? Is there too much commemoration going on? An industry of commemoration – book publishing, conferences, pageants, cultural festivals, exhibitions, films, etc? Are we, in Conor Cruise O'Brien's words, commemorating ourselves to death, 'sleep-walkers, locked in some eternal ritual re-enactment'?[60] Or are we developing a new, inclusive culture of commemoration? Without having answers for all these questions, Dan Mulhall's foreword and, I would hope, this volume as a whole point with some confidence to an Ireland neither blind to its multi-faceted past nor to its plural and diverse future.

I

1

'Who fears to speak of '98?' historic commemoration of the 1798 rising

PETER COLLINS

Introduction

The Society of United Irishmen, founded in Belfast in October 1791, itself originated, to an extent, in commemoration. The previous July there had been enthusiastic anniversary commemorations of the fall of the Bastille with their ally France. This was repeated in July of 1792 and 1793 in Belfast and Dublin. For the United Irishmen these commemorations were good propaganda and a means of establishing an affinity with the French Revolution, which they sought to emulate. During successive periods of commemoration of '98, many in turn have similarly sought to establish an affinity with the United Irishmen. However, there was an initial period in which many understandably distanced themselves from the events of 1798.

The aim of this chapter is to analyse the often conflicting motivations of those involved in commemoration of '98, and also the attitudes of their Loyalist opponents, particularly northern Presbyterians, who were actual descendants of the United Irishmen. It will look at the impact, on the politics of their time, of commemorations of '98, in 1848, 1898, 1938, 1948 and 1998. On this, Kevin Whelan has written,

> The 1798 rebellion was fought twice: once on the battlefields and then in the war of words which followed in those bloody footprints. The struggle for the control of the meaning of the 1790s was also a struggle for political legitimacy. … The interpretation of 1798 was designed to mould public opinion and influence policy formation: the rebellion never passed into history because it never passed out of politics.[1]

Retreat from '98

Soon after the failed rising, the 'spin-doctors' began putting 'side' on what had happened. Understandably there was a retreat from the legacy of the United Irishmen, by many former adherents. Also their opponents were soon to the fore with hostile versions of '98. The seminal Loyalist account was Sir Richard Musgrave's highly partisan *Memoirs of the Various Rebellions* (Dublin, 1801). Musgrave made the link between 1798, 1690 and 1641, portraying each as a phase in the continuing Catholic campaign to overthrow Protestant hegemony in Ireland. In Musgrave's account, a wedge was driven between the risings in Wexford and Ulster. The former was a sectarian Catholic peasant jacquerie, the latter a misguided, if understandable, reaction by Presbyterians to political and social, economic and religious strictures. Highlighting, in very colourful language, atrocities such as the barn-burning tragedy at Scullabogue, Musgrave set out to foment division where the United Irishmen had sown unity. His book set the agenda for Loyalist interpretations of 1798 for many generations.

Archbishop Troy of Dublin was concerned to distance the Catholic Church from the rising and to mitigate any Loyalist back-lash against the members and property of his church. In addition, he wanted to ensure that the good relations, between the Church and the government, following the ending of the Penal Laws, should continue. The hierarchy supported the Union, which they expected to deliver them from the anti-Catholic Irish parliament and introduce Catholic emancipation. Furthermore, the Church had opposed the United Irishmen, fearing an anti-clerical secular republic, similar to that commemorated, to a very great extent, in the media.

A great difficulty for the Church was to explain away the involvement of the minority of priests like John and Michael Murphy in the rising in Wexford. Troy expressed his fears on this issue: 'We all wish to remain as we are and we would so were it not that too many of the clergy were active in the wicked rebellion or did not oppose it.'[2] James Caulfield, Bishop of Ferns, in whose diocese Wexford lay, anathematised those few Wexford priests who had participated in the rising: 'Excommunicated priests, drunken and profligate couple-beggars – the very faeces of the church.'[3]

In order to persuade Britain to grant Catholic emancipation and eventually an Irish parliament, Daniel O'Connell sought to distance himself from revolutionary nationalism. His own version of his activities in 1798 was that he had been a member of the Dublin Lawyers' Yeomanry and opposed the Rebellion. O'Connell's nationalism was wholly Catholic, with little or no place for Protestants. Furthermore, he denied that Catholics and Protestants had made common cause in '98, and stated that Catholics bore the brunt of brutal repression unleashed on them, as a result of a rebellion of which they were not the authors. In 1825, when asked if there were any Catholics among the United Irishmen he replied:

> There were scarcely any among the leading United Irishmen who were almost all Dissenters. In the North, the lower classes of United Irishmen were at first Dissenters: it spread then among the Roman Catholics and as it spread into the southern counties, and took in the population, it increased its number of Catholics. In the county of Wexford, where the greatest part of the rebellion raged, there were no United Irishmen previous to the rebellion and there would have been no rebellion there if they had not been forced forwards by the establishment of Orange lodges and the whippings and torturings and things of that kind.[4]

Many Presbyterians began to disengage from their adherence to the United Irishmen very soon after 1798. Undoubtedly the stories of sectarian atrocities against Protestants in Wexford, such as the Scullabogue massacre, had an effect. O'Connell's campaigns frightened many Presbyterians into a new pan-Protestant alliance. O'Connell's foe, Revd Henry Cooke, invoked the memory of Wexford in 1798: 'The unhappy men and women who fell victims at Scullabogue barn and Wexford Bridge have been the political saviours of their country. They live in our remembrance. Their deaths opened the eyes of many thousands in Ulster.'[5] Many northern Protestants, especially Presbyterians, had prospered since the Act of Union, and they feared that the Dublin parliament, espoused by O'Connell, would undo this. In the mid-nineteenth century, relations between Catholicism and Protestantism hit a long-time low. The Catholic 'Devotional Revolution' was mirrored in the increasingly evangelical trend in Protestantism, culminating in the so-called 'Great Awakening' of 1859. By this stage, the United Irish influence in Presbyterianism was dead.

Rehabilitating '98

The sectarian interpretation of '98 was greatly reinforced by George Cruickshank's hostile and grotesque cartoons, in W. H. Maxwell's *History of the 1798 Rebellion in Ireland* (London, 1845). Cruickshank, famous as Charles Dickens' illustrator, produced shocking illustrations such as the piking of prisoners at Wexford Bridge and the burning barn at Scullabogue. Cruickshank's simian and racist characterisations of the Irish were taken up by *Punch* and other English journals. The memory of the United Irishmen and the events of '98 had become a travesty. From this low point, they experienced a rehabilitation, due to the work of Dr R. R. Madden. Madden's *United Irishmen, their Life and Times* (London, 1842–7) gave a very positive view of the United Irishmen. Madden's book had a tremendous impact, primarily in nationalist quarters, both in reviving interest in the United Irishmen, and reinstating their reputation.

Young Ireland and 1848

This influence was particularly strong on the Young Irelanders, who claimed for themselves apostolic succession from the United Irishmen. The Young Ireland leader Thomas Davis (1814–45) was engaged in a biography of Wolfe Tone when his own life was cut short. Tone's grave, at Bodenstown, had authoritatively been identified by Madden, in 1842. Davis made it the focal point of commemoration and homage to the martyr. The following is an extract from Davis' poem 'Tone's Grave', published in *The Nation*, 25 November 1843:

> In Bodenstown Churchyard there is a green grave
> And freely around it, let winter winds rave
> Far better they suit him, the ruin and the gloom
> Till Ireland, a nation, can build him a Tomb.

Young Ireland erected a black marble memorial to Tone, at Bodenstown in 1844, though they eschewed ceremony in order not to embarrass O'Connell in his relations with the government. This was an indication that the memory of the dead of '98 was still a controversial topic.

Mood music, for lasting remembrance of the United Irishmen, as well as contemporary support for the Young Irelanders, was provided by the popular Irish melodies of the day, especially those of Tom Moore. In Moore's 'She is Far From the Land', an Irish exile mourns her dead patriot lover, following the Emmet postscript rebellion of 1803. However, of utmost importance in this respect was 'The Memory of the Dead', known popularly by its first line, 'Who fears to speak of Ninety-Eight?'. It was written in 1843 by John Kells Ingram, son of a Church of Ireland rector, while a student at Trinity College, Dublin. It was published in the Young Ireland paper the *Nation* and later, set to music, it became the anthem of subsequent '98 commemorations.

> The Memory of the Dead[6]
>
> Who fears to speak of Ninety-Eight?
> Who blushes at the name?

When cowards mock the patriot's fate,
Who hangs his head for shame?
He's all a knave and half a slave
Who slights his country thus,
But a true man, like you, man,
Will fill your glass with us.

We drink the memory of the brave
The faithful and the few
Some lie far off beyond the wave,
Some sleep in Ireland too;
All, all are gone; but still lives on
The fame of those who died
All true men, like you men
Remember them with pride.

Ingram later regretted writing it, believing that it had affected his subsequent academic career. O'Connell acidly commented, 'The bird that once sang so sweetly is now caged within the walls of Trinity College.' In 1848, the 50th anniversary of '98, Young Ireland attempted a rising, an act of the utmost commemoration. However, it was on a much lesser scale than '98, ending in fiasco. That year, due to the Young Ireland failure and the disastrous impact of the Great Famine, which many nationalists viewed as genocide, there was no cause for celebration, no will for commemoration.

The Fenians

The next link in the chain of emulation and commemoration came with the Fenians, also known as the Irish Republican Brotherhood (IRB). In 1863, their newspaper the *Irish People* serialised extracts from Miles Byrne's *Memoirs*, which had just been published posthumously.[7] A veteran of '98 and the Emmet sequel of 1803, Byrne had gone into exile in France, where he became a distinguished soldier. He portrayed the United Irishmen as a cohesive, revolutionary, ideologically-based society. Their clear aim of a democratic, secular republic had captured the imagination of great masses of the Irish people. He dispelled the accusations that the rising in Wexford was driven by sectarianism, that it was a peasant jacquerie or that there was no Protestant participation and leadership in that county. For the Fenians, Byrne provided evidence that their present-day secular republicanism stood in direct relation to that of the United Irish patriots.

The Fenians realised the potency of the memory of the martyred dead and popularised graveside commemoration. These commemorative obsequies lent credibility to the Fenian claim to be heirs of the United Irish mantle. Their first monument to '98 was a stone celtic cross, dedicated to Fr John Murphy, at Boolavogue. Paid for by a Fenian '98 club from Dublin, it was unveiled on 29 September 1878. The Catholic Church remained opposed to the United Irish memory. The cross had crossed pikes carved on it, causing the local parish priest to object, describing the '98 club as a den of 'communists and freemasons'.[8] He would not allow the memorial to Fr Murphy on church property, and forbade parishioners from attending the unveiling. Worse still, he forced the closure of local pubs on the day. The Boolavogue PP's action was in line with the blanket condemnation by Ireland's first cardinal, Paul Cullen, who described the Fenians as 'Godless nobodies' for whom 'Hell was not hot enough, nor eternity long enough.' The cardinal's attitude also extended to the rising of 1798 in which 'all our patriots were tinged with infidelity, the two Sheares, Emmet etc.'[9]

Fr Kavanagh's 'faith and fatherland' version of '98

The Church gradually adopted and shaped commemoration of '98 to conform more to Catholic nationalism than the secular republicanism of the Fenians. It had a major weapon in the person of Fr Patrick Kavanagh, a Franciscan historian from Wexford. Fr Kavanagh's *A Popular History of the Insurrection of 1798* (Dublin, 1870, with nine further editions up to 1928) posed a very different view of 1798. Kavanagh portrayed the rising in Wexford as defence of their homes and churches by a 'morally pure' Catholic peasantry, led by their heroic priests. They had risen only as a last resort in self-defence against Loyalist and military attack. In this version, the Society of United Irishmen and, by implication, Protestants had no place. 'When Wexford stood at bay, the United Irishmen were not to be found'.[10] For generations, this 'Faith and Fatherland' version of '98 would be the dominant mainstream nationalist interpretation. By the centenary year, the Fr Murphy memorial had been moved into the churchyard at Boolavogue. This was a symbol of the extent to which the Church accepted the Kavanagh version of '98.

The 1898 centenary

The 1898 centenary became the occasion for a contest, within nationalism, over who owned the commemoration of '98. The Fenians, claiming the revolutionary mantle of the United Irishmen, had a track record of commemoration. However, they remained on the margins of politics and continued to incur the enmity of the Catholic Church. Constitutional nationalists, by definition opposed to the insurrectionist nature of the United Irishmen, were at first lukewarm or hostile. The Parliamentary Party had been divided since the demise of Parnell and the failure of the Home Rule Bill of 1893. There was a solid Conservative and Unionist majority in the House of Commons, and Home Rule appeared to be dead. In 1897, nationalists had to witness the celebrations of Queen Victoria's jubilee, with many buildings in central Dublin decorated with loyalist flags and bunting. They were keen, therefore, to use the centenary of '98 as a counterblast to the jubilee and a means to restore their self-respect and morale. A National Commemoration Committee, set up early in 1897, primarily an IRB initiative, had as its president the veteran Fenian/Young Irelander, John O'Leary. The parliamentarians, led by Dillon and Redmond, eventually jumped onto the gathering centenary bandwagon, not without opposition from the Fenians. However, the Fenians maintained overall direction of the national commemorative events through their investment of enthusiasm, time and effort. At regional and local level, the constitutionalists, commanding the support of the local constituency organisations, press and clergy, were more in control.

The main focus of the commemorations nationally was the erection of a monument to Wolfe Tone in Dublin. Also, '98 clubs were set up to raise memorials, all over the country. In Ulster, the organisation of commemoration was fragmented. Joe Devlin, the Dillonite parliamentarian, controlled the '98 clubs in Belfast. In Derry and Tyrone, they were organised by the Irish National Foresters. Elsewhere in Ulster, the Fenians dominated the '98 clubs. Due to its sectarian geography, '98 monuments could not be safely erected in the north. Therefore, the northern '98 clubs had to content themselves with the fabrication of ornate banners, depicting United Irish leaders and '98 scenes. These banners were startlingly similar in design to those of the Orange lodges. Indeed, many of the Ulster '98 clubs employed firms like Bridgetts of Belfast, the principal Orange banner-makers.

The centenary celebrations began, on New Year's Eve 1897, with torchlight parades all over nationalist Ireland, the largest being in Dublin, Belfast, Limerick and Cork. In Belfast, a group climbed to MacArt's Fort, the scene of the Cave Hill compact. Here, in 1795, Tone, Russell, McCracken, Simms and Neilson had sworn 'never to desist in our efforts, until we have subverted the authority of England over our country and asserted our independence'.[11] After lighting a dozen pitch-barrels and reaffirming the United Irish oath, the commemorative group joined the main Belfast parade on the nationalist Falls Road. In some parts of Belfast and Ulster there was hostility, and there were attacks on marchers by loyalists.

Another parade, along Belfast's Falls Road on Monday 6 June 1897, the anniversary of the Battle of Antrim, was attended by many thousands of marchers and onlookers. Again, these commemorations were confined to the nationalist heartland of the city. Afterwards, the banners of the '98 clubs were carefully wrapped and stored. Some would be used during the march on the Falls Road in 1948. In August, the foundation stone for the proposed Wolfe Tone monument in Dublin was hewn from MacArt's Fort. It was processed from the Falls Road to the railway station and set on board the Dublin train. As it was impossible to site the monument in Belfast, birthplace of the Society of United Irishmen, this symbiotic link was the next best thing. When the foundation stone arrived in Dublin, it lay in state for two nights in the old Newgate Gaol, with all its melancholy associations with the United Irishmen. On the morning of 'Lady Day', 15 August, a feast day laden with Catholic association, now by popular ascription 'Wolfe Tone Day', the foundation stone was placed on a lorry and carried in procession, with great solemnity. It was flanked by an ornately costumed Irish National Forester guard of honour, with many bands and banners, and followed by a huge throng. There were many contingents from the North, among whom pride of place was given to a girl, dressed in green and gold, portraying Betsy Grey, the legendary heroine of the Battle of Ballynahinch. This was the greatest commemoration of revolutionary nationalism ever seen in Dublin.

The parade followed a three-mile route, passing places associated with Tone and Emmet. The whole procession took three hours to reach the designated site of the monument at Stephen's Green/Grafton Street. This site was chosen as a deliberate assertion of nationalist territorial imperative, in the Unionist heartland of Dublin. It would become a place of assembly for future nationalist parades and demonstrations. John O'Leary presided at the very moving and symbolically orchestrated stone laying ceremony, flanked by Irish Party leaders Dillon and Redmond. This show of unity was soured by the radical Maud Gonne's refusal to share the platform with the constitutional politicians. O'Leary pronounced himself a living connection with 1867 (the year of the failed IRB rising), 1848 and, by implication, 1798. He was presented with an ornate trowel, sent from America by Tone's granddaughter, which had been touched by as many of the martyr's descendants as possible. O'Leary tapped the stone six times, to represent Ireland's four provinces and America and France. In conclusion, the band struck up the 'Memory of the Dead', the virtual national anthem of the centenary commemorations.[12] Whilst this was indeed the high point of the commemorations, there was to be an anti-climactic denouement to the whole Wolfe Tone monument project. When the centenary year ended, the parliamentary politicians lost interest in the Tone monument, leaving it to the IRB who, through a mixture of incompetence and corruption, failed to see the project to completion. Eventually, they suffered the galling usurpation of the site by the Dublin Fusilier Boer War memorial, known to republicans as 'Traitors' Arch'. It is tempting to interpret this as a metaphor for the failure of nationalism to best unionism up to that point. The Wolfe Tone monument foundation stone has been installed in the Croppies' Acre Garden of Remembrance, dedicated on 22 November 1998 at Collins Barracks in Dublin.

Local monuments

In many local areas, the lasting centenary commemorative act was to be the erection of a permanent memorial to the martyrs of 1798. There was a keen sense of a national deficit in patriotic monuments, compared to other countries, and especially given the number erected to the loyalist cause throughout Ireland. This was rather forcefully given expression by the Nationalist MP, Sir Thomas Esmonde, at the stone-laying ceremony in Wexford Town:

> ... while there are monuments in plenty to the alien representatives of English misrule in Ireland, the monuments commemorative of great Irishmen, of great events in Irish history, are few and far between. Our towns are studded with memorials of English kings, of English Lords Lieutenant.[13]

Most of the '98 statuary, particularly the work of Ireland's leading monumental sculptor, Oliver Sheppard, was highly influenced by the Fr Kavanagh interpretation of the Rising. Thus many of the figures in the monuments were representations of heroic peasantry in working clothes, rather than United Irishmen in uniform. Sheppard's Enniscorthy monument shows a flag-draped Fr Murphy pointing the way to a young peasant insurgent. In many monuments, the clear association was made with religion, with some adorned with rosary beads or crucifixes. In others, a female figure represents Ireland and/or 'Mary of the Gael'.[14] Many were bedecked with other symbols of nationality, such as harps, shamrocks, Irish wolfhounds and round towers. In Co. Wexford, there was virulent rejection of Redmond's proposal of a round tower monument on Vinegar Hill. It smacked too much of the constitutionalism of O'Connell whose burial place in Glasnevin was thus adorned.

In many cases, the siting of '98 monuments had an historical/political significance. 1898 was also the year in which the Local Government Act handed over control to mostly nationalist-dominated councils. Now they were able to place monuments in areas, such as town centres, which had previously been Loyalist-controlled. Nevertheless, this was a transitional period and a number of monuments were sited on the periphery in some areas. Perhaps most galling to nationalists was the refusal, by Lord Portsmouth, to allow a monument to be erected at Vinegar Hill, on his property.

Due to factors of time and expense, several years elapsed before a number of monuments were put in place. By that stage, they had become unfashionable in some quarters, particularly with constitutionalists wishing to project a less militant image of nationalism. Many of the centenary monuments were simply not very good art, a fact with which Maud Gonne found herself in agreement with W. B. Yeats, even though she was involved in stone-laying and unveiling ceremonies. Yet she recognised their educational/propaganda value.[15]

Nationalist propaganda was undeniably disseminated in the outpouring of high quality cartoons, portraying 1798 and other historical themes. These were mostly published in supplements with the popular monthly periodicals and national weekly newspapers, such as the *Shamrock*, the *Irish Emerald*, the *Weekly Freeman* and *United Ireland*. These cartoons by, among others, J. F. O'Hea, J. D. Reigh, Walter C. Mills, Thomas Fitzpatrick and Phil Blake also filled a vacuum in the school history curriculum which, largely for political reasons, contained little or no Irish history.[16] From a nationalist perspective, this gap was also filled by the histories of A. M. Sullivan, the novels of Charles Kickham and the plays of Dion Boucicault, P. J. Bourke and Yeats, notably the latter's celebrated *Cathleen Ni Houlihan* (1902). Ballads such as Robert Dwyer Joyce's 'Boys of Wexford' and P. J. McCall's 'Boolavogue' and 'Kelly the Boy from Killane' also followed the Kavanagh interpretation of '98.

Low art was also a part of the centenary year as commemorative merchandising, some of it pure kitsch, made its appeal to popular taste. For instance, the Belfast jewellers Wightman & Co. advertised, in the nationalist *Shan Van Vocht*, jewellery made from the chips left over from the cutting of the Wolfe Tone foundation stone. These were polished and incorporated into shamrock-shaped scarf pins, harp-shaped brooches and celtic cross pendants. A range of centenary perfumes was marketed by the Dublin chain of chemists, Leonards. There was even a centenary cycle manufacturer. A northern distillery, not normally associated with the nationalist cause, proclaimed, 'True patriots drank Bushmills in 1798.' A huge range of decorated handkerchiefs, ceramics, posters, postcards and novels portrayed the 'Faith and Fatherland' version of '98. These manifestations of commemoration, in their way, were contributing to the end-of-century process of invention of the nation.

Protestant participation in the Ulster commemorations was limited to a small but high-profile group of nationalists, notably Alice Milligan and the antiquarian and Hibernicist Francis Joseph Bigger. Bigger, a member of the Church of Ireland and a prominent solicitor and Freemason, wrote and published *Remember Orr*, the life of the United Irish Presbyterian martyr William Orr.[17] It was the only one published of Bigger's series of the *Lives of the United Irish Leaders of the North*. Alice Milligan, a Methodist, originally from Omagh, along with her Catholic colleague, Anna Johnston (aka Ethna Carbery) ran the *Shan Van Vocht*. This appeared from January 1896 until its demise in early 1899, and was a vehicle for nationalist propaganda and Irish culture. The 1898 commemorations filled much of its column space with ballads, essays, reports of visits to graves and battle sites, etc. The attitude of Protestant nationalists to participation in the centenary was in stark contrast to the attitudes of the vast majority of their co-religionists.

Loyalist hostility to the centenary

The rising in Ulster in 1798 had been a mainly Presbyterian affair. Somewhat ironically, in 1898 it was being commemorated, primarily by Catholics, in areas with little or no connection with the events of 1798. By June 1898, there was only one '98 club, in Down, a county where the United Irishmen had been out in great numbers. Presbyterians were by 1898 far removed from the United Irish ideals of many of their forebears, and viewed the commemorations with hostility. Religious antipathy between Catholics and Protestants had proceeded apace during the nineteenth century. Since the Act of Union, Presbyterians and other Protestants had closed ranks, politically and theologically. Most Presbyterians believed that their United Irish forebears had been fighting for political and religious equality or tenant rights. These had now been achieved.

Fortunately, loyalist hostility to the '98 celebrations was mainly confined to the columns of unionist newspapers. The unionist *Belfast Evening Telegraph* described the commemorations as the ''98 microbe'. However, some violence was fomented as a result of the June parade on the Falls Road; it was mainly confined to loyalist areas such as the nearby Shankill Road. Trains carrying participants back from the Dublin '98 celebrations in August were stoned and their occupants molested outside the station in Belfast. There was a minor sectarian riot in Stewartstown, Co. Tyrone. In Sandy Row, Belfast, during the 1898 'Twelfth' commemorations of the Battle of the Boyne, an Orange Arch bore the legend 'Scullabogue Barn is ever green'. This was commemoration of the other side of 1798.

If there was nothing like the sectarian hatred and violence engendered during the recent Home Rule campaigns, the destruction of the Betsy

Grey gravestone graphically illustrated the extent of loyalist hostility in the north. Betsy Grey, slaughtered with her brother and lover while fleeing from the battlefield at Ballynahinch, was a heroic figure for nationalists in 1898. Although romanticised in a recent book, to most northern Unionists she represented part of their history which had finally to be exorcised.[18] A monument had been erected in 1896 by her great-nephew at Ballycreen, outside Ballynahinch. Nationalist excursions to decorate the graves of martyrs and lay wreaths at hallowed '98 spots had elicited, from their opponents, the sneering epithet 'Charabanc Nationalists'. When nationalists tried to hold a commemoration at the grave of Betsy Gray, on Sunday, 1 May 1898, an affray ensued and the monument was destroyed. The incident was reported, from different perspectives, in nationalist and unionist newspapers, each side citing it to vilify the other.

The speech of Revd L. A. Pooler, shortly afterwards, at the 1898 'Twelfth' commemorations in Ballynahinch, gives a good illustration of the changed Presbyterian attitudes since 1798. From his perspective, the main aims of the United Irishmen had now been fulfilled. He was happy to say that every constitutional reform which the Volunteers desired, and every grievance of which the United men complained, had found a remedy long ago by a parliament of the United Kingdom. If an inhabitant of Ballynahinch in 1798 could stand there that day he would see great changes. He could see signs of industry and prosperity all around; he could see the descendants of the United men in thousands praising God for the Union, and wearing Orange sashes.[19]

Commemoration of '98 in the twentieth century

As a result of the ultimate failure to erect the Wolfe Tone monument in Dublin, the focus in the 1900s switched to his grave at Bodenstown. Since 1891, annual Fenian commemorations had taken place here on the Sunday in June nearest his birthday. This continues to be the main focus of republican commemoration. The divisions and splits in republicanism down the years have resulted in many separate commemorative parades to Bodenstown churchyard, in some cases, carefully timed to avoid confrontation. However, there were lasting gains for nationalism from the 1898 commemorations, notably the reunification of the Parliamentary Party in 1900, under John Redmond. A new generation, seeing the Fenians as the true successors of '98, joined the organisation. They gave it a new vigour and direction, which was to lead to the Easter Rising of 1916. Patrick Pearse, one of this new generation, was a leading exponent of the efficacy of graveside commemoration. Speaking at a massive IRB commemoration at Bodenstown in 1913, Pearse described Tone as 'the greatest of Irish Nationalists'.

The work of commemoration was carried on by enthusiasts, and the National Graves Association (NGA) was set up in 1926, for the upkeep of patriot graves and monuments. As well as Tone's at Bodenstown, '98 monuments in NGA care include Bartholomew Teeling at Collooney, Co. Sligo, Roddy McCorley at Toomebridge, Co. Antrim, and the Croppy Boy/Pikeman at Tralee, Co. Kerry. National bodies, like the Irish National Foresters, Ancient Order of Hibernians and Gaelic Athletic Association, have kept the memory of the United Irishmen alive in the names of their branches. In 1938, Fr Patrick Murphy, of Glynn, Co. Wexford, believing that he would not live to see the 150th anniversary of the '98 rising, organised commemorations in his county. The priest became so associated with commemoration that he was accorded the epithet "98".

The Wexford 1938 commemorations seemed to capture the national mood, and their observance spread throughout nationalist Ireland. A youthful Conor Cruise O'Brien was one of the leading participants in the 1938 commemorations, which accorded with his then anti-partitionist views.

1948 in the South

For the sesquicentenary in 1948, there were huge rallies and parades in Co. Wexford. Fr Patrick Murphy actually did live to see and take an organisational role in the 1948 anniversary. The inter-party government of John Costello sponsored several official events, one of which was a large gathering at the Hill of Tara. This Church and State 'concelebration' involved prelates and government ministers, contingents of the Irish armed forces, representatives from the rebel counties of 1798 and a firing-party composed of the Old IRA. The official commemorations climaxed in a massive parade through the capital, involving nationalist organisations, ranging from the Anti-Partition League to the Catholic Boy Scouts of Ireland. While most of the floats and tableaux depicted 1798, there were representations of other eras, providing lines of affinity down the generations. Prominent among these was a representation of the scenes in the burning GPO during the 1916 Rising, based on the famous watercolour by Walter Paget, *The Birth of the Republic*. A small group of left-wingers and advanced Republicans, mostly in the Dublin area, used the commemorative year to propagate the radical ideas of the United Irishmen. In September, the commemorative year was crowned for many, when the Taoiseach, John Costello, announced that the government would move to set up a republic, thus fulfilling the aim of the United Irishmen.

1948 in the North

In the North, the 1948 commemorations took place against a background
of increasing sectarian polarisation. For the first time, commemorations
were allowed by the unionist government, which had previously used
Orders in Council to ban nationalist monuments, e.g. the memorial to
Roddy McCorley, the United Irishman, at Toomebridge. The
Commemoration Committee in Belfast was largely made up of
nationalists, ex-internees, and anti-partitionist socialists, the latter from a
mainly Protestant background. The Committee was described wrongly by
the *Belfast Telegraph* as 'Presbyterians to a man'. The Committee gave
notice of a rally, to be held on 13 September at a bomb site known as
'Blitz Square' off High Street, in Belfast city centre. The site was just
across the street from the place of execution of Henry Joy McCracken.
The rally was banned by the authorities and the Committee instead
participated in a march to Cave Hill. The 1795 declaration of the United
Irishmen was read, followed by an oration. The Cave Hill assembly
passed without incident. A commemorative '98 ceilidh had been
organised in the Ulster Hall, in the centre of Belfast, for 17 September.
The hall was owned by the unionist-dominated Belfast Corporation and,
predictably, the application for its use was turned down. This decision
was clearly discriminatory and the Commemoration Committee
successfully challenged it in the High Court. That night, in a packed
Ulster Hall, the organisers triumphantly went ahead with the ceilidh.

By now, as well as being part of the commemoration of '98, it had
become an expression of nationalist defiance of unionist repression. On
18 September, United Irish graves were visited at Clifton Street, Mallusk
and Templepatrick, and wreaths were laid, in some cases by surviving
relatives. The centrepiece of the 1948 commemorations in the North was
a parade, on 22 September, again confined to the nationalist Falls Road.
Thousands marched and many more watched. Among the marchers were
old men who as young boys had marched in the 1898 parade. Banners
surviving from the centenary parade were again unfurled. The march
finished at Corrigan Park with a rally attended by some 30,000.

Continuing unionist hostility

By 1948, strongly pro-partitionist unionist attitudes had been copper-
fastened by the separate experiences of the two parts of the island in the
recent war. In the North, the newly introduced benefits of the Welfare
State made Irish unity an even less attractive prospect. The declaration of
the Republic, in the South, made Unionists even more determined to

remain British. For many years after 1948, commemoration of the United Irishmen remained the preserve of republicanism. They were preaching to the converted, as most Protestants remained hostile. Indeed, during the most recent Troubles, loyalist paramilitaries took symbolic action against various United Irish monuments. The Ulster Volunteer Force (UVF) blew up the memorial to Wolfe Tone at Bodenstown in 1969. This was replaced in 1972. The statue of Tone, by Edward Delaney, installed in Stephen's Green, Dublin, in 1967, was bombed by the UVF in 1971. In the same year, they bombed Jemmy Hope's gravestone, at Mallusk, near Belfast.

Recent commemorations

In the last decade, despite the overall conflict, there has been a gradual thaw in northern Protestant attitudes to the United Irishmen. In 1991, the bicentenary of the foundation of the Society of United Irishmen, there were commemorative events, in most cases organised by non-political groups. A group of academics from North and South, involved in the major reworking of the history of the 1790s, organised a two-stage conference on the United Irishmen, in the Ulster Museum, Belfast, and Trinity College, Dublin. A permanent outcome of the conference was an edited collection, based on the various talks.[20] On 14 October 1997, the exact bicentenary date, over 600 people, from all communities, crammed into the Elmwood Hall at Queen's University for 'A Brotherhood of Affection'. This was a highly successful commemorative evening of songs, music, dancing, drama and lectures. Both events were grant-aided by the Cultural Traditions Group of the Northern Ireland Community Relations Council, a body set up by government to foster community relations and explore cultural diversity. These grants were awarded due to the cross-community nature of these events and their organisers. It was an important early official recognition of the efficacy of studying and commemorating the United Irishmen as part of our common heritage and history.

In 1997, the United Irishmen Commemoration Society (UICS) was set up in Belfast, involving mainly the same enthusiasts as in 1996. They aimed to organise events and disseminate information for the bicentenary commemorations in 1998. The UICS held a regular, well-attended programme of lectures at the Linen Hall Library in Belfast. By 1998, UICS membership had reached 250, representing a cross section of the community. As such, it is typical of many of the groups involved in the recent commemorations in the North. This has set the bicentenary apart from previous anniversaries in composition and emphasis. An example of

The Orange Order Memorial at Thiepval, set apart from the official Ulster Division Memorial (photograph by Tommy Kirkham).

Mural in east Belfast commemorating Pte. McFadzean VC and VVF 'hero' William Millar, featuring a wreath of poppies (photograph by Ian McGill).

this new direction occurred just prior to the commencement of the bicentenary. On Tuesday, 14 October 1997, an evening of lectures and Irish harp and uileann pipe music was held by the Remember Orr Society, at Templepatrick Old Presbyterian Church. This commemorated William Orr, the Presbyterian United Irishman, executed on that date in 1797. It set the scene for the bicentenary year, a major factor of which has been the reclamation by Presbyterians of a part of their history long banished from their communal memory.

The bicentenary in the North

The bicentenary has generally not been controversial or politically divisive. It is perhaps too early to fully comprehend why this has been so. Involvement in the recent commemorations has sprung from a variety of motivations, political, cultural, and historical. Many in the North, during the bicentenary, have viewed the United Irishmen through their own particular prisms. In the past, one side's commemoration has invariably been seen as triumphalism or coat-trailing by the other. '98 commemorations were perceived as the preserve of nationalists or republicans, both by friends and enemies. Interestingly, there have been comparatively few bicentenary commemorative events organised by republicans. In that quarter, there seems to have been a desire to eschew negative publicity, possibly arising from the exigencies of the peace process. There have been relatively few examples of the world-famous political murals devoted to the theme of the United Irishmen. Conspicuously absent during the bicentenary year was a major '98 parade on the Falls Road.

The Orange Order, which played a major part in defeating the United Irishmen in 1798, showed particular interest. Many of its Presbyterian members are descendants of United Irishmen. The Order held a 1798 exhibition in Comber, Co. Down. A colourful Battle of Antrim re-enactment, on Saturday 6 June 1998, was organised by the Ulster Heritage Museum Committee, a cultural body with close links to the Orange Order. During the year, members of the Order engaged in debate with other bodies on the legacy and present-day relevance of the ideas of the United Irishmen. Many Unionists commemorated the involvement of many of their forebears in armed struggle against the government in 1798, empathising with the reasons for such action then. This in no way compromised their opposition to its present-day manifestations, nor their own position as Unionists.

There was opposition to the commemorative events at the start of the bicentenary year. Some believed that all commemoration causes strife and should be avoided. Others, hostile to the United Irishmen, saw the bicentenary as propaganda for current republicanism. In the event, far from causing resentment and division as in the past, the commemoration of the United Irishmen and their ideals has provided a positive cross-community focus, much in keeping with the times.

The involvement of public bodies has been important. The Northern Ireland Community Relations Council (CRC), through its Cultural Diversities programme, funded many commemorative events, exhibitions, and publications. I was awarded a Cultural Traditions Fellowship to act as organiser of the UICS and to write a book on the history of commemoration of 1798. The CRC also funded an Outreach Officer to promote community involvement in the excellent 1798 exhibition 'Up in Arms', at the Ulster Museum. Belfast City Council also provided very generous funding to both the UICS and the Ulster Museum for the bicentenary. There were excellent exhibitions in the Belfast Central Library, the Down County Museum, Lisburn Museum, and the Linen Hall Library, Belfast. Many extensive commemoration programmes were organised by local councils, both nationalist- and unionist-controlled. There were several major '98 theatre productions in Belfast, including John Gray's dramatisation of Revd James Porter's *Billy Bluff and Squire Firebrand*, a new play, *Tearing the Loom* by Gary Mitchell, in the Lyric Theatre, and a reprise of Stewart Parker's *Northern Star*, in the appropriate setting of the eighteenth-century Rosemary Street Presbyterian Church.

The bicentenary in the South

In the South, commemoration programmes, locally and nationally, were greatly assisted by the government's Commemoration Committee. There were major '98 exhibitions at the National Commemoration Centre, Enniscorthy, Co. Wexford, and the 'Fellowship of Freedom' exhibition in the Collins Barracks annex of the National Museum of Ireland in Dublin. Political parties and movements, per se, seemingly absented themselves from commemorative events. In general, commemoration programmes were organised by committees composed mainly of local government representatives and officials, local historians and other enthusiasts. As in the North, some were no doubt motivated, to an extent, by opportunities for tourism. The largest of the local programmes in the south was Comóradh '98, centred in Wexford, as befits the county most heavily involved in 1798. There were many other local commemoration programmes, particularly in areas directly involved in 1798, such as Dublin City, North County Dublin/Fingal and Meath, Carlow, Wicklow,

Kildare, Mayo, Sligo, Leitrim, Longford and Donegal. In addition, there were many one-off events elsewhere. Government commemorations, involving ministers and units of the armed forces, took place, notably at Killala, Co. Mayo, with French official and military participation, as in 1798. The Taoiseach, Bertie Ahern, concluded the government's programme with the opening of the 'Croppies' Acre' Garden of Remembrance at Collins Barracks, Dublin.

Conclusion

There has been much column space devoted to '98 in local and national papers. The big gain, in terms of books, has been the outpouring of excellent local accounts of the events of that year, supplementing the national overviews. Whilst historians have recently produced a colossal number of books and articles, they have also been heavily involved in researching and writing for television networks, RTÉ, TnaG, BBC and UTV, which have all screened programmes or series on 1798. The newest media was employed in the shape of CD-Roms and Internet websites. It is indeed the case that today no one 'fears to speak of '98', except perhaps because the subject has been exhausted.

2

History à la carte? historical commemoration and modern Ireland

MARY DALY

I

Between 1995 and 1998 Ireland commemorated two of the major events in modern Irish history: the sesquicentenary of the Great Famine, and the bicentenary of the 1798 uprising. Both anniversaries have prompted an extensive series of conferences, lectures, exhibitions and public spectacles together with more lasting memorials in the form of museums and interpretative centres. And while many of these commemorations have been organised by local historical and community groups, the anniversaries have attracted a level of official patronage that is comparable only with the attention devoted to the fiftieth anniversary of the 1916 rising in 1966. In this chapter I propose to examine the programme of official commemorations during the years 1995–98, looking first at what has been commemorated, and what has been ignored; secondly at the tone of the official commemorations; and then, by looking in more detail at the commemoration of the Great Famine, to examine the similarity and divergence between the popular and official commemorations. Finally, it is important to ask what this recent wave of commemorations reveals about attitudes towards Irish history and specifically towards the wider question of revisionism.

The Irish Government's commitment to commemorating the Famine and 1798 is indicated by the presence in the Department of the Taoiseach in Upper Merrion St. (the hub of government) of a person who is wholly dedicated to commemorations. Each of the past three governments has designated a junior minister who is specifically responsible for the official commemorative programme, though other ministers, particularly the Taoiseach, are not slow to become involved. Since 1995 the annual estimates of the Taoiseach's Department have included a budget for these programmes, though the government has also drawn heavily on private sponsorship. When the office was originally established in 1994, the commemorative committee, which was drawn from public servants, was instructed to deal firstly with the Famine, then 1798, and lastly the millennium. (The millennium was dropped from this committee's remit early in 1995 shortly after the collapse of the Fianna Fáil–Labour government and its replacement by a coalition of the Fine Gael, Labour, and Democratic Left parties.) The omnibus nature of the responsibilities suggests that its activities were motivated by something wider than historical scholarship. There is no evidence to suggest that the decision to launch a programme of commemorative events came from historians. Indeed, at times historians have been akin to uninvited guests, though less so in the 1798 commemorations than in the case of the Famine.

II

The last major official commemoration before the current wave was the fiftieth anniversary of the 1916 rising. The Troubles in Northern Ireland followed shortly after 1966, and prompted considerable heart-searching over the impact of Irish history on contemporary events, and questions as to whether or not the 1966 commemorations had prompted a renewed wave of militant nationalism.[1] This heart-searching let to a reassessment of the history curriculum that was taught in primary and secondary schools, and a new set of school textbooks was written to take account of these susceptibilities. After 1966 the anniversaries of major historical events attracted at best low-key commemorations, (as in the case of the 50th anniversary of the founding of Dáil Éireann in 1969),[2] and sometimes almost nothing at all. The only memorable celebrations were those organised at a local level, such as the 1988 celebration of Dublin's millennium, Cork's 800th anniversary in 1985, the 300th anniversary of the Treaty of Limerick in 1691. The 75th anniversary of the 1916 rising was marked, or not marked, largely by embarrassment.[3]

Hence there is immense significance attached to the revival of official interest in commemorations after years of inactivity. At this stage it is not clear what prompted the change of heart, one factor may have been the commemoration of the bicentenary of the French Revolution[4] and the benefits that commemorations appeared to offer for tourism, employment and national prestige. By the 1990s the Irish tourist industry had been actively engaged in promoting heritage tourism for many years, and Americans and Australians were encouraged to visit Ireland in search of their ancestral roots. During the 1980s, when there was considerable unemployment among young people – many of them holding either the school Leaving Certificate or a university degree – the Irish Government and the state manpower training agency poured resources into projects that were seen as contributing to heritage tourism: compiling databases from old parish registers, deciphering and cleaning headstones in old graveyards, and establishing heritage centres or local museums. Similar projects were being funded at this time in Northern Ireland.[5]

There is little doubt that the decision to commemorate the Great Famine was prompted primarily by non-historical concerns (this is true of most commemorative events), and that non-historical concerns also impinged strongly on the commemoration of 1798. Before we examine these issues, it is interesting to note the anniversaries that were ignored by the official commemorative calendar during the years 1995–98. Bureaucrats prefer a neat and tidy schedule; history is not necessarily a tidy event, anniversaries clash and overlap. At an early stage it was decreed that the Famine commemoration would commence in September 1995 – one hundred and fifty years precisely from the time when the potato blight was first reported in Ireland – and end by the summer of 1997 to make way for the commemoration of 1798. The last official event was the unveiling of a Famine memorial in Co. Mayo on 20 July 1997; the 1798 commemoration was officially launched exactly six months later on 20 January 1998.[6] The duration and timing of the government's Famine commemorations almost exactly mirrored the British government's involvement in the real famine of the 1840s, though the British government did not officially end its programme of special relief measures until August 1997, or one month later.[7] One consequence of this timing is that the later stages of the famine from the autumn of 1847 have again been ignored, despite the fact that a majority of famine victims probably died after this date; evictions peaked in 1850 and the peak years for emigration were 1851 and 1852. This policy of discrete commemorative programmes also meant that Bantry Bay in 1796 was omitted from the official programme,[8] perhaps wisely since any undue attention to Hoche, the commander of the French fleet, and the man who was responsible for the massacres in the Vendée, might have proven rather uncomfortable, particularly given the tendency in many official speeches to relate the past to the present. Events marking the centenary of the 1898 Local Government Act, which inaugurated democratic local government in Ireland, were postponed until 1999, the anniversary of the first elections in order not to clash with 1798.

The official concentration on two major events, the Famine and 1798, meant that other anniversaries attracted scant attention. A comparison between the commemorative programmes of 1945–48 and 1995–98 is instructive in this respect. The Famine commemoration of the 1940s was a low-key affair: the GAA played the 1947 All-Ireland final in New York

– the only All-Ireland final to be played outside Ireland; in 1945 the Irish Folklore Commission's distributed a questionnaire specifically relating to folklore about the Famine, and the government provided funding for a scholarly study of the Great Famine.[9] By contrast, the centenaries of the deaths of Thomas Davis and Daniel O'Connell attracted considerable public attention,[10] as did the centenary of the 1848 Rebellion and the 150th anniversary of 1798.[11]

On this occasion O'Connell was relegated to a one-day conference at Maynooth, which was attended by President Mary Robinson, former Taoiseach Garret FitzGerald, the Chairman of the Reform Club and the Speaker of the House of Commons, Bernard Weatherill, though not apparently by any member of the Irish government or any formal representative of Dáil Éireann. The theme of the conference, which was organised by the National University at Maynooth, was the National Question, and papers examined current issues such as Ireland's monetary policy, so that the connection with O'Connell was somewhat incidental. Otherwise the only other gesture marking this anniversary was the opening of an O'Connell heritage trail in Co. Kerry.[12] O'Connell's eclipse probably owes much to his Catholicism; Catholicism is out of favour in Ireland at present – at least among the political and intellectual elite. By contrast, in the early years after independence the most successful commemorative occasions were the celebrations marking the centenary of Catholic emancipation in 1929 and the Eucharistic Congress, which celebrated the 1500th anniversary of the coming of Christianity to Ireland.[13] In the aftermath of civil war, Catholicism offered a common ground to over 90 per cent of the population of the Irish Free State, (though not of course to Protestants).[14] By 1997, however, O'Connell's Catholic nationalism was out of favour; it is equally possible that publicising his message of non-violence might have presented certain political difficulties. William Smith O'Brien and the 1848 rebellion have attracted an Andy-Warhol-measure of attention, with a visit by the Taoiseach, Bertie Ahern, to Ballingarry in July 1998, and plans to turn the Widow McCormack's house, though not apparently the more famous cabbage patch – which was the setting for this rather inglorious – rising into an interpretative centre. But, as Minister of State Avril Doyle (the minister responsible for commemorations from December 1994 until June 1997) remarked, '1798 in Wexford was not cabbage-patch skirmishes',[15] so 1848 has been relegated in favour of a greater battlefield. Other 1848 commemorations have been largely masterminded by Irish-Australians. Descendants of 1848 leaders, such as Michael Doheny, have visited Ireland, unveiling plaques, etc. and conducting what can best be described as private commemorations.

Thomas Davis was undoubtedly the major loser in latter times. In September 1945, the centenary of his death was marked by a week of lectures (including one by Sinéad de Valera), parades, concerts, wreath-layings, art exhibitions and several commemorative volumes. For neutral Ireland, denied the opportunity to celebrate VE Day or VJ Day, it provided an opportunity for military parades and illuminated buildings and seems to have been consciously used as such. Éamon de Valera, who played a prominent role in the Davis centenary, emphasised his love of the Irish language and wish to unite Orange and Green. One centenary essay emphasised Davis's place as a founding father of an independent Ireland and a seminal influence on the socio-economic policies of Fianna Fáil.

> In truth never was Davis better worthy to be read than now, when the means have been won to build up on three-quarters of our land a life like that which he envisaged and described: a nation based on a populous country-side of peasant proprietors and towns of free artisans; the whole people devoted to religion and homely ways; the rulers spring from the folk and answerable to them. The schools patriotic and popular; learning and science, arts, letters, Press and other institutions all directed by public-spirited zeal for the community.[16]

Although it would have been difficult to present such a memoir in the 1990s, Davis's apparent fall from favour is puzzling, though the Irish language is no longer widely acknowledged as a central element in Irish identity. However, it is surprising that the Young Irelanders were not in greater favour in the Ireland of that decade, in the light of their commitment to an Irish nationalism that included people of different religions and ethnic backgrounds.

III

This brings us to the Famine and 1798. Both commemorations have involved governments (and ministers) drawn from the two main Irish political parties, Fianna Fáil and Fine Gael. Perhaps the first point to note is the bi-partisan approach that has been adopted to both events – indeed Fine Gael's Avril Doyle (Minister for State at the Department of the Taoiseach) and Fianna Fail's Síle de Valera (Minister for Arts, Heritage, Gaeltacht) used identical phrases in major speeches about 1798.[17] However there are important distinctions between the tone of speeches on the Famine and those on 1798. Whereas there has been a strong editorial line on 1798, which emphasises an official version of the history and almost forbids any alternative interpretations, the ministerial speeches on the Famine adopted a much softer, much vaguer tone. Most if not all included references to pain, memory, therapy, grieving; the fact that only now are we in a position to remember the Famine because it is now distant from us; how much better life was in the 1990s because of the modern Welfare State; the Irish Famine as an international event. There are numerous references to the diaspora; parallels between the Famine of the 1840s and contemporary famines in the Third World; Ireland's empathy with Third World suffering as a consequence of our Famine experience.[18]

However, the government commemoration of the Famine went to considerable effort to play down any element of sectarianism; several speeches emphasised the contributions that the all the churches made to famine relief. One of the first events in the official commemorative calendar in September 1995 was an ecumenical service in the Church of Ireland Cathedral in Tuam. References to blame and responsibility were either absent or such as to suggest that we were all to blame. The Famine was presented as an all Ireland event, with Minister Doyle travelling to Derry to launch the Teagasc exhibition in February 1996. However in contrast to the 1798 commemoration, where the National Museum unveiled a major exhibition (in association with the Ulster Museum), there was no official Famine exhibition, though one was originally planned. The closest to an official exhibition was the exhibition organised by Teagasc, the state's agricultural advisory service, which concentrated heavily on agricultural aspects of the disaster, with displays of pre-Famine varieties of potatoes, opportunities to taste lumper potatoes, and a practical demonstration of how potatoes were planted in the so-called lazy beds; this also devoted some space to the theme of famine in the Third World.

The strong emphasis in all ministerial speeches on pain, memory and therapy was reflected in many of the commemorative events that were organised by local groups. There were candlelight processions to work-houses, (e.g. the processions to Macroom workhouse from surrounding districts which took place in May 1997), or to the sites of Famine graves; the marking of Famine graveyards; the commissioning of sculptures, paintings, etc.; the unveiling of plaques on the sites of former workhouses (as in Ennistymon, Co. Clare). In Birr, Co. Offaly and Bawnboy, Co. Cavan, the anniversary of the Famine prompted local efforts to restore disused and abandoned workhouses. This form of 'new-age' commemo-ration, or commemoration as a form of national therapy, has achieved wide support in the Irish media, particularly from *Irish Times* columnist John Waters. Unfortunately it indicates a defective memory and under-standing of the Irish past. If the Irish Famine was not commemorated in the past by formal monuments or official ceremonies, this did not mean that it had been forgotten.[19] Indeed even the most casual examination of the speeches of Irish politicians, reports written by public servants and other written records throws up recurring references to '47, to famine, where the terms are used in such a manner as to indicate that they are part of a commonly understood discourse.[20] The wave of commemorations reflects the gestures of a population that is now more urban, that is less in touch with rural Ireland and with its past. The memory of the Famine is no longer part of a long-standing tradition; rather it now has to be made intelligible to people who find it distant to their everyday lives. The commemorations are an indication of the changes that have taken place in Ireland since the 1940s.

Many of Avril Doyle's speeches employed themes, and indeed phrases, that can be traced to earlier speeches by President Mary Robinson. The title given to Avril Doyle's speech at the opening of a conference in Dublin Castle on 'International perspectives of the Great Famine': 'First World Country – Third World Memory' is a phrase that President Robinson employed on many occasions. A careful examination of the text of President Robinson's speeches suggests that, unconsciously or otherwise, she set the editorial line for much of the official Famine commemoration, specifically in the emphasis that was placed on the Irish diaspora, the Third World and the factors that are common to Ireland in the 1840s and modern famines. In August 1994 at Grosse Île in Quebec – a quarantine station where thousands of Famine emigrants died – President Robinson referred to her visits to Rwanda and Somalia.[21] When she opened the Famine Museum at Strokestown in May 1994, at a time when the government was only beginning to consider a possible programme of events to commemorate the Great Famine, the *Irish Times* headed its coverage with the caption: 'President compares unemployed youth to people exiled by Famine'. The contrast that Avril Doyle drew in a speech at the opening of the Cork Archives Famine Exhibition between modern social welfare programmes and the situation at the time of the Famine could be seen as an implicit rebuttal of that argument. President Robinson's speech at Strokestown contained several references to Somalia and South Africa; she also remarked that the Famine emigrants had greater freedom of movement than the youth of modern Ireland who faced restrictions if they wished to emigrate to the United States.[22]

Robinson's most important speech on this subject was probably her address to both Houses of the Oireachtas in February 1995. This was given the title 'Cherishing the Irish Diaspora', and she made the commemoration of the Great Famine her central theme. The speech contained the by-now-familiar references to Africa, the diaspora, voluntary aid workers and praise for the National Genealogical Programme. Speaking specifically of the Famine commemoration, she emphasised that 'the commemoration is a moral act'. It offered an opportunity to understand 'economic vulnerability' in the present; to connect the Irish diaspora of the past with modern refugees and modern victims of world hunger. 'This imaginative way of interpreting the past' was, she believed, something that could be shared with 'our Diaspora'.

The practice of drawing analogies between the Great Famine and famine in the Third World predated the recent anniversary of the Great Famine; it goes back at least to Bob Geldof's Live Aid, and perhaps to an earlier date. In 1989 AFri, an organisation that is engaged in raising public awareness about poverty and hunger in the Third World, reprinted an abridged version of Canon O'Rourke's 1874 book, *The Great Irish Famine*, and for some years AFri has organised a 'Famine Walk' in Co. Mayo to retrace a route taken by Famine victims in the 1840s in an effort to persuade the Westport Board of Guardians to grant them assistance. Perhaps the most explicit attempt to identify the Irish Famine with modern famines in the Third World is found in the Famine Museum at Strokestown where artefacts and information on modern Sudan and Ethiopia are juxtaposed with material relating to Co. Roscommon in the 1840s, without any attempt to distinguish between the two. In this presentation the World Bank is depicted as the agent of global free-trade capitalism that bears the primary responsibility for modern famines, much as the policies favoured by the British government did in Ireland during the 1840s.

This tendency to see the Great Famine as analogous to modern famines emerges also in many recent books, notably Margaret Kelleher's *The Feminization of Famine*.[23] It reflects the current intellectual vogue for an eclectic approach that ranges freely across time and distance. In fact such comparisons do considerable injustice to the Great Famine, in that the mortality in recent famines is relatively low when compared with the numbers who died in Ireland in the 1840s. Such comparisons also considerably understate the real cost to Britain or indeed to the world of the 1840s of providing adequate relief for Ireland; it would cost much less at present in real terms to provide adequate relief to Third World countries.[24]

Linking the Great Famine with a critique of global capitalism and the policies that are currently being pursued by the World Bank might present certain problems for the Irish government, given its zealous and effective pursuit of foreign investment, its commitment to the European Community and European Monetary Union and its active membership of the World Bank. However, this has not happened, because the issue has never been pressed to its ultimate conclusion, and successive governments have to date successfully evaded the potential pitfalls that might emerge from this quarter.

The second major theme in the Famine commemoration – the importance that was assigned to the diaspora – has presented potentially greater pitfalls. In many respects the attention that the official commemoration has given to Irish communities overseas and the descendants of Irish emigrants is a good thing. Irish history has tended to neglect the history of the Irish overseas, except in so far as Irish emigrants made a contribution to the cause of Irish freedom. Until recently, however, few Irish students would have learned about Irish-America or the Irish in Britain.[25] The official programme commemorating the Famine included a ministerial visit to Liverpool, the city that probably suffered most from that calamity.[26]

In North America the commemoration of the Famine raised a number of controversial issues. The timing of the anniversary has proved to be extremely important, because 1995 was also the 50th anniversary of the ending of the Second World War, and this led to renewed interest in the Nazi death camps and the Jewish Holocaust; the opening of Holocaust museums in Washington and in other American cities, notably Boston, and the introduction of the Jewish Holocaust as an item on the curriculum in the public schools of several American states. Just as the Holocaust has come to be regarded as a key element in the Jewish-American identity, part of their founding myth, the Great Famine has increasingly assumed a similar role for Irish America; indeed it has done so for a long time. The estimated 1.5m emigrants who arrived before 1845 tend to be passed over (perhaps the fact that so many were Ulster Protestants has been a factor in this), and there is little recognition of the fact that the size of the Irish community on the eve of the Famine was an important factor in attracting large numbers of emigrants during the years 1845–55.[27] As for the long period of mass emigration from the 1860s to 1929, this is often viewed as a long-term consequence of the Famine. In the past, Irish nationalists and Irish-Americans have tended to deny that Irish men and women emigrated in pursuit of better economic opportunities, just as the Germans, the Swedes or the English did.[28] In the case of Irish America traditional badges of identity are disappearing fast: religious practice has waned; marriages are increasingly being contracted with people from other ethnic groups; Irish Catholics no longer send their children to parish schools where they are taught by Irish-born priests and nuns, and increasingly the local Catholic clergy no longer come from Ireland, or even from Irish-American families. Except in isolated instances such as South Boston, most Irish-Americans now live in suburbia, not in predominantly Irish communities. However, in a country that now emphasises multiculturalism, rather than the melting pot, the Famine offers a soft, emotional form of Irish identity, an opportunity to empathise with their past.

There is also a certain element of competition, whether with Italian-Americans who erected monuments to Christopher Columbus in 1992, or with the emphasis on Holocaust studies. In Canada, the proposal to open a heritage centre at Grosse Île became a major cause of contention between some Irish-Canadians, who wished the site to become exclu-sively a memorial to the Famine Irish, and Parks Canada, who wanted to remember all immigrants to Canada. Grosse Île was used as a quarantine station from 1832 until 1937. In 1909 a memorial was erected to the over 3,000 Irish people that died there in 1847.[29] The dispute would appear to have been resolved amicably.

In the United States there have been campaigns in several states to include the Irish Famine in the syllabus for Genocide and Holocaust studies. (The Armenian Massacre is also part of this syllabus in some US states). The draft syllabus that was submitted to the New Jersey Commission on Holocaust Education in the state of New Jersey resembles an inflammable mixture of the writings of two nineteenth-century authors, Canon O'Rourke, a parish priest of Maynooth, and the Young Ireland leader, John Mitchel.[30] Among the reasons given for the impoverishment of the Irish (and consequently an important cause of the Famine) are all the landmarks commonly found in traditional nationalist summaries of 800 years of English misrule: the Statutes of Kilkenny (1366), the Reformation, Oliver Cromwell, the Penal Laws. The teachers' notes that have been provided barely mention the potato; they make no reference whatsoever to the growth in population; neither do any of the selected readings that were provided. One section in the notes for students is headed 'Irish starve amid plenty' – the source is inevitably John Mitchel; some of the citations from modern scholars have been edited in a manner that distorts their argument into a more anti-British version than is apparent in the full text.[31]

Irish-Americans (much more than the Irish in Britain) have undoubtedly influenced the commemorations of the Great Famine. Perhaps this should not surprise us, since many of the dominant images of the Famine over the past 150 years come from the works of John Mitchel, which were written and first published in the United States. The term 'Holocaust', which is widely applied to the Famine in Irish-American circles, has not been commonly used in Ireland and there has been very little reporting of the inclusion of the Famine in Genocide and Holocaust studies courses.

Once again the timing of the commemoration is important, because the influence of Irish-America has been at a peak in recent years. The Northern Ireland crisis forced the Irish government to establish contacts and influence on Capitol Hill and among the wider Irish-American community, in an effort to thwart the fundraising and public relations efforts of republican sympathisers;[32] the wave of undocumented Irish immigrants during the 1980s brought a new awareness of Irish-America within Ireland.[33] In addition, it became common to draw rather sweeping analogies between the emigrants of the 1980s and those of the Famine years. Fundraising groups, such as the Ireland Fund, have deliberately employed memories of the Famine, or images of poverty and unrest in contemporary Ireland to elicit support;[34] the presence of Jean Kennedy-

Smith as US Ambassador to Ireland has added to this influence. Thus, if the Irish government saw the Famine as an opportunity for building stronger links with the Irish community overseas, this was by no means a one-way traffic. Irish-American money has funded Famine-related events and memorials, such as the Strokestown Museum and the construction of replicas of two 'coffin ships' – the *Jeanie Johnston* at Fenit in Co. Kerry and the *Dunbrody* in New Ross, Co. Wexford.[35]

One consequence of this focus on the diaspora has been the suggestion that the Irish overseas are the true victims of the Famine; that they have a superior standing as its victims over those who live in Ireland. The catchphrase, 'We are the survivors of the famine', recurred in so many discussions on the Famine that eventually it became a cliché. This interpretation suggested that those who died, and those who emigrated carry equal status as Famine victims (It is doubtful that people who lived in nineteenth-century Ireland would have seen matters in this way). In turn it has been suggested that this superior victimhood means that expatriates are in a better position to interpret the Famine, and to understand it, than those remaining in Ireland.[36]

Another consequence has been a lack of interest in the microhistory of the Famine: – i.e. how it affected land ownership, population, the distribution of land, and class interests within Ireland. The tendency to gloss over these issues was also evident in television documentaries which were often targeted at overseas markets. For a global market, a global interpretation is undoubtedly much more attractive, and it is this image of the Irish emigrant as an exile, a victim of the Famine; a victim of British misrule, that has often prevailed. As I have already noted, the old topic of Britain's responsibility was given a modern gloss by equating nineteenth-century laissez-fare economics to global capitalism. The question of Britain's responsibility also came to be linked with the IRA ceasefire in Northern Ireland, because it has been suggested that while the conflict in Northern Ireland continued, people were afraid to mention Britain's responsibility for the Famine (or indeed to voice any sympathy for Irish republican heroes of the past); however with the ceasefire it was again permissible to do so.[37] Again, the issue became entangled with Germany's responsibility for the Holocaust and with the demands that the Emperor of Japan apologise to former allied prisoners of war and their families for the manner in which they were treated by the Japanese. The statement by British Prime Minister Tony Blair admitting that the 'people of Ireland were failed in their hour of need by the Government in London' was a response to demands from some quarters in Ireland for a formal apology.[38] What is clear is that the Great Famine is now an international event, and although there is much merit in ending the long-standing practice of regarding Irish history as *sui generis*, at present this comparative dimension has probably obscured our understanding of the history of the Famine, rather than added to it.

From the global let us turn to the local, as President Robinson suggested. As noted, the Famine was marked by many local commemorations. Indeed it offered the ideal commemorative event, since all parts of Ireland could justly claim to have experienced it, whereas other anniversaries, such as 1798, were necessarily concentrated in certain areas. The Famine commemoration undoubtedly produced some valuable local information, which was mainly drawn from local newspapers or the minutes of local workhouses; indeed the commemoration actually unearthed some missing volumes of minutes.[39] Unfortunately the detail and complexity of the local accounts appear to have made little impact beyond the research seminar or the dedicated local amateur historian, perhaps because the outcome is an extremely rich and complicated series of Famine narratives – all different – and this necessarily leads to a loss in clarity. Many Irish people who became interested in the Famine during the years 1995–97 preferred to concentrate on pain and therapy, on commissioning works of art or restoring buildings and clearing disused graveyards. There was remarkably little interest in moving from a generalised empathy to specifics, by discovering precisely what categories of people were most likely to die, when they died or why. Lectures on these subjects, which attempt to examine the outcome on the basis of age, gender, marital status, or socio-economic condition, rarely provoked specific questions or much evidence of interest.[40] Indeed, regardless of the specific subject of a lecture, the questions tended to follow well-trodden paths. Almost every session at the official conference on international aspects of the Great Famine in Dublin Castle was followed by a question on the export of food from Ireland during the Famine, irrespective of whether the preceding paper had examined the impact of famine in nineteenth century India on births and deaths, the famine in Finland in the 1860s, the impact of the potato blight on continental Europe during the 1840s, or women and the Irish Famine. It seemed that successive questioners, having failed to get the wished-for answer on the first occasion, hoped that they would eventually succeed. Indeed, while scholars such as James Donnelly and Joel Mokyr have concentrated their criticism over Britain's responsibility for the Famine on the sum of money that the exchequer made available for famine relief and they have compared the almost £70 million that Britain spent on the Crimean War with the estimated £7.3 million that was provided for Irish famine relief[41] – the wider public tends to argue the case for Britain's guilt by referring to the export of food during the Famine years. The image of Irish people starving while enormous quantities of food were exported from Ireland, which was crafted by John Mitchel in the mid-nineteenth century, and Mitchel's belief that Ireland was capable of feeding many more than its population of eight million even at the height of the Famine is still widely accepted as correct, despite the impeccable scholarship of Austin Bourke and Peter Solar showing that neither argument is correct. According to James Donnelly, even a cursory check of trade figures that were readily available during the nineteenth century would have disproved this argument.[42] Otherwise, at both Dublin Castle and at many local seminars, questions from the floor generally concentrated on a traditional nationalist analysis, which sees the Famine as merely one piece in a story of conquest that stretches over seven or eight hundred years. One speaker from the floor at Birr criticised a lecturer for failing to mention the major causes of the Famine – Oliver Cromwell and the penal laws; the preceding paper had examined mortality in the Birr area during the Famine years. Another requested a list of names of those who were guilty of causing the Famine, but further questioning revealed that he wanted a list of guilty people in Whitehall, Westminster, Dublin Castle and other distant locations, not a list of guilty people in Birr. In other words, he was not prepared to countenance any suggestion that some people in the locality might have died because of the actions or inaction of landlords, land agents, middle-men, larger farmers, exploitative grain dealers, negligent poor law officials, and members of the board of guardians.

This unwillingness to investigate the local impact of the Famine is regrettable, because there remain many unanswered questions concerning the differences in both the timing and the severity of the Famine that can simply be explained either by the poverty or the population density in each area. These topics are of particular relevance if we are to understand how the Famine unfolded after the summer of 1847, a chapter of the Famine story that is generally ignored and one that has been largely ignored during the recent wave of commemorations. Perhaps the suggestion that we are the survivors of the Famine may have some validity after all, since many of these questions relate to the local economy, local elites and property relations. Indeed, the focus in recent commemorations on pain, memory and therapy has promoted a tendency to gloss over such details. Similarly the assertion that we were all victims of the Famine, if only as suffering from some form of national post traumatic stress disorder, obscures the reality that there were substantial differences in the impact of the Famine between different regions and different social classes.

Another dimension of the 150th anniversary was the inclusion of Ulster in the Famine story. Traditional versions of the Famine suggested that Ulster was largely spared this disaster; the index to Cecil Woodham-Smith's best-selling book, *The Great Hunger*, does not include the word 'Ulster'. As to the explanations given for Ulster's escape, in the past they varied from the mid-nineteenth-century providentialist version that the Famine only affected improvident Catholics, not hard-working God-fearing Protestants; to the suggestion that better relations between landlords and tenants, and the Ulster custom provided the answer, or that the population of Ulster was more dependent on oatmeal and therefore less affected by the failure of the potato. In fact the impact within the province of Ulster varied considerably, with south and south-west Ulster, counties Monaghan, Cavan and Fermanagh being severely affected; Donegal getting off very lightly indeed and a limited impact in east Ulster (much less than is now suggested in a reversal of the traditional interpretation). At the moment the inclusion of Ulster has again served to confuse rather than enlighten: a lot of the distress in Antrim, Armagh and Down that has been attributed to the Famine in recent times was due to the final collapse of domestic spinning and the financial crisis in 1847.[43] Although Ulster shares some features of the Famine with counties such as Clare or Mayo, there are important differences. Ulster communities were much less reliant on the state, indeed they were often reluctant to accept public money; Ulster landlords were more arrogant about their ability to relieve distress without outside intervention and their attitude may resulted in people dying.[44] Interestingly some of the new work on Ulster has begun to pinpoint the deteriorating relationship between landlord and tenant during Famine years, and the evidence that east Ulster, at least, then saw itself as a place apart. Although the more prosperous poor law unions of east Leinster and Ulster were asked to contribute towards the cost of local relief in the poorer areas of the west of Ireland, the Ulster unions were alone in refusing to pay.[45]

IV

Before bringing this chapter to an end, I wish to look very briefly at how the 1798 Rising has been presented in official speeches. Unlike the official commemoration of the Famine, which was something of a rushed affair, there was considerable advance planning for the bicentenary of 1798, and the commemoration benefited enormously from the fact that the minister in charge of commemorations, Avril Doyle, represented Co. Wexford in Dáil Éireann. The stronger didactic tone in the official speeches commemorating 1798 suggests that this was regarded as a much more sensitive commemoration, one that offered more immediate parallels with contemporary Ireland (the Third World is comfortingly far away). It would seem that the Irish government sought to use the bicentenary of 1798 in order to bolster the peace process, just as the commemoration in 1898 was used by Irish nationalists to re-invigorate their movement. Irrespective of party politics, ministerial speeches have emphasised that the United Irishmen included men and women from all traditions, and there has been considerable emphasis on Presbyterian republicanism. In a manner that recalls the traditional Irish nationalist narrative, 1798 has also been presented as a step on the road to democracy. Visitors to the 1798 Museum in Enniscorthy, which was opened to mark the bicentenary, walk across the Bridge of Democracy which begins in Athens and ends at Wexford. In the Enniscorthy museum and in official speeches there is considerable emphasis on 1798 as an all-Ireland event. Although at first glance the gloss is open to several interpretations, including perhaps a two-nation version, it has often tended to be simplified into a reincarnation of the traditional Irish republican vision of Irish history – the long march to freedom and belief that in every Ulster Unionist there beats the heart of a United Irishman, if only Britain would withdraw from Ireland.[46]

Both of the commemorations reveal much more about contemporary Ireland than about the actual history of either the Famine or 1798. There are some common themes: the emphasis that was placed on the international dimension, on the diaspora, on the role of women in the case of 1798, though less so in the Famine;[47] the playing down of any sectarian dimension; and the prominence that has been given to what has been termed 'the catastrophic dimension of Irish history'.[48] However there are some differences between the two events; there is a single official narrative of 1798 – one that is to a large extent a reprise of the traditional republican narrative. In the case of the Famine, although a clear narrative of the Famine exists – the Famine as yet another example of Britain's effort to conquer Ireland – this was not the official line; indeed, at times the official version of the Famine appeared to have been detached from history and suspended in some postmodernist timeless zone in a manner that resembles the treatment of the Holocaust.[49] This probably reflects an effort to walk a tightrope between the potential pitfalls of offending either Irish-America and a section of Irish public opinion, and the alternative peril of antagonising Britain. Perhaps the most worrying feature of both commemorations has been the decided lack of curiosity about the internal dynamics of Irish society in the 1790s or the 1840s, and a continuation of the long-standing tendency to blame the outcome on external factors. There has been an unwillingness to confront some of the messier aspects of these historical events, whether this was sectarianism in 1798, which cannot simply be dismissed as a construct that was imposed by mischief-makers, or the reshaping of Irish society as a consequence of the Famine – whether this took the form of ethnic cleansing as appears to have been the case in Co. Fermanagh, where the proportion of Catholics living in some areas containing good agricultural land fell sharply between the 1830s and the 1860s, (most of the Catholics that disappeared had probably been cottiers or labourers), or the consolidation of holdings that took place in the immediate aftermath of the Famine. As a consequence, both commemorations exude a certain air of complacency, which was very much in keeping with Ireland in the late 1990s, enjoying as it was, a period of unprecedented economic prosperity.

In 1988 Roy Foster noted that in the world of Irish history 'academic revisionism has coincided with popular revivalism'.[50] Popular revivalism has been very much to the fore during these occasions though it is often wearing new garments, and there has also been a substantial injection of academic post-revisionism. For many people both commemorations have offered what could be described as comfort history – a return to the old familiar story, though for nationalist Ireland this tends to be a history of discomfort and catastrophe.

These commemorations pose interesting dilemmas for academic historians. Lecturing to local gatherings serves as an important reminder of the gap between academic debate and what is of interest to a popular audience. Commemorations also offer the lure of media attention, the possibility of enhanced book sales, television fees, plus the danger that to profit from these events it might be desirable to bring the analysis into line with what is politically correct or in favour. There is a further danger that opinions that were heavily qualified and balanced in an interview are edited into sound bites designed to give a different impression. In recent times a number of television documentaries that were produced to mark the anniversaries of events in Irish history have included statements that were factually inaccurate. These are not trivial matters. Despite the remarkable increase in the number of Irish people with second and third-level education, an ever-smaller proportion of the population now studies history. Consequently historical knowledge and understanding is more likely to come from commemorative events, tie-in television programmes, heritage centres or films. The continuing large sales of the so-called *Famine Diary*, several years after it was exposed as a fraud, is one indication of this.[51]

However, we should probably also keep these concerns in perspective; the men and women of Wexford who spent much of 1998 dressing up and parading as pike persons have probably already lost interest; within twelve months, many were probably be found rehearsing some futuristic pageant for the millennium. For many young Irish men and women, I suspect that Irish history is a very marginal concern.

Appendix

A

Just as the landscape of Ireland still bears the physical scars of the disaster so the people of Ireland bear the emotional scars of that appalling tragedy. In every county of Ireland can be found the unmarked remains of the

Famine. Potato ridges, deserted villages, paupers' graveyards and still in some places the dreaded workhouses are there to remind us of our past.

But the emotional scars are there too. Until recent years the pain of the famine was too close to allow us properly to confront the memories of these days. ... We need to mourn our dead and to grieve for our loss. It is time for us to come to terms with the disaster. We need the therapy of grief. The 100th anniversary of the Famine was still too close; the pain still too acute; for people to commemorate the tragedy. We now have the opportunity to begin the grieving, and the healing, process.

...

Helplessness in the face of such suffering led people to avoid talking about the Famine and contributed to what has been called a 'Famine Amnesia' in the past. But the Famine was not forgotten. The response of the Irish people to appeals for famine relief in modern times has been very generous. This has clearly grown from a folk memory of the Famine. Our own Famine taught us to respond generously to the needs of others.

(Speech by the Minister of State Avril Doyle T.D. at a mass for the victims of the Famine in Our Lady of Lourdes Church, Caltra, Ballinasloe, Co. Galway, 16 November 1995).

B

'... for almost 3 million Irish men women and children, the annual potato harvest was the one equivalent of the Social Welfare system. Its loss could be compared to the effect of the collapse of today's Social Welfare system, if such an unthinkable act were to happen. The historical research project may seem as little more than an academic study but the reality for our people was a matter of life and death. When the potato failed there was no Social Welfare, no Local Development Partnership, no County Enterprise Boards, no Urban and Village Renewal programmes, to assist. The Social Welfare system of the time was woefully inadequate for the challenge it had to face.

(Address by Minister of State Avril Doyle T.D. at the opening of the Cork Archives Famine Exhibition called 'Our Dark Legacy' in the Cork Public Museum, 16 November 1995.)

C

A central theme of the Government's commemorative programme has been precisely to make explicit the international aspects of the Irish Famine . ... Our Famine confers a unique responsibility on us in terms of world hunger, we are a first world country with a third world memory. As such, we as a people have contributed on both a personal and national level to relieving global hunger....

Consideration of the Famine also forces us to recognise that we must assume a far greater recognition of our responsibilities towards – our connection with – our diaspora, working creatively in a process of 'globalisation'. Part of that equation is the role of massive emigration – which, looked at in a positive sense, laid the foundation for our diaspora. That responsibility involves us in a more considered, supportive and communicative relationship with our diaspora. Half of all Irish people born in Ireland since 1841 have emigrated. While there are currently five million people on this island, there are at least seventy million in the Irish diaspora.

In this sense too, Ireland as a country has to face the complexity of the world.

Circling the cultural wagons creates a stifling stasis, immured behind cultural tariff walls, and with a tightly policed cultural cordon sanitaire. This effort at constructing a cultural cocoon necessarily involves a retreat into an idealised past rather than an openness to the future. At its best, the result is populist nostalgia, a cloying elegy for a lost world. At its worst, it involves racist, xenophobic and cultural chauvinisms, unrelenting in its hostility to otherness. Ireland can no longer afford this reactionary modern mobilisation under faded ancient banners; it involves a souring and thinning of meaning, an impoverishment of identity, within a sterile survival straitjacket. We as a nation can no longer afford the comforting but dangerous illusion of unitary identity, a seamless, stable tradition. Our identity now is multiple and plural, overlaid by overlapping layers.

It is impossible to hermetically seal the local from the global, to indulge in the fantasy of undisturbed residence within the warm embrace of a primary world.

(Speech by Minister Avril Doyle T.D. at 'International Perspectives on the Great Irish Famine' Dublin Castle, 8 and 10 May 1997.

D

This year we begin to commemorate the Irish Famine which started 150 years ago. All parts of this island – north and south, east and west – will see their losses noted and remembered, both locally and internationally. This year we will see those local and global connections made obvious in the most poignant ways. But they have always been there.

Last year, for example, I went to Grosse Île, an island on the St. Lawrence River near Quebec city. I arrived in heavy rain and as I looked at the mounts which, together with small white crosses, are all that mark the mass graves of the 5,000 or more Irish people who died there, I was struck by the sheer power of commemoration. I was also aware that, even across time and distance, tragedy must be seen as human and not historic, and that to think of it in national terms alone can obscure that fact. As I stood looking at Irish graves, I was also listening to the story of the French-Canadian families who braved fever and shared their food, who took the Irish into their homes and into their heritage.

[THERE FOLLOWED TWO PARAGRAPHS IN IRISH ABOUT THE IRISH LANGUAGE AS SPOKEN IN NEW YORK, TORONTO AND SYDNEY].

And so, the weight of the past, the researches of our local interpreters and the start of the remembrance of the Famine all, in my view, point us towards a single reality: that commemoration is a moral act, just as our relation in this country to those who have left it is a moral relationship. We have too much at stake in both not to be rigorous. We cannot have it both ways. We cannot want a complex present and still yearn for a simple past. I was very aware of that when I visited the refugee camps in Somalia and more recently in Tanzania and Zaire. The thousands of men, women and children who came to those camps were, as were the Irish of the 1840s, defenceless in the face of catastrophe. Knowing our own history, I saw the tragedy of their hunger as a human disaster. We, of all people, know it is vital that it be carefully analysed so that their children and their children's children be spared that ordeal. We realise that while a great part of our immediate concern for their situation, as Irish men and women who have a past which includes famine, must be at practical levels of help, another part of it must consist of a humanitarian perspec-tive which springs directly from our self-knowledge as a people. Famine is not only humanly destructive, it is culturally disfiguring. The Irish who died at Grosse Île were men and women and indeed children with plans and dreams of future achievements. It takes from their humanity and indi-viduality to consider them merely as victims.

Therefore it seemed to me vital, even as I watched the current tragedy in Africa, that we should uphold the dignity of the men and women who suffer there by insisting there are no inevitable victims. It is important that in our own commemoration of famine, such reflections have a place. As Tom Murphy has eloquently said in an introduction his play *Famine*: 'a hungry and demoralised people becomes silent'. We cannot undo the silence of our own past but we can lend our voice to those who now suffer. To do so we must look at our history, in the light of this commem-oration, with a clear insight which exchanges the view that they were inevitable victims in it for an active involvement in the present applica-tion of its meaning. We can examine in detail humanitarian relief now and assess the inadequacies of both. And this is not just a task for historians. I have met children in schools and men and women all over Ireland who make an effortless and sympathetic connection between our past suffering and the present tragedies of hunger in the world. One of the common bonds between us and our diaspora can be to share this imaginative way of re-interpreting the past. I am certain that they, too, will feel that the best possible commemoration of the men and women who died in that famine, who were cast up on other shores because of it, is to take their dispossession into the present with us to help others who now suffer in a similar way.

Therefore I welcome all initiatives being taken during this period of commemoration, many of which can be linked with those abroad, to contribute to the study and understanding of economic vulnerability. I include in that all the illustrations of the past which help us understand the present. In the Famine Museum in Strokestown there is a vivid and careful retelling of what happened during the Famine. When we stand in front of those images I believe we have a responsibility to understand them in human terms now, not just in Irish terms then. They should inspire us to be a strong voice in the analysis of the cause and the cure of conditions that predispose to world hunger, whether that involves us in the current debate about access to adequate water supplies or the protection of economic migrants. We need to remember that our own diaspora was once vulnerable on both those counts. We should bear in mind that an analysis of sustainable development, had it existed in the past, might well have saved some of our people from the tragedy we are starting to commemorate. We need to make these connections.

(Speech by Mary Robinson, to both Houses of the Oireachtas, 2 February 1995).

E

If the 1790s can be seen as the pivotal decade in the evolution of modern Ireland, then an honest and accurate understanding of it is not just of scholarly interest but has important implications for current political and cultural thinking. It is precisely because of its enduring relevance that 1798 has never passed out of politics and into history. A window of opportunity was opened in Ireland by the impact of the American and French Revolutions: that moment was brilliantly seized by the United Irishmen who imaginatively created a vision of a non-sectarian, democratic and inclusive politics, which would attract and sustain all Irish people in all their inherited complexities. Rather than seeing religious, ethnic and political diversity as a disabling problem, the United Irishmen saw it as a glorious opportunity, to construct a wider, more tolerant and generous vision of Irish identity. Rather than grimly clinging to a divisive past, the United Irishmen sought to create a shared future ...

The enduring legacy of the United Irishmen was their momentous ability to bring Dissenter, Anglican and Catholic together in a shared political project. Now, as we know from more recent scholarship, that generous project was deliberately derailed by counter-revolutionaries in the 1790s, largely through the injection of sectarianism to break the United Irishmen's non-sectarian appeal. We are still living with the consequences of that defeat. The United Irish project of an inclusive, democratic, non-sectarian Ireland remains uncompleted: understanding the reason for its momentous defeat in the 1790s can help us to ensure that history does not tragically repeat itself in the 1990s.

In an eerie way the problems of the 1790s are still with us today, 200 years later. Like the fall of the Bastille, the Fall of the Berlin Wall signalled the collapse of old certainties at the beginning of the decade. But as in the 1790s the outcome of what had seemed to be an event ushering in a glorious new European epoch was uncertainty and eventually European conflict. ... The 1990s equally saw, not the dawning of a new age of freedom, but the grotesque horrors of Bosnia. Equally in Ireland, the 1790s began with a glorious, optimistic sense of sweeping political change leading to a bright future. In the 1990s the peace process began in a similar warm glow of optimism. There are, therefore, instructive parallels between our two decades at both the European and the Irish level. Given the delicate state of the peace process, we need to learn all the lessons that Irish history can teach us – and the 1790s is particularly instructive.

... Firstly, we must discard the now discredited sectarian version of '98, which was merely a polemical post-rebellious falsification. Secondly, we must stress the modernity of the United Irish project, its forward looking, democratic dimension, and abandon the outdated agrarian or peasant interpretation. Thirdly, we must emphasise the essential unity of the 1798 insurrection: what happened in Wexford was of a piece with what happened in Antrim and Down.

(Speech by Avril Doyle T.D. at launch of Friends of Comóradh '98 at Johnstown Castle, Wexford, 24 November 1995).

F

I want to pick out three elements highlighted by this Exhibition, Firstly, we must continue to never entertain a sectarian version of '98. Secondly, we must stress the modernity of the United Irish project, its forward looking, democratic dimension. Thirdly, we must emphasise the essential unity of the 1798 insurrection: what happened in Wexford was of a piece with what happened in Antrim, and Down.

(Speech by Síle de Valera, T.D., Minister for Arts, Heritage, Gaeltacht and the Islands at the opening of the 1798 Exhibition in the National Museum, Collins Barracks on Monday 25 May 1998)

G

We are commemorating a number of things this year. We are first of all commemorating the dawn of the democratic age in Ireland, where people sought equal civil rights, parliamentary reform and religious emancipation, and, in the context of their refusal, the right to national independence.

Secondly, we are commemorating the most sustained effort in Irish history, to reconcile and unite what were then three communities with different religious beliefs and ethnic backgrounds. The initiative for this came from humane and enlightened people of all traditions ...

Thirdly, we commemorate the suffering and sacrifices made by the thousands of people, who died or were wounded, or who were transported, in the course or, or in the aftermath of, the rebellions. Many of them were caught up in an impossible position, forced to defend themselves against tyranny and oppression. But there were also many honest and honourable loyalist victims who were civilians caught up in the Rebellion in Wexford and elsewhere ...

Fourthly, we commemorate the events of the rebellion in their own locality, in Wexford ...

Fifthly, we commemorate the political alliances, especially with revolutionary France, which tried to give some assistance, but also with radicals and the United men in Scotland and England. Today, we are partners in the European Union with France, Germany, Spain and other countries with which we have historic ties, as well as with Britain ...

Sixthly we commemorate the subsequent contribution made by Irish participants in the building of new countries, noting the United States and Australia ... (and Newfoundland).

(Speech by Taoiseach Bertie Ahern at the launch of the official programme of commemorations for 1798, 20 January 1998).

3

The poppy my father wore: the problems facing Irish nationalists in commemorating the two world wars

TONY CANAVAN

I

In the run up to St Patrick's Day 1996, the TV presenters on BBC Northern Ireland wore a shamrock in honour of the occasion, except for one, Donna Traynor, who explained that she felt that as a symbol of Irishness the shamrock might be offensive to the Unionist community and she preferred to be perceived as being neutral. Her decision aroused little comment and caused no concern among the management at BBC Northern Ireland. However, when eight months later, Donna Traynor made it known that she would not be wearing a poppy for Remembrance Sunday because as a symbol of Britishness it might be offensive to nationalist viewers, her bosses made it clear that this was regarded as a serious misdemeanour and Ms Traynor was told to wear a poppy or else be 'assigned to other duties.'[1]

In 1997, Oakgrove Integrated College in Derry initiated a cultural policy which it believed would promote tolerance among its students. The proposal was that staff and students would observe a minute's silence on United Nations Day, Armistice Day and on 30 January, the anniversary of Bloody Sunday. As well as this, it was proposed that people in the college wear a black ribbon on the anniversary of Bloody Sunday and a poppy on Armistice Day. Following protests from Protestant parents and the intervention of local DUP councillor Gregory Campbell, 'angry that the Bloody Sunday anniversary should be equated with Armistice Day', the policy was withdrawn.[2] What these episodes show, if nothing else, is that the wearing of a poppy in Northern Ireland is not entirely a voluntary nor indeed a non-political act.

That tens of thousands of nationalist Irish men and women served with the British armed forces in both world wars is beyond dispute. Some estimate that over 150,000 enlisted in the First World War and 50,000 in the Second.[3] Yet, their status, role and place in Irish society have been matters of dispute. Since 1918, the issue of commemorating the war dead has been fraught with problems leading to controversy, anger and hurt. Despite the numbers involved, there is little or no official, public commemoration of them in the Republic. Rather, in both the Republic and in the nationalist community in the North, there has been a collective amnesia regarding the soldiers and sailors in British service. The children and grandchildren of those who made the ultimate sacrifice in the two world wars must remember them in private, if at all. Some people alive today may not even be aware that a family member was in the British Army because it is something that is just not talked about. This is particularly the case with the first war since a different attitude prevails in relation to the second. Yet, on the other hand, there is a growing recognition of the part played by Irish people in the two world wars. They are included in the Republic's National Day of Commemoration, the highlight of which is a ceremony in the former Royal Hospital at Kilmainham (Ireland's equivalent to Chelsea) attended by the President and members of the government. Those who had family members in the British forces have in recent years found the confidence to go public and organise commemorations of them.

However, there are still enormous problems facing those from the nationalist community who wish to recognise the role of their forebears who fought in the British forces. In 1997, by chance, the inauguration of Mary McAleese as President of Ireland was on 11 November, and her first official duty as president was to attend the memorial service in the Protestant St Patrick's Cathedral the following Sunday. The questions of her attendance, and of whether or not she should wear a poppy, caused much discussion and comment in the media, provoking debate on the commemoration of the Irish men and women from the nationalist tradition who served with the British Armed Forces. This controversy illustrated not only that there are those in the nationalist tradition who want to commemorate the war dead, but also that there are still many who have problems with it. It is those problems that I wish to look at in this chapter, particularly in relation to Remembrance Day and the wearing of the poppy.

II

The problems can be divided into two categories. The first is the opposition within the nationalist community to any recognition of those who fought in the British forces. Because of Britain's historical role in Ireland, and the continued presence in Northern Ireland, many nationalists believe that it is inappropriate to participate in the British state's commemorative events. Others take the more hardline view that those who served Britain were traitors to Ireland who are best ignored. On account of this, and other considerations, there are serious obstacles to nationalists' commemorating their war dead within their own community.

In the other category, we can identify the barriers placed by the hostility of the Northern authorities and the Unionist community to the idea of acknowledging nationalist involvement in the two world wars, and the fact that they have appropriated the commemoration of the war dead as a means of expressing their Protestant–British identity in a manner that makes it impossible for nationalists to participate without denying their own identity and expressing support for those hostile to them. While it may be true that Unionists have occasionally acknowledged nationalist involvement in the British armed forces, the circumstances in which they do so raise doubts about their sincerity. For example, some Orange spokesmen in 1998 made reference to this as a rejoinder to the Garvaghy Road residents' opposition to the Order's march on the anniversary of the Battle of the Somme. However, in general commemorations in Northern Ireland have tended to have an exclusively Unionist and Protestant character.

The first, and obvious, problem in the way of nationalists' commemorating the war dead is the opposition from republicans and some hardline nationalists who continue to regard those who fought in the world wars, at the very least, as dupes and more often as traitors. From the ending of the First World War until today, republicans have openly opposed the Remembrance Day commemoration and any involvement by Irish people in the British Armed Forces. For example, in 1936, republican dissidents killed Boyle Somerville, a retired admiral, because he was helping local unemployed men in County Cork to join the Royal Navy. In the modern Troubles, British Legion halls were attacked by the IRA, and the infamous 1987 Enniskillen bombing, which killed eleven people, had as its target the Remembrance Day ceremony. Many republicans sincerely believe that it is wrong to honour those who fought and died in British uniform, while their opposition has caused others to question the legitimacy of commemoration or simply intimidated them from openly commemorating the world wars. Such opposition is well known and needs little further explanation.

However, even moderate nationalists find the general tone, or character, of the official Remembrance Day at the very least unsavoury and, at worst, offensive. It offers no recognition of the separate identity of the Irish who died in these wars. Instead they are subsumed into the British paradigm and portrayed as patriotic Britons who fought for king and empire (which while this may be true of some Ulstermen, it does not represent the Irish as a whole). The fact that, as was the case in the first war, they enlisted to help secure an autonomous Irish parliament, or, as with the second, that they were volunteers from a neutral country is ignored. Many nationalists would be happy to participate in an Irish commemoration of the war dead, if it were that. They are uneasy about taking part in the official British commemoration because they believe that the Irish involvement, in the First World War in particular, was different from mainstream British. There is a recognition that those who fought in British uniform did so from a complex combination of motives, the least of which was defence of king and empire. As Keith Jeffery has observed, Irish people had at the very least an ambivalent attitude toward the First World War if not outright confusion as to why the war was fought at all. As the poet Tom Kettle said, the Irish soldiers 'died not for flag, nor king, nor emperor.' According to Jeffery, even Sir William Orpen, an artist accepted by the British establishment, conveys in his paintings a distinctly Irish disillusionment with the war. The popular feeling in Ireland is reflected by writers in works such as Yeats's 'An Irish Airman Foresees His Death' and, more forcefully, and more typically, in Sean O'Casey's *The Silver Tassie* and Liam O'Flaherty's 'The Return of the Brute'. In the latter two, the war is portrayed as a brutal dehumanising struggle which left Irish soldiers saddened and disillusioned by their involvement.[4]

Moderate nationalists look at the British, and in particular Unionist, commemoration of the wars and do not recognise their own experience. Instead, they might look to the example of, say, Australia or New Zealand where the official commemoration does not follow Britain but is held on Anzac Day, 25 April. They would feel, too, that the Australian attitude to commemorating their dead is more in keeping with the Irish. Perhaps most movingly exemplified in Eric Bogle's ballad 'And The Band Played Waltzing Matilda', Australia remembers with pride that her soldiers fought well and bravely but also with sorrow and indignation that young men's lives were lost in futile battles such as Gallipoli.

In contrast, those who want nationalists to commemorate the Irish dead not only want it as part of the British commemorations but in acknowledgement of a British heritage. For instance, John Bruton, a former Taoiseach, said in 1997, '[T]he sacrifice in the last war, and in the first world war, are part of a larger shared experience going back for a thousand years.' And, 'in this commemoration we remember a British part of the inheritance of all who live in Ireland.'[5] He appeared to be saying that those who enlisted in 1914 and 1939 did so for British, not for Irish, motives. Another campaigner for Ireland to participate in Remembrance Day, Paddy Harte, a former Fine Gael T.D., says Irish people today should be grateful to those who died in the First World War 'to defend democracy.'[6] However, most nationalists do not believe that the sacrifice of Irishmen in that war was responsible for the democracy they enjoy today but rather that Irish soldiers were sacrificed by Britain for her own ends. John Robb, chairman of the New Ireland Group, has identified the essence of the pro-remembrance arguments to be that Irish people should acknowledge their relationship to Britain in a way that ignores 'the trauma which has been inflicted, in this century alone, by British imperial power'. Robb says that

> the decision to wear or to refrain from wearing the poppy became in part, for some people at least, a statement about their relationship with the British state rather than an exclusive expression of remembrance of those killed and bereaved and a tangible support for those who continue to suffer.[7]

By extension, we might also say that for some the wearing of a poppy is a statement about their relationship to the Irish Republic. Whether deliberately or not, those who argue in favour of the poppy appear to do so in terms repudiating the legitimacy of the Irish state. Speaking of people, North and South, who wear the poppy, even Paddy Harte admits that 'in the eyes of Catholics they have made it far too British and they have worn it with such triumphalism they make it difficult for Catholics to wear.'[8] Individuals and organisations, such as the British Legion, who want official recognition in the Republic of the Irish who died in the British Army, are noticeably absent from the official National Day of Commemoration ceremony in July.

Opposition from within the nationalist community is not all based on anti-British prejudice; there is also what we might call principled opposition, which would find sympathetic echoes among left-wing and pacifist thinkers in Britain, Australia and elsewhere. While willing to allow that Irishmen who volunteered for the British Army were not traitors, they object to the jingoistic character of the official Remembrance Day. They reject the focus on patriotism and glory, especially with regard to the First World War, which makes no allowance for the fact that many joined the army simply to escape poverty or in search of adventure, and that too often their lives were sacrificed to no end. As Eamon McCann, the noted commentator, has put it,

> When we think of the Somme, as we should every year, we should rage against those responsible for sending the young men of Ulster, and from all other corners of Ireland and Britain, to die so uselessly in such droves. ... The main protagonists were competing sets of robber-barons, British and German capitalisms, [which] fought for the 'right' to rule the world. Or, rather, they didn't fight at all. They never do. They summoned the lower orders to do the fighting, and dying, for them.[9]

In the same vein, others see wearing the poppy as a gesture of support and approval of a military tradition which they find immoral. They argue that it is not possible to separate honouring Irishmen who died in the world wars from an imperial tradition that encompasses, as one journalist from the North put it, a 'catalogue of massacres and crimes committed by [the British] army, Amritsar, Bloody Sunday (twice), Aden, Cyprus, Malaysia'.[10] For them, to wear a poppy on Remembrance Day is to signal approval of an imperialistic and military tradition that is better deserving of critical scrutiny.

III

This brings us to the third element in nationalist opposition to partici- pating in the official Remembrance Day – the role of the British Army in the Troubles. While the British Army may have entered Northern Ireland in 1969 to restore order and protect the nationalist community, the situa- tion soon changed to one where the army was the spearhead of security operations against the nationalist community. Events such as the Falls Road Curfew in July 1971 and the introduction of internment in August alienated nationalist opinion from the security forces. Add to this the fact that the British Army has been found guilty by international courts of the violation of human rights in Northern Ireland, and that the security forces have been responsible for 11 per cent of the deaths in the Troubles (204 of them civilians),[11] and one can appreciate that many nationalists would be reluctant to participate in an event which expresses unqualified support for the Army. Nell McCafferty, the well-known journalist from Derry, has summed up her own feelings:

> The poppy is not a symbol of remembrance of all who died in both World Wars. It is specifically dedicated to those who have served, and are currently serving in British forces since 1914, and money from sales is used for their benefit.[12]

For many Irish people, the poppy presents a dilemma because not only is it in remembrance of the war dead but also a symbol of support for the British Army today. Paddy Hayes, secretary of the Organisation of National Ex- Servicemen (representing veterans of the Irish defence forces), spoke in November 1997 of buying a poppy but choosing not to wear it – they were on sale again on the streets of Dublin for the first time in decades:

> How could I, with the trouble in the North and British soldiers still in occupation there? I was remembering those Irish people who fought

in the world wars but who can tell the difference between buying, wearing, supporting and remembering?[13]

IV

We can appreciate then that there are a number of factors within the nationalist community that both collectively and individually prevent formal commemoration of the two world wars. However, obstacles within the nationalist community are matched, if not surpassed, by Unionist exclusion of nationalists. From its very inception, the northern statelet was meant to be a 'Protestant state for a Protestant people'. The idea quickly gained root that the sacrifice of the Ulster Division at the Battle of the Somme in 1916 had earned the Ulster Unionists the right to their own state. If, as in 1925 in Portadown, a war memorial was unveiled in a ceremony involving both Catholic and Protestant clergy,[14] such ecumenism was soon squeezed out in the face of sectarian rhetoric which emphasised only the Protestant dead. It was primarily the Ulster Division's sacrifice at the Somme which was honoured and commemorated and which was used in decade after decade to justify the existence of Northern Ireland. Catholic involvement in the war was ignored and the Catholic population portrayed simply as the enemy within the border. In March 1934, for example, Basil Brooke, the Northern Ireland Prime Minister, stated that '99 per cent [of Catholics] are disloyal'.[15] Wearing the poppy, like the Orange sash, became a public symbol of Unionism.

Increasingly also, official commemorations in Northern Ireland took on an Orange hue as the Orange Order played a prominent role in them. On Remembrance Day, representatives not just of the military and the government but also of the Orange Order laid wreaths on war memorials while sporting poppies on their sashes. Under the auspices of the Orange Order, commemoration was extended to July and lodges marched to church services on the anniversary of the Battle of the Somme. Parades that are contentious today, such as at Dunloy in Co. Antrim, Bellaghy in Co. Fermanagh and the Garvaghy Road in Portadown, began in the 1920s as First World War commemorative events.

Although Winston Churchill praised Northern Ireland's role in the Second World War, the unionist establishment was afraid that its efforts were not duly appreciated. The number of people from the Republic who volunteered to fight in the British Armed Forces or who did vital work in the wartime industries – estimated at around a quarter of a million[16] – unnerved the Stormont government. To make matters worse, only one Victoria Cross was awarded to anyone from Northern Ireland, and he was a Catholic from West Belfast. The Unionist establishment's neglect of

James Magennis VC illustrates their unease at formal, indeed royal, recognition of the Irish Catholic contribution to Britain's war effort. Their response to Magennis's award was to drag from retirement Ulster heroes from the First World War, like Robert Quigg VC, who were, of course, Protestants. In the end, Magennis thought it better to live in England since not only was he given a hard time by Unionist Belfast but he was ostracised by his own community because he was a British war hero. Even after his death, Belfast City Council declined to erect any memorial to him until the balance of power in the council shifted away from the Unionists in 1998.[17] In Northern Ireland after 1945, the Second World War commemorations were subsumed into those of the First World War and took a similar Unionist Orange character. Catholic ex-servicemen or the relatives of Catholics who had died in the war found little welcome at these occasions.

Three decades of communal violence understandably polarised attitudes even further and this is true also of attitudes to Remembrance Day. For Unionists, wearing the poppy became an act of defiance in the face of republican violence and a public affirmation of their political allegiance. Wearing or not wearing a poppy became a political test, as the Donna Traynor case shows. For Unionists the poppy was a part of their, and only their, cultural identity. Wearing a poppy started earlier in the year so that it could be seen on lapels from the beginning of October. In 1997 a company in Derry, Coats Viyella, in an effort to lessen tensions in the workplace, instructed their employees to wear a poppy no earlier than six days before Remembrance Day (which is the official military regulation). Some workers were suspended for ignoring this instruction. This unleashed a storm of protest from Unionist politicians and activists who demanded the right to wear a poppy whenever they wished. The company's action was characterised not as displaying disrespect for the dead but as an attack on the 'Protestant-Unionist community.' Gregory Campbell, the DUP councillor, and Glen Barr, a loyalist local community activist, intervened on the suspended workers' behalf. The factory was picketed and David Trimble, the Ulster Unionist Party leader, raised the issue with the Prime Minister in the House of Commons.[18]

Perhaps more disturbing for nationalists is the increasing tendency among Unionists, in particular Orangemen, to write completely out of history Catholics who fought and died in the world wars. There appears to be a concerted attempt to portray service in the British Forces not just as a Protestant monopoly but almost as an Orange one. The corollary of this, of course, is that Britain owes the Unionist community, and the Order in particular, a debt. One writer makes the claim that 'upwards of two hundred thousand Orangemen served throughout the Great War'.[19] Another Unionist historian describes how the men of the Ulster Division at the Battle of the Somme

> went over the top at zero hour on that Saturday wearing their Orange
> sashes and with cries of 'No Surrender!' and 'Remember 1690!' At
> one stage in the heat of battle when men of one unit appeared to be
> faltering, their company commander, Major George Gaffiken,
> successfully rallied them by whipping off his sash, holding it high for
> them to see and shouting, 'Come on boys! No surrender!'[20]

This image of the Somme has received widespread acceptance in the
Protestant community although it is not supported by contemporary
accounts and receives no mention in official histories. In fact, it is worth
pointing out that army regulations forbade soldiers from participating in
organisations like the Orange Order.[21] Still, the belief prevails among
many unionists that they and they alone fought and died in the two world
wars. It would seem that they are either ignorant of, or deliberately
ignore, the contribution made by Irish nationalists. This view reached its
apogee at the height of the Drumcree stand-off in 1998 when the Order
published a full page advertisement in Northern Ireland papers arguing
for their right to march down the Garvaghy Road. Prominent in this
advertisement was the claim that

> those who gave their lives in defence of civil liberties, principally at
> the Battle of the Somme, where the British Army suffered massive
> casualties – 5,000 Ulstermen, many of whom were members of the
> Orange Order, faced a whirlwind of bullets and died in one day
> fighting, to defend Europe against tyranny.[22]

Such an attitude has gone to the extreme of finding the official monument
to the 36th (Ulster) Division at Thiepval unsatisfactory because it does
not specifically commemorate the Protestant dead. In 1993 the Orange
Order erected its own monument at Thiepval, specifically to the
Orangemen who died in the First World War. The unveiling ceremony
was conducted by James Molyneaux MP, then leader of the UUP, the
Orange Grand Master, Revd Martin Smyth MP, also in the UUP, and the
Lord Mayor of Belfast, Hugh Smyth of the Progressive Unionist Party,
the party associated with the UVF.

Acts such as this send a clear signal to nationalists that there is no
place for them in unionist commemoration of the world wars – and interestingly Unionist emphasis is almost entirely on the Battle of the Somme
alone. However, the symbolism of wearing the poppy goes even further
in being associated not just with Unionist politics but with loyalist paramilitaries. From the beginning of the Troubles, many Protestants have
worn the poppy in remembrance also of members of the security forces

killed since 1970, but the poppy has also been employed by loyalists for their own dead. Loyalist paramilitaries see themselves, and would like to be seen, as equally legitimate forces in the defence of the Protestant state. By using the poppy they are seeking to establish a legitimate connection between their members and those who fought and died in British uniform. The poppy has been used in murals in memory of dead loyalists, in wreaths placed at world war memorials and, of course, on lapels to honour the loyalist dead.

There are a number of murals in memory of loyalists in Belfast and elsewhere that employ the poppy wreath, but the direct association between the loyalist dead and dead servicemen is shown starkly in a mural near the Cregagh Road in East Belfast. Covering an entire gable wall, the mural has at the centre a representation of a war memorial – a statue of a First World War soldier in mourning – and on its left is portrayed Private William McFadzean, while to the right is William Millar. This is all encompassed in a single wreath of poppies with the scroll 'For God and Ulster'. Private McFadzean was posthumously awarded the Victoria Cross for bravery in the First World War; William Millar was a member of the UVF shot dead by the RUC while carrying out an act of terrorism.[23] One does not have to be a trained anthropologist nor a political scientist to read the message being conveyed here.

At Belfast City Hall in November 1997, after the official ceremony of remembrance was over, another was held in which a wreath of poppies bearing the initials UVF was laid alongside those placed by the Duchess of Kent, the Secretary of State, the Lord Mayor and others. That this wreath was for the present-day UVF and not its 1912 predecessor was clear, as among the official wreaths was one in honour of the 36th (Ulster) Division which the UVF became on being absorbed into the British Army. When officials at City Hall did not see fit to remove this tribute to an illegal organisation, nationalist councillors protested; despite this the wreath was allowed to remain. That officials at City Hall and the other, Unionist, councillors saw no problem with thus honouring the UVF was a cause of unease in the nationalist community.[24]

It can be quite clearly seen then that the unionist community, from politicians to loyalist paramilitaries, view the commemoration of the war dead as something special to them and that wearing the poppy symbolises a Protestant–British identity. The message sent out to the nationalist community is that 'No Catholics need apply'. Unionist commemorations, and here the term includes official events in Northern Ireland also, focus almost exclusively on the Protestant war dead and portray service in the Armed Forces as an act of loyalism. Nationalist involvement is not only ignored, but traditionally Nationalists have been cast as the enemy within the frontiers of Northern Ireland. These events have an inbuilt ambiguity about them. For many nationalists observing these commemorations it is often difficult to tell who they are honouring: the military casualties alone or also those who fought to defend 'Protestant Ulster'? The consequence is that even those nationalists who would wish to openly and publicly honour the dead of two world wars dare not do so as it would be interpreted as denying their own identity and expressing support for loyalist organisations.

Nationalists, then, are excluded by Unionists from participation. Unionists do not want to acknowledge Nationalist involvement in the two world wars as they believe this would dilute their claims to their own state. At the same time, the commemorations themselves have increasingly assumed a character which privileges the role of the Orange Order and in some instances honours loyalist paramilitaries. Under such circumstances, nationalists would find it impossible to participate even if they wanted to.

V

While the problems facing nationalists who wish to acknowledge the role played by their community in the First and Second World Wars are enormous, reinforced by history and politics, the situation is not entirely bleak. In the Republic of Ireland attitudes to history are changing. One consequence of the Troubles and of the debate over the revision of Irish history has been that people are taking a fresh look at the past and what it means to us today. A more complex and less judgemental view is emerging. One manifestation of this is the increasing acknowledgement of the British military tradition in Ireland and in particular the nationalist involvement in the First World War (those who fought in the Second World War have always been viewed differently). In the Republic, a decades-long attitude of official ignoring, indeed of denigration, of those who served in the British Army is steadily giving way to a more honest appraisal. The Royal Dublin Fusiliers Association and the Royal Munster Fusiliers Association, made up mostly of people whose family members served in these regiments, are a sign of increasing confidence in this area. Through exhibitions and lectures, they have increased public awareness of the issue and fostered a greater appreciation of the motives of and the part played by Irishmen who joined the British Army in 1914. They have now the confidence publicly to stage commemorative events with flags and wreaths in memory of their forebears who fought in British uniform, and to date these have not been met with serious objections. In 1997, for example, seven such ceremonies were held, including a wreath-laying at the War Memorial Gardens at Islandbridge on the Saturday prior to

Remembrance Sunday. Similar events were held in 1998. In the wider political field, the attendance of Tom Harte, a leading member of Sinn Féin, at a ceremony in the War Memorial Gardens to mark the 50th anniversary of the end of the Second World War illustrates that even republican opposition can be diluted. Fine Gael has always been sympathetic to the concept of commemorating the Irish who served in the British forces, and recently the present Fianna Fáil led government announced financial support for the Messines Tower, a memorial to be built in Belgium to those from all parts of Ireland who died in the First World War. It is also worth reiterating that the National Day of Commemoration is an official public event which honours 'all those Irish men and women who died in past wars or on service with the United Nations',[25] and this includes those who served in the British armed forces. However, in the North, despite the peace process, not much seems to have changed. In the wake of the Good Friday Agreement, we can only wait and see if the more tolerant and open attitude that has emerged in the Republic will have any influence there.

4

Memory, forgiveness and conflict: trust-building in Northern Ireland

PAUL ARTHUR

The trouble about memory is that it develops its own defences, against truth-telling and in consequence against history.[1]

History is a priori amoral; it has no conscience. To want to conduct history according to the maxims of the Sunday school means to leave everything as it is.[2]

Historiography is less and less a matter of finding out how things really were, or trying to explain how things happened. For not only is historical truth irrelevant, but it has become a common assumption that there is no such thing. Everything is subjective, or a sociopolitical construct … So we study memory, that is to say, history as it is felt, especially by its victims.[3]

Memory and reconciliation

The years of the 'Troubles' have left a deep feeling of mistrust between the communities in Northern Ireland. Since the ceasefires of 1994 and 1997, trust-building has been a slow process, and often a painful one. It involves coming to terms with a violent past, in order to build a peaceful future. We seem to be living in a confessional age. Priscilla Hayner has identified no less than fifteen truth commissions – predominantly in Africa, Asia and Latin America – in the two decades after 1974. She asserts that 'truth commissions can play a critical role in a country struggling to come to terms with a history of massive human rights crimes.'[4] The thrust of this chapter is not to suggest that we rush thoughtlessly into adapting a format that appears to have worked in another context. Rather we should take note of practice, good and bad, elsewhere whilst being conscious of local conditions in a time of transition and trust-building. Kader Asmal, the Minister of Water Affairs in the South

African government, was conscious of the fundamental leaps which transition could entail. Borrowing from Gramsci, he asked:

> If the old order is dying and the new is not yet born, can there be reconciliation simply through an assertion that new structures and new arrangements will be set in place? Is reconciliation between victim/survivor and the over-lord possible on the basis of a Caliban and Prospero relationship, between master and servant?[5]

These questions are pertinent to the current political climate in Northern Ireland and in relations between Britain and Ireland in the wake of the Belfast Agreement. Not only does the Agreement embrace institutional change but implicit in its discussions on rights, on decommissioning, on policing and justice, on prisoners, and on validation is a recognition of attitudinal change. It is explicit when it addresses reconciliation:

> ... it is essential to acknowledge and address the suffering of the victims of violence as a necessary element of reconciliation ... It is recognised that victims have a right to remember as well as to contribute to a changed society ... An essential aspect of the reconcilation process is the promotion of a culture of tolerance at every level of society.[6]

Our primary concern is with these matters and we intend to examine them obliquely.

History and memory

> One of the sound foundations of a political society is a true knowledge of its past. ... But the affirmation of the rights of memory does not mean that the past must become the only, or the main value.[7]

In their efforts to deal with the past, new democracies have given victims their chance to speak. Wrongs have been exposed. A few culprits have been punished. These are considerable achievements. And by investigating the sins of the former regimes, the new governments have invited their own people to judge them by a higher standard of behaviour. This is the most important achievement of all. The trials and truth commissions of recent years have not really been about the past. Rather, and rather more sensibly, they have been about building trust, about building a future in which the rule of law prevails, especially over the rulers themselves.[8]

It was St Augustine who delineated three aspects of memory-time – anticipation of the future, present attention and past memory – as well as

the three faculties of the soul – will (towards action), intellect (of articulated reality) and memory (establishing identity).[9] Following Augustine,
we can look on history as a scientific discipline and memory as a vital
part of culture. As the historian Jacques Le Goff wrote:

> There is no people, no nation, no identity without memory, and no
> democracy without a free memory ... Memory and history have adja-
> cent, connected but not identical objectives. Memory is an existential
> work, history must also inform life and collective life but the priority
> imperative is of scientific truth ... The worst is oblivion.[10]

We shall see that history is not without its flaws; we may note the public
silence about the Holocaust during the first decade of Israel's existence;
and the Israeli example has resonances in the Irish conflict. There is in
Ireland a whole literary tradition devoted to the creation of moral and
symbolic capital. It can be found in some of the poetry from the seventeenth century onwards when the old Irish aristocratic order disappeared
and 85 per cent of Irish land was transferred into the hands of English
colonists, all of which affirmed the dispossession of an entire caste.[11] In
the present conflict it can be seen in some of the work of playwrights like
Brian Friel, Frank McGuinness and Gary Mitchell.[12] Equally, there is no
shortage of novelists and poets who are tackling the issues thrown up by
'The Troubles'. Like Israel, Ireland has wrapped itself in ambiguity
because it

> would be unnatural for any society enduring the traumas of nine-
> teenth-century Ireland, including not only colonization, but famine,
> depopulation, language loss and religious revival, not to have devel-
> oped protective layers of ambiguity.[13]

Some of this can be found in the manner in which we commemorate the
past. Commemoration in Ireland has been called a 'pitched battlefield of
opposing ideologies, more divisive and triumphal than healing and cele-
bratory'.[14] Parading is the most obvious manifestation of this practice.
Neil Jarman, who has described parades as 'expressions of culture,
displays of faith and acts of domination; ... intimately linked to the wider
political domain', calculates that there were 3,500 parades held in the
north of Ireland in 1995, loyalist parades outnumbered republican
parades by around nine to one.

> Loyalist parades are essentially triumphal expressions of a collective
> determination, a celebration of strength in unity and in brotherhood,
> while republican parades commemorate the continued resolve in
> defeat and the determination to carry on the fight. ...

> [These acts] of performative commemoration complete a circle
> between the past and the present, and thus make the future certain. ...
> The celebration and commemoration of past events and heroes aims
> to guide action in the present, and so the recurrent celebration of
> martial heroes and military victories helps to legitimise and sustain
> faith in a violent solution to Ulster's problems.[15]

In this context, he says, memory 'becomes less a means of conserving a
distinct lineal history than a generator of meaning.'[16] Moreover,
following Ernest Gellner's dictum that a consciousness and memory had
to be created for newly emerging nation states, parading had a role to play
particularly for Unionists who had a complicated case to sell in relation
to the British state: 'They had to blend High Culture and folk tradition
rather than choose an either-or solution. Once the folk culture of parading
was civilised and tamed, it was then refocused as a vehicle to define and
display the nature of Unionism.'[17]

Given this frequent and highly visual display of memory, the casual
observer might conclude that there was no place for silence, for forgetting, for erasure in the Irish conflict. [S]he would be wrong. Michel-
Rolph Trouillot maintains that there are four crucial moments when
silences enter the processes of historical production: fact creation (the
making of sources); fact assembly (archives); fact retrieval (narratives);
and the moment of retrospective significance (the making of history in
the final analysis). He believes that effective silencing does not require a
conspiracy, nor even a political consensus, but that its roots are structural.
It is due in part to uneven power in the production of sources, archives,
narratives: 'Mentions and silences are thus the active dialectical counterparts of which history is the synthesis.'[18]

Two other factors in the production of history are relevant to this
discussion. One concerns the ordering of facts: 'As sources fill the historical landscape with their facts, they reduce the room available to other
facts.'[19] In finding the space for certain facts, the writer is engaged in an
act of exclusion. Second, some facts are 'unthinkable' in the framework of
Western thought. Trouillot had in mind the slave-led Haitian Revolution
(1791–1804): 'The unthinkable is that which one cannot conceive within
the range of possible alternatives, that which perverts all answers because
it defies the terms under which the questions were phrased'.[20] In terms of
Irish history, one could cite nineteenth-century British security policy as
an example of the unthinkable: 'If, therefore, the enforcement of the law
provoked disorder, as it appeared to do in Ireland, the fault lay in English
eyes not with the law but with the people.'[21]

It might also be added that some facts are embarrassing and hence
there is a need for erasure. The Great Famine beginning in 1845 is a case
in point. The economist Amartya Sen has written that 'in no other famine

in the world was the proportion of people killed as large as the Irish famines in the 1840s'.[22] The literary critic Terry Eagleton states: 'If the Famine stirred some to angry rhetoric, it would seem to have traumatised others into muteness. The event strains at the limit of the articulable, and is truly in this sense an Irish Auschwitz.'[23] Yet if one examines the literature there is remarkably little written until fairly recently, and much of that carries great simplicities:

> It is plain from much writing about the Famine that two things happened in its aftermath. One, people blamed the English and the Ascendancy. Two, there began a great silence about class division in Catholic Ireland. ... The Famine, then, had to be blamed on the Great Other, the enemy across the water, and the victims of the Famine had to be this entire Irish nation, rather than a vulnerable section of the population'.[24]

Silences can be common, too, in societies in transition. In Guatemela, for example, the truth commission concluded that approximately 93 per cent of human rights violations can be attributed to the army and only three per cent to the guerrillas – yet both sides seemed not interested in having these cases exposed. There may be a similar reluctance in Ireland. The daughter of one of the 'disappeared' has stated: 'When the tourists visit the IRA graves, I want them to see my mother's and ask questions about what happened her. The disappeared were part of Irish history whether the Provos like it or not. I don't want them ever forgotten.'[25]

Forgiveness and the culture of necropolis

Why not leave the past behind? You cannot reconcile with the present if you cannot reconcile with the past. Equally important is Primo Levi's concern with oblivion. It can be seen in a remark from an inmate of Majdanek concentration camp:

> Should our murderers be victorious, should they write the history of this war ... their every word will be taken for gospel. Or they may wipe out our memory altogether, as if we had never existed ... But if we write the history of the period ... we'll have the thankless job of providing to a reluctant world that we are Abel, the murdered brother'.[26]

It is not difficult to empathise with this latter position, but in the light of experience we need to be aware of its shortcomings. Levi need not have feared that the Holocaust would be consigned to oblivion because 'far from forgetting the most recent and horrible chapter in the long book of

Jewish suffering, the remembrance of it grows in volume the further the events recede in the past.'[27]

This issue is explored by Ian Buruma who extracts a sobering lesson from the role that Holocaust studies are playing in Israeli civic education. He sees it as a form of secular religion and quotes the historian, Saul Friedländer, who described it as a 'union of kitsch and death', the former defined by Buruma as 'an expression of emotion which is displaced, focussed on the wrong thing ...'[28] The more general danger in all of this is that it 'becomes questionable when a cultural, ethnic, religious, or national community bases its communal identity almost entirely on the sentimental solidarity of remembered victimhood. For that way lies historical myopia and, in extreme circumstances, even vendetta.'[29] His conclusion that Levi's fear 'was not that future generations would fail to share his pain, but that they would fail to recognise the truth' is apt. And one of the obstacles on the quest for truth is that:

> the tendency to identify authenticity in communal suffering actually impedes understanding among people. For feelings can only be expressed, not discussed or argued about. This cannot result in mutual understanding, but only in mute acceptance of whatever people wish to say about themselves, or in violent confrontation ... you cannot argue with feelings. Those who try are not denounced for being wrong, but for being unfeeling, uncaring, and thus bad people who don't deserve to be heard.[30]

Buruma is not arguing against Holocaust studies. Indeed he supports the building of the Holocaust museum in Berlin because, with its library and document centre, it will be more than a colossal monument – 'In the new plan memory will go together with education. Literature, of fact and fiction, about individual and communal suffering, should have its place'.[31] He recognises too that history is important and that there should be more of it. Nor does he baulk at the notion of fostering tolerance and understanding of other cultures and communities but warns that 'the steady substitution of political argument in public life with the soothing rhetoric of healing is disturbing.'[32]

This is a powerful health warning. To raise questions about how we tackle painful memories of victimhood is not to belittle the sufferings of others. Although he is alarmed at 'the extent to which so many minorities have come to define themselves above all as historical victims',[33] Buruma is not indifferent to the plight of victims. No doubt he would agree with the opinion of Marie Smyth that the question of whether we should remember,

> is usually asked by people who have a choice. For many ... there is

> no choice about remembering … [it] is not an option – it is a daily
> torture, a voice inside the head that has no 'on/off' switch and no
> volume control.[34]

Although Buruma quotes an Israeli friend on the perception that everyone
wants to compete with the Jewish tragedy in 'the Olympics of suffering'
he would not take issue with Smyth's implicit question: Are there hierarchies of pain and responsibility? He is simply putting this in a wider
context by making two general points. One is implicit. It is our tendency
to be cavalier with concepts and meanings. The use of the word
'Holocaust' is an example. Buruma offers as evidence two books
published in recent years. One, *The Rape of Nanking: The Forgotten
Holocaust of World War Two*, has a self-explanatory title. The second,
Reports from the Holocaust, is a book about Aids. He could have added
David Stannard's *American Holocaust: Columbus and the Conquest of
the New World*. He did not intend to diminish the scholarship and intent
of these authors in making the point that a concept can be retarded
through reproduction. When Buruma claims to detect a new Romantic
age which is anti-rational, sentimental and communitarian, and which is
encapsulated in the reference to Diana as the 'Princess of Hearts' and in
the appeals of Clinton and Blair to the community of feeling, he may be
reflecting (what Matthew Arnold called in another age) our bias against
'the despotism of fact'.

The second point concerns the appropriation of historical trauma for
political purposes. Again we refer to Primo Levi. Israel and the special
encounter between the Zionist revolutionary collective and the Jewish
remnant after the Holocaust provides a useful reminder. Idith Zertal has
explored the role of remembering and forgetting in the evolution of the
Israeli state. She detects a change in Israeli society in the years of the
capture and trial of Adolf Eichmann, 1960–62, in which a process begins
that replaces the silence and denial regarding the Holocaust. She remarks
that in a 220-page textbook of Jewish history published in 1948, one page
was devoted to the Holocaust, compared to ten pages on the Napoleonic
wars. An official Holocaust Remembrance Day became mandatory only
in 1959 but a year later more than a quarter of educational institutions
ignored the event. But the Eichmann trial had a profound effect on Israeli
society:

> It changed the face of Israel, psychologically binding the past-less
> young Israelis with their recent past, and revolutionizing Israelis' self
> perception … It was also a major step in the shaping of the Western
> post-Holocaust culture and the effort to grapple with the history and
> memory of the Holocaust.[35]

Zertal notes that Susan Sontag 'immediately and succinctly grasped the fundamentally paradoxical essence of this great event' in an essay she published in 1964. Sontag described the trial as 'the most interesting and moving work of art in the past ten years', and while it was primarily a great act of commitment through memory and the renewal of grief, yet it 'clothed itself in the forms of legality and scientific objectivity' – catharsis through the rule of law. Zertal carefully traces this growth in the ideological weight of the Holocaust for internal Israeli politics beginning with Ben-Gurion and not being adequately challenged until 1988.[36]

In an essay in *Ha'aretz* published in March 1988, Professor Yehuda Elkana, a survivor of Auschwitz,

> made a direct connection between the project of systematically instilling lessons of the Holocaust into Israel's national consciousness and mental fabric through commemoration, education and indoctrination, and the violent 'exceptional' acts employed by Israeli soldiers and settlers toward Palestinian civilians during the first months of the Intifada.[37]

His plea to let go of the Holocaust and 'to position themselves in favour of life, to dedicate themselves to the building of the future and to cease dealing morning and evening with the symbols, ceremonies and lessons of the Holocaust'[38] appears to have fallen on deaf ears more than a decade later. Elkana's is an eloquent testimony to the paradox of reducing 'memory' to its complexity and seduction.

All of the above would seem to suggest that we approach memory, the remembrance of the past and the idea of a truth and reconciliation commission with great caution. And yet it is imperative that we deal with the past, that we tackle the question of oblivion and the lack of communication which leads to an inability to resolve conflict. In her comparative research Marie Smyth posits the idea of positive revenge:

> … recognising the harm that has been done to you, you refuse to allow the harm to determine the rest of your life. You become determined to lead a positive life, to make a positive contribution, and not let the perpetrator win by resisting the damaging effect and triumphing over them'.[39]

Barely a decade after the defeat of the Nazis Hannah Arendt addressed similar concerns through the power to forgive and the power to promise:

> The possible redemption from the predicament of irreversibility – of being unable to do what one has done though one did not, and could not, know what he was doing – is the faculty of forgiving … Without being forgiven, released from the consequences of what we have

done, our capacity to act would, as it were, be confined to one single deed from which we could never recover; we would remain the victim of its consequences forever, not unlike the sorcerer's apprentice who lacked the magic formula to break the spell. ...In contrast to forgiving, which – perhaps because of its religious context, perhaps because of love attending its discovery – has always been deemed unrealistic and inadmissable in the public realm, the power of stabilization inherent in the faculty of making promises, has been known throughout our tradition.[40]

But, as Byron Bland notes, she does not mention forgetting. Instead she argues that revenge, which is the alternative to forgiveness,

is merely a reaction that stands in contrast to the unpredictable and unexpected character of forgiveness. ... Forgiveness sets aside revenge ...[T]he only really viable – and therefore moral – option is to identify, thereby remembering the villany of the past, but then to displace this legacy of humanity to the margins of societal concern.[41]

Conclusion

At a colloquium in the Aspen Institute's Conference Center in Maryland in the autumn of 1988, a group of individuals from societies in transition gathered to ask the question of what to do with former torturers in their midst:

The participants ... worried this question around the table several times ... until Thomas Nagel, a professor of philosophy and law at New York University, almost stumbled upon an answer. 'It's the difference', Nagel said haltingly, 'between knowledge and acknowledgement. It's what happens and can only happen to knowledge when it is officially sanctioned, when it is made part of the public cognitive scene.' Yes, several of the panellists agreed. And that transformation, offered another participant, is sacramental.[42]

This chapter has been concerned with acknowledgement. It has avoided being prescriptive and has concentrated instead on complexity, on memory and history, on remembering and forgetting, on catharsis and on feeling as the necessary preconditions for mutual trust. It has worked on the assumption that Northern Ireland has been 'a victim-bonded society in which memories of past injustices and humiliation are so firmly entrenched in both communities' that collective memory can be seen as a major obstacle in the business of trust-building: a society in which victimhood can be defined as the 'political economy of helplessness'.[43] The Belfast

Agreement of April 1998 and the Hillsborough declaration of April 1999 are both honest attempts at confronting the egoism of victimization.[44]

If we need any reminder of the strength of feelings remaining in Northern Irish society we may look no further than the reaction to the suggestion in the Hillsborough declaration that there should be a day of national reconciliation. The mixed messages which that evoked in different communities suggest that we should be cautious in assuming that a Northern Ireland version of South Africa's TRC might provide the answer. Instead a more modest suggestion might be that we build on what has been achieved since the Belfast Agreement was signed.[45] We recognise the progress that is being made by acknowledging that reconciliation and trust are processes and not products. By addressing the issue of the merits or otherwise of a Truth and Reconciliation Commission for Ireland we are addressing the issue of memory and forgiveness, and of reconciliation itself.

5
The rivers to Drumcree

OWEN DUDLEY EDWARDS

We propose more immediately to consider our RIVERS; and let not
the reader deem the plan too contracted, for it is far otherwise. It has
been chosen after much thought, and will supply us with an inex-
haustible range of subject. A river is at all times the opening scene of
human civilization: on its shore the wigwam of the savage first sends
up its wreathing volumes of smoke; and by-and-by the settlement is
formed, and some chief chosen to give laws to the community. Then
ships come from far, and commerce struggles into being: new
productions, both of nature and art, are introduced; new thoughts are
imparted to the simple-minded colonists; lines of towns and cities are
marked out, and the virgin country passes into the hands of a foreign
possessor. We witness these things in our own day; and so was it with
Ireland ages ago.

> Charles Lever, 'Irish Rivers – Introduction'[1]
> *Dublin University Magazine*, 26 (September 1845)

So we beat on, boats against the current, borne ceaselessly into the
past.

> F. Scott Fitzgerald, *The Great Gatsby* (1925), last words

I

Ireland is a country of rivers; Scotland is a country of mountains; Wales
is a country of valleys; England is a country of villages.

The conceit may be as useless as any: and make your own by all
means, and good luck to you; but print deafens me to your rejoinder.

Mountains visibly make Scottish history, above all in the dichotomy
between Highlander and Lowlander, real and imagined. Valleys make
Welsh history, whether in the industrial mine-pitted south-east, or the

insulated myth-spotted north-west. Villages make English history, and typify the more sophisticated, most urbanised, most civilised quarter of our archipelago: maypoles and Farmer Giles and bitter beer and Brontë parsonage and Clun quietest under the sun and Roman roads and village greens and village cricket and RAF airfields down the road in summer 1940. Likewise the Irish rivers carry their stories of national identity – identity of pagan and of Christian, identity of Catholic and of Protestant, identity of native and of settler, identity of victor and of victim, identity of male and of female; identity of human and of spirit.

We silently assent to the historical consciousness of rivers at the Welsh Marches, or the Thames Estuary, or Bannockburn. Yet they are curiously less personified than the Irish variety, give or take suitable legends. No doubt other ladies baptised rivers by drowning in them, as did the eponymous heroine of the Shannon:[2]

> There is a singular myth which, while intended to account for the name of the river Shannon, expresses the Celtic veneration for poetry and science, combined with the warning that they may not be approached without danger. The goddess Sinend it was said, daughter of Lodan son of Lir, went to a certain well named Connla's Fairyland. 'That is a well', says the bardic narrative, 'at which are the hazels of wisdom and inspirations, that is, the hazels of the science of poetry, and in the same hour their fruit and their blossom and their foliage break forth, and then fall upon the well in the same shower, which raises upon the water a royal surge of purple.' When Sinend came to the well we are not told what rites or preparation she had omitted, but the angry waters broke forth and overwhelmed her, and washed her up on the Shannon shore, where she died, giving to the river its name [Irish, *Sionnain*].

Thus T. W. Rolleston (1857–1920) told his fellow-enthusiasts of the Irish Renaissance (and the British public that bought them) where to find Ireland's Faust, female and riverborne through the longest stream of water in these islands. The Shannon thus destroyed and immortalised an intellectual; the Hellespont merely drowned and commemorated a dizzy girl unable to hold on to a flying ram's back. The primacy of Irish womanhood goes back to the ancient cults of river-goddesses,[3] but the independence, intellectualism, courage, and vanity, give the legends strong character, and Rolleston's version of it fed his own times whose Gaelicists, feminists, intellectuals, and scientific pioneers united identities and disputed their primacies. The Irish Renaissance would reconsume itself in 1939 when James Joyce (1882–1941) gave *Finnegans Wake* to the bewildered world, centred on his own eastern river Liffey, personified in its female epiphany Anna Livia Plurabelle and amphibious to the reader from the book's opening words:

riverrun, past Eve and Adam's, from swerve of shore to bend of bay, brings us by a commodius vicus of recirculation back to Howth Castle and Environs.

The great salutation of the encircling Liffey begins later, her uxorial crises enthralling attendant washerwomen/ducks as they wash his befouled garments in her stream while indicting his diabolic misconduct in Phoenix Park past which her current rolls:[4]

O

tell me all about

Anna Livia! I want to hear all

about Anna Livia. Well, you know Anna Livia? Yes, of course, we all know Anna Livia. Tell me all. Tell me now. You'll die when you hear. Well, you know, when the old cheb went futt and did what you know. Yes, I know, go on. Wash quit and don't be dabbling. Tuck up your sleeves and loosen your talk-tapes. And don't butt me – hike! – when you bend. Or whatever it was they threed to make out he thried to two in the fiendish park. He's an awful old reppe. Look at the shirt of him! Look at the dirt of it! He has all my water black on me.

He is Professor H. C. Earwicker, whom she brides, hides, cradles, surrounds, whereas the hero Fionn again (the Phoenix of the Park being an Anglicisation for 'Fairwater', *Fionn-uisge*, her water his water and resurrection of the fire-consumed his essence) he sleeps in gigantic embodiment of Dublin she permeating his form, slumber, being, banks (and Brays), source of mouth resuscitated, revivificated, reJoyced, Awake, Finnegan beginagain!

Rivers drowning their godparents may be the future – or the death – of culture and literature no less than the cradle and the birth, the waters bearing the embryo, the womb with a view. Antiquity worshipped the potential agent of death: the river-god's dues may forfend the river-death. Victorian Ireland listened to Thomas Babington Macaulay (1800–59) and his *Lays of Ancient Rome* (1842) where Horatius seeks the aid of the river Tiber all too likely to drown him (Macaulay's idea of it was inspired by the worship of the Ganges he saw in India, but his own paternal Scots Gaelic ancestry may have contributed more).[5]

'Oh, Tiber! Father Tiber!
To whom the Romans pray,
a Roman's life, a Roman's arms,
Take thou in charge this day!'
So he spake, and speaking sheathed
The good sword by his side,
and with his harnass on his back
Plunged headlong in the tide.

...
Never, I ween, did swimmer,
In such an evil case,
Struggle through such a raging flood
Safe to the landing place:
But his limbs were borne up bravely
By the brave heart within,
And our good father Tiber
Bore bravely up his chin.

Macaulay neatly combines the brave swimmer's efforts to resist the river-death and the river's brave effort to help him to defeat it. Like Joyce, Macaulay is in-again, out-again (Finnegan) vis-à-vis Christianity: his footnotes firmly cite the support of the Blessed Virgin Mary to swimmers in the Ballad of Childe Waters in the first canto of *The Lay of the Last Minstrel* (1805) by Walter Scott (1771–1832). His Irish poetic disciples would be numerous, but the laurel falls on Samuel Ferguson (1810–86) with his *Lays of the Western Gael* (1865), in which, we will notice later, the struggles of mortal man and enemy-or-ally sacred river go beyond death and even wake.

But even in English the Irish versifiers were riverborne long before Macaulay, and verse – and worse – are the most lasting, and hence most seminal, expressions of river-running. Thomas Moore (1779–1852) would conscript a river for his melodies at the drop of a note, especially when he could get two – and even three – for the length of one. The Avon, the Avonbeg, and the Avoca in Co. Wicklow gave him 'The Meeting of the Waters' in 1807, and posterity would endow it with fresh magic when it proved to have heralded the birthplace of Charles Stewart Parnell (1846–1891) many years after its own conception. Moore was not being parochial in his compliments, having just come from Jefferson's Washington, DC about which his charity elegantly unveiled a multitude of sins.[6] Parnell's natal identification with the lyrics of so eminently patriotic yet cosmopolitan a poet harmonised with the Parnell myth during and after the hero's lifetime. Since Parnell would supply yet further antecedents for Joyce's Finnegan, the rivers' womb-waters are all the more romantically commemorated before the birth they would produce. Parnell's hard-bitten pragmatism might seem far from so humanely sentimental yet sociable a song, but he had his sentiment – it was to prove his Nemesis – and the song was certainly familiar to him, possibly occasionally sung by him. Joyce was certainly conversant with it, and is even more appropriately at home in the Dublin description of Moore's statue above the ladies' and gentlemen's lavatories in College Green as 'The Meeting of the Waters'. Yet the close of the verses prophesied a cruel irony for Parnell, who died in Brighton, his party broken, his friends at loggerheads, his beloved Katharine for whom he had sacrificed all being forever barred from his ancestral home:[7]

> Sweet vale of Avoca! how calm would I rest
> In thy bosom of shade, with the friends I love best,
> Where the storms that we feel in this cold world should cease,
> And our hearts, like thy waters, be mingled in peace.

Tom Moore was Catholic, the Parnells Protestant but, long before the Cromwellian ancestors of the 'uncrowned King of Ireland' had set foot in Ireland, a more formidable poet and settler than any Moore or Parnell had paid his predatory poetical portion. Edmund Spenser (1552–99) sang the beauties of Ireland strictly from the voice of an English Elizabethan conquistador, the natives being distasteful if ultimately removable blots on the pastoral and profitable landscape. He shared with Gaelic poets a freedom in his disposition of natural phenomena in his Muse's service. In *The Faerie Queene* Book IV Canto xi, he conscripted the Irish rivers as wedding party for the nuptials of the Thames and the Medway. Rather akin to the Texan who marvelled at what God could have done, if only He had had the money, one idly speculates on what Spenser might not have made of canals or river drainage awaiting their cues from the eighteenth, nineteenth and twentieth centuries. But, as Professor Alastair Fowler pointed out:

> The Canto, I would suggest, is far from being merely descriptive. It is a festival piece, celebrating a visionary England – and Ireland – united in friendly alliance, and married to a sovereign whose policy promises a strong and prosperous peace. ... We can no longer speak of Spenser's formal construction as loose. If anywhere, we should expect to find looseness in a catalogue of rivers. But what we actually find in the wedding of Thames and Medway [symbolising England and Elizabeth] canto is a high degree of formal organisation – 'narrow verse' in which there would literally be no room for a single additional stanza or extra river.

Dr Patricia Coughlan falls in with Professor Fowler's fine numerological proof of a craftsmanship as cunningly conceived and structured as Joyce's own:

> ... the beauty of perfect order is imputed by the genial personification of Munster mountains and streams. The river-marriage episode in IV. xi uses the attendance of the Irish rivers in a general procession to prefigure optimistically the acquiescence, in fact withheld, of the inhabitants in the conquest and plantation.

This may be unduly charitable. Spenser's preoccupation with Irish landscape as inviting English colonisation seems little troubled by aboriginal objections: English conquest will not be deterred by them or their makers, and if the latter are swept aside along with the former, it is the natives' own fault. Such is the clear message of his *View of the Present State of Ireland*, written in 1596, and the Irish rivers flow along their inviting beds in *The Faerie Queene* as one of the most poetic forms of advertisement for potential immigrants known to economic history.[8]

> There was the Liffy rolling downe the lea,
>   The sandy Slane, the stony Aubrian,
> The spacious Shenan, spreding like a sea,
>   The pleasant Boyne, the fishy fruitfull Ban,
> Swift Awniduff, which of the English man
>   Is cal'de Blacke water, and the Liffar deep,
> Sad Trowis, that once his people overran;
>   Strong Allo tombling from Slewlogher steep,
>   And Mulla mine, whose waues I whilom taught to weep.
>
> And there the three renowned brethren were,
>   Which that great Gyant *Blomius* begot,
> Of the faire Nimph *Rheusa* wandring there.
>   One day, as she to shunne the season whot,
>   Vnder Slewbloome in shady groue was got,
>   This Gyant found her, and by force deflowr'd
>   Whereof conceiuing, she in time forth brought
>   These three faire sons, which being thence forth powrd
>   In three great riuers ran, and many countreis scowrd.
>
> The first, the gentle Shure that making way
>   By sweet Clonmell, adornes rich Waterford;
> The next, the stubborne Newre, whose waters gray
>   By faire Kilkenny and Rosseponte boord,
>   The third, the goodly Barow, which doth hoord
>   Great heapes of Salmons in his deepe bosome:
> All which long sundred, doe at last accord
>   To ioyne in one, ere to the sea they come,
>   So flowing all from one, all one at last become.
>
> There also was the wide embayed Mayre,
>   The pleasaunt Bandon crownd with many a wood,
> The spreading Lee, that like an Island fayre
>   Encloseth Corke with his deuided flood;
>   And baleful Oure, late staind with English blood:
>   With many more, whose names no tongue can tell.
> All which that day in order seemly good
>   Did on the Thamis attend, and waited well
>   To do their duefull seruice, as to them befell.

Fowler's fascinating numerological argument is founded first of all on the numbers of rivers Spenser used, the eighteen listed above (IV. xi. 41–4) matching eighteen famous rivers of the world (IV. xi. 20–1 between which two groups fall forty-five English rivers.

Spenser naturally required a predominance of English rivers – but the case for the river as Ireland's in the geographical symbolism of the archipelago is unimpaired. It was from his Irish domicile that Spenser was inspired to think of rivers, and his Irish rivers derive from his own experience or fellow-conquistadors' accounts, where his English rivers are largely book-learned as are those of the rest of the world. The use, almost certainly by invention, of a rape-legend to introduce the Barrow, Nore, and Suir is ominously suggestive for the political purposes of the verses. *Blomius* seems born of a classicist's mind: Slieve Bloom, the mountain where Spenser has the rivers (known locally as 'the three sisters') rise is correctly *Sliabh Bladhma*, the mountain of flame. In fact only the Barrow rises in it. *Rheusa*, deeper classicism, is from the Greek verb 'to flow'. If Spenser plays the fool by classicising Irish language sources when on Leinster rivers (with Munster vagaries as he points out for the Suir), he is much more formally the well-instructed resident on Munster rivers proper. He knows his Irish Gaelic, and even parades his knowledge of the correct name where many tiros use the English form. 'Awniduff' is an attempt at *Aibhne dubha*, the black rivers. The otherwise useful P. W. Joyce insisted the reference was to the Ulster Blackwater, tributary to the Ban, and that the Munster Blackwater, in whose valley Spenser had his estates, was known as Broadwater; but the near-contemporary document he cites gives both names. *Slewlogher* is *Sliabh Luachra*, the mountain of the rushes. Allo is a tributary to the Munster Blackwater flowing past the house where my mother was born and raised, at Dysert, between Banteer and Kanturk, north Cork. The ironies of the English poet trying hopelessly to shape his mouth into the aspirates and gutterals of the Gaelic speech are manifold: he heard beauty in its tones, as Wordsworth did in testifying to the Scots-Gaelic singing-girl whom he identifies as 'The Solitary Reaper' and, like Wordsworth, Spenser may make us even more aware of the beauty of the Gaelic by his inability to come to full terms with it. Being a conquistador he expresses his identification with natural beauty by insisting he owns it: 'Mulla' is 'mine', and his name for it is assumed to abbreviate *Cill na Mullach*, the church of the mountain tops, an old name for Buttevant (north of Mallow) where he had his seat, the river there being generally known as Awbeg (i.e. *Abha beag*, the little river). Equally, 'Oure' seems to be his version of Glenmalure, Co. Wicklow, where his patron, Lord Grey de Wilton, had been defeated by Fiach MacHugh O'Byrne on 25 August 1580, two weeks after his arrival as new Lord Deputy with Spenser as his secretary.

It was the beginning of Spenser's Irish life, climaxing in a 3000-acre estate, ending – under the age of 50 – in his last year of life, 1599, as he fled to England, with his castle burnt and one of his children killed. It was a cruel legacy Ireland left him in the end; he left its landscapes in the lush, predatory prose of his *View of the Present State of Ireland* (not published until 1633 and hence left to inspire Cromwellian settlers) and in the sublime poetry of *The Faerie Queene* and *Colin Clouts Come Home Again*. He was the evangelist of a new Ireland, and the euthanasiac of the old.

In 1844 Spenser was remembered for celebrating 'most of the Irish rivers' by James Roderick O'Flanagan (1814–1900), a genial Catholic lawyer whose affection for Daniel O'Connell (1775–1847) did not forbid his turning a literary penny in what O'Connell termed 'that monstrous liar, the *Dublin University Magazine*', once he had established his pota-mology in *The Blackwater in Munster*. O'Flanagan's deference to Spenser matched his book's civility to prominent squirearchical subscribers, but both in the book and in his subsequent contributions to the *DUM*'s 'Irish Rivers', O'Flanagan was happy to trail some pagan pre-Tudor traditions. In any case Protestant antiquarians, many of whom began by accusing Roman Catholicism of refurbishing and perpetuating paganism, often settled for stressing that it, also, was a mere modern invader, by comparison with Pagan Ireland. Yeats, Synge, Shaw and O'Casey all play with the idea, which surfaces in more cosmopolitan form in Oscar Wilde.[9]

The great people of Gaelic Munster were the MacCarthys, taking their descent from the fourth-century chieftain Eoghan Mór, as also did many of their satellite tribes, chief of whom were my mother's family, O'Sullivan. Clan Eoghain was also a designation for McAuliffe (MacAmhlaoibh), with a castle near Newmarket, not far from the Blackwater at Kanturk: Spenser or Spenser's patrons and their Cromwellian successors displaced many a McAuliffe, O'Sullivan and MacCarthy. 'The Castle of Dromore' (a poetical enlargement of Dromore House, owned by the Newman family in O'Flanagan's book) is a lullaby ostensibly by Sir Harold Boulton (1859–1935), English heir to a baronetcy and claimant also for authorship of the 'Skye Boat Song', 'All Through the Night', 'Glorious Devon', 'The Song of Kent', and others. Wales would make him a bard, Scotland seems to have made him a Jacobite, and Ireland may or may not have the credit for his conversion to Roman Catholicism. His *Who's Who* entry retreats to 'editor and part-writer' of at least some of his work, though his many slim volumes make less qualification. Presumably he found airs and texts from local sources: the most famous songs ascribed to him are far better than compositions unquestionably his. 'The Castle of Dromore' is probably a Gaelic song in the original – Boulton's version includes Gaelic words, although a translation into Gaelic by the founder of the Gaelic League and future President of Ireland, Douglas Hyde, is less felicitous. The air was composed, or at least 'arranged', by the future Sir Arthur Somervell (1863–1937), who put songs to Tennyson's *Maud* and some of Housman's *Shropshire Lad* – it is Gaelic enough to carry its content, and lullaby enough to quieten its auditors. The theological accuracy may bespeak the care of the convert, but its blend with pagan antecedents is authentic enough for any indigenous Corconian, while most Cork Catholics would appreciate the perfect statement of the Virgin Mary as intercessory without divine claims:

> Bring no ill-wind to hinder us – my helpless babe and me,
> Dread spirits of the Blackwater, Clan Eogha[i]n's wild banshee;
> For Holy Mary, pitying us, in heaven for grace doth sue –
> Singing hushaby lullaloo lo lan, sing hushaby lullaloo.

I recall a folk version restricting the Blackwater spirits to one, with 'lo lan' as '*mo gheall*' (my love, my pledge); the rest of that line is probably a hybrid of Gaelic and English, leavened by illiteracy or preliteracy in transcription of versions from oral rendition, whether the infirm author be Boulton or another. The banshee is famous far beyond Ireland, the lachrymose lady (or fox or other spirit embodiment) whose cry announces the imminent death of one of the family she haunts. The name – *bean sidhe* – simply means a woman fairy. As a rule she is a harbinger of doom, but not its cause, so we might expect the dread spirits to work doom and the banshee to announce its imminence. This particular banshee is that entity attached to the MacCarthys (and O'Sullivans and McAuliffes), and is identified as Clíodhna, or Cliona, whose various origins include status as a fairy who fled from Tír na n Óg, the Land of Perpetual Youth, with her curly-haired mortal lover; once in Ireland, he went to hunt for food, she was lulled to sleep on the beach of Glandore, in south-west Cork, and was then brought back to Tír na n Óg by a great wave sent to abduct her by her true sovereign, the sea-god Mananaan Mac Lir. The roar of *Tonn Clíodhna*, the wave of Clíodhna – still perfectly audible during a northeast wind in Glandore Harbour betweeen Skibbereen and Ross Carbery, is by now taken to mourn for her beloved family chieftains rather than for the lost boy. But her principal palace, according to the great Irish lexicographer Father Patrick Dinneen, is at Carraig Clíodhna (the rock of Clíodhna), once again in the neighbourhood of Kanturk – whose local castle, once a MacCarthy fortress, seems the obvious antecedent for 'The Castle of Dromore', rather than the civil residence of the Newmans, and their seventeenth-century war-profiteer predecessor, Sir Richard Kyrle (fl. 1666).

Invocation of Clíodhna on the death or downfall of MacCarthy (or O'Sullivan or O'Callaghan) was appropriate for the bard in use of pathetic fallacy, especially for the great Irish Gaelic poet Aodhagán Ó Rathaille (?1670–?1736) who proudly commemorated his family's bardic service to the MacCarthys throughout the previous two millennia; but James Stephens (?1882–1950) suggests that the unavoidable sound of the wave might lead Ó Rathaille to curse the banshee's pessimism:[10]

> O Wave of Cliona, cease thy bellowing!
> And let mine ears forget a while to ring
> At thy long, lamentable misery…

Ó Rathaille in general assumes Clíodhna's feelings to be benevolent towards family members whose misfortunes she vigorously deplores, but a more critical spirit towards the ambiguity of fairy treatment of mortals may link her to such practices as sundered herself from her lover so long ago. It is also possible that folklore transmitted to new men – Newmans – in possession of former Gaelic territory enjoyed a more malevolent quality. If the Boultons and Somervells captured the Castle, their suppressed informants may have hardened the hauntings with which they credited it.[11]

O'Flanagan tells a story, engagingly prettified according to the romantic specifications of the 1840s ('with an etheriality caught from that dreamland, Germany' beamed the *DUM* in looting it):[12] and this would seem to identify the destructive spirit with the presumably female family fairy. O'Flanagan's version seems to be set in the later fifteenth century when Gaelic lordships were impeded by encroaching descendants of Normans, but holding much of their own. In keeping with the poetry of Sir Walter Scott, the rude Gaels (as their future supplanters and Spensers would have seen them) become knightly figures of high snobbery, but if O'Flanagan suggests English inheritance by primogeniture, there is also a hint of Gaelic traditional insistence on a future chieftain being the best qualified. McAuliffe of the Castle has but one child, the beauteous Mealane (a diminutive of Mella, presumably, *Mealla* in Irish-Gaelic, a name much associated with ancient Irish holy women, but unsuccessfully so in this case).

> 'Who was like to Mealane, the fair-haired daughter of McAuliffe? Whose step was lighter in the dance? Whose voice sweeter in the song? Who was like to Mealane?'
>   Years have passed since the events I am about to relate. The proud wall has crumbled into a mass of ruin, and the proud race who held the lordly towers are extinguished: yet never has the beauty of Mealane been surpassed, or the graceful figure of the damsel equalled.

'My daughter shall be the bride of a hero', the aged sire would say. 'Now that old age hath stricken my limbs, and years rolled heavy on my nimble feet, I can no longer wield the spear, or chase the fleet flying stag; but as God has not blessed me with sons, I may be the grandsire of them. My Mealane shall be the bride of a hero.' These words were not spoken unheard: they were echoed abroad by fame, and the surpassing loveliness of the Lily of the Valley, as she was commonly called, and the widespread possessions of the McAuliffes, (to all of which she was sole heiress) soon procured her many suitors; but one was preferred to all: he was O'Herlahy [Ó hIarfhlatha i.e. the descendant of an under-lord; the O'Herlahys were an ecclesiastical-linked family with lay patronage over the nearby church of St Gobnait at Baile Mhúirne, but their own name specifically means inheritors of lower chieftains' rank], chief of Carrigduve [*Carraig Dubh* i.e. Black Rock]. Having found favour in the eyes of the fair lady, the suitor next urged his claims before the grey-haired sire. The elder thus answered his deep entreaties.

'The Lord of Blackrock is young in years; his name is not known in the council, not his prowess in the song of the bard. Go into a foreign land, O'Herlahy; let thy sword be fleshed in the blood of the infidel, and I will grant thee my daughter. Mealane shall be a hero's bride.'

The heart of O'Herlahy murmured in silence at the delay, but he could not refuse the terms. The spirit of the sire was as unyielding as the stubborn rock that, thrown in the midst of the ocean, stands unmoved in the blast; the waves lash it in vain, and mounted up to the craggy sides, tumble back into their liquid bed. He led the hardy sons of Erin; they joined the gallant troops led by Fernando [II of Aragon in the 1480s] to crush the Moorish infidel; but at the walls of Granada the brave O'Herlahy was taken. Five years he lingered in captivity; he thought of his absent country, and the image of his love was never forgotten. The favourite of the Algerine Dey became enamoured of the noble prisoner; she procured his freedom, and would have accompanied his flight, but the love he bore another forbade; he returned to Spain, and had revenge on his captors. His companions were fired by his example; they rushed into the thickest of the battle, and ruin and death marked their gory career. The Moors fled [1482–84], never again to rule in Spain. The king embraced the brave youth, and gifted O'Herlahy with the proudest order of Spanish chivalry. With joy he returned to Ireland, no obstacle between him and the possession of his love.

It was towards the hour of noon. At the castle of McAuliffe, every thing betokened joy and hilarity. From the opposite side of the Aun-Daluagh the hills rose covered with waving forests, and parties of pleasure were either roving the shady alleys for a walk, or traversing in search of game: a number of cooks were hard at work in the ample kitchen of the castle; parties in groups were arriving every moment at the portal, and the major-domo, with his liveried attendants, was marshalling each to his apartments, who were bidden guests to witness the marriage between the fair heiress of McAuliffe to the brave chief of Carrigduve, O'Herlahy. Dressed in her nuptial robe of virgin white, the lovely Mealane appeared to have well deserved the *soubriquet* of the Lily of the Valley. Her fair flaxen hair, secured by a golden chaplet, gave a stately air to her graceful bust; her blue eyes sparkled with uncommon vivacity, and her slight figure, as it glanced to and fro, reminded one of the graceful bendings of the flower after which she was named; her cheek was pale – rather too pale; but all said that the situation in which she stood occasioned the total absence of colour. Once or twice during the afternoon she was observed to start suddenly, and when uncalled for cry out, 'I come! I come!' As if to calm her spirits, she said she would try a short walk. O'Herlahy rose to accompany her.

'No, my dear lord; I bid you stay', she said

'What! may I not go with you?'

'Not now, no now', she said mournfully.

'Nay, then, I will follow you.'

'If you do, I go not forth. Abide here till my return.'

Mealane walked forth; but the evening wind whistled gently down the glen, like the sighing of unseen spirits, and yet she came not back. The clergyman who was to perform the ceremony arrived, and the bridegroom was waiting, but no bride. A peasant who had just returned from the opposite of the Aun-Daluagh, said he saw a white figure near a large tree; but when he spoke he received no answer, and went on his way wondering. O'Herlahy buckled on his trusty armour, and was resolved to win his bride or perish. He went forth alone; the night was still and lonely. Every rock, tree, hill, and glen was streaming with the bright light which beamed from the full moon; the heavens were clear, and studded with myriads of glittering stars, which twinkled in the intensity of the blue sky. O'Herlahy paused on the banks of the Aun-Daluagh, and gazed on a panorama of beauty; yet his heart was ill at ease for the loss of his beloved, and the tears came to his eyes, as turning round he looked on the castle of McAuliffe crowning the hill: lights issued from every window, yet sad were the hearts within.

He crossed the stream, and approached the oak tree, the oldest in these parts. A figure in white reclined beneath the branches; he stole cautiously. 'Mealane!' At the sound of his voice the figure rose up, and waving her white hands to bid farewell, was borne along the course of the stream, as though under the guidance of some powerful spirit, and fled towards the rock, which opened to receive her. It closed immediately, and since there has been no trace of the fair Mealane; but often the nightly wanderer sees the fluttering of the white drapery about Mealane's Rock. O'Herlahy married a less supernatural lady, and the lands of McAuliffe passed to strange hands.

It has kinship with Moore's *Melodies*: sound in his case story in O'Flanagan's, is tamed, drawing-roomed, and brought into the taste of the time. Eighty years before, James Macpherson (1736–96) had made respectable the stories of the old Fianna or Fenian warriors and repackaged them in ornate romantic language; and the success of his attempt in drawing polite society behind his Gaelic lore was a secret vindication of the Highlands against an age of improvement whose votaries despised Celtic civilisation and indeed denied the possibility of its existence. O'Flaherty had produced a socially acceptable version of an old Blackwater folk legend, and had Victorianised Munster Gaelic lordships of the late fifteenth century with cunning use of fashionable history such as Washington Irving's *The Conquest of Granada* (1829) and William H. Prescott's *Ferdinand and Isabella* (1837), to say nothing of Byron's *Don Juan* (1818–24). But for all of his need to tailor his emancipated Catholicism to his Protestant patrons, the end of the story packs its own punch. 'Strange hands' take over McAuliffe's lands, and the civilisation of their *ancien régime* by any standard is no whit inferior to the highest pretensions of Victoria's Munster, let alone Spenser's. As to the plot, its roots are no doubt numerous in international as well as Blackwater folklore, yet it also reaches forward to themes in very different works – the close of Anthony Trollope's short story 'La Mère Bauche', the opening of Bernard Shaw's *Arms and the Man*, the plot of Joan Lindsay's *Picnic at Hanging Rock* (filmed 1975). The dread spirit of the Blackwater exercises an ascendancy far beyond the rationality of the love-betrayed suicide girl in 'La Mère Bauche', who surrenders her life on being summoned by the man who has deserted her, whereas Mealane gives away her mortal life when her too faithful true hero calls her. (Trollope has learned his novelist's trade studying the *DUM* of the early 1840s.)[13] *Arms and the Man* has the heroine forced to admit she does not want the gallant military hero after all her high posturings over his courage: and O'Flanagan's tale might bear such an interpretation with a clue or two but in fact gives not the faintest suggestion of it.[14] Even the Australian gentilities of boarding-school girls in 1900 may end in unsolved mystery, but the mystery at least leaves enough psychological fodder for the enthusiast. O'Flanagan's story abides no question, it would seem.[15] The best we can suggest is that the wild banshee, notoriously insistent on ancient lineage, summoned the girl lest she throw herself away on the outshoot of an inferior family tree. Here again there would seem a coded message. If the O'Herlahy hero is unacceptable, for all of his heroism, slaughtered Muslims, seduced houris, cheering Spanish kings and approving McAuliffe, what would the snobbish fairies think of the English nouveaux riches?

II

O'Flanagan's tale subtly enough suggests that the victimised Mealane becomes a spirit of the Blackwater herself, much as in the romantic imagination of the day the Flying Dutchman might now be destroyer and now victim, or in Greek legend Scylla the innocent girl enchanted by Circe becomes the horrific peril of passing sailors, or Sinend becomes the soul of the Shannon that drowned her. The idea of the river enforcing virginity suffuses the Blackwater legend (though there does seem an implication that before O'Herlahy had found success and glory Mealane would have enjoyed mutual discovery with him). Charlotte Grace O'Brien (1845–1909), daughter of the 1848 revolutionary 'leader' William Smith O'Brien (1803–64), captured such a moment in 'A Lament of the Shannon' in 1878, but from the grim day-to-day lives of the people, not from their high folklore:[16]

> Oh! do you remember that night –
> That night when the tempest was born,
> And the shriekings and weepings ere morn
> Chilled the heart of the bride with affright? –
> Oh! do you remember that night?
>
> Oh! do you remember that night –
> That night when the feet of the dead
> Were borne in to the bridal bed
> By the young men silent and white? –
> Oh! do you remember that night?
>
> Oh! do you remember that night –
> That night the waves beat on the shore:
> Rippling and laughing, they bore
> His poor broken body to sight? –
> Oh! do you remember that night?

Charlotte Grace O'Brien could be political enough, fighting for better conditions for emigrants, reform of Irish land laws, alleviation of human suffering. But she dealt in facts of life: the enforced virginity commanded by her Shannon is a tragedy, to be realised, not to be rhapsodised. But sometimes the river takes its due in her verse because a marriage has been consummated rather than in seeking to prevent it. 'The River' makes its own lyricism the instruments of the doom it tells:

> Poor Mick was trotting on to the town,
> The side car under him going;
> He looked on the water swollen and brown,
> He looked on the river flowing.

The day was drear and heavy and dank,
A sleety wind was blowing,
And the river creeping up over the bank
Was in to the roadside going.

Now all that day till the night drew near,
For the wind was bitterly blowing,
Poor Mick sat gossiping here and there,
While the river was steadily flowing.

'And why would he lave? 'tis a cruel night;
Oh, why should he be going?
Bide ye here till the morning light,
For the blackest wind is blowing!'

'The wife will be wanting her bread and tay
And oil for to light her sewing –
Myself never minded the roughest day
Or the blackest black wind blowing.

'Gi' alang, old mare! get up out of that!
For sure 'tis home we're going!'
He buttoned his coat and settled his hat,
Nor thought of the river flowing.

But cold and drear and dark was the night,
The sleety wind was blowing,
And where the road that morning was right,
The river's edge was flowing.

Movrone! for the childer, Movrone! for the wife,
They listen the north winds blowing,
Movrone! for the gasping struggling life,
Movrone! for the river flowing.

The morrow's morn saw the trembling mare,
Saw the river muddily flowing,
Saw boys and men seeking here and there,
Though the soft south winds were blowing.

Oh! the early sun is fair to see
And the winter'll soon be going,
But deep and dank and dark lies he,
Though the sweet south winds are blowing.

It quietly sets aside the comedy of Burn's 'Tam o' Shanter' and the tragedy of Kingsley's 'The Sands of Dee' and makes its own achievement in its simplicity. It catches crowd-conscious folk song assonances. It turns on the sure element of the road suddenly becoming the murderous river. Its pathetic little domestic boastings and kindnesses become lures more captivating than any witches or cattle ownership. And in the midst of the repetitive Movrone! (*Mo bhrón*, i.e. 'my grief!'), it makes us feel a man drowning.

The river as guardian of virginity came into its own with the Foyle (Spenser's 'Liffar deep', apparently). For this purpose the Foyle has to be masculine: the Shannon might jealously snatch the bridegroom from his bride, the man from his wife, but the Foyle had more altruistic work to do. Charlotte Elizabeth Tonna (1790–1846) produced a sharply feminist personification of Derry resisting the Jacobites, and while her own broken-down first marriage to a suspiciously Irish-sounding (and Catholic-sounding) officer, Captain Phelan, receives little commemoration, the poem is an old favourite, being reprinted as recently as 1987 (if not later) in *The Orange Lark*, a convenient anthology for the Orange marcher and singer commencing with an imprimatur from David Trimble.[17]

The Foyle's masculinity ambiguously guards the feminised Derry's feet or chastity belt against Jacobite importunity, and does so (whether or not her Orange singers know it) in celebration of her Catholic thirteenth-century temple and the Protestant commerce that followed her incorporation in 1609 under the investment of London capital:

> Where Foyle his swelling waters
> Rolls northward to the main,
> Here, Queen of Erin's daughters,
> Fair Derry fixed her reign;
> A holy temple crowned her,
> And commerce graced her street,
> A rampant wall was round her,
> The river at her feet;
> And here she sat alone, boys,
> And, looking from the hill,
> Vowed the Maiden on her throne, boys,
> Would be a Maiden still.

The Foyle's masculinity is presumed to blend with that of its audience: but since Protestant Derry wants to commemorate above all the Apprentice Boys who closed the gates on Jacobite authority, the audience becomes significantly deficient in mature masculinity. So are the heroes under commemoration, the unpatriarchal fathers; frustrating the rapist required by the storyline, Alexander Macdonnell (d. 1699), Third Earl of Antrim arriving with a Catholic regiment on 7 December 1688:

> From Antrim crossing over,
> In famous eighty-eight,
> A plumed and belted lover
> Came to the Ferry Gate:
> She summoned to defend her
> Our sires – a beardless race –
> They shouted 'No Surrender!'

> And slammed it in his face.
> Then, in a quiet tone, boys,
> They told him 'twas their will
> That the Maiden on her throne, boys,
> Should be a Maiden still.

The next stage suggests that the Foyle's example and his disciples' demands result in conditions akin to the women's sex strike against war in Aristophanes' *Lysistrata*. The relevant pope (Alexander VIII) actually supported William III, not James II, but the 'Pope's commission' has a more symbolic usage and Charlotte Elizabeth Tonna was certainly correct in crediting James with a vigorous sex life and hence presumably pain on denial:

> Next, a crushing all before him,
> A kingly wooer came
> (The royal banner o'er him
> Blushed crimson deep for shame);
> He showed the Pope's commission,
> Nor dreamed to be refused;
> She pitied his condition,
> But begged to stand excused.
> In short, the fact is known, boys,
> She chased him from the hill,
> For the Maiden on the throne, boys
> Would be a Maiden still.

Sexually denied James would have been 'in short', inspiring speculation on the home-life of Captain and Mrs Phelan, who may herself have envied Derry. She certainly had a sense of humour, a ribaldry denied in Unionists and feminists alike by their enemies. But the commemorative nature of the poem seems to turn on Derry's reconstitution as a local authority under the Irish Municipal Reform Act passed on 10 August 1840, when landlord control was abolished and ratepayer control was substituted, all at the behest of Daniel O'Connell on whom the Whig Government of Lord Melbourne still depended. Tonna defied the oratory of the former and the authority of the latter:

> Nor wily tongue shall move us,
> Nor tyrant arm affright,
> We'll look to One above us
> Who ne'er forsook the right;
> Who will, may crouch and tender
> The birthright of the free,
> But brothers, 'No surrender!',
> No compromise for me!

We want no barrier stone, boys,
No gates to guard the hill,
Yet the Maiden on her throne, boys,
Shall be a Maiden still.

Derry itself was being rapidly increased in population by Roman Catholic immigration, as pointed out in the Maynooth MA dissertation on Derry 1825–1850 by Mr John Hume (later MP, MEP, Nobel Laureate etc). Tonna was employing Protestant populism in the landlord interest, it seems, and would not be the first or last patrician to try such a tactic. In fact, Tory democracy was a working political system in Ulster decades before Disraeli or Lord Randolph Churchill had an inkling of it.

Whatever Tonna's political intent, the work became a firm favourite with Roman Catholic and nationalist anthologists in the early twentieth century.[18] James had been an English king, and the brave men and women (or boys and girls) of Derry were Irish in rebellion against him, however much they might have disliked the identity. The most popular textbook in Irish history, James Carty's *A Class-Book of Irish History* (1929), was a fervent evangel of Irish nationalism. It was ready enough to speak of the 'superb courage and loyalty' of Irish Jacobites, but declared:[19]

The defence of Derry against the forces of King James is one of the most memorable episodes in Irish history. It is one in which all Irishmen should take pride.

Macaulay's description of the city's relief by the *Mountjoy*, the *Phoenix*, and the *Dartmouth* breaking the boom across the Foyle (the conclusion of which is engraved on the walls of Derry) was added as an appendix to the relevant chapter by Carty. Carty (1901–59) was justly held in esteem as a distinguished scholar by Éamon de Valera (1882–1975), but it is unlikely that his opinion of the place of the siege in Irish nationalist ideals would have been supported in Derry's Bogside. It is an important, if neglected, point of divergence of Irish Catholic nationalist commemorative traditions.

If the Foyle is sexually somewhat monastic and authoritarian about it, what is to be said of its neighbour slightly to the south, the Erne? William Allingham (1824–89) produced a beautiful lyric 'The Winding Banks of Erne; or, The Emigrant's Adieu to his Birthplace', but while excellent of its kind it is *genriste*: it is topographically admirable, but the river remains in its landscape. It recalls Spenser's 'Sad Trowis, that once his people overran', also on the Donegal–Sligo border. The Erne loomed large in a famous Gaelic poem in Spenser's day, Róisín Dubh', widely credited to Red Hugh O'Donnell's bard (Gaelic equivalent of speech-writer), and O'Donnell's war in Munster would account for Spenser's final expulsion. James Clarence Mangan (1803–49) produced a high Romantic version for the 1840s:[20]

> Over hills, and through dales,
> Have I roamed for your sake;
> All yesterday I sailed with sails
> On river and on lake,
> The Erne, ... at its highest flood,
> I dashed across unseen,
> For there was lightning in my blood,
> My Dark Rosaleen,
> My own Rosaleen!
> Oh! there was lightning in my blood,
> Red lightning lightened through my blood,
> My Dark Rosaleen.
> ...
> O! the Erne shall run red
> With redundance of blood,
> The earth shall rock beneath our tread,
> And flames wrap hill and wood,
> And gun-peal, and slogan-cry,
> Wake many a glen serene,
> Ere you shall fade, ere you shall die,
> My dark Rosaleen!
> My own Rosaleen!
> The judgement hour must first be nigh,
> Ere you can fade, ere you can die,
> My Dark Rosaleen!

Rivers of blood are remarkably unpleasant visions. Thomas Jefferson (1742–1826) wrote to John Adams (1736–1826) in 1823 that to obtain universal republicanism 'rivers of blood must yet flow ... yet the object is worth rivers of blood': there is something of a Roman aristocrat patronising a gladiatorial show about Jefferson.[21] Macaulay's Huguenot poem 'Ivry' (1824) ascribes such a memory of the Massacre of St Bartholemew's Eve to its narrator on the eve of battle:[22]

> There rode the brood of false Lorraine, the curses of our land;
> And dark Mayenne was in midst, a truncheon in his hand:
> And as we looked on them, we thought of Seine's empurpled flood,
> And good Coligni's hoary hair all dabbled with his blood;
> And we cried unto the living God, who rules the fate of war,
> To fight for his own holy name, and Henry of Navarre.

Apart from the Bann (1641) and the Boyne (1690), whose blood-empurplement is obvious enough, the red river of Irish history is not the Erne, but the Slaney, diagonally across the island from it in Co. Wexford. The reason is simple: the final defeat of the Wexford insurgents of 1798, described in the touchingly artless phrase of the popular ballad 'Boulavogue':

> At Vinegar Hill, o'er the pleasant Slaney,
> Our heroes vainly stood back to back ...

The work of P. J. McCall (1861–1919), it was published for the centenary of the Wexford Rising, an emotive performance of little subtlety, but that conventional 'pleasant' has a chill no contrivance could produce. McCall's verse, often taken for folk poetry, drew on old ballads, though in the words of the conscientious Swiss Georges-Denis Zimmermann 'he never borrowed more than half-a-line at a time'. His antecedent here is uglier, commemorating moments of victory, not yet defeat:

> To Enniscorthy we marched quite easy, [pronounced 'aisy']
> > Where Orange blood died the Slaney stream; [pronounced 'shtrame']
> To the market-house they ran for shelter,
> > But that stately building we soon set in flame.

The date is unknown, but it is much nearer the events, as the Gaelic internal vowel rhyme-scheme shows (aisy/Slaney/shtrame/flame; 'shelter' may have been lengthened to match with 'building', sounding like 'belding', though as the Gaelic language grew more distant, these rules were less and less rigorously applied). It also brings us closer to the savagery of the insurrection: dotty Protestant fears about the revival of the fires that burnt mid-sixteenth century Protestants in the reign of Mary Tudor sound less dotty as we hear the rejoicing at the burning alive of enemies. An allied song rejoices in the barn at Scullabogue where Protestants were burnt by supporters of the rebels.

A strongly Ulster Protestant Unionist voice, Colonel William Blacker (1777–1855) produced his own brand of romanticism in 1837, 'Oliver's Advice':[23]

> They come, whose deeds incarnadined the Slaney's silver wave –
> They come, who to the foreign foe the hail of welcome gave;
> He comes, the open rebel fierce – he comes, the Jesuit sly;
> But put your trust in God, my boys, and keep your powder dry.

Blacker, a Dublin University graduate, was consciously drawing on Spenser, whose knowledge of the heavy sanding of the riverbed inspired his 'sandy Slane' (phonetically sound enough, too, for the Irish name –

Sláine – ends in a half-elided 'e' rather than the fully 'y' termination).
'Charlotte Elizabeth' attempted to rationalise it:

> I know what a clamour has been raised by that song, the burden of
> which is Cromwell's advice to his troops on crossing a river. ...
> Cromwell was a heartless, hypocritical aggressor; but it does not
> follow that his advice abstractedly was wrong. Ahitophel gave excel-
> lent counsel, though from a bad motive, and for a bad purpose. ...
> You know that I can go as far as the Quakers do in reprehending and
> denouncing even defensive warfare; but with all these feelings
> unchanged, and desiring rather to fall beneath the hand of an assassin
> than to send his unprepared soul before the judgment seat, I heartily
> concur in the propriety of presenting such an aspect as shall, humanly
> speaking, preserve us both unharmed.

Admittedly, Blacker seemed to want his bloody rivers on both sides of his
verse, when he commends his hearers to follow

> The Power that nerved the stalwart arms of Gideon's chosen few,
> The Power that led great William, Boyne's reddening torrent through

But from his opponents the same verdict on the Slaney returns:[24]

> But the bold sun of Freedom grew darkened at Ross,
> And it set in the Slaney's red waves ...

The Erne might have run somewhat red during the Jacobite/Williamite
wars of 1688–91 when the Protestant settlers fled to the safety of Derry or
Enniskillen, and such figures as the future playwright George Farquhar
(1677–1707) found their homes burnt out, thus accounting for his future
presence as one of the youngest combatants at the Boyne. But neither
Farquhar nor anyone else seems to have so described it. Mangan, possibly
under the stimulation of Macaulay on the Seine, was at least prepared to
make the Erne's empurplement an item on a revolutionary agenda, which
was thrilling enough provided one did not look too closely at realities on
the Slaney. The original Gaelic text did not bear him out: in one way it
went further, in another it simply played with pathetic fallacy:[25]

> The Erne will flood strongly, and hills will be torn,
> The sea will become red waves and the sky into blood,
> Each glen of the mountains throughout Ireland and bogs will shake,
> One day, before my black little rose will die.

There is even some doubt as to whether the poem is patriotic in its origin,
and modern scholars suspect it may have been a love poem by a some-

what hysterical priest who had fallen in love with a girl. It was appropriate Irish Victorianism that so theologically and erotically indelicate an antecedent should be obliterated by a longed-for bloodbath.

III

Why the Boyne?

Commemorating the Shannon, the Blackwater or the Liffey is perpetual tourism, with the cream of the joke that Joyce, the supreme iconoclast, supplies the peak of the tourist attraction. Commemorating the Avoca or the Slaney is pageant backdrop. Commemorating the Foyle and the Erne, in the sieges of Derry and Enniskillen, makes sense enough, especially when the rise of a politicised and militarised Catholicism is making so much headway. The eighteenth century gave little enough cause for Derry Protestants to unite in commemoration of an event when the more numerous Presbyterians had gallantly supported the more vulnerable episcopalians, who then (in fear that the Church of Ireland would be Presbyterianised like the Church of Scotland) turned on their former comrades and reduced them to second-class citizenship above Catholics alone. But when the pariah had become the patriarch to the extent that Daniel O'Connell carried more weight in Melbourne's Ireland than any single Irish Protestant of whatever sect, let Derry remember the days of old, 150 years old in precise terms. Besides, in the words of Rory Fitzpatrick, in his sympathetic portrait *God's Frontiersmen: The Scots-Irish Epic* (1989):[26]

> Water, in springs and rivers, has a spiritual and practical significance in the history of the Scots-Irish. Rivers to a restless people were a means of transport or a barrier to progress, but for settlers established for a generation or two they could become a focus of local patriotism, or perhaps *pietas*, as in the valley of Virginia. Water has the obvious symbolism derived from Revelations: 'Then he showed me the river of the water of life, bright as crystal, flowing from the throne of God'.
> ...
> The first evangelical river in Ireland was the narrow trout burn called Six Mile Water which winds through the rich farmlands of mid-Antrim. On the banks of this stream [the Scotsman Robert] Blair and his fellow ministers tackled the problem of ungodliness among their fellow settlers, and their unfitness to build the new Zion. On a summer day the four ministers would preach in turn for perhaps two hours each; the endurance of early Presbyterian congregations was phenomenal. But then the whole audience, old and young, was involved in something which was of the utmost importance and often very dramatic. Andrew Stewart attended the Six Mile Water Revival

as a boy of eight and heard Blair preach; 'his hearers ... fell into such
anxiety and terror of conscience that they looked on themselves as
altogether lost and damned ... I have seen them stricken and swoon
with the Word – yea a dozen a day carried out of the doors as dead'.
This tradition of evangelism is still alive and kicking ...

... and in Catholic as well as Protestant churches: I remember seeing
schoolboys carried out unconscious from sermons on Hell. But however
valuable Fitzpatrick's illustration of the place of rivers in Ulster
Protestant *mentalité* from its beginning in the early seventeenth century,
why commemorate the battle of the Boyne?

Out step the Orangemen on the Twelfth of July, to celebrate a battle in
1690 whose Protestant combatants believed had taken place on the First
of July, and which became the Twelfth for all British subjects in
September 1752, when Britain accepted the reform proclaimed by Pope
Gregory XIII in February 1582. Out step the Orangemen on one pope's
instructions, to celebrate the Dutch English king fighting in another
pope's cause, against another King, the English English one, whose
Catholic monarchical support was limited to the near-schismatic Louis
XIV of France. Out step the Orangemen glorying in the name of a river
lying in its totality beyond the boundaries of Northern Ireland, knowing
that any actual return by the Orangemen to the River Boyne would place
them at the mercy of an Irish Roman Catholic electoral majority owning
no allegiance to the British Crown or United Kingdom. Is there on the
face of the earth a spectacle so absurd as a people commemorating their
past and asserting their identity by invocation of a part of their island
proclaimed purdah by their whole philosophy? It is as though the Scots
were to celebrate their national identity, not as Bannockburn but as some
point in the former Scots domain of Cumbria to which the celebrants
would never go. There is nothing ridiculous in commemorating William
III (of England), II (of Scotland), I (of Ireland), the last hero king of the
British Isles, and it would be well for the Orangemen to commemorate
above all William's brave leadership of his own country, the United
Netherlands, against its French invaders from 1672 to 1678, to prevent
whose return he acquired England, conciliated Scotland, and conquered
Ireland between 1688 and 1691. But the analogy is ignored, and the irrelevance enshrined. It is not William the defender they recall but William
the conqueror, regardless of the abhorrence with which the celebrants
look on most of the territory William conquered. William's own cry that
it was a land well worth fighting for they might, with consistency, recall:
he could be taken as alluding to what he encountered from Carrickfergus
to Dundalk, rather than the green, grassy slopes of the Boyne beloved by
them in song but not in sight.

Or is it William the conqueror they commemorate? Is it not in fact William the deliverer, whose advent saved them from popes and popery, knaves and knavery, slaves and slavery, brass money and wooden shoes, etc.?[27] But if so, why the Boyne? Aughrim – admittedly won without William's presence – was what consolidated Protestant ascendancy in Ireland, won in 1691, on the twelfth of July (the Protestant one, this time, thus making its date 23 July in our, Gregorian, dating).

Let us look a little closer at the Boyne. First of all, it has no mere casual supernatural associations like drowned girls to gratify folklorists, or female embodiments to awaken Finnegans. Most great Irish rivers no doubt had their divine cults, but the Boyne's ancient theological associations are still vehement and vocal where its rivals have made do with more modern folk-lore or poetic personification. The Boyne in ancient Irish legend is female, raped or seduced by the pot-bellied Dagda, thereby giving birth to Aonghus Óg, possibly the most loveable god in all pagan antiquity, and certainly the god of love, not in the wayward, supposedly Puckish fashion of Eros or Cupid, but in tenderness and compassion for lovers on the fron-tiers of tragedy. Aonghus, like many another god, is invoked on more than one side of Irish conflicts: thus Seán Clárach Mac Domhnaill likened Bonnie Prince Charlie to him in the afterglow of the '45 (with clear assumptions his audience would recognise what was intended in the simil-itude).[28] The combatants in 1690 may not have been thinking of him – after all, William III, James II, Marshall Schomberg, Patrick Sarsfield, the Revd Dr George Walker (now Bishop-elect of Derry), the future playwright George Farquhar, and the rest of them, had enough on their minds as it was – but posterity obligingly made good the deficiency.

The Christianisation of pagan traditions (one of whose long-term allergic side-effects was the Reformation) had given plenty of scope to monkish or bardic reinventors of folk epic, among them, somewhat snob-bishly, the conversion of Irish hero-kings to Christianity before its arrival in Ireland. One story told how Conor Mac Neasa, the king served by Cuchulainn and the Red Branch Knights, died of rage on learning of the (contemporary) crucifixion of Christ: the devout Catholic nationalist Timothy Daniel Sullivan (1827–1914) made a good ballad of 'The Death of King Conor Mac Nessa' in the mid 1860s, reaching poetic heights when the life of Christ is recounted to the king, significantly by his druid (hailed by Conor as 'O priest').[29] Another, less dramatic but slightly more plausible, made a comparably exemplary end for Cormac Mac Airt, High King in somewhat uneasy proximity to Fionn Mac Cumhaill and his warrior band. Cormac being High King at Tara injured his eye in combat late in life and withdrew to Clethech (Sletty) near the Boyne. One version of the story was quoted by William Wilde (husband of the poet, father of the playwright) in his contribution to the *DUM*'s 'Irish Rivers', afterwards his *The Beauties of the Boyne and its Tributary the Blackwater* (1849). It made a strange unity of purpose between Cormac and the pagan deities he had repudiated:[30]

> And he (Cormac), told his people not to bury him at Brugh (because it was a cemetery of idolators); for he did not worship the same god as any of those interred at Brugh; but to bury him at Ross-na-Righ, with his face to the east. He afterwards died, and his servants of trust held a council and resolved to bury him at Brugh, the place where the kings of Tara, his predecessors, were buried. The body of the king was afterwards thrice raised to be carried to Brugh, but the Boyne swelled up thrice, so as that they could not come; so that they observed that is was violating the judgment of a prince to break through this testament of the king; they afterwards dug his grave at Ross-na-Righ, as he himself had ordered.

Wilde (surely the greatest Irish topographer of his time)[31] continued:

> And, again, 'The nobles of the Tuatha de Danaan were used to bury at Brugh.' And the Dagda, as well as Boinn … were also interred in this place. The river here well deserves the name of Brugh-na-Boinne, (the broad Boyne)

– this is Victorian euphemism for 'the broad-bellied/great-breasted Boyne' but a more probable translation is the 'fairy fort of the Boyne' –

> which it still retains. Some ancient pagan remembrances and super-stitions attached to this locality, up to a very recent date; and, at a pattern which used to be held here some years ago, it was customary for the people to swim their cattle across the river at this spot, as a charm against certain diseases, as in former times they drove them through the Gap of Tara.

Wilde was unusual for his time in investigating superstitions with scientific interest rather than for social reproach or theological reprobation.

The Annals of the Four Masters, more correctly the *Annals of the Kingdom of Ireland* prepared by the Franciscan friar Micheál Ó Cléirigh (1575–1645?) and his three colleagues in 1632–36, left the Boyne out of the story but gave the pagan clergy a more active role:[32]

> AGE OF CHRIST, 266. Forty years was Cormac, son of Art, son of Conn, in the sovereignty of Ireland when he died at Cleithech, the bone of a salmon sticking in his throat, on account of the sorcery [*Siabhradh*, also meaning 'demonical rage'] which Maoilghenn, the Druid, incited at him, after Cormac had turned against the Druids, on account of his adoration of the God, in preference to them. Wherefore

a devil attacked him, at the instigation of the Druids, and gave him a painful death.

Revd Geoffrey Keating (1570?–1645?), correctly Seathrún Céitinn, was preparing his *Forus Feasa ar Éirinn* about the same time. It was known to Wilde's fellow-Academicians and fellow-scholars chiefly in the 1857 translation by John O'Mahony (1815–77) who co-founded Fenianism the following year:[34]

> Soon after, a meal was prepared for the king, and he began to eat of a salmon from the Boinn. Thereupon the demons of the air came and attacked him, at the instigation of Maelghenn, the druid, and by them the king was slain. Other accounts say that he was killed by a bone of a salmon, that had stuck in his throat and choked him; he was engaged in eating of that fish when the demons had attacked him.
>
> When he found the symptoms of death upon him he commanded his relations not to bury his body at Brugh, on the Boinn, where several of the preceding kings of Temhar (Tara) were laid. And then (when contrary to his instructions), the host was bearing him thither, the demons thrice opposed the progress of the funeral, by raising an immense flood before it, in the river; for these spirits did not wish to allow his body into an idolatrous cemetery, by reason for his having believed in the True God. But the fourth time, the men that carried the body entered with it into the swollen stream; but there the current of the Boinn swept off their burden, and bore it along to Ross-na-Righ. There the corpse was separated from the *Fuad*, or bier, and hence the ford of Áth-Fuaid, the ford of the bier, on the Boinn, has its name. It was retained at that place, and a grave was made for it, and it was buried, at Ross-na-Righ.

Keating noted that many years later Columcille [i.e. St Columba] came to Ross-na-Righ, found Cormac's head there, buried it and said thirty masses over it, so that a church was now there.

These narratives are all of Catholic authorship, yet all concede considerable effectiveness to the pagan authorities, clerical or divine. The mid nineteenth-century growth of interest in Gaelic scholarship was particularly well served by Wilde's friend (and poetic elegist) the Ulster Protestant poet antiquary Samuel Ferguson. Ferguson seems to have shared the hostility of his fellow-Protestants for the new Roman Catholic clerical power so ruthlessly organised after 1850 by Paul Cardinal Cullen (1803–78); he also seems to have had common ground with many of the evangelical clergy whose attempts at proselytism had strongly advanced Irish literature before the Great Famine. Politically, Ferguson had green moments, but they were much less visible after 1860. His *Lays of the Western Gael* (1865) were consciously in the tradition, and drawing on the plots, of Scott's *The Lay of the Last Minstrel* and Macaulay's *Lays of*

Ancient Rome; but they evidently also owed some cutting edge to the vigorously Protestant spirit of Macaulay's 'Ivry', 'The Armada' and 'The Battle of Naseby', frequently republished with the Roman poems. Ferguson's contemporaries would have had little difficulty finding an anti-Catholic resonance in 'The Burial of King Cormac'. By way of a start, Paul Cullen's Ireland was abounding in the ostentation of Catholic commerce. The faithful competed in bourgeois Catholic respectability as they bought their sacred statues and holy pictures:

> 'Crom Cruach and his sub-gods twelve',
> Said Cormac, 'are but carven treene;
> The axe that made them, haft or helve,
> Had worthier of our worship been.

> 'But He who made the tree to grow,
> And hid in earth the iron-stone,
> And made the man with mind to know
> The axe's use, is God alone.'

Keating makes this a conversation about worship of a golden calf in which Cormac declines to participate, refusing to worship a creation from his own artificer and saying it were better to worship the artificer; and that he worshipped only the God of heaven, of earth, and of hell. But the scholar in Ferguson cried out against so obvious an intrusion of the book of Exodus into the Celtic theogany.[34] Good Protestant hostility to worship of any human (especially the pope, bishops or priests) enhanced the axe rather than the artificer in framing Cormac's ironical preference to idolatry, as Ferguson tells it. Irish evangelical Protestantism insisted that salvation came from Jesus alone, and ferociously denounced all images, icons, cults of the Virgin Mary and the Saints.[35]

> Anon to priests of Crom was brought –
> Where, girded in their service dread,
> They ministered on red Moy Slaught –
> Word of the words King Cormac said.

Priests. Not druids. Priests. The image in the minds of Ferguson's Irish readers, Catholic or Protestant, would be modern Catholic priests in chasuble, amice, alb, cincture, maniple, stole, vestments for celebration of the sacrifice of the Mass. And Moy Slaught (unmentioned by the four Masters or Keating, but supported by a scholarly footnote in Ferguson) had a sinister resemblance to Maynooth (especially in the Irish language):[36] St Patrick's College, Maynooth, its state income augmented by a controversial increase in 1845, trained the Roman Catholic bishops of tomorrow and hosted the deliberation in which the Roman Catholic bishops of today determined the limits of their laity.

> They loosed their curse against the king;
> They cursed him in his flesh and bones;
> And daily in their mystic ring
> They turn'd the maledictive stones,
>
> Till, where at meat the monarch sate,
> Amid the revel and the wine,
> He choked upon the food he ate,
> At Sletty, southward of the Boyne.

(The latter rhyme succeeds only when the poem is read in an Ulster accent.) Ferguson might be thinking of the fate of certain Catholic opponents of the bishops, but would also have remembered Catholic clerical support of agrarian agitation against landlords, hitherto monarchs of all they surveyed. His fellow-Protestant contemporary W. E. H. Lecky (1838–1903), wrote a bitter indictment of Roman Catholic clerical dictatorship in its mastery and deployment of popular control: it appeared only a year or so before Ferguson's poem was written, closing the first edition of Lecky's *Leaders of Public Opinion in Ireland* (1861).[37]

> High vaunted then the priestly throng,
> And far and wide they noised abroad
> With trump and loud liturgic song
> The praise of their avenging God.
>
> But ere the voice was wholly spent
> That priest and prince should still obey,
> To awed attendants o'er him bent
> Great Cormac gather'd breath to say, –
>
> 'Spread not the beds of Brugh for me
> When restless death-bed's use is done:
> But bury me at Rosnaree
> And face me to the rising sun.
>
> 'For all the kings who lie in Brugh
> Put trust in gods of wood and stone;
> And 'twas at Ross that first I knew
> One, Unseen, who is God alone.
>
> 'His glory lightens from the east;
> His message soon shall reach our shore;
> And idol-god, and cursing priest
> Shall plague us from Moy Slaught no more.'

Cormac's deathbed affirmation as to his funeral arrangements certainly has the best warrant in Ferguson's sources, but again the manner of repudiation of material objects for salvation (Catholic scapulars, rosaries, pictures, holy water, etc.) recalls Irish Protestant evangelism in full flower, as shown, say, in Carleton's story of a deathbed where Catholic adjuncts are repudiated.[38] The glory Ferguson hopes from the east would presumably be the supersession of Catholic obsessions by British civilization: in the narrower sense, that British evangelicalism would find friends and converts in Ireland, the east's day had ended with the Great Famine. After 1851 the prospects of proselytism were almost entirely over. But its ghost could still write poetry.

The poem now changes, rather like a river-course, and new demands on our loyalty appear: in place of the vicious priests we meet Cormac's normally supportive councillors and, much more emotively, the devoted soldiers who have saved his life.[39] It is not Robin Hood against the sheriff and the bishop any more, but Robin Hood against Little John and Will Scarlet.

> Dead Cormac on his bier they laid: –
> 'He reign'd a king for forty years,
> And shame it were', his captains said,
> 'He lay not with his royal peers.
>
> 'His grandsire, Hundred-battle, sleeps
> Serene in Brugh: and, all around,
> Dead kings in stone sepulchral keeps
> Protect the sacred burial ground.
>
> 'What though a dying man should rave
> Of changes o'er the eastern sea?
> In Brugh of Boyne shall be his grave,
> And not in noteless Rossnaree.'
>
> There northward forth they bore the bier,
> And down from Sletty side they drew,
> With horseman and with charioteer,
> To cross the fords of Boyne to Brugh.
>
> There came a breath of finer air
> That touch'd the Boyne with ruffling wings,
> It stirr'd him in his sedgy lair
> And in his mossy moorland springs.
>
> And as the burial train came down
> With ridge and savage dolorous shows,
> Across their pathway, broad and brown
> The deep, full-hearted river rose;
>
> From bank to bank through all his fords,
> 'Neath blackening squalls he swell'd and boil'd;
> And thrice the wondering gentile lords
> Essay'd to cross, and thrice recoil'd.

Then forth stepp'd grey-hair'd warriors four:
They said, 'Through angrier floods than these,
On link'd shields once our king we bore
From Dread-Spear and the hosts of Deece.

'And long as loyal will holds good,
And limbs respond with helpful thews,
Nor flood, no fiend within the flood,
Shall bar him of his burial dues.'

With slanted necks they stoop'd to lift;
They heaved him up to neck and chin;
And, pair and pair, with footsteps swift,
Lock'd arm and shoulder, bore him in.

'Twas brave to see them leave the shore;
To mark the deep'ning surges rise,
And fall subdued in foam before
The tension of their striding thighs.

'Twas brave, when now a spear-cast out,
Breast-high the battling surges ran;
For weight was great, and limbs were stout,
And loyal man put trust in man.

But cre they reach'd the middle deep,
Nor steadying weight of clay they bore,
Nor strain of sinewy limbs could keep
Their feet beneath the swerring four.

And now they slide, and now they swim,
And now, amid the blackening squall,
Grey locks afloat, with clutching grim,
They plunge around the floating pall.

While, as a youth with practised spear
Through justling crowds bears off the ring,
Boyne from their shoulders caught the bier
And proudly bore away the king.

Aubrey de Vere (1814–1902), Ferguson's Catholic convert contemporary, has Boyne drown 'with one black wave / Those Twelve on-wading' after which he removes Cormac 'with glee'.[40] Ferguson is more economical. We never discover whether his four 'loyal' and 'brave' (good emotive Protestant, even Orange, traits) die in their loss or live in their shame, and we have come to like them too much for their misplaced devotion, to want to know. For all that the funeral is girt in pagan, i.e. Catholic, superstition – the professional laments, the wakes, the keens, the *Dies irae* are all implied – the four warriors are Cormac's men both against what they see as his delirious judgement and against his clerical enemies whose magic they read as dishonour to Cormac's burial having taken his life. Ancient

Irish texts support Ferguson's version – the Boyne intervenes because the king's wishes are ignored – but Keating sees pagan enchantment as animating the Boyne, and Ferguson lets Cormac's Old Guard embody Keating's view. As a scholar Ferguson would have given Keating respect he would not grant to a modern priest (Máire Mhac an tSaoi has remarked that Ferguson's zeal drew him far into enemy territory.)[41] Ferguson is playing Macaulay's trick in 'Horatius' where the reader, supporting Horatius, is nevertheless slightly drawn to the chivalrous if ruthless Lars Porsena and his 'ranks of Tuscany' who 'Could scarce forbear to cheer' when Horatius survives his first dive into the river.[42] But our sympathy carries its distancing. We begin to realise that Cormac's old friends are *old* friends, that whatever the merits of their pagan camaraderie and codes, their time is over, and they are defeated by a river suddenly young. The spirit animating the Boyne is not the demon described by Keating or the fiend suspected by the four, but the athletic youth to which the four once aspired: Aonghus Óg, in fact, Aonghus the Young.

But Aonghus is surely part of the paganism which above all else discredited Catholicism? To the pre-famine evangelicals whence Ferguson's passion had arisen, yes; but Ferguson was evolving towards a newer Irish culture, the mood of John Millington Synge (1871–1909) and W. B. Yeats (1865–1939) as they confronted Catholic puritanism with the surviving pre-Christian traditions of love and laughter, and answered the charge that they were invaders, strangers, blow-ins by indicting Catholicism as the newcomer foreign to ancient Irish custom and belief. Yeats knew his trade when he invoked the shade of Ferguson, whose repudiation of paganism here is transformed into its rejuvenescent celebration. Aonghus the Young is in excellent metamorphosis, his epiphany in his own simile as spear-throwing youth. Behind Aonghus there is the river-god of greater antiquity, his mother, and entities far older than that mother. But where is Jesus? Oscar Wilde (1854–1900), for one, would have no problems with the equation of Aonghus and Jesus. The Ulsterman C. S. Lewis's Martian theology in the *Out of the Silent Planet* series renders Jesus as 'Maleldil the Young'.)[43] Ferguson might seem a less obvious exponent of such a link, but the interment of Cormac by unknowing shepherds once the Boyne has done its work, makes its own association with the Christian theophany.

> At morning, on the grassy marge
> Of Rossnaree, the corpse was found,
> And shepherds at their early charge
> Entomb'd it in the peaceful ground.
>
> A tranquil spot: a hopeful sound
> Comes from the ever youthful stream,
> And still on daisied mead and mound
> The dawn delays with tender beam.

Round Cormac Spring renews her buds:
In march perpetual by his side,
Down come the earth-fresh April floods,
And up the sea-fresh salmon glide;

And life and time rejoicing run
From age to age their wonted way;
But still he waits the risen Sun,
For still 'tis only dawning Day.

The final statement is one of startling individualism. This superficially agrees with evangelism, demanding as it does the personal moment of Christian witness, but evangelism insists even more on having its church. But Cormac ends in pure isolation. Earlier versions assume final acceptance of his Rossnaree interment: nobody knows he is there, in Ferguson's poem, apart from the shepherds who do not know who he is. There is one Maupassant-like possibility: the salmon may know. Celtic lore associated the salmon with wisdom, and Cormac's malicious death by salmon is now arched by his benevolent burial beside salmon. But the new Celticism as the new individualism would be crucial to the Irish Renaissance, whether in Wilde, Yeats, Synge or Joyce.

Whether he lives to see the risen sun or not, Ferguson intends to win. It may not be a Protestant victory in the new Ireland, but at least it will end the Catholic tyranny so bitterly assailed by Lecky and others. Lecky as a historian was the champion of the oppressed Catholics of the eighteenth century, and as a contemporary the opponent of the oppressor Catholics of the nineteenth century. But for all of Lecky's – and Ferguson's – anger at the way Catholics were dishonoured and impoverished by the penal laws after the victory of William of Orange, they are Williamites. The Boyne is their symbol of victory, a victory they intend to renew by claiming Irish intellectual leadership even as they are losing political control.

For good or evil, the Boyne was the river of Irish Protestant rule. But when the Protestant rulers had lost, politically, and later, culturally and intellectually, the Boyne meant nothing. The Orange Order had once been a mighty organisation across the entire archipelago, across the whole island of Ireland. Its survival in Northern Ireland alone might still proclaim its might, but the Boyne has no place in that survival. 'No surrender', cried the Orangeman. 'Not an inch', intoned James Craig, their greatest leader. The Boyne had surrendered long, long ago. It had surrendered on good terms: it got excellent conditions of land purchase, fine grants for its intellectual pleasure-grounds, ceremonial dignity for the princes or moderators of its churches, lucrative directorships in the boardroom, prominent political positions for Protestants potentially closed to those of comparable talents from the majority religious faith. But these were Napoleonic adornments at St Helena. The Boyne courses through the richest grazing soil in the Republic and bears its kings no more.

IV

The Boyne flows down to the sea and, in common with most of the world's rivers, finds its mouth polluted by the greed and waste of humanity, collected in a port, in this instance Droichead Átha, the bridge of the ford – interesting over-precaution, belt and braces, as the English say – anglice Drogheda (which the Irish pronounce 'Dro' as in 'dropsy', 'head' as above body, 'a' as indefinite article; which the Scots and some Ultonians pronounce 'Drocheda',[44] 'Droch' as in 'loch' the rest as Irish; which the informed English pronounce 'Drawdah', 'Draw' as for artist or potboy, 'dah' as in diminutive paternity; and which the uninformed English pronounce 'Droydah').[45] In the seventeenth century it was anglified as 'Tredagh', which in the absence of personal instruction we must take to have been pronounced 'tray-dah', a desperate attempt to put substance on the elided gutterals and quicksilver aspirates of the Gaelic (which sounds now like 'dhru-hadh aw-ha' and may have sounded like that then). The seventeenth century was its century, and it is Oliver's town. But which Oliver? The great Roman Catholic Church holds Oliver's head, the head of St Oliver Plunket (1625–81), martyred during the Popish Plot in London where he was hanged, drawn and quartered in 1681, after twelve years as Archbishop of Armagh.[46] From a strictly Roman Catholic standpoint, no more horrifying crime could be committed: the execution of Anglican King Charles I – the execution of the Roman Catholic King Louis XVI – pale by comparison. The Primate of All Ireland was the high priest of high priests, greatest of all the Lord's anointed: no pope or cardinal sacramentally ranks above their fellow-bishops, by whom alone the power of ordaining priests is transmitted, and in the act of consecration at Mass the priest holds the place of God Himself.[47] Macaulay (1800–59) evidently had Plunket in mind in seeking to bring home to his British audience the horror in Hindu eyes of the judicial murder of Nuncomar (or Nandakumar) in 1775:[48]

> He was the head of their race and religion, a Brahmin of the Brahmins. He had inherited the purest and highest caste. He had practised with the greatest punctuality all those ceremonies to which the superstitious Bengalees ascribe far more importance than to the correct discharge of the social duties. They felt, therefore, as a devout Catholic in the dark ages would have felt, at seeing a prelate of the

highest dignity sent to the gallows by a secular tribunal. According to their old national laws, a Brahmin could not be put to death for any crime whatever.

But Macaulay was writing in 1841: seventeenth-century Irish Catholicism had supped so full with horrors that another bishop may simply have added another sacred name to the martyrology – after all Oliver Cromwell and his merry men had hanged the Roman Catholic Bishops of Ross, Clogher and Emly within the space of a year. It was in the nineteenth century that resurgent, respectabilised Catholicism commemorated its martyred Archbishop, and in the lines of the Catholic convert Aubrey de Vere recalled not the profitable perfidy of his perjured accusers nor the institutionalised cruelty of his judges and executioners but the cowardice of his fellow-Catholic Charles II. It is essentially a commemoration of the debt owed by the British to Catholic subjects, not the title of the Irish to revolt:[49]

> Why crowd ye windows thus, and doors?
> Why climb ye tower and steeple?
> What lures you forth, O senators?
> What goads you here, O people?
>
> Here there is nothing worth your note –
> 'Tis but an old man dying:
> The noblest stag this season caught
> And in the old nets lying!
>
> Sirs, there are marvels, but not here:
> Here's but the threadbare fable
> Whose sense nor sage discerns, nor seer;
> Unwilling is unable!
>
> That prince who lurk'd in bush and brave
> While bloodhounds bay'd behind him
> Now to his father's throne brought back,
> In pleasure's mesh doth wind him.
>
> The primate of that race whose sword
> Stream'd last to save that father,
> To-day is reaping such reward
> As Irish virtues gather.
>
> His Faith King Charles partakes – and hides!
> Ah, caitiff crowned, and craven!
> Not his to breast the rough sea tides;
> He rocks in peaceful haven.
>
> Great heart! Pray well in heaven this night
> From dungeon loosed, and hovel,
> For souls that blacken in God's light,
> That know the truth, yet grovel.

This last reflects de Vere the Catholic convert received into the Roman Catholic Church by the future English Cardinal Henry Edward Manning (1808–92), both having rejected their natal Protestant episcopalianism in 1851: de Vere believes that many of his fellow-Protestants are afraid to adopt Roman Catholicism in clinging to their respectability. In Ireland certainly the notion that Roman Catholicism was socially retrograde and Protestantism socially desirable was crucial in the nineteenth century (the identification of Roman Catholicism as the true snob religion by Evelyn Waugh (1903–66) lay in the future). But beyond individual considerations, de Vere's commemoration of Plunket commemorates the perjured state. De Vere, from the stance at Ferguson's polar opposite, commemorates with the same intent, that the state might yet be saved. But the Manning-baptised de Vere is thinking of the United Kingdom of Great Britain and Ireland, while the Ulster-born Dublin-based Ferguson has a purely Irish agenda. De Vere's Irish Catholicism had big stakes in Britain; Ferguson's Irish Protestantism might hope for British support and influence, but it was in business for itself. Ferguson's state was certainly to remain the United Kingdom: but it was Ireland's redemption he sought.

The Boyne was Plunket's, far more than it was William's or James's, for the Archbishop was a Meathman, and so, for most of its course, is the river. In fact he was resented in Armagh as from a family of English origin resident in Ireland for a mere 400-odd years, instead of the Gaelic Ulsterman local Catholicism would have preferred: Catholic clerical resentment and rivalry had paved some of the road to the scaffold. Commemoration of Plunket, especially in the early twentieth century, had very firm purposes: his elevation from beatification to canonisation. Ireland likes to call itself the island of saints and scholars, but very few have been canonised (which reflects less on the quality of Irish sanctity than on the cool relations between Rome and Ireland down the centuries). Canonising Plunket meant that he had formally died for the faith (which he had) and that therefore the Franciscan Friars could forget about the part played by their order in anger against his judgement in favour of their Dominican rivals, and that Armagh Gaelic nationalists could dismiss the tradition of Gaelic deficiencies in support for the murdered Archbishop. Persons with no such historical guilt to assuage (be the consciences of Crossmaglen what they may) could urge his cause with vehemence. The most substantial historical work on Plunket for many years remained the multi-author *Blessed Oliver Plunket – Historical Studies* (1937) to which my father, Robert Dudley Edwards, on the eve of co-founding *Irish Historical Studies* as the journal of scientific historical writing in Ireland, contributed two essays: the publishers were the League of Prayer for the Canonisation of Blessed Oliver Plunket.[50] No barriers were felt to exist between comprehension, commemoration, and

canonisation – and the technique of *advocatus diaboli* should be as necessary an adjunct to the first of these categories as it is to the third; it is only
the second which may not easily bear it. But the Plunket campaign
resulted in extensive prayer-recitals from Catholic schoolchildren, whose
difficulty in recollecting the precise roles of historical characters in close
proximity resulted in orisons for the canonisation of Blessed Oliver
Cromwell. The latter would greatly have disapproved of such conduct, as
of all other popish antics, but it seems only charitable to hope that he may
have changed his mind by now, finding the sanctified condition to his
liking. He certainly loved God well enough, however much he resembled
fellow-Christians of all camps in using Him as an alibi, and in failing to
see Him in his Irish neighbour. For Oliver Cromwell is no martyr of
Drogheda; it was Drogheda that was the martyr.

Boyne commemorations are frequently jolly enough, indeed the more
historical the jollier: William's displeasure that the lamentably slain
Bishop Walker of Derry had forgotten his clerical status so far as to take
part in the battle, Sarsfield's request that the victors and vanquished
change kings and fight over again, James's complaint of the flight of his
cowardly Irish troops received with congratulations on his Majesty's
having won the race – with lines like these a myth is as good as a mile.
The Battle itself is replayed annually at Scarva, Co. Down, with the
Newry Canal adjoining rather than a self-assertive river (and in testament
to eastern Ulster industrialisation the type of water course is symbolically
apt). Its good humour, pageantry, and sense of entertainment wins it
many friends:[51] arguably its highest realism is in conveying the battle of
the Boyne itself as something *unreal* by now. The traditional joke tried on
severe observers afterwards is for an Orange marshal to inquire 'Who
won?' The battle commemorated can only be the Boyne, since it was
William's only one in Ireland, but Derry, Enniskillen and Aughrim are
supposedly also commemorated, the Ulster sieges being dragged on the
battlefield because there is little Ulster about the major battles (apart from
Walker getting himself killed at the Boyne, like an unwanted gift unin-
tentionally broken). Even the leading dramatis personae are reinvented.
Schomberg, the great Huguenot general killed at the Boyne must be
there, partly in celebration of the one of the cheerier Ulster folk songs:[52]

> Then horse and foot we marched amain,
> Resolved their ranks to batter;
> But the brave Duke Schomberg he was slain
> As he went over the water.
> Then William cried, 'Feel no dismay
> At the losing of one commander,
> For God shall be our King to-day
> And I'll be general under.'

Thus the mythical Protestant William: in reality his brave readiness to put himself in danger where Schomberg had fallen was a reassuring 'you will be my guards today' to the shaken troops. He would probably have felt that God's clerical status would have forbidden His enlistment in any martial activity, as it should have forbidden Walker. The folk song was sound in other respects, recording William's dismissal of his wound with the wry codicil that it had come near enough 'Pray come no nigher!' King James and King William parade at Scarva, James supported by Patrick Sarsfield, whose place is a little ambiguous. On the one hand, he was the leading Irish Catholic general in the field (although much sidelined at the Boyne itself apparently by jealous rivals), and hence presumably a vital symbol of the Irish Catholic defeat; on the other, Macaulay's much-quoted *History of England* makes Sarsfield the only unquestionable hero (however minor) on James II's side:[53]

> His intrepidity, his frankness, his boundless good nature, his stature, which far exceeded that of ordinary men, and the strength which he exerted in personal conflict, gained for him the affectionate admiration of the populace. It is remarkable that the Englishry generally respected him as valiant, skilful, and generous enemy, and that, even in the most ribald farces which were performed by mountebanks in Smithfield, he was always excepted from the disgraceful imputations which it was then the fashion to throw on the Irish nation.

Ulster Protestantism was of necessity obliged to borrow much of its literary affections and affectations from the Britain whence it had come, and it preserved them longer than the parent culture would. But the benevolence of Boyne pageant, however crudely stressing who won, required no terror figure: if it did it could have made much of the brutal French general Rosen, who drove the Protestant women and children between besieged city and besieging army so that they would be starved or killed in the sight of the Derry garrison. But this would bring in a note of vulnerability. King James was different. King William would always beat King James, in spite of James's brave Irish general.

Yet pageant seems much more indigenous to Ulster Protestant commemoration than to the Catholic's. Certainly there were successful Catholic processions and pageants down the centuries, those taken up in urban centres under Cullen stinging Ferguson into his line about 'trump and loud liturgic song' and thinking their expectation of future power 'The praise of their avenging God'.[54] In Belfast such processions prompted riots encouraged by employers to divide Catholic and Protestant workers, and were assailed because the triumph of one set of marchers would seem to spell the peril of another where jobs were concerned. But Catholic pageant knows itself inferior to the real thing:

the Mass, in which the greatest of all occasions for self-identification is recreated before its audience, Christ's offer of His own sacrifice for humanity to His Father, its fulfilment, and its realisation in the consecrated bread and wine now the Body and Blood of Christ eaten by His priest and followers. Any attempt to call up a glorious past pales by comparison: yet this re-enactment becoming a reality in worshippers' eyes happens every Sunday. Protestant pageant, on the other hand, has not such invincible competition to face. The anti-ritualism of Ulster Calvinists and evangelicals gives freedom to their political votaries to be religious while denying they are being religious, to make their politics a ritualistic religion while denouncing ritualists and their clerical influences. And the result was that Protestant pageant made for one of the most astonishing achievements in modern history: the non-violent Ulster revolt against legally constituted governmental authority in 1912–14, when guns were imported, army mutiny was threatened, violent resistance promised, the Tory party conscripted into declarations of treason and, in the greatest political pageant of British history, the Ulster Covenant was signed, invoking the traditions of Scottish Covenant against the king, while quietly ensuring that all impulses to irregular sectarian violence would be channelled into the rebellion which would never be called on to face government troops. Sir Edward Carson (1854–1935), Sir James Craig (1871–1940) and its other leaders had been stimulated by the success of non-violent agrarian and constitutional nationalist agitation under Parnell, and threatened violence as he never did; but he never played rebellion by pageant and ritual as they did. In the Ulster Covenant, Ulster Protestantism found its own mass.

And then war broke out in August 1914 and the Ulster Volunteers went into battle on behalf of the government they had so vehemently defied just before. And the Ulstermen found themselves with a shooting war as part of their ritual after all; and the ritual contained a sacrifice – themselves; and the sacrifice was made at a river, the Somme.[55]

It was not a sacrifice which could ever have its pageant beyond silence on Remembrance Day, and in that silence on 8 November 1987 the Irish Republican Army exploded its bomb killing eleven holding their commemoration. By so doing the IRA fuelled another form of commemoration: not the triumphant Boyne, but the horror-haunted Bann.

James Orr (1770–1816), son of an Antrim weaver, did his duty as a United Irishman in the Battle of Antrim in 1798, as a weaver poet in the movement's *Northern Star* and in two volumes of poems, one posthumous. Orr dreamed of an Ireland emancipated from the reactionary politics of his fellow-Protestants, at the same time as the Wexford insurrection was taking lives on harshly sectarian grounds, and troops on either side did their bit to incarnadine the pleasant Slaney. Orr was impressively representative of the new, frontier, linguistic culture emerging from migrant Scots in Ulster conscious of their forefathers' land and their present host culture, and as such he won praise from John Hewitt (1907–87) and others for his Scots-Irish verse. His poetic proficiency in that Ulster weavers' speech asserts how conscious he was of his special place both in Ireland and in the archipelago, but in an appeal in pan-Irish terms he had to employ formal English at its most flowery as the cultural common ground. Thus began 'The Irishman':[56]

> The savage loves his native shore,
>		Though rude the soil and chill the air;
> Then well may Erin's sons adore
>		Their isle, which Nature formed so fair.
> What flood reflects a sore so sweet
>		As Shannon great, or pastoral Bann?
> Or who a friend or foe can meet
>		So generous as an Irishman?

He won his pan-Irish audience all right: I heard the verse quoted in a remote Kerry pub in summer 1965, which speaks well for both the time and the space it conquered. Orr's Ulster dialect poetry and its themes reflect slightly excessive derivation from Robert Burns (1759–96), and even when his is appealing to Irish patriotic sentiments by English conventional forms, there is an echo of Burns in society.

The invocation of Shannon and Bann might seem reminiscent of Burns's tributes to Allan or Afton waters, and no doubt his master's voice speeded the plough. But by his discard of his Ulster language Orr adds an Irish identity to his habitual Ultonian Scots, or Caledonian Ulster, and his river-choices proclaim both: the giant river of Ireland, indeed of the archipelago, contrasted to the heart of Ulster Scots settlement. There is also a geographical opposition, with historical coloration: the Shannon seals off the most Gaelic section of Ireland, Connacht (and Clare), this becoming the frontier across which the Cromwellian supposedly herded the Catholic aborigines as an alternative destination to Hell, and, more realistically, on which the Dutch learned the real strength and weakness of Gaelic Irish defence in the conflicts at Athlone and Limerick in 1691; the Bann surrounds the most Scottish section of Ireland, traditionally linked to the southwestern Scottish coast by Irish conquest and later by Scottish military enterprise long before the great plantation of the early seventeenth century. If there are river symbols of ethnic identity in Ireland, these are they.

As to Burns's apparent challenge to Ireland's river runnings, he used a river when his poem wanted one. Had he sought a typification for Scots as Orr did for the Irish, he had the Ness or the Clyde, but what use did he make of them? If a poetic Scot wants water, a loch supplies her or him, as Loch Katrine did for Scott, and Loch Lomond for the doomed Jacobite soldier to die at Carlisle. But when Burns's verse and songs moved across the Ireland where Gaelic was dying in the early nineteenth century, the Irish – Catholic, Protestant, Gael, Borderer, from one end of the island to the other – made him their vernacular, so much so that in the early twentieth century the brand name of an Irish cigarette, confident of its local popularity, was marketed with likenesses of poet and river: 'Sweet Afton'. If Orr had lived, he would have found his chances of becoming a front-rank Irish poet in popularity all the greater had he stuck to Ulster speech at its most Burnsian. He was never more Irish than when he was never more local.

The Bann is the oldest part of Ireland known to have supported a human population, somewhere like 6000 BC when Mesolithic people made their way from what is now Scotland. They spread out from there over the next 3,000 years and seem to have overlapped thereafter with Neolithic invaders, some moving northward from Brittany and Spain. It has been a widespread superstition in both Protestant and Catholic cultures in Ireland that there has been very little interbreeding: the doctrine has been articulated in various forms by persons as intelligent as Jane ('Speranza') Lady Wilde (1821?–1896) and Michael Collins (1890–1922).[57] It is of course nonsensical: today the effective second-in-command of the IRA/Sinn Féin, Martin MacGuinness, and that of the Ulster Unionists, Ken Maginnis, bear what in all respects but spelling is the same name, i.e. in its Gaelic form Mac Aonghusa, son of Aonghus, for all we know a claim to descent from our amiable divine child and animator of the Boyne. Equally, it seems childish to deny the possible growth of affections between the opposite sexes of surviving Mesolithic and intrusive Neolithic settlers. There is this charm about their juxtaposition: the original settlers, less sophisticated technologically, derive from northern and eastern lands, the second group, more advanced in their manufacturing skills, enter Ireland from the South. Much of the ethnic dispute in Ireland has been between persons conscious of finding themselves living in different phases of history; our stone age ancestors may have had the same sense as pushy southerners confronted archaic northerners.

The Bann received its settlers from stone age to gunpowder age, and the proximity of Scotland would have kept up the number of its products on Bannside over the centuries. St Patrick may have been among them. Missionaries, no less intransigent and fierce than he, arrived there about 1100–1200 years after him, no doubt seizing on the Bann as a new Jordan where new John Baptists could preach, convert and baptise. Like John their work was no doubt primarily limited to their fellow-members of their own sect; but like Jesus whom he baptized, and like the Peters who followed Jesus and the Pauls who embraced His memory, the Scots

Protestants may have sought to win converts from beyond their own ethnic ranks. Their attempts to Protestantize, no less than their part in the landgrab from Catholics, may have increased the mounting hostility from the native population, and in 1641 it exploded.

1641 is the true year of Protestant Ulster commemoration, not 1689 or 1690. My sister Ruth quotes some instructive doggerel in her study of Orangeism *The Loyal Tribe* (1999) where the link is ultimately made in a local account of the Portadown massacre during the insurrection of the displaced Catholic former owners. It is significantly anachronistic, terming the rebels 'Fenians' which implies something like 250-year longevity at least, just as its exaggeration of victims is approximately tenfold:[58]

> At least ten hundred faithful souls, in Portadown were slain,
> All were the deeds of Popery, their wicked ords to gain:
> But God sent down brave Cromwell, our deliverer to be,
> And he put down Popery in this land, us Protestants set free.
>
> King William soon came after him and planted at the Boyne,
> An Orange Tree there, that we should bear in mind
> How Popery did murder us, Protestants did drown,
> The bones of some can still be seen, this day in Portadown.

Doggerel though it be, it has linguistic erudition: 'ord' means the point of a weapon, and also the beginning, an archaic usage now, but available in a community cherishing its older vocabularies. Cromwell seldom gets a mention in Orange song, especially with the hijack of William's title 'Deliverer': so unmentionable was Cromwell by William's day that his Lieutenant General of cavalry in Ireland, the regicide Edmund Ludlow (1617?–92), was forced to flee from an order for his arrest when he returned to England after the Glorious Revolution.[59] William's first awareness of European politics as a Dutch child of three or four would have been of his country at war with Cromwell, the killer of his grandfather Charles I. Ruth notes that after the formation of the Orange order, Portadown Orange processions initially took place in November: the massacre of the Protestant prisoners in 1641 was at the beginning of November. There would be a church service in July, and the procession ultimately shifted there nominally for convenience, actually to sink the commemoration of defeat into one of victory. It is this which lends the peculiar venom to confrontation over the Drumcree marches today: Catholics see the Orange parade as triumphalist, asserting the Protestant supremacy; Protestants nominally acquiesce in this thesis, but secretly cherish the event primarily as the memory of their day of doom, and of their dead. It is important that November is still a month of the dead for Portadown: for pious Catholics, it is the month of prayer for souls in purgatory in hopes that they will the more rapidly be admitted to Heaven, and for pious Protestants, it is the month of memory of the Ulster Protestant martyrs, whether on the Bann, on the Somme, or elsewhere in the war against God's enemies. But November is the protest of silence, the poppy alone speaking. July vindicates the memory of Bann martyrdom but in victorious form. To abandon their march is to betray their martyrs; yet to assert the festival from the perspective of defeat is to belie their fiercely male chauvinist culture. A martyrs' memorial march would win wider support, but it would seem to admit the possibility of defeat, not to speak of encouraging the IRA and its siblings in deeds of inhumanity as hideous as any in the wildest legends of 1641. And they have a point. Some IRA songs, including those sung by supporters of Glasgow Celtic, are as ugly celebrations of mass murder in the recent past as any hate-filled Gaelic chant of the 1640s or romantic lunacy of the 1840s. So they march at Drumcree with drums and songs, but in the heart a deeper silence.

The insurrection of 1641 inaugurated one of the worst known cases of what we may term the Confessional Interpretation of History: the assumption that the history of one's own ethnic or confessional or national or class or gender or gender-preference group must be squeaky-clean as a vindication of one's self and validation of one's agenda. Greater and more self-important garbage it would be hard to find save in the converse, the use of history to demean one's opponents. Am I the better Roman Catholic because St Francis preached to the birds or the worse because Pope Alexander VI poisoned the cardinals? I may be the better or the worse if I study them with a view to their imitation, in letter or in spirit: the Confessional Interpretation insists that I am the better or the worse because of the conduct of my fellow-Catholics, regardless of what – other than apostasy – I may do. Cromwell gave us bad leadership here. When he massacred the Drogheda garrison (who were probably mostly his fellow-English by birth or descent) he could have cited the habitual procedures of generals of the Thirty Years War (of which the commander he faced at Drogheda was a veteran). He actually gave the credit, and hence the blame, to his habitual consultant, God (about Whom I believe him to have been thoroughly genuine: he took it as Divine rebuke when the weather held back his campaign).[60] And he also justified the slaughter as being revenge for the massacres of innocent Protestants in 1641 (not at Portadown alone, but in Augher, Belturbet and more general if less authenticated cases). It was the excuse of a weak man (a man resorting to extreme violence is clearly weak), if one at his wits' end at the world's end (in several of the term's meanings). He did fairly well with the limited wits (i.e. the almost unbelievable ignorance about Ireland) available to him. And we must not assume his priorities were as

Irish as posterity has made them: what he did in Drogheda and Wexford[61] against Royalist commanders was intended as a lesson to British Royalists, and that was probably his prime motive. To Cromwell as to many other English over history, Ireland was a useful laboratory for demonstration and experiment, whether in military severity or in land reform. But the argument about the Drogheda and Wexford massacres as just punishment created chains of recrimination became chains of causation: if there had been no massacres in 1641, there would have been no massacres in 1649. As I write, we seem on the verge of discovery that if British troops had not murdered a dozen or so people in Derry thirty years ago, Mr Gerry Adams and his associates would not have been under the urgent necessity of blowing the rest of us up ever since. The Orangemen were right to cold-shoulder Cromwell, likeable as he is: we really did not need instruction in the politics of who-began-it. His massacres may be understood when allowance is made for his peril and fear of a terrible vengeance if his British enemies were to triumph; but his excuses made him the progenitor of every Irish thug from his day to ours. William III is a colder fish, intellectually rather than emotionally attractive, but William was really anxious to get rid of the recriminatory rubbish which wasted so much time. Naturally the Orangemen in commemoration worship a Cromwell in William's clothing.

But the Bann commemorates its tragedy, and the Boyne, whether at Drogheda or Oldbridge or Brugh is of little relevance: the dead in the Bann were dead, regardless of who might do what to whom when. The depositions from surviving witnesses and alleged witnesses to the massacres of 1641 had crucial parts to play in persuading Scotland and England to intervene in Ireland independently of the king, whom many of them saw as an ally of the Irish Catholic insurgent leaders: Charles I had probably done no more than give the vague promises which politicians habitually aggrandise above the level of serious performance, whether in the making or the deploring, and the massacres, were almost certainly on a level of command not planned beyond local hysterical revanchists, but that was bad enough. Montrose (1612–50) was almost certainly executed in the end for having brought to Scotland as his allies Irish Catholic troops viewed as implicated in the massacres and Charles I owed his fate in part to similar if more baseless reasoning. Cromwell might assert that his ruthlessness in Ireland was intended to finish recrimination for good and all: a few strong blows, and the whole matter was over, the good (if still alive) ending happily and the bad unhappily, which, as the younger Wilde's Miss Prism says, 'is what fiction means':[62] but the Marquis of Montrose was hanged in Edinburgh well after Drogheda and Wexford. And the unending spiral of recrimination was the basis for the Restoration maintaining most of Cromwellian land confiscation:

commemoration is immeasurably intensified by the memory of who once
had the land and whether they can reclaim it, and how. The hysterical
fears of Irish support for James II in 1688–91 derived from the folklore
of the horror of 1641. In 1713 a sermon from the Revd John Ramsay
'preach'd to the Protestants of Ireland now in London' on 23 October in
fulfilment of parliamentary demand for a national day of recollection,
rallied public opinion against any offer of the Crown to the Jacobite
claimant, James II's son James (a decided possibility in default of any
other descendants of Charles I to succeed the dying Queen Anne):[63]

> Common Prudence wou'd warn us to prevent their occasioning such
> another anniversary. Must *Ireland* serve only as a grave to bury our
> galent [*sic*] and best Men, and a Gulf to swallow *England's*
> Treasures? Must 30 or 40000 *Britains* be sent over once in thirty
> Years to reduce it, or find untimely Graves there? Is there no Manure
> for that Kingdom but *English* blood? Is the soil so fertile as to answer
> the cost of being so often dunged and fattened?

A Stuart in London meant a massacre in Ulster, argued Ramsay. A
Hanoverian succeeded, in name at least, in 1714, and the penal legislation against Irish Catholics reduced the need for further anniversaries: it
had become quite a season for zealous Protestants and the protection of
the agrarian capital rewarding their piety, running from late October to
the Fifth of November – and that it had now been established to cover
Hallowe'en, All Saints' Day and All Souls' Day (31 October–2
November) has its own logic. Protestantism, however sanctimonious
about pagan survivals in Catholicism, knew a trick or two whence to
usurp symbols from both.

   Catholics and their sympathisers, including the great Edmund Burke
(1729–97), made efforts to rectify the black legend of 1641 – sometimes
to the level of denying much of what was certainly true – but it was not
until the effective return of Irish Catholics into power politics that the
debate really intensified, and here once again the use of commemoration
for capital gains received some of its strongest support from British
politicians and intellectuals, headed by Thomas Carlyle (1795–1881) and
his crude disciple James Anthony Froude (1818–94). Carlyle, a prema-
ture literary impressionist, interpolates one of his innumerable elucida-
tions exasperating and stimulating – and comic, now involuntarily, now
intentionally, now God knows which – into his great edition of *Oliver
Cromwell's Letters and Speeches* (1845, 1846):[64]

> [A] certain terrible fact, which the Irish Imagination pretends to treat
> sometimes as a chimera, might profitably return, and reassert itself
> there. The Massacre of 1641 was not, we will believe, premeditated
> by the Leaders of the Rebellion; but it is an awful truth, written in

sun-clear evidence, that it did happen; – and the noble-minded among the men of Ireland are called to admit it, and to mourn for it, and to learn from it! To the ear of History those 'ghosts' still shriek from the bridge of Portadown, if not now for just vengeance on their murderers, yet for pity on them, for horror at them; and no just man, whatever his new feelings may be, but will share more or less the Lord Lieutenant Cromwell's old feelings on that matter. It must not be denied, it requires to be admitted! As an act of blind hysterical fury, very blind and very weak and mad, and at once quite miserable and quite detestable, it remains on the face of Irish History; and will have to remain till Ireland cease, much more generally than it has yet done, to mistake loud bluster for inspired wisdom, and spasmodic frenzy for strength; – till, let us say, Ireland *do an equal act* of magnanimous forbearance, of valour in the silent kind! Of which also we have by no means lost hope. No: – and if among the true hearts of Ireland there chanced to be found one who, across the opaque angry whirlwind in which all Cromwell matters are enveloped for him, could recognise, in this thunderclad figure of a Lord Lieutenant now about to speak to him, the veritable Heaven's Messenger clad in thunder; and accept the stern true message *he* brings – ! – Who knows? That too, we believe, is coming; and with it many hopeful things.

It reads as though Carlyle, in secret fear that some Irish Catholic nationalist might agree with him, transformed his harangue in mid sentence to the much more improbable demand that Cromwell be accepted as an archangel, thus taking canonisation a stage further: Michael, Gabriel, Raphael, Cromwell, have they not kinship, at least in final syllables? It would have served Carlyle right had any Gaelic scholar pointed out the undoubted fact that some Gaelic poets in Cromwell's time did hail him as a messenger of God – sent to punish those of the Irish who had insufficiently obeyed the most sectarian demands of the Papal Nuncio Archbishop Giovanni Battista Rinuccini (1592–1653) in the complex multi-factional Irish conflicts of the 1640s. As it was, John Mitchel (1815–75) the leading Carlylean in Young Ireland, indignantly denied the Bann massacre in a tedious treatise at the end of his life, but adopted Carlyle's methods of proof by declamation by announcing in the midst of the Great Famine that a fearful murder had now been committed on the mass of the Irish people.[65]

Carlyle's effect on Mitchel shows the anger of a prose as sublime – and ridiculous – as his: the wand works different results when the apprentice follows the sorcerer. If the apprentice has some literary sorcery of his own, as Mitchel had, it makes his theft of his master's wand more effective. Mitchel could play with the sublime. Froude could only be sure of the ridiculous:[66]

When will the Irish Catholics, when will the Roman Catholics, learn
that wounds will never heal which are skinned with lying? Not till
they have done penance, all of them, by frank confession and humiliation – the Irish for their crimes in their own island – the Catholics
generally for their yet greater crimes throughout the civilized world
– can the past be forgotten, and their lawful claims on the conscience
of mankind be equitably considered.

It is a moot point whether Froude's prescription amounted to a revival of
extreme penitential public rites from the high (papist) Middle Ages or to
a foundation of the International Court of Human Rights. That it clearly
required a world dictatorship (by Froude) was no doubt inevitable:
Carlyle might limit himself to idealisation of Cromwell, Froude could
hardly restrict his eloquence to so dead a shrine as that. Every historian
his own Cromwell! And so, whatever their confessional or ethnic prefer-
ences, Froude led the future Irish historians on their way to history by
tribunal. Froude's most attentive audience in the USA seems to have been
the writers and readers of the *Irish World*, which oscillated in the 1880s
between support for Irish Home Rule and for Irish dynamite war in
England. Both Carlyle and Froude needed their massacres to justify their
hero cults but, in G. K. Chesterton's words:[67]

> Froude … carries far beyond Carlyle the practice of worshipping
> people who cannot rationally be called heroes. In this matter the
> eccentric eye of the seer certainly helped Carlyle: in Cromwell and
> Frederick the Great there was at least something self-begotten, orig-
> inal or mystical; if they were not heroes they were at least demigods
> or perhaps demons. But Froude set himself to the praise of … a much
> lower class of people; … There is a sort of strong man mentioned in
> Scripture who, because he masters himself, is more than he that takes
> a city. There is another kind of strong man (known to the medical
> profession) who cannot master himself; and whom it may take half a
> city to take alive. But for all that he is a low lunatic, and not a hero;
> and of that sort were too many of the heroes whom Froude attempted
> to praise.

On that showing Carlyle did not cause Hitlers, as he has so often been
accused of doing: he caused Mitchels and Froudes, and they caused
Hitlers. The Hitlers would always claim fellowship with Carlyle afterwards. Everyman his own Cromwell naturally works itself out as
Everyman his own Hitler. Carlyle for all of his elucidation kept the documents, and hence their time, before his readers: he asked for acceptance
of his version of the past as a sort of moral improvement for its own sake.
Froude demanded acceptance of his version as a preliminary to future
politics. And as Yeats summed it up, Mitchel simply demanded war.
Carlyle's closer but less uncritical admirer (Sir) Charles Gavan Duffy

(1816–1903) took the most characteristic controversial method of all, denial and reaffirmation:[68]

> We deny and have always denied the alleged massacre of 1641. But that the people rose under their chiefs, seized the English towns and expelled the English settlers, and in doing so committed many excesses, is undeniable – as is equally their desperate provocation. The ballad here printed is not meant as an apology for these excesses, which we condemn and lament, but as a true representation of the feelings of the insurgents in the first madness of success.

We may extract a few verses from Gavan Duffy's poem in question, 'The Muster of the North':

> Pity! no, no, you dare not, priest – not you, our Father, dare
> Preach to us now that godless creed – the murderer's blood to spare;
> To spare his blood, while tombless still our slaughtered kin implore
> 'Graves and revenge' from Gobbin Cliffs and Carrick's bloody shore!
>
> Pity! could we 'forget, forgive', if we were clods of clay,
> Our martyred priests, our banished chiefs, our race in dark decay,
> And, worst of all – you know it, priest – the daughters of our land
> – With wrongs we blushed to name until the sword was in our hand?
>
> Pity! well, if you needs must whine, let pity have its way –
> Pity for all our comrades true, far from our side to-day:
> The prison-bound who rot in chains, the fearful dead who poured
> Their blood 'neath Temple's lawless axe or Parsons' ruffian sword.

And the culminating argument is Cromwell's own, the logic of the bloody Book of Joshua, with its massacres of civilian populations undertaken in the name of God:

> Our rude array's a jagged rock to smash the spoiler's pow'r –
> Or, need we aid, His aid we have who doomed this gracious hour;
> Of yore He led His Hebrew host to peace through strife and pain,
> And us He leads this self-same path, the self-same goal to gain.

Modern psychological interpretation will be interested in the inability of the insurgents to contemplate rape without their own reassuring phallic symbols. The theologian will also notice the Calvinism of the Catholics: the hour of Protestant Nemesis is God-appointed, 'doomed' (in the interesting appropriation of the Scots legal term). Yet the poem was used as an approximation of reality within 'histories' denying any Catholic massacre of Protestants (while insisting on Protestant massacre of Catholics at Islandmagee, as indeed there had been). A. M. Sullivan (1830–84), proprietor and editor of the Dublin *Nation* in succession to

Gavan Duffy, produced the most popular Irish Catholic nationalist historiographical justification, *The Story of Ireland* (1867), with denial of
Catholics' homicides and inspirational lines from Gavan Duffy alongside. Froude's hysterics quoted earlier appeared a few years after
Sullivan. Resurgent Orangemen hurried back to the depositions of the
witnesses of the 1641 massacres, whether the narratives seemed wild or
sane, credible or lunatic, and passionately extolled the veracity of them
all, the leading Ulster historiographical defence of the depositions being
by Lord Ernest Hamilton MP, who, as the son of the Duke of Abercorn
and the sibling of four other Tory MPs, knew well enough the fruits of
commemoration, judiciously deployed.[69] The Sullivans had played the
same game for Catholic nationalist political purposes.

   Not until we get back to the heart of real Orange commemoration does
something like sanity and fair play return. R. M. Sibbett, the prime filio-
pietist historian of Orangeism, made his touching protests in *On the
Shining Bann* (1928):[70]

> [W]ith this rhetorical flourish [Sullivan] throws over board facts well
> attested. But that is not the way to make the world better. Suppression
> of truth no matter in whose interest, is always bad, inasmuch as it
> tends to destroy moral fibre, and open the door for every other evil.

It is not only the ghost of Sullivan that is shamed. Sibbett was ready
enough to try fairness:

> [T]he Roman Catholics at the time of the great Rebellion, and the
> Puritans, occupied much the same position with regard to matters of
> conscience. They were standing separately, but none the less deter-
> minedly, against efforts made in high quarters to compel acceptance
> of a form of faith and church government that they did not want.

Few comments by hagiographers can claim to be as reasonable and as
perceptive as that. His version of the massacres is not more uncritical
than Lord Ernest's, but is clearly the work of a much more honest historian with far less of an economic stake in his own arguments. Sibbett
supplies the most hideous river story any commemoration could ask; ('At
Portadown so large was the crowd of men, women and children driven
into the Bann that the Irish were able to cross dry shod over their
bodies'). But his simple honesty punctures the disingenuousness of the
Duffy–Sullivan denial/celebration of the Catholic mass murderers: if
Duffy was right about the *mentalité*, he was himself the best witness as
to the likelihood of massacre by the insurgents.

   Once interrogated, Duffy's poem has more to yield. The 'Graves and revenge' cry is supposedly in answer to the massacre of Islandmagee. But, as even Froude had the wit to notice, Islandmagee (whose numbers of victims he carefully reduced below comparable levels on the other side) took place on 9 January 1642: Catholic massacres of Protestants had been going on for the previous year, with Portadown Bridge, on 1 November, over two months before Islandmagee. Duffy may be very sound in imagining the general logic behind Catholic insurrection (and massacres, where there were massacres): but the cry of 'Graves and revenge' is purloined from the Bann. 'Revenge!' would be much used by Young Ireland and subsequent nationalist poetasters – the cry of the Irish Brigade at Fontenoy in 1745 supposedly recalling English dishonour of the Treaty of Limerick – and in the folklore of 1919 an English priest visiting Dublin and seeing a wall daubed 'SINN FEIN' asks the cab-driver 'wot is this sin fine?' to be answered 'Revinge, beJasus!' It has duly justified its place as the Irish sin fine, the crime we most deeply honour. But the most stirring expression of the cry for revenge comes from Protestant traditions of 1641:[71]

> Elizabeth the wiffe of Captain Rise (Rhys?) Price late of the parish and County of Armagh, ... prisoner ... of ... Manus O'Cane ... liberated on the arrival of Owen roe O'Neill ... And they hearing of divers apparitions and visions that were ordinarily seen neere Port-a-downe bridge since the drowning of the children and the rest of the Protestants there; ... and ... being all together at the water-side, there, near the said bridg, about twylight in the evening, then and there upon a sudden, there appeared unto them a vision of spiritt assuming the shape of a woman waste-high in the water with elevated and closed hands, her haire dishevelled, very white, her eye seeming to twinkle in her head, and her skin as white as snowe, wch. spiritt or vision, seeming to stand upright in the water, divulged, and then repeated the word *Revenge! Revenge! Revenge!*

So the hidden Protestant commemoration was looted for the public Catholic commemoration. But in fact the woman in the river symbolises the closeness of all three traditions: Protestant, Catholic, pagan.

V

> He met a Fisherman who was drying his nets and he asked him what name the river had. The fisherman said it had two names. The people on the right bank called it the Daybreak River and the people on the left bank called it the River of the Morning Star. And the Fisherman told him he was to be careful not to call it the River of the Morning Star when he was on the right bank nor the Daybreak River on the

left, as the people on either side wanted to keep to the name their fathers had for it and were ill-mannered to the stranger who gave it a different name. The Fisherman told Flann he was sorry he had told him two names for the River and that the best thing he could do was to forget one of the names and call it just the River of the Morning Star as he was on the left bank.

Padraic Colum (1881–1972) made a wonderful story for children in *The King of Ireland's Son* (1916), woven from so many threads of folklore, and so sure of itself within its own framework that it resists critical unwinding quite firmly. Where Colum adorns or originates, where what folk tale goes whither, becomes endless yarns. What he intended by this conflict of river nomenclature we can dispute – it plays no part in the story.[72] The one lesson that seems clear is that the Daybreak River is a beautiful name, and so is the River of the Morning Star.

In fact, about the one thing people do not seem to have disputed in our river conflicts are the names of the rivers themselves. Brian Friel (b. 1929) has written a moving play of the cartography of ordnance mapping and its violence to local placename culture and identity, *Translations* (1981): its history is disputable, its artistry is not. Language does not account for the place of topographical divergence: Dublin and Donegal are derived from Gaelic words, but they are not the words for those counties in Gaelic.[73] If anything we have been looking at conflict with topographical agreement: the people might dispute who owned the river-fish, river-beds, river-banks, river-valleys, but their poetic and imaginative hold on the rivers become fluid, and intermingle. The drownings from so many different motives, the memories, the personifications, the totems, the taboos cross the cultures often with little realisation of their transition. The folktale of the Blackwater's Dread Spirit or whatever lured the MacAuliffe girl to her destruction comes to us in the stilted language and cultural reassemblage of Victorian gentility (without spoiling a good story): was O'Flanagan's told-to-the-Protestants version so remote from its origin as to leave different cultures of one time more unified than the same cultural strain at different times? The fifteenth-century version, if any, was probably of a far poorer society, though not necessarily of a less cosmopolitan one. They were more European then, in many ways, than we are.

The traditions, however transmitted, are purloined as we have seen for various purposes. Identity has to be reinforced by commemoration, and commemoration needs to recruit what it can get regardless of its ultimate alienation. The recruitment of tradition itself becomes river-like: now meandering across linguistic, religious, even landowning disputes, now forced into intense mutual barter in the high tide of 1840s romanticism. Commemoration no doubt is really based on the personal satisfaction of the commemorator, but what is the intent for the audience? It must be primarily for the converted, with the slight fear that they have to be kept in good commemorative temperature lest (tell it not) they backslide, or foreslide, or diminish their faith or betray it. But there is always the hope of commemoration making its new converts and (to purloin a thesis from Brian Friel's *Dancing at Lughnasa* (1990)) the hidden problem of what credal tenets are to be traded in the process, and how far and how much and how many and for how long.

The Revd Charles Kingsley (1819–75) makes one of the greatest charms of his *The Water-Babies* (1863) its readiness to anticipate all the questions its child audience may have, and if it has lessons to teach, it laughs at itself in the teaching. In the process the hero, Tom, now a dead chimney-sweep and live water-baby, finds the river:[74]

And what sort of river was it? Was it like an Irish stream, winding through the brown bogs, where the wild ducks squatter up from among white water-lilies, and the curlews flit to and fro, crying 'Tullie-wheep, mind your sheep'; and Dennis tells you strange stories of the Peishtamore, the great bogy-snake which lies in the black peat pools, among the old pine-stems, and puts his head out at night to snap at the cattle as they come down to drink? – But you must not believe all that Dennis tells you, mind; for if you ask him:

'Is there a salmon here, do you think, Dennis?'

'Is it salmon, thin, and ridgmens, shouldthering ache out of water, av' ye'd but the luck to see thim.'

Then you fish the pool all over, and never get a rise.

'But there can't be a salmon here, Dennis! and, if you'll but think, if one had come up last tide, he'd be gone to the higher pools by now.'

'Sure thin, and your honour's the thrue fisherman, and understands it all like a book. Why, ye spake as if ye'd known the wather a thousand years! As I said, how could there be a fish here at all, just now?'

'But you said just now they were shouldering each other out of water?'

And then Dennis will look up at you with his handsome, sly, soft, sleepy, good-natured, untrustable, Irish gray eye, and answer with the prettiest smile:

'Shure, and didn't I think your honour would like a pleasant answer?'

So you must not trust Dennis, because he is in the habit of giving pleasant answers: but, instead of being angry with him, you must just burst out laughing; and then he will burst out laughing too, and slave for you, and trot about after you, and show you good sport if he can – for he is an affectionate fellow, and as fond of sport as you are – and if he can't, tell you fibs instead, a hundred an hour; and wonder all the while why poor ould Ireland does not prosper like England and Scotland, and some other places, where folk have taken up a ridiculous fancy that honesty is the best policy.

As a good Christian Socialist, Kingsley can hardly be expected to understand capitalism. But he was writing a fairy story, and, like Tom, perhaps he never saw the Irishwoman behind him, although she ultimately went before him:

> For just before he came to the river side, she had stept down into the cool clear water; and her shawl and her petticoat floated off her, and the green water-lilies floated round her head, and the fairies of the stream came up from the bottom and bore her away and down upon their arms; for she was the Queen of them all; and perhaps of more besides.

And while we may never hear Dennis's version of the story (authentic though Kingsley's dialect and landscape was, for a Victorian cleric), and he would not give it to us since our honours would like a pleasant answer, and even when (and it is 'when') Dennis (more correctly 'Denis') stops giving pleasant answers the new ones may not be accurate either, we may at least wonder how far the Irish Queen of the Fairies did work her will on Kingsley, who commemorated her as he did, because without her the world was one of unfortunate boys being sent up hot chimneys by drunken sweeps, and so, in the end, he ended like Dennis, closing *The Water-Babies* with a very good metagraph for the historian:[75]

> But remember always, as I told you at first, that this is all a fairy tale, and only fun and pretence: and, therefore, you are not to believe a word of it, even if it is true.

II

6

In the shadow of Calton Hill

RAY BURNETT

The histories of Ireland and Scotland contain many shared moments, events and individuals of common significance. Yet the received memories and commemorations of these linkages are as different as the ties are frequent, each nation ascribing a different reading, a different set of referral points to their presentation of the past, locating the same people and events on a different political–cultural axis, each indicative of a diverging and differing agenda. This chapter is concerned with one specific common moment, the 1790s, one particular shared individual, James Connolly (1868–1916), and with the linking moment of 1848. The focus is not on the events or individuals themselves but on the *process* of commemoration. It seeks to outline how this commemorative process occurred within a specifically Scottish prism on the common contested political terrain of 'Great Britain & Ireland' and within a particular location of space and place – the urban landscape of Edinburgh, in the shadow of Calton Hill.[1]

It is a shadow in three senses of the term. Firstly, as a physical feature relating to a sense of place. The events of the 1790s and 1848 occurred on or around Calton Hill and Connolly's Edinburgh life and activities were also within its proximity, the long cast of its shadow. Secondly, in the sense of a lingering cloud denying the light of a new dawn, a shadow that has yet to dispel or be dispelled by action. For the communal events and individual contributions represented by the encoded story of the hill and its environs contain a call to political action, an exemplar of political praxis, which remains undiminished over the years and which casts a metaphorical shadow over the moment of Edinburgh and Scotland's political present and future. Thirdly, a shadow that provides an orientation, a direction of travel, either the constitutional, parliamentary route of Scotland's Whig–Liberal–Labour–New Labour–Conservative caravan to Westminster, or Edinburgh's alternative radical road of constitutional deconstruction and extra-parliamentary mobilisation. Throughout the latter decades of the twentieth century, Calton Hill itself, as the rational location, and one preferred by popular will, of a re-convened Scottish

Parliament, cast the same unchanging shadow over the 1990s as it did over the 1790s, a brooding backdrop to Holyrood, highlighting the shifting tectonic plates and emergent fault lines fracturing the still contested terrain of 'Great Britain & (Northern) Ireland'.

I

> We rejoice that you do not consider yourselves as merged and melted
> down into another Country, but that in this great national Question
> you are still Scotland – the Land where Buchanan wrote, and Fletcher
> spoke, and Wallace fought.
>   *Address from the Society of United Irishmen, 1792.*[2]

The events of the 1790s are a critical juncture in the history of Scotland's political and national development. This was the decade that shaped all subsequent political discourse in Scotland. It is from this pivotal moment that the metanarrative of the 'forward march of labour' and the first stirrings of 'political democracy' are traced.[3] From this decisive moment, Westminster is fixed upon as the referral point for political change and party organisation and the primacy of parliamentary constitutional reform, mediated through Anglo-Brit parties, is asserted over popular and insurrectionary risings. Historians differ in their interpretation of Scotland's revolutionary decade, the extent to which there was a revolutionary dimension to events, the degree to which they were distinctively Scottish. From what may be termed the minimalist-Unionist perspective, the 'Pike Plot' of Watts and Downie is an isolated desperate aside, the insurrectionary wider stirrings of Angus Cameron and his followers an adventurist irrelevance. Callender, Mealmaker and the United Scotsmen are a short-lived and peripheral flurry and the memorials of Watson, Muir and the Paris exiles, like the reports of Jacobin agents, are but inflated rhetoric with no purchase on a quiescent reality. In this hitherto dominant reading Muir, Palmer, Skirving, Gerrald and Margarot were arrested, tried and transported for advocating nothing more than political and parliamentary reform. Their perspective was firmly 'British'; any expression of Scottish sentiment was precisely that – mere emotion and no more. Ireland, if discussed at all, was an external measure of dissimilarity rather than an integral component of the dominant problematic of English expansionism, colonialism and the 'three kingdom' state.[4]

Implicit to this chapter is an alternative, contrapuntal reading of the 1790s that takes cognisance of the central overdetermining structural feature of the moment, which was that neither the political terrain of 'Great Britain' nor of 'Great Britain and Ireland' was settled. It was in fact a deeply contested 'three kingdoms' formation in which the state's integument was brittle and the state's repression in inverse proportion to its fragility. The 1790s were a seminal, not a given, critical juncture in imposing the lineage of the incorporating state. Although in later dominant labourist portrayals of events the decade assumes significance as a key moment in the inventing of a merged and melted down Anglo-Brit labourist tradition, close scrutiny of Scottish political and popular culture in these pivotal years makes it clear that the notion of being a free 'Briton' was reflective of an aspirational political ideal rather than any manifestation of an ascribed, unified, new 'national' consciousness. The radical movement in all three kingdoms connected into this notion to a greater or lesser degree, but it was in a sense of being political 'Britons', not being British. There was a shared ideal, resonant with common values, giving cohesion and unifying purpose to three discrete movements, each organically and deeply rooted in their own distinct national–popular cultures, enabling the enhanced strength of a unified movement to mask the actuality of a plurality of movements. In Scotland, beyond the Friends of the People was the creative, spontaneous and volatile popular voice of radical protest, articulated as much in the cultural and linguistic subalternity of popular song, urban disorder, rural outrage, military disaffection and the carnival of riot as in the political treatise on national subordination. The outcome of '98 and the contingencies of history have ensured that the potential capability of these overlaid components of a vitiated national culture to fuse their disparate subaltern strands into an oppositional national-popular bloc has seldom been acknowledged, far less assessed. Such an acknowledgement requires recognition of Edinburgh as the street theatre in which the national subaltern performed. It is a glimpse of this alternative performance which the 'official' commemorative process in the city has persistently denied.[5]

II

The truth is, that if they had only been properly tried, and properly punished, the idea of raising a monument to their memory would never have occurred. *It is not to them that the Memorial is erected.*
Lord Cockburn[6]

The initiative for a memorial to Thomas Muir and his associates came from the leading parliamentary radical, Joseph Hume MP. The idea emerged in the context of the Reform Bill campaign of 1831–32, not in Edinburgh but in London where it was launched at a meeting of reformers from the three kingdoms at the city's Crown and Anchor Tavern.[7] Hume was a constitutional Whig reformer in the Foxite tradition. The Member of Parliament for Montrose, he personified the core binary of the self-colonised with a sublimated national identity and a career embracing Scotland, England, Empire and the East India Company.[8] When the noted English radical Major Cartwright died in 1824, a committee had been formed to raise a monument to his memory, with Hume a prominent member. In 1831 a public dinner was held in London to mark the erection of the Cartwright monument and Hume was invited to preside. He took it on himself to ask Peter MacKenzie, the noted West of Scotland reformer, to attend. MacKenzie had just published his *Life of Thomas Muir* with its account of the events of the 1790s in Scotland.[9] An outburst of commemorative statuary in London, Dublin and Edinburgh had expressed the relief and gratitude of the ruling elite at the defeat of the state's enemies at home and abroad over three pivotal decades of revolutionary threat, insurrection, popular insurgency and protest. Now Hume wrote to MacKenzie expressing his irritation at the proliferation of monuments to 'conquerors and statesmen', men 'of questionable utility and humanity and good government.' He wanted to redress the balance by erecting a monument to the true 'patriots' who had acted more 'meritoriously' and in the best interests of the people:

> I think the time has now arrived when we should raise, as of old, statues in honour of honest, virtuous, and unfortunate Martyrs in the Cause of Liberty.[10]

Triggered, it seems, by MacKenzie's own mediated reformist text, Hume recognised the value of promoting Muir as a figure inscribed with the values, aspirations and determined commitment of the burgeoning reformist cause. He therefore wrote to MacKenzie in Scotland urging him to

> take measures immediately for erecting a monument which will hand down to posterity his name in connection with the other Scottish sufferers in the cause of freedom.[11]

Hume would contribute his own financial 'mite', he was confident his fellow countrymen would come forward to support the friends of reform in Scotland and as a result they would have a memorial which would both, 'stand as a beacon to future Governments, to avoid acts of tyranny and oppression' and serve as encouragement to all 'honest and independent men' in their perseverance in the advocacy of 'those great principles on which alone Governments can be permanently secure, and the people free, independent, virtuous, and happy'. MacKenzie readily accepted Hume's invitation to the London dinner where, at the latter's request, he proposed the toast of the 'Scottish Martyrs' to an assembly which included some of 'the best of English and Irish reformers'.[12] Hume acted on the opportunity of the occasion by heading up a monument subscription sheet which soon accumulated £1,100 from an impressive list of aristocratic and parliamentary reformers.[13] The campaign for a commemorative memorial to the 'martyrs' of the 1790s was launched. It was, however, from its inception an exercise in commemorative reductionism. Hume subsequently outlined 'the Object we have in View' to his Edinburgh contact, Tait, as being:

> The perpetuating of the recollection of the atrocious acts of the Scottish Bench against honest Reformers in the worst time of Tory misrule.[14]

This would be a commemoration of Muir without Paine or Paris, 1793 without '98, parliamentary reform without popular insurgency. The 'martyrs' were having their cause redefined, retrospectively.

The initial proposal initiated by Hume had made clear the political limits as to who and what was to be commemorated. Further difficulties and constraints subsequently emerged over how and where the proposal should be taken forward and its implementation became a protracted affair. The original idea, as envisaged in London, was that there should be two monuments, one in London and another in Edinburgh. Those who favoured a London dimension argued that although the trials and sentences of transportation had taken place in Edinburgh, the focus of 'national' political reform was Westminster. It was also pointed out that, with only two of the condemned men being Scots, they were most appropriately commemorated as the 'British Political Martyrs'. When it became likely that only one monument would be proceeded with, the Scots proposed that, in relation to their own national focus, all the money collected should be sent to them for the erection of one monument in Edinburgh. The London Committee, however, were insistent that the original resolution 'that Monuments must be erected in both Capitals' should be adhered to and for good measure they rejected the plans sent by the Edinburgh committee with the snubbing observation that the drawing was 'unnecessarily ornamented and not pure and correct in character'[15] This was not merely a matter of acknowledging the physical location of events. The men had been tried and sentenced under Scots law by the Scots judiciary, the keystone of Scottish civil society and the embodiment of a distinct post-Union surviving national identity, a distinctiveness underlined by the enduring memory of Lord Braxfield's vengeful strictures being handed down in the auld Scots tongue.[16] Edinburgh was the specific location where this national political culture could be mediated through a specific matrix of place and space, the dense, intimate urban landscape of the old town and the new.

In March 1837 a public meeting of leading reformers was held in the
Waterloo Rooms, in the shadow of Calton Hill, to progress plans to
commemorate the 'Political Martyrs of Scotland'. A succession of advocates, lawyers, baillies and councillors and surviving family associates
came forward to formally propose a series of resolutions outlining their
reasons and purpose in proposing the erection of a monument to the
'martyrs' in the capital. They felt it was a duty 'especially incumbent
upon the reformers in Scotland' to take the lead in expressing their gratitude. While the recognition of the justice of their cause was now univer-
sally recognised, they felt it necessary to

> express the strongest disapprobation of the shameless injustice by
> which the early reformers were sacrificed, and of the servility which,
> for a season, degraded the tribunals of Scotland into the ready tools
> of an unscrupulous faction ...[17]

Therefore they were now commencing a public subscription 'in connection
with the subscription begun in London and other places' and they made it
clear that while they had no wish to dictate to 'other communities':

> It is our opinion that no locality is so well adapted for the site of a
> public monument to the First Martyrs of Political Liberty in Scotland,
> as the scene of their persecution, and of the short-lived triumph of
> their oppressors.[18]

Such a national monument, claimed the motion of Thomas Muir Moffat
and William Muir, would serve as 'an enduring record of their deeds, and
an encouragement to the men of future times to emulate their heroic
example'.[19] Edinburgh Town Council had already agreed in principle to
provide a site for the monument on Calton Hill but five years later the
monument committee and their key representatives on the Town Council
were still struggling to bring the plan to fruition against a significant
reluctance on the part of the more conservative and fearful Whigs and a
tenacious rearguard action by a network of power and influence within
the dominant order in the city who sought to retain their effective control
over its cultural landscape, not least the iconography of the urban landscape and the skyline which encased the commanding heights of Calton
Hill. Their objections were summarised by Lord Cockburn. There were
the objections on basic principles, namely that the men and their objec-
tives were not worthy of commemoration. 'If the reform was bad, the
martyrdom was foolish.' They had done more harm than good.

> The broaching of the doctrines of universal suffrage and annual
> parliaments – absurd at any period, but worse than absurd in 1794 –
> very greatly retarded the progress of all liberal opinion in Scotland.[20]

They were, in effect, the enemies of liberty. Any rational man could see that, which was why so many 'good Whigs' were withholding their support from the proposed monument. This was what led Cockburn to state that it was '*not to them that the Memorial is erected*'. It was not the absurd ideas and foolish actions of the men transported that were being commemorated so much as the ineptitude of the Scottish judiciary of the time.

The core objections, however, were to the monument's proposed location. The Calton Hill and its environs were a physical testimony to the fact that political hegemony occupies space and place. By the 1830s the hill and the Old Calton Burial Ground had become a repository of Edinburgh's neo-classical taste in commemorating its chosen cultural icons, Dugald Stewart, Robert Burns, William Playfair, David Hume the historian, David Hume the philosopher.[21] In its Waterloo Place approach, with the incomplete columns of the National Monument and the functioning Nelson column, Calton Hill also reflected the dominant classes' endorsement of the military achievements of Empire in their capacity as North Britons.[22] With their own monument proposal, the reformers were intruding into a Tory pantheon.

It also offended dominant tastes and sensibilities in what Cockburn termed its 'abominable' design. The privileged location of the hill and the old burial ground merited a construction of a grander design than could ever be achieved by the modest amount of money available.

> This noble eminence ought to be left sacred to such structures as all may sympathise with. The Astronomical Institution, and the monuments of Stewart, Playfair, and Burns, are edifices that can create no pain, or division of opinion.[23]

Cockburn's reflections capture perfectly the sensibilities of Edinburgh's elite as to the political–cultural values inscribed on the Calton Hill skyline and surrounds. The broad sweep of urban elegance which incorporated in its passing the Old Calton Burial Ground was a 'splendid terrace' which all could enjoy through the 'associations only elevated by beautiful works of art'. They reminded them of science and 'great men'. They brought forth 'unanimous reverence'. Few 'merely political characters' could do the same. Even then they should not be obtruded 'on those public walks, which it is useful that all should be in the habit of resorting to, and with worthy thoughts'. There should be nothing discordant in such a situation.[24]

On Wednesday 21 August 1844 the foundation stone of the monument was finally laid. The tone of the occasion was set by the formal notices in that morning's *Scotsman* inviting 'Subscribers to the Monument, and all friends of Parliamentary Reform, and enemies of Persecution' to attend the laying of the foundation stone in the Old Calton burial ground by Joseph Hume MP. Later, the Committee and Subscribers, honoured with the presence of Hume and of Sir James Gibson-Craig in the Chair, would dine in the Royal Hotel, Princes Street, where 'those who are disposed' could join the elect gathering at 10/6d a ticket. As the day progressed, the *Scotsman*, Hume and Gibson-Craig between them made clear the parameters of commemoration: it was to be remembrance by social and political confinement; the Friends of the People without the people; the rhetoric of reform masking the reality of containment.[25]

In its morning editorial the *Scotsman* had given a new 'spin' on the story of the 1790s, narrowing the moment to an issue of the dangers of 'judicial tyranny' as evinced by a Pitt administration which had sought 'high game' in England by using the 'convenient instruments' of a packed jury, a vengeful judiciary and the catch-all charge of 'sedition' provided in Scotland. The unfortunate 'martyrs' were now rescued from their association with the 'men of no property', disturbing ideas and dangerous activities to be re-packaged by Edinburgh's Whig philosophical reformers in their own image and likeness as models of respectability and constitutional propriety. Muir had been a member of the bar, 'gentle, kind, accomplished, pious'; Skirving had been the 'respected pupil, of Dr John Brown of Paddington; Gerrald had been 'an Englishman of fortune and family', a protégé of that illustrious scholar Samuel Parr, 'a pupil not less distinguished than loved'. In short, the *Scotsman* assured its genteel readers:

> The men who suffered in this crusade were not turbulent, violent, or in any sense of the word, bad citizens. They were not of the class which times of excitement are too ready cast up – men of desperate fortunes and characters, with nothing to lose and something to gain by convulsions. ...[26]

The *Scotsman* concluded its editorial homily on 'The Political Martyrs' with a fierce denunciation of those who had had the temerity to suggest that Muir and his associates represented anything other than the most moderate and modest of political aspirations.

> Perhaps of all the vile things done in that chapter of atrocities, the meanest, if not the worst, was the attempt, systematically made, to confound the opinions and the acts of these men with the disturbance of the public peace, and a partiality for the enemies of their country.[27]

At the laying of the foundation stone ceremony in the Old Calton Hill cemetery, Joseph Hume's address reiterated a similar theme, castigating Pitt as the instigator of repression and the Scottish judiciary for being his willing instrument and the disgrace of Scotland. He also refuted those who denigrated the 'martyrs' as men who sought to promote disturbance and dissension. They were men of the highest character whose station in life 'might have been injured but could not have been improved by confusion'. Muir's political career is presented as ending with his trial and transportation as a martyr to parliamentary reform. His adventures subsequent to Botany Bay are outlined, but it ends with his welcome to France as a victim of past injustice, not as an active political figure deeply involved with his fellow Scottish and Irish exiles in the revolutionary politics of Paris and the competing schemes for landings and insurrections. All trace of context, linkage to deeper political thought, is erased. A brief mention of Paine served only to dismiss his ideas as an irrelevancy as Hume firmly relocated the men being commemorated in a new narrative as 'the pioneers of the cause in which we are all engaged'.[28]

When the select gathering of some 200 Edinburgh worthies reconvened for dinner, their chairman Sir James Gibson-Craig admitted he had been initially reluctant to take part in the proceedings but had been persuaded to do so to make clear the grounds on which many had agreed to subscribe to the erection of a monument:

> For great pains have been taken to hold us up as the friends of annual parliaments and universal suffrage and that the monument is to be consecrated to these principles. Now, I think it due to the memory of Lord Holland and to the Duke of Norfolk, the Duke of Bedford, and many other subscribers to say, that we never entertained them – we have always disclaimed them having been convinced that the constitution could not survive many months after their adoption.[29]

What he did not admit was that Lord Dunfermline, the nephew of Lord Abercromby, one of the trial judges, had also prevailed on him to chair the dinner to make sure that the reputation of the capital's judiciary was not savaged.[30] His lordship need not have worried. To an approving audience, Gibson-Craig gave a gloss on the events in the capital in the 1790s which fully exonerated all the law lords concerned. It was hard to imagine what the mood in the city had been like unless you had been involved. The great hopes and deep fears evoked by the French Revolution had divided society. On looking back they could now see that things had been done when judgement was clouded and people thought they were acting for their lives. The trials and sentences, especially that of Muir, had undeniably been unfair but the one offence Muir had committed was to conduct his own defence. Gibson-Craig revealed that Lord Erskine had been willing to act on Muir's behalf but Muir had rejected the offer. A juror he knew had told him that Muir had condemned himself through his speech in defence; Erskine would have secured his acquittal. All the sentences had been unjust, the juries had been packed, but that was the way it was in those days. However, even the jury had been astonished at the severity of Muir's sentence. They were about to bring their concerns before the judges but 'some hot-headed zealot' had sent a letter to the jury chancellor threatening to assassinate him and it thereby became 'impossible for the jury to proceed further'. However, the severity of the sentences had shocked many into recognising the need for a general reform of the Scottish Judiciary and things were much better now. The monument was therefore being erected to express their gratitude and respect for the memories of the martyrs but also to warn judges and juries that if they wanted the rule of law to be respected, then they must

> never allow themselves to be swayed by any fanciful theories of expediency or of a supposed necessity of acting on a 'wholesome vigour beyond the law' but that in the exercise of the sacred duties committed to them, they will be guided by the law, and by nothing but the law.[31]

The chairman knew his audience and the town well. By his allusions to close friends and relatives who had counselled and confided, the insider knowledge of sentiment and opinion on the Scottish bench, the passed-on memories of the people and events they were now reflecting on, Gibson-Craig was only articulating the felt experience of many in a city where the legal profession reigned supreme. The political outcome of the campaign for parliamentary reform may be ultimately determined at Westminster, but it was also an issue that had to be contested on the terrain of Scottish civil society, a landscape with its own distinctive topography, the salients of which the rising Whig ascendancy had to occupy and fortify with their own cultural armoury. In his earlier address, Joseph Hume had also drawn on this deep sense of place, so critical to the sensibility of the gathering when he had referred to his own recollections of the 1790s and his own young student days in Edinburgh. He knew that this was a city in which memory lingered like mist on the hill. But he also knew that Edinburgh's urban landscape of tributary commemoration had to be contested:

> I do not think we have been hasty in raising a monument to the memory of those who suffered at that time. We see monuments to their persecutors – men who had no right, on the part of the people, to receive any mark of respect; and yet in every street we see monuments erected to them. But up to this hour we have never erected a monument to the memory of those persons.[32]

They were hardly in every street, but the monuments to 'their persecutors' were certainly prominent, most notably the imperial 150-foot pillar in St Andrew Square, crowned with the uncrowned 'King Henry of Scotland', Henry Dundas, 1st Viscount Melville raised by the city's Tories in 1822, and the George Street statue of William Pitt which the Edinburgh Pitt

Clubs had erected in 1833.[33] The established order had been shaping the profile of the town's northward expansion, providing an exemplary urban gaze, encoded with the icons of order and stability, for its rising middle-class residents. This was why the issue had provoked such a tenacious rearguard action. As well as defining themselves in opposition to the established order and authority, the patrician Whig reformers were also defining themselves in relation to their more dangerous political flank, the universal suffragists, the radicals, the new disturbing forces gathered around the People's Charter. For the Chartists themselves were also intent on commemorating that day, and the tone of their ceremony was markedly more direct, rooted in social rather than philosophical reform, with a burning sense of moral indignation and anger.

III

> They might erect a monument to their memory – monuments were the order of the day – but he was sure that if these men were now present, and could give them an advice, that advice would be to take up the work for which they suffered – and thus raise the noblest monument to their memory, and pay the highest tribute of admiration to the principles for which they struggled.
> *Baillie Stott, Calton Hill, 21 August 1844.*[34]

When some four hundred members of the Complete Suffrage Association assembled, 'respectably attired in black clothes', leaving Middle Meadow Walk to walk in procession past the scene of the trials of 1793–94 in Parliament Square, down the High Street and across to the ceremony at the Old Calton Burial Ground it was a most docile demonstration.[35] Yet, the simple act of walking through the heart of the town was significant. It gave the commemoration different co-ordinates of time and place, identity and ownership. This was a memorial act outwith the parameters of MPs and a Westminster orientation. It was out on the streets of Scotland's capital. By occupying a different public sphere it relocated the past not only in the present, but in the future – the aspiration of 'complete suffrage' still to be attained. It re-positioned politics not in the confined, limited party dialogue of London parliamentary constitutionalism but in the swirling discourse of Edinburgh subalternity. For behind John Dunlop of Brockloch and the worthies of the CSA were the unrepresented and unvoiced masses. In the passion of Patrick Brewster and his associates echoed the felt experience of 'universal man'. The moment was not pivotal, the state was more secure, yet in the 1840s the language, the rhythms, the cadences of the 1790s can be heard re-emergent. In its own prescient way, the rhetoric of 1844 presaged '48 as 1794 portended '98 and the 'wretches of Ireland' once again spoke directly to 'the rabble of Scotland' in a demotic dialect of dissent with a French accent.[36]

In his opening remarks to the 3,000 and more gathered on the Calton Hill to remember the martyrs at the 'unofficial' meeting above the burial ground ceremony, Stott, the chairman put a different gloss on the act of commemoration when he simultaneously placed it in the passive context of a 'debt of gratitude under which Scotland lay to them' and the active framework of a call to 'take up the work for which they suffered' thereby raising 'the noblest monument to their memory'. To an audience largely composed of Chartists and Repealers it was a call unlikely to fall on deaf ears. The Revd Patrick Brewster, the main speaker, took his cue from the chairman. Describing the event as 'a glorious day for Scotland', he conveniently ignored the actual nationality of the martyrs and assured the gathering that,

> [t]hough their names were not emblazoned in the proud roll of Scotland's chivalry, yet they gave their lives for their country, and their spirits would ever continue to exercise an influence over her destinies, while the names of their persecutors would continue to be held in fame and infamy.[37]

They were to be honoured because they had acted on their principles and underlined the lesson that 'slavery was the curse of God upon cowardice'. Brewster, as a fierce champion of the poor of Paisley, brought a social dimension to the notion of 'freedom' as well as a firm notion of the need for struggle and a clear idea as to the enemy. The history of the country abundantly proved that the nobility always looked to their personal interests in preference to those of the nation. In every struggle for freedom they were to be found on the side of the oppressor against the oppressed, making laws not to feed the hungry but to 'pamper idleness and plunder industry'. The patriots whose memory they had met to cherish had sought no personal aggrandisement, instead they had given their lives 'for the world's freedom, for the emancipation of universal man'. He agreed with the chairman that:

> work has yet to be completed, and no monument to the merits of the martyrs of 1794 would deserve the name which did not include the realisation of these just and equitable principles of popular govern-ment for which Muir and his associates had endured the obloquy and scorn of a prejudiced age.[38]

John Dunlop of Brockloch brought the gathering on Calton Hill to a close and re-opened proceedings in the evening at a packed soirée in the Waterloo Rooms. The speeches were of a different tenor and urgency to those at the formal dinner. The sense of 'unfinished business' evoked on

Calton Hill was carried over and apart from the generalities of Joseph Hume and Dr Marshall of Leith there was a blunt directness in the contributions. Dunlop began his remarks by referring to Edinburgh itself, 'this city of monuments' on none of which could be found engraved the inscription of liberty. He singled out for particular comment, by implication if not by name, Dundas, high on his commemorative column in St Andrew Square, a dark force reared aloft, frowning down on the busy millions beneath 'who dared to think of themselves as capable of self-government'. Dunlop made clear that what they were commemorating with their own monument was more than simply a matter of judicial oppression. He cited Muir and Palmer on the moral nature of 'the cause', Skirving's dictum that 'the price of liberty is the establishment of the social band', and Gerrald's calls for annual parliaments and universal suffrage, to emphasise his point that, 'the opinions and struggles of these pioneers of reform were identical with their own'. The point was reiterated by the son of William Skirving who made a short speech stating that they remained far from the martyrs' goal of 'full and fair' representation because of the lack of 'fixed principle' to secure their goal. The contemporary relevance of events was forcefully made by Glendonwyn Scott, responding to the toast of 'Honour to Mr O'Connell and the Political Martyrs of Ireland'. Scott made a direct comparison to current events in Ireland, pointing out the 'singular coincidence' that they were meeting to honour the martyrs of Scotland who had been 'branded with the name of felon, upwards of fifty years ago',

> on the very day they had laid the foundation stone of a monument to the memory of the dead – the Martyred Patriots of Scotland – they found it an imperative duty also to express their sympathy for and to honour, the living martyrs of a like tyranny and injustice in Ireland! The trials of Daniel O'Connell and the repeal martyrs of Ireland.[39]

There was some open dissent when Patrick Brewster finally spoke, drawing the evening to a close with a vote of thanks to Hume. He invited controversy by taking issue with Hume's interpretation of suffrage, but it was his barbed reference to the Princes Street monument to Sir Walter Scott, currently under construction, which drew a hostile response. Brewster said he was pleased to see a monument to the martyrs finally being erected, but

> there was one monument being raised in this city to which he looked with very different feelings. The rich tracery and very different proportions of that structure showed that it was not erected by the poor, but by the opulent. This was a monument to a man who had never shown himself favourable to the liberties of the people, and whose fine genius only rendered his writings the more dangerous. His was the song of the syren lulling to repose.[40]

The mingled response of hisses and applause suggests that even then radical Scotland had difficulty separating out Scott the writer from Scott the reactionary Tory. Unperturbed, Brewster then alluded with approval to the Calton Hill's monument to Burns, using it for a further swipe at the Tories for having the temerity to hold a recent demonstration of honour in memory of the poet, and to the display which they had made of his sons who had been paraded for the purpose of showing how finely they had succeeded in taming the lion's whelps.

> It was time enough for that party to produce their admiration of Robert Burns when they should have adopted his sentiments, and when they should have begun to exert themselves to hasten the day
>   'When man to man the world o'er
>   Shall brithers be an' a' that.'[41]

An oblique recommendation for a 'metaphorical' adoption of the sentiments contained in 'Scots wha hae wi' Wallace bled' brought his contribution to a close. A brief exchange between Hume and Brewster followed. It ended amicably enough but the evening, as indeed the day as a whole, had demonstrated all too clearly the tensions involved in the *process* of commemoration. The underlying politics, the discord between passive tribute and active memory, the divergent reading of past figures and events, above all the spoken silences. Alluded to only by their absence, the ghosts at the table were the wider ranks of martyrs and exiles of the 1790s and subsequent insurrectionary moments – the 'other' Muir, Watts, Downie, Mealmaker, Cameron, Watson, Callender, the anonymous ranks of United Scotsmen, the men and women of Tranent, Bonnyrigg and Strathaven, Baird, Hardie and Wilson. There had been a fleeting echo of them when Dunlop said:

> He would invoke the spirit of a better age and remember, with the patriots of '93, that this was the land where Buchanan wrote, where Fletcher spoke, and Wallace fought, and that here also Adam Smith reasoned and Muir and Skirving suffered.[42]

This was a striking evocation of the language and sentiment of the 1790s, the very tropes of Drennan's United Irishmen's Address which had led to Muir's arrest and transportation.[43]

Reflecting on the day's events with satisfaction, the *Scotsman* revealed how the original plan had been to place the monument high on the top of Calton Hill. The committee had obtained consent for this location but some neighbouring residents had threatened interdict in 'a spirit of paltry spite'. The committee had therefore abandoned the original plan and settled for the Old Calton Burial Ground. Yet although the foundation stone had just been laid, the *Scotsman* had been informed by reliable Edinburgh source that efforts were to continue to prevent its completion:

> It is said that sundry people of high Tory sentiments are in dread that the bones of their relatives will not rest in peace in the vicinity of such an object.[44]

With unconcealed contempt it asked whether there would be any less 'dispeace' if the men commemorated had actually been buried on Calton Hill, or whether interdict would have been sought against 'the body of any individual being there buried on account of the political opinions expressed by him, or, being so buried, against the place of sepulture being marked by a tombstone or monument? And in a barbed taunt hinting at family complicity in the transportation sentences by the objecting Calton Hill residents it concluded:

> Will the stone obelisk desecrate the spot because the dust it commem-orates is not below it, but is scattered over the various quarters of the world? Are there any Goldsmith hall jurymen buried in that grave-yard, that survivors are so anxious for the undisturbed repose of the dead?[45]

There seems little doubt that the Edinburgh legal establishment were indeed concerned that the monument would involve a 'name and shame' inscription regarding the judges who had presided over the initial trials of 1793–4. As Lord Cockburn had noted in November 1844:

> The names of the judges will, no doubt, be perpetuated on the column. So visible a condemnation of judges is not to be found else-where in Europe.[46]

However, as Cockburn's additional comment – 'Would that their conduct had made it contemptible!' – made clear, their conduct in 1793–4 had been so shamelessly vindictive and partisan that even the most conserva-tive opponents of reform felt unease at the conduct of the Scottish bench which had earned it such sustained notoriety and contempt. This did not deter them from a final rearguard action. Early in 1845 bills of suspen-sion and interdict were raised in the Court of Session. The legal argument was that it was an inappropriate use of a burial ground to erect monu-ments, particularly political monuments, which gave offence and which were in honour of men convicted of crimes and not buried there. Although, as Cockburn noted, the reports of the court proceedings made no mention of the political dimension, all of Edinburgh knew that it was a political issue, 'a party struggle on both sides' as he acknowledged.[47] Lord Jeffrey was on the bench that considered the interdicts. He did not agree with the insinuation that the promoters of the commemorative monument sought to encourage contempt for lawful authority. Even if there were those who did, they were bound to be disappointed. In an insightful commentary on the success of the moderate, parliamentary reformers to emasculate, strip down and reconstitute the aspirations of the 1790s, Jeffrey observed that

> [t]he evil of any lesson in such a form depends wholly on the spirit in which it is read, and not on the purpose with which it may have been promulgated, and I have no fear of it now being read, by the people of this country, in any but a safe and salutary sense.[48]

The crisis was over, the threat had receded, the state was secure and Scotland and Edinburgh's political elite could afford to be sanguine, confident in the reinforcement of established values which the very design of the monument implicitly evoked:

> The thoughts, which such a monument suggest, even to those most opposed to the views of its founders, are naturally of a solemn and a sobering character.[49]

If grievance over the memory of the 1790s were to continue in the city, it would only be because of 'those who continue, on either side, to cherish sentiments so uncharitable'. And where better to 'soften down' any residual feelings of anger than in 'that scene where the wicked cease from troubling and the weary are at rest, and where everything should remind us of our own frail mortality'.[50] Lord Cockburn thought Jeffrey's opinion, which he had read to the Court, was 'singularly beautiful'. In the event the threatened appeal did not materialise. On Friday 26 September 1845 the 140-foot monument was capped with its final copingstone and the needle was completed. In October Hume was back in the city to mark the event.[51] Cockburn had doubts over the claim that Hamilton's design was a copy of Cleopatra's needle:

> However, nothing that sticks up without smoking seems to me ever to look ill in Edinburgh. This pillar adds to the general picturesqueness of the mass of which it is a part.[52]

Two years later, in August 1846, there was still no inscription. Cockburn thought it was 'fortunate for surviving friends that they have the delicacy to pause'. Various inscriptions were discussed. Lord Dunfermline suggested linking their aims and sentences to the subsequent passing of the Reform Bill and of the legislation abolishing transportation for sedition, but in the event the Committee, to Cockburn's surprise, 'exceeded even this moderation' and in 1847 engraved the two inscriptions that are there today:

> To the memory of Thomas Muir, Thomas Fyshe Palmer, William Skirving, Maurice Margarot, and Joseph Gerrald. Erected by the friends of Parliamentary Reform in England and Scotland, 1844
> 'I have devoted myself to the cause of the People; it is a good cause; it shall ultimately prevail; it shall finally triumph.' – Speech of Thomas Muir in the Court of Justiciary on the 7th of January 1794.[53]

In the event it was as reserved, muted and passive as possible. Ireland, the national–popular and the revolutionary were erased from all memory. It was left to Cockburn to give the surprised and relieved verdict of the Edinburgh establishment on this final outcome:

> A sparing inscription. How the judges' names are omitted I cannot understand. For it is in truth, their monument.[54]

IV

> For a nation to be free it required but arms and a knowledge of their use.
> Edinburgh Street Handbill, 1848[55]

At the laying of the foundation stone the *Scotsman* had commented favourably on the fact that 'two totally distinct classes of Reformers' had come together despite the occurrence of 'some incidental bickering', united in commemorating the past. It did, however, warn the more radical reformers of the dangers of false friends. The advocates of universal suffrage were urged to draw from the monument event the realisation that their true friends were the moderate parliamentary reformers. Even if they did not go along with their demands for more extensive reform, they were nonetheless their true allies. They should remain united against those who claimed to befriend them but were in fact their 'bitterest enemies', a thinly-veiled reference to the more radical Chartists and Repealers who had made up a not insignificant section of the 3,000 who had gathered that day on Calton Hill outwith the containment of the formal ceremony. The unspoken worry was that amongst those who had reclaimed the hill were those who were motivated not by a desire for passive commemoration but from an active residual memory. As the leaders of 'responsible' and 'respectable' reform in Edinburgh were all too aware, the commemorative process they had been engaged in always carried the risk that others would seek to reaffirm the memory of the dead through deeds and actions rather than by an impassive inscription on mute stone. Within months of the final completion of the monument the residual memory had become a reality. In 1848, not just the rhetoric and aspiration but the applied spirit of revolution was once more on the political agenda. The radical press of Edinburgh echoed the configurations of 1798: France and the Republic, Ireland and rebellion, Scotland and the need to emulate them by deed and action. The warning signs had been there in 1844 at the Waterloo Rooms meeting when Glendonwyn Scott had raised a direct comparison with Ireland's 'Political Martyrs' and spoke of how they had now gathered on Calton Hill to honour the martyrs of Scotland who had been 'branded with the name of felon, upwards of fifty years ago'. The implication was clear. Political felony was no dishonour, unjust laws, repression and the denial of democratic rights should be actively resisted by whatever means necessary. Dunlop had invoked the patriotic rhetoric of the earlier revolutionary age, now others in the city were once again issuing a call to its 'citizens'.[56]

The tone had been set in Glasgow where John Mitchel and Fergus O'Connor spoke in March. As in '98, the cause of Ireland and the cause of Scotland were presented as inextricably linked. John Daly went well beyond the passive line of the 'moral force' Chartist leaders Dunlop and Brewster. Prayers and petitions, Daly told the assembled crowd, were the weapons of slaves and cowards. Arms were the weapons of the brave and the free and they could best help Ireland by keeping an army in Scotland.[57] The same divide between 'passive obedience' and 'physical force' with its attendant personality clashes had deeply divided the Chartist movement in Edinburgh no less than elsewhere in Scotland, and in 1848 the 'physical force' wing was dominant. The tensions implicitly hinted at in 1844 now surfaced in a more explicit form and on the same location, the now familiar radical rallying ground of Calton Hill.

On 10 April over 10,000 people passed by the 'Political Martyrs' monument to gather on the hill above, fearful of an imminent crackdown under Grey's sedition bill. There was much talk of arbitrary arrest, telegram wires being cut, the threat of state repression. John Grant told the crowd that 'the time was now come when it was the duty of every man, for his own undivided safety, to arm himself'. If they did not depend on themselves, they ran the risk of being butchered. Henry Rankine agreed. It was no longer the time for speeches but for action. A revolution might not benefit any class, but they had to show their hard taskmasters that they would be slaves no longer, that they were prepared to die by the sword rather than by hunger. Robert Hamilton urged the need for everyone to purchase a musket or a pike. The leading moderate, Robert Cranston, sought to deflect the insurrectionary fervour by closing the meeting with a call for Edinburgh Town Council to support the universal suffrage resolutions and to receive deputations, but the insurrectionary wing was in the ascendancy and mobilising.[58] The following evening the Waterloo Rooms, where Joseph Hume and Patrick Brewster had clashed and Glendonwyn Scott had raised the honouring of 'felons', were once again crowded as the Chartists and Repealers of Edinburgh met together to condemn Grey's sedition bill and the prosecution of the Irish leaders, Smith O'Brien, Mitchel and Meagher. This time the moderate Scott and his Town Council ally Baillie Stott found themselves outflanked. Robert Hamilton announced that he 'intended to talk sedition'. He had advocated moral force for the last fourteen years and was now tired of it. The government did not have enough force to put down the working class:

> Just let everyone of them make the same stand as he did and the government would find that the gaols would not be sufficient to hold them all.[59]

Hamilton concluded on a conciliatory note. He did not wish to 'butcher the aristocracy' – although they well deserved it. Glendonwyn Scott sought to disassociate the more moderate Repealers from such sentiments, and the meeting quietened down to a concluding motion thanking Baillie Stott and supporters of the Town Council motion for universal suffrage. A few days later Ernest Jones was the speaker in the Waterloo Rooms as the insurrectionary fervour continued. On 17 April a crowd estimated at 25–30,000 were once more on Calton Hill. The talk was now of working with England to form a 'National Guard' armed to uphold a 'National Assembly' if it declared itself for a parliament. An Edinburgh contingent of 1,600 had been agreed at a public meeting. By the end of the month 120 recruits were duly enrolled in the Adam Square Hall under the command of Donald MacKay. They were armed with lances and muskets.[60]

In June a further evening demonstration was called to march the route from Bruntsfield Links to Calton Hill by Middle Meadow Walk and 'the Bridges', the route taken by the universal suffragists to the foundation of the monument in 1844. They assembled under the banner of a Highlander armed with a broadsword and the motto 'Let them turn the blue-bonnets wha can'. The tenor was unmistakably insurrectionary. The press reported 'a foreign-looking individual' on the hustings waving a tricolour, and Henry Rankine spoke strongly in terms of emulating the French Republic when he told the gathering that:

> the knowledge of chemistry had now entered the workshop of the artizan, and that he was possessed of a power, as that of Warner's Long Range, wherewith to claim and defend his rights.[61]

Hamilton, who spoke of the need to get guns and bayonets to repel brute force with brute force, followed the combustible upholsterer who was reported as having asserted that:

pikes were easily made, and that the young and spirited men of Scotland should go to Ireland and help the Irish people, and that at one time you would have been satisfied with the charter as the law of the land, but that now you would accept of nothing else than a republic, and that they would soon obtain one.[62]

The demonstrators then crossed the Meadows heading for Calton Hill but there was trouble with the police at Middle Meadow Walk and they were stopped entering George IV Bridge. The following Monday a meeting was held in the Waterloo Rooms to discuss the police actions and a hand-bill was circulated in the city:

> For a nation to be free it required but arms and a knowledge of their use.[63]

Such explicit references to the need to take up arms was an unambiguous echo of Edinburgh's David Downie, Robert Watts and the 'Pike Plot', of George Mealmaker, Angus Cameron and the United Scotsmen, of Baird and Hardie, Robert Wilson and the ill-fated rising of 1820. The presence of Skirving's son on Calton Hill in 1844 had been a reminder that the judiciary and Edinburgh establishment were not alone in nursing personal memories of the events of the 1790s. The old town would have had more than its fair share of old radicals with their memories and a younger generation willing to listen and to commemorate in an active and applied mode.

The clearest indication that there was a subaltern world of insurrectionary Edinburgh drawing on a collective memory, sense of tradition and a legacy of struggle, came on Monday 24 July when an emergency meeting of over a thousand of the city's Chartists and Repealers gathered on Calton Hill to express sympathy with the situation in Ireland. Archibald Walker, editor of the Edinburgh Chartist newspaper, the *North British Weekly Express*, chaired the meeting.[64] A resolution by Samuel Macdonald was passed expressing the meeting's indignation with the conduct of the Government to Ireland as being base, unprincipled and cowardly. Their acts of injustice had provoked rebellion, the motion asserted, and the Irish people were justified in resisting 'even unto the death'. Macdonald hinted that it was time for Scotland and Edinburgh to be up and doing but he, at least, was careful not to be explicit. Peter Duncan was less cautious. Supporting Macdonald's call, Duncan referred to the recent insurrection in France which he termed 'a labourers' war' in which workmen had been betrayed by priestcraft and foreign gold. France, he declared, would never be quiet until the rights of labour were granted, adding:

> It was the same thing in Ireland and the sooner the battle began the better.[65]

Chartists of this country, he urged, needed to give more than sympathy – they must *do* something. As the resolution was carried by loud acclamation, Henry Rankine then spoke openly of the extent of insurrectionary organisation in Edinburgh. It was the first public acknowledgement that more than a monument in the Old Calton Burial Ground and an innocuous inscription had commemorated the memory of the 1790s and the actions of successive political martyrs. He told the gathering that there were a 'great many' clubs in the city, with a hundred men in each club organised into ten companies under a leader, thereby enabling them to muster at an hour's notice. After this remarkable piece of intelligence from Rankine, the chairman closed the meeting, exhorting those present to disperse quietly and orderly, making their way separately back down into the city.[66] That this was no idle boast was confirmed in a letter to the Glasgow Chartists from James Cummings, an elderly shoemaker in the city, which the authorities had intercepted only two days previously. Cummings, it transpired, had long been involved in the secret armed clubs organising in the city. The intercepted letter gave a clear picture of the sense of commemorative continuity that pervaded the working-class districts of the Old Town, an insurrectionary tradition that was the common cause of both Scots and Irish. Rankine had given the names of several of these clubs when he had spoken to the gathering on Calton Hill. Cummings' letter confirmed these details and also gave a breakdown of membership (in brackets). Four commemorated the Irish tradition: the Emmet Club, the O'Connor Club, the Mitchel Club (56) and the Faugh a' Ballagh Club. One, the Washington Club (25) evoked the American Revolution and its republican tradition. The remainder commemorated Scotland's radical and national tradition: the Wallace Club, the Burns Club (25), the Gerrald Club (26), the Muir Club (200), the Baird and Hardie Club (20) and the Edinburgh Guard (500). The average membership as detailed confidentially by Cummings was less than the hundred per club claimed by Rankine. It was nearer two dozen per club although with two hundred men in the Muir Club and five hundred in the Edinburgh Guard, the total number of armed men in the city given by Cummings actually exceeded Rankine's public claim.[67]

Two days after the Calton Hill meeting, the authorities made a series of arrests, including Henry Rankine and James Cummings.[68] When they raided the offices of the *North British Weekly Express* in the Royal Exchange on the High Street, they found more incriminating letters and 'two flags belonging to the body of the United Irishmen'.[69] The men were detained on a variety of charges, including attendance at secret clubs and illegal meetings, and arming to overthrow the government. The following Monday, 31 July, some 15,000 Chartists and Repealers were again on Calton Hill, this time on a protest demonstration against the arrests. John

Grant was to take the chair but he was picked up on the steps approaching the Hill. There were warrants for others but they evaded arrest. The men were held in the Calton Gaol, and as the protest procession passed by it paused opposite the gaol to raise a cheer for the inmates.[70]

The invocation of Muir and Gerrald (not to mention Burns), the substantial membership of the Muir Club and the possession of flags belonging to the United Irishmen make it clear that the memory of the 1790s in Scotland and '98 in Ireland was still very much alive in subaltern Edinburgh. The dedication of a club to John Mitchel also shows that it was an organic national–popular culture. The leaders were brought to trial under new legislation and a Scottish judiciary determined to show that the partisan failings of 1793–4 would not be repeated. Cummings was charged with chairing a meeting

> which was to form an illegal and disloyal body to compel by force of violence an alteration of the laws and constitution of the realm. By procuring and using guns and pikes, in order to levy war.[71]

A prolonged wrangle ensued as to the competency of the new statutes on sedition and conspiracy under Scottish law. The comparisons with the political trials of 1793–4 were not lost on a directly involved Lord Cockburn who later noted:

> If anyone who had heard the trials of 1793 and 1794, and had then left this country, had come back, and been present at this trial, it would not have been more easy to have convinced him that he was again among the same people.[72]

It had been the Calton Hill meeting at which Henry Rankine had first made public the existence of gun clubs that had 'excited the attention' of the authorities. The illegal organisation of gun clubs by the city's Chartists and Repealers had already been a matter of public notoriety. And as the memory of radical Edinburgh was later to recall, at the foot of Carrubber's Close, running north from the High Street, the Chartists maintained an arsenal in Whitefield's, an old chapel near Robert Cranston's coffee house and looking directly over to the 'Political Martyrs' monument and Calton Hill.[73] This was probably the main arsenal for the five hundred members of the 'Edinburgh Guard' but the principal location for most of the clubs was on the other side of the High Street, down in the poorest quarters of the Old Town, the district with the highest Irish immigration. As the *Scotsman* confirmed from 'informed reports',

> it was in the Cowgate where 'a number of clubs regularly assemble to discuss and to mature their seditious and treasonable plots.'[74]

It was here, in the working-class heart of Old Town Edinburgh, James Cummings the old shoemaker had advised his Glasgow associates, that the feeling amongst the city's residents was 'decidedly warlike'. The general topic of conversation was 'arming, and street-fighting'. Some club members had even purchased their own muskets at £1 each and 'a great many had provided themselves with arms'. In twenty years Cummings had never known such a strong feeling of resistance to the government. He also revealed that Irish papers were read avidly in the city, particularly the *Felon*. This was corroborated by the *Scotsman* source, which reported that:

> The Irish Felon of general notoriety, is regularly received by a butcher in the Cowgate, in large quantities, and the treason which is proscribed in the land of its publication is retailed here to eager sympathisers.[75]

As in 1798, however, the cross-fertilisation of radical national agendas between Scotland and Ireland, which the authorities and established orders of both countries dreaded, did not materialise. No sooner had the crisis apparently heightened than it was over. The same edition of the *Scotsman* that carried the account of the protest meeting on the Calton Hill, also carried an editorial scornfully rejoicing at the collapse of rebellion in Ireland:

> On Saturday the 29th of July, the Irish Rebellion of 1848 commenced, and apparently ended, in a bog called Balough.[76]

V

> 'The past?' Aye, boy, the method's past, the deed is still the same,
> And robbery is robbery, yet though cloaked in gentler name
> Our means of life are still usurped, the rich man still is lord,
> And prayers and cries for justice still meet one reply – the sword!
> James Connolly, *The Legacy*[77]

The *Scotsman*'s observations on the Cowgate revealed more than the shift in the reading tastes of radical Edinburgh. It also reflected the changing nature of the Old Town, the growth of its immigrant Irish community bringing a new energy to Edinburgh's working-class politics, its proximity to the Southside university quarter giving it a curious overlap with the emergent socialist groups that were to flourish in the city in the latter half of the nineteenth century. Around its spinal axis of the High Street, the orientation of public politics switched from north to south, away from the Calton Hill to the open meeting spaces of the Meadows. At its heart were the densely packed tenements and closes connecting the Southside down to the Cowgate and up to the High Street, embracing the privileged and the law courts of Scotland, the poor and the struggles of the present and the enduring memory in stone of the country's national past. Here, as in decades past, the political and social aspirations of Scotland and Ireland came together in an overlap of struggle.

In 1898, it was a place familiar to a man again re-visiting his native Edinburgh and his elderly father in the Lawnmarket, taking brief time out from writing and organising around the centenary commemoration in Ireland of the 'Year of '98'. Keen to launch his own radical socialist newspaper, he had called on a comrade in Glasgow to borrow £50 for the project. Back in Edinburgh's Old Town he met up with an old friend and mentor who spoke in even broader Scots than himself and who would give him a poem on Wolfe Tone to appear in his new publishing venture. In Leith he met up with another comrade he had known in Dublin. The Edinburgh man back in town was, of course, James Connolly, the comrade in Glasgow, Keir Hardie, the mentor in the Old Town, John Leslie, the comrade in Leith, George Yates, who had left Dublin the year before at the time of the anti-Jubilee demonstrations which had marked the commemoration of Queen Victoria's long reign in that city.[78] It was within this matrix of place, commemorative events and subaltern publications, Dublin and Edinburgh, the Jubilee of 1897 and the '98 Centenary of 1898, Keir Hardie's *Labour Leader* in Glasgow, Alice Milligan's *Shan Van Vocht* in Belfast and his own *Workers' Republic* in Dublin that Connolly developed his seminal writings on nationalism and socialism. They were ideas which had gestated from his formative years in Edinburgh and his development within the socialist movement in Scotland, a contribution which distinguish Connolly as an outstanding example of Gramsci's organic intellectual.[79] As Victor Kiernan has noted, Edinburgh's James Connolly, 'banished from political activity by a firing-squad when Gramsci was just entering it', was like Sardinia's Antonio Gramsci, himself an embodiment of 'how enormous a leap an individual mind can make when caught up by a progressive historical movement'.[80]

Within months of leaving Edinburgh for Dublin in 1896, Connolly was engaged with the politics of commemoration. He outlined the acuity of his approach to the commemorative process in relation to the 'variety of agencies seeking to preserve the national sentiment in the hearts of the people' in an article published in the *Shan Van Vocht* in January 1897:

> Now traditions may, and frequently do, provide materials for a glorious martyrdom, but can never be strong enough to ride the storm of a successful revolution.
>
> If the national movement of our day is not merely to re-enact the old tragedies of our past history, it must show itself capable of rising to the exigencies of the moment.[81]

An opportunity to demonstrate this capability 'of rising to the exigencies of the moment' was brilliantly taken in connection with the royal Jubilee celebrations to be held in Dublin later that year. An alliance of Maud Gonne and her cultural nationalist associates with Connolly's socialist and republican comrades marched through Dublin behind a red flag showing a royal crown on a pike and the legend *Finis Tyranniae*, a hand-cart carrying the black coffin of 'The British Empire' and a labourers' band playing the Dead March. Stopped by the police on O'Connell Bridge, Connolly seized the commemorative moment with inspiration, and to rousing cheers, the demonstrators acted on his instructions and threw the coffin into the Liffey as the Edinburgh voice of the 'Scotto-Hibernian' cried: 'Here goes the coffin of the British Empire. To hell with the British Empire!'[82] The following month, Connolly was back in Edinburgh. It is difficult to imagine that if economic necessity had not forced him to leave Edinburgh for Dublin the previous year, this most fertile political imagination would not have drawn on the strong Scottish and Irish republican traditions of his native city to ensure that the voice of radical subalternity and its message *Finis Tyranniae* would not have disturbed the douce loyalty of Scotland's capital in like measure, though perhaps without such exigent theatricality.

The counter-Jubilee demonstrations were, however, a spin off from the principal commemorative event on which Connolly's attention was focused, the forthcoming centenary of the 'Year of '98'. In Dublin a committee of the respectable and responsible had organised themselves in a Centennial Association to shape the tenor and content of the commemoration of '98 and Wolfe Tone in a manner not dissimilar to that of the Edinburgh worthies of 1844 who had set their own imprint on that capital's commemoration of Thomas Muir and the Scottish 'Political Martyrs' of 1793–4. Bolstered by the loan he had secured from Keir Hardie, his comrade in Glasgow, Connolly spent July of 1898 in Edinburgh's Old Town with his elderly father and his old comrades of the left before returning to Dublin to make his own distinctive commemorative contribution. In his earlier *Shan Van Vocht* article on how to commemorate tradition, Connolly had argued that any national movement needed to demonstrate that its nationalism was not 'merely a morbid idealizing of the past' but was also 'capable of formulating a distinct and definite answer to the problems of the present' and the needs of the future.[83] With the launch of *Workers' Republic* in August 1898 he applied this approach to an analysis of the contemporary social and political background to the Wolfe Tone and '98 commemorations, not least in his scathing observations on Dublin's Lord Mayor and the other honoured guests at a commemorative Mansion House banquet:

> Poor Wolfe Tone. Lived, fought and suffered for Ireland in order that
> a purse-proud, inflated windbag should exploit your memory to his
> own aggrandisement.

Connolly concluded his observations on the centenary commemorations by noting:

> The mixed character of all speeches in connection with the '98 move-
> ment, at the banquet and elsewhere, proves conclusively that our
> middle-class leaders are afraid to trust democracy.[84]

This was precisely the appraisal the Edinburgh radicals had made of their own middle class in 1848 as they had gathered on Calton Hill to pledge their own commitment to 'democracy' in Scotland and Ireland, and the Edinburgh resonance in the thinking and writing of Connolly in these initial months in Ireland are striking. In early August 1898, alongside his own article in the first issue of *Workers' Republic*, Connolly had published a poem on Wolfe Tone by his old Edinburgh mentor, John Leslie.[85] Most likely he had been given it, or perhaps commissioned it, when he had been with Leslie in Edinburgh a few weeks earlier. Given Connolly's undoubted interest in history, his avid capacity for reading, his penchant for poetry, song and the 'living stream' of the radical tradition the Edinburgh contribution to his formative influences is an intriguing question. Born to a Scottish father and Irish mother in Edinburgh's Old Town, the older John Leslie shared the same enthusiasm for poetry, song and the history of the radical and socialist movement.[86] A regular contributor to the Social-Democratic Federation's *Justice* on both Scottish and Irish affairs, he had significantly written of James Fintan Lalor, describing him as 'the shrewdest and the most far-seeing, indeed, the ablest of the men of '48' and urging his comrades in Scotland and Ireland to read Lalor's 'little known and neglected *Faith of a Felon*'. Leslie also described Lalor's *Irish Felon* as 'perhaps the ablest news-paper ever edited upon Irish soil'.[87] This was, of course, the same journal that the local butcher had sold 'in large quantities' to an avid readership of 'eager sympathisers' in and around Edinburgh's Cowgate in 1848. What was the memory of this when Leslie became active in the Edinburgh movement in the 1880s? What were the memories of '48 in Ireland and Scotland in the Cowgate when James Connolly was born there only twenty years later in 1868? Desmond Greaves speculated that Connolly's decision to publish excerpts from Lalor's *Faith of a Felon* and *The Rights of Ireland* 'may have come from the republican Fred Ryan' after Connolly attended a lecture and participated in the subsequent discussion shortly after his move to Dublin in April 1896.[88] However, given John Leslie's strong interest in Lalor already expressed in his

*J*ustice articles in 1894, and the attested contemporary popularity of Lalor's writings in Edinburgh, is it not more probable that Connolly's original interest formed in Edinburgh, an absorbed enthusiasm which the Dublin lecture merely reinforced? The question becomes even more intriguing when we reflect on the fact that shortly after James was born, the family moved from the Cowgate up to Carrubbers Close. The young Connolly spent his formative years in a family home only yards from where the Edinburgh radicals of 1848, the men of the gun clubs commemorating Wallace and Burns, Muir and Gerrald, Emmet and Mitchel, had housed their arsenal. The foot of a close which he would have known well looked directly across to Calton Hill, the monument to the Political Martyrs, the memory of the 1790s and of '98, the United Men of Scotland and Ireland. It was, as it remains, a political urban landscape infused with the memory across history, space and place of the felon, the radical and the rebel, a pantheon of subalternity which after 1916 would include James Connolly himself.

VI

> Apostles of freedom are ever idolized when dead but crucified when living.
>
>   James Connolly, *Workers' Republic, August 1898*[89]

In 1968 Edinburgh and District Trades Council decided to mark the centenary of James Connolly's birth in the city by unveiling a plaque in the Cowgate close to the spot where he had been born in June 1868. Even this modest gesture of recognition had been difficult to organise in a city with a tenacious streak of indigenous Protestant anti-Catholicism, anti-Irish prejudice and a pronounced Unionist loyalism that transcended the Labour – Tory political divide. It was quietly announced by the *Edinburgh Evening News* under the heading 'Edinburgh's own rebel is remembered' as the short lead item in a regular column on local Edinburgh people. The report reflected the profile that the trade unionist organisers were anxious to attach to the occasion:

> [A] plaque will be erected to his memory – not as a 'rebel' but as the founder of the Irish Socialist Republican Party and as an 'international trade union leader'.[90]

The apostle James was to receive limited idolization, an emasculated commemoration not dissimilar to the constrained confined tribute of the 'Political Martyrs' monument. The Cowgate plaque was unveiled in June 1968 by the Counsellor from the Irish Embassy in London. Amongst those present were surviving family members, a daughter from London and Senator Mrs Nora Connolly O'Brien from Dublin, a nephew, John Connolly from the Canongate, and two nieces from the Edinburgh housing scheme, Craigmillar.[91] Trade unionists from the United States and New Zealand were amongst those invited to a reception in the North British Hotel (the irony of the venue doubtless lost on the London loyal leaders of the Scottish trade union movement) hosted by Edinburgh and District Trades Council 'in honour of the man who became the city's most famous union leader'.[92] Even with this minimised nationalist profile there were sectarian threats. Gerry Fitt had been due to give a talk on the 'Life and Times of Connolly' to a gathering at the YMCA but he was called back to Belfast. Protestant Action Society Leith branch were disappointed. As the *Evening News* put it, 'Change of Plan foils protest at "Rebel" talk' and their intended demonstration was called off.[93] Five days after the £100 plaque was erected it was stolen. It was revealed that the organisers of the commemoration had earlier received phone calls and threats from Protestant Action threatening to break up the commemoration. The Cowgate had been daubed with anti-Catholic and anti-Irish slogans.[94] The secretary of the Trades Council said:

> It has taken us many years of hard fighting to see it erected. In that time we met opposition from many quarters, but this has come as a real slap in the face.[95]

All Edinburgh knew who was behind the removal of the plaques, except it would seem, the staunch stalwarts of the Edinburgh police who provided those all too aware of the city's dark sectarian underside with the memorable quote:

> To our knowledge the plaque has been stolen and the CID are investigating, but as yet we have no idea who might be responsible.[96]

It was replaced, higher up, with invisible bolts. The Trades Council announced that they would ask the Scottish Trades Union Congress to rename their Summer School Scholarship the 'James Connolly Scholarship' but nothing came of it.[97] The commemoration was to be a one-off affair. Although long overdue, in the context of a long Britified Scottish labour movement, a timorous and a Scottish national movement ambivalent to Ireland and republicanism, and an Edinburgh which had long echoed to a rancorous bigotry against all things ostensibly Catholic or identifiably Irish, it was no small achievement.

Under the heading, 'One of the rebel band who were going to take over the castle' in the local column of the *Edinburgh Evening News*, the occasion also brought a personal recollection from 70-year-old Michael

Rogers, who reckoned he was the only survivor of a small company of around thirty Irish Volunteers Connolly had raised and commanded in Edinburgh in 1913. According to Rogers:

> We were armed with rifles and drilled in the Moulders Hall in the High Street. James had a plan for the company to take over the Castle by going in as visitors but we didn't want to antagonise the Scots. We disbanded when war broke out and most of us eventually joined the British Army.[98]

Rogers added that he had been in Egypt when his former 'commander' was executed and had only heard of Connolly's death a year later when he was wounded and returned to a depot in Ireland.[99]

Referring to this claim in a footnote to his 1968 James Connolly Centenary Lecture, Owen Dudley Edwards cited it as further evidence of the tendency for Connolly's actions in 1916 to lead to a retrospective enhancement of his earlier career with improbable, apocryphal accretions, memories of a man 'always on the boil' for armed action. If not a complete fabrication, then, at best, the 'most charitable' interpretation was that it was a reminder of Connolly's sense of humour, an embellishment in which 'some light reference was recalled as evidence of long-cherished plans'.[100] Certainly the central claim that in 1913 Connolly had found time to raise, arm and organise a company of 'Irish Volunteers' (*sic*) in Edinburgh cannot be squared with events. In 1913 Connolly was living in Belfast and totally absorbed in events in Ireland. After intense trade union activity in Belfast early in the year he went to Dublin in August to assume a leading role in the great Dublin lockout. In September he was back in Belfast recuperating from gaol and hunger strike in Dublin. The following month he did return to Edinburgh, where he is on record as speaking at meetings in Leith and on his previous old pitch of the East Meadows, before going on to other speaking engagements in Kilmarnock and Glasgow. However the visit, his last to his native city, lasted only a matter of a few days before he returned to Ireland.[101] The timing of the visit is nonetheless significant in terms of the development of notions of organised, armed volunteer bodies. At the end of October Connolly had returned from Scotland to Ireland to immerse himself once more in the Dublin struggle. Within a month the idea of the Citizen Army was born out of the intensification of the lockout struggle against armed scabs, the inauguration of a 'Civic Committee', a 'drilling scheme' for Dublin workers by Captain Jack White, and the ideas being promoted by Connolly. Only a fortnight after his return from Edinburgh he was telling a meeting of Dublin workers called to celebrate the release from gaol of Larkin:

> Listen to me. I am going to talk sedition. The next time we are out for a march I want to be accompanied by four battalions of trained men with their corporals and sergeants. Why should we not drill and train men as they are doing in Ulster? But I don't think you require any training (laughter).[102]

It may well be that the 'light reference' charitably ascribed to Connolly's well attested sense of humour may, in fact, have been a somewhat more serious notion being given a gestational airing in discussion with Edinburgh comrades at some close gathering, quite possibly in the Moulders Hall. Whatever the truth of the matter, the claim was the last living testimony in his native city to the man older members of the city's labour movement proudly used to recall had 'gaun tae his death wi' a guid Edinbra accent'.[103]

In 1986, a brief moment of left Labour control of Edinburgh District Council coincided with the anniversary of context of the 1936 outbreak of the Spanish Civil War, the 1926 General Strike and the 70th anniversary of the execution of Edinburgh's 'most famous son', as he was deemed in a House of Commons commemorative motion by Leith Labour MP, Ron Brown. The District Council mounted an exhibition, produced a poster and published an accompanying booklet, 'Sing a Rebel Song'.[104] It was to be the last commemoration of Connolly from a predominantly Scottish and Edinburgh perspective, the only one to give equal prominence to his nationalism, his socialism and the significance of his contribution to political culture. By the 1990s there was a pronounced shift in emphasis, and throughout the decade Connolly commemoration in the city was increasingly located within the context of the conflict in the north of Ireland. A 1991 headline in the *Sun* Scottish edition, 'Storm as council lefties let IRA pals have party', referring to a meeting held by the James Connolly Commemoration Committee in Edinburgh City Chambers at which the Labour MP Denis Canavan and others addressed the issue of the H-Block hunger strikes, summed up the level to which coverage of all matters deemed 'pro-nationalist' had dropped.[105] It was a low point of political culture in Scotland in which intolerance thrived. In 1993 when the capital's James Connolly Society proposed a march and a subsequent commemorative meeting in the City Chambers, the Lothian Loyalist League distributed a leaflet urging their supporters to 'come tooled up' to stop the march.[106] From Leith, J. G. MacLean, who in a previous letter had compared Connolly to Myra Hindley, wrote to the *Evening News* to express the view of Connolly held by Edinburgh's Protestant Action:

> Connolly will be long remembered, but in the same way as Attila the Hun, Hitler, Franco and Himmler.[107]

There was a heated debate in the District Council at which the SNP Lord Provost, Norman Irons, voiced his objection to the proposed meeting in the City Chambers, saying that a line had to be drawn at the presence of a Sinn Féin speaker and sympathisers with the IRA in the City Chambers. The police expressed their opposition to the march and after emotional pleas from those whose grandfathers had been in the British Army in 1916 and the family of a soldier killed while serving with the Royal Scots in South Armagh, who urged the Council to 'Stand up to the IRA', the march was banned.[108] The following year permission was again given for the march to go ahead. In a tactic resonant of Paisleyite responses to the early Civil Rights marches in the north of Ireland, a spokesman for the Pride of Midlothian Independent Loyal Orange Lodge declared:

> The threat of IRA supporters marching through Edinburgh is enough to incite people to violence against them.[109]

The march went ahead with a 500-strong police presence. The *Evening News* coverage pictured British National Party and other neo-Nazi supporters amongst the Loyalist protesters in the Grassmarket giving Nazi salutes from behind the police cordon.[110] The shift of context from Edinburgh to an exclusively 'Orange/Green' fault-line was now virtually complete. The confusion as to what the commemoration was all about was perhaps best summed up in the paradoxical comments of the Sinn Féin guest speaker who, referring to the loyalist protesters and giving an assurance that the march represented no threat to the Protestant religion or 'way of life', said:

> This is not 1690 or 1969. Let us leave history where it belongs, in the past.[111]

By 1996 the James Connolly Commemorative March was accepted as an annual Edinburgh event and a standard route was agreed for what the political editor of the *Evening News* insisted on describing as a 'Republican parade' and a 'traditional flashpoint between Catholic and Protestant extremists'.[112] Certainly representatives of organised labour, the trade union movement, the Labour Party, the Scottish National Party were conspicuous by their absence. This invited criticism that the commemoration had become a 'set piece in sectarianism' although the organisers have persistently pointed out that extensive invitations are issued to the organised labour and nationalist movements in Scotland to participate but that with equal regularity they decline.[113] By the end of the 1990s, nonetheless, attitudes became more relaxed and in 1998, against a backdrop of the continuance of the IRA ceasefire in Ireland, it was even being mooted that the capital could erect a statue 'to honour rebel

Connolly', a proposal which was now being presented as a potential 'money-spinner'.

When the 1990s process of re-defining the commemoration of Connolly as an unwelcome importation of what was deemed to be the 'sectarian conflict' of the north of Ireland rather than a rightful celebration of an outstanding Edinburgh political organic intellectual and activist began, the Edinburgh journalist Ian Bell gave his own reflective assessment of what had happened to the memory of the man who was his own great-uncle. It was hard, he felt, not to feel ambivalent about the Edinburgh commemorative march. If Connolly had lived, both Ireland and Scotland, perhaps even the United States, would have been very different countries. As both a socialist and a nationalist, he straddled a political divide which still seemed too wide for many contemporary politicians. As a result, his greatness was still too little recognised. This was particularly the case, Bell felt, in Edinburgh itself where Connolly deserved far better from his home town that he had thus far received. For a working-class Edinburgh boy he had led an extraordinary life, one, still, it seems, too extraordinary for the tastes of the modern capital.

> Connolly was the most internationalist of nationalists, sincere but dangerous. When he committed himself to the Irish revolution he established a legacy which the land of his birth has never been able to digest.[114]

To this it could be added that Edinburgh, as a particular place of deep-embedded historical political memory, has always had difficulty in coming to terms with the more radical and challenging aspects of its eventful past. There has been a persistent fear of the radical, a fear of the national, a cringe resultant from the Britification of our political culture. It was epitomised in the inability of one of New Labour's most ultra-Brit Labour MPs to countenance the expressed national will that the site of the reconvened Scottish Parliament should be on the prominent location of Calton Hill because the latter represented 'a nationalist shibboleth'.[115] From the 1790s through the 1840s to the 1990s the subaltern struggles of Calton Hill cast a long shadow.

In August 1968, only two months after the Connolly commemoration, a small commemorative gathering was also held in the Old Calton Burial Ground, beside the 'Political Martyrs' Monument to mark the anniversary of the banishment of Thomas Muir to Botany Bay in 1793. The meeting was organised by the Workers' Party of Scotland (Marxist-Leninist), a tiny Maoist group committed to promoting awareness of Scotland's radical past and the achievement's of Enver Hoxha's Albania in equal measure. Significantly no parliamentary representatives deigned to grace the monument erected by the 'friends of parliamentary reform', but a cluster of Labour councillors from Edinburgh, Fife and the West, a few Scottish Nationalist activists and some cultural nationalist figures including the writers Naomi Mitchison and Douglas Young were on the platform and a message was read from Chris Grieve (Hugh MacDiarmid).[116] Each strand touched on the emasculated tradition of extra-parliamentary action and national–popular aspirations. The leading Edinburgh Labour councillor and activist, Jack Kane, declared that courage and self-sacrifice would always be needed and that

> In these days when our Movement seems to have lost direction, and when we are looking for the way forward, we can draw inspiration from the pioneers.[117]

Referring to the proliferation across the capital's urban landscape of a statuary reflective of respectable Presbyterian hagiography, Naomi Mitchison made the same comparisons first voiced by Patrick Brewster in 1844:

> Thomas Muir and the Martyrs represented the real Scotland, and not the theologians whose statues decorated this city. The Martyrs represented the eternal veritas and struggles of the Scottish people.[118]

However, it was left to Elizabeth Mein, a former Edinburgh councillor, to give a glimpse of the enduring radical memory within the capital when she recalled how her great-great-grandfather had been one of a small group in the city who had organised and carried meals to Thomas Muir and his comrades while they were in prison awaiting deportation. Elizabeth Mein had already put in print her own personal memories of the events of 1848 and the arms dump in Carrubbers Close in a little-known booklet on the Edinburgh radical and Chartist, Robert Cranston.[119] Yet the modest turnout and the marginal political status of the event organisers were indicative of the extent to which the collective memory of Muir, as of Connolly, has been steadily erased from the city's political landscape. Hopes were expressed that the event might become an annual event, the 'first of a new series of commemorations'. A 'Thomas Muir and the Martyrs' committee was formed to ensure annual commemoration, to develop related historical and literary work and to organise a proposed delegation to Chantilly, France on the forthcoming anniversary of Muir's death there, but the initiative petered out.[120] Thirty years later, it seems that the process is even more complete. It is not just Connolly's Edinburgh legacy that has been eclipsed, or the memory of subaltern resistance in the city, the expressive radicalism of the organic components of our national–popular culture, but this wider setting of the 'other Muir', the transnational and international axis of Dublin–Edinburgh–

Paris which has also been eroded. Thomas Muir died in exile and ultimate obscurity in Chantilly on 24 January 1799. While all Ireland will commemorate '98 and Wolfe Tone, in Scotland the bicentenary of Muir's early passing was a commemorative moment nearly as forlorn and forgotten as his lonely death.

7
Contrary heroes:
industry, ethnie and 1848

CHRISTOPHER HARVIE

I would show you … with great eloquence that all Ireland's failures
have been due to her incapacity for believing in success or happiness
– for talking like Lefanu whilst Irishmen are going out into all lands
and putting them on as a shepherd putteth on his garment. As long as
Ireland produces men who have the sense to leave her, she does not
exist in vain.

George Bernard Shaw to Charlotte Payne-Townshend, 4 November
1896[1]

Measuring distances

Two forces contended for the soul of industrial Europe: nationalism and
materialism. The latter was itself divided into free-market internation-
alism and Marxism, but these divisions were never absolute, and in that
most unideological of regions, the British islands, matters were not seen
so schematically. Only in the 1960s, when economic development began
to stumble, did 'the peculiarities of the English' feature. Paradoxically,
this coincided with an interrogation of the nationalist historiography
which had been dominant in the 'exceptional' state: the Republic of
Ireland. 'Revisionism' had Scots and Welsh parallels, with the success of
T. C. Smout's *A History of the Scottish People* (1969) and Kenneth O.
Morgan's *Wales in British Politics* (1963). The aim of both was to relate
national experiences to the diffused impacts of European social evolution
and Britain's leading role in it; yet they also reflected a greater awareness,
within the 'materialist' mainstream, of the regional inflection of its
components.

As nationalism and globalisation in 1989–91 disrupted both cold war
historiography and the influence of 'Anglo-Marxism', English historians

problematised a 'national' experience they had regarded as 'un-English' even to enquire about. This meant, in Raymond Williams' phrase, 'measuring the distance' between the historical discourses within the archipelago.[2] Particularly about the 1840s, when free-trade-materialism was confirmed, but alongside an unequal development which enabled British nationalism to contrast triumphalist Anglo-Saxonism with an apparently antithetical Celticism. Consonant with the decay of Empire and Marxism, this confrontation has survived.

Linda Colley's influential *Britons: Forging the Nation, 1707–1837* (1992) reprises much Victorian ideology in seeing Protestantism behind a British nationalism mature by Victoria's accession. This discounts not only industrialisation but more mysteriously the incorporation into the United Kingdom of 5 million, mostly Catholic, Irish in 1801. In what appears as a mirror image the Irish arch-revisionist Conor Cruise O'Brien, in *Ancestral Voices* (1994), sees an equally intolerant Catholic nationalism, personified by Paul, Cardinal Cullen, fusing the secular *ressentiments* of Protestant Young Ireland with the anti–enlightenment evangel of ultramontane Catholicism.[3]

Yet one can argue that in the 1840s the argument about revolution, though it fed in Ireland two patterns of socio-economic development, and drove their governing discourses in different political directions, had what amounted to a common language and 'myth-kitty'. The discourse stemmed from one milieu and even – to a great extent – from one man: Thomas Carlyle.

The arch Anglo-Saxonist? The confederate of Froude and Buckshot Forster? The great non-appearer in both 'remembrancer' and 'revisionist' accounts?[4] Carlyle's influence on Young Ireland gets registered, rather sheepishly.[5] Owen Dudley Edwards sees it fulminating away, along the road to the Post Office, and close reading of most 'nationalist' texts in *any* of the 'British' countries will yield dozens of sightings.[6] But one can claim more: if one Carlyle-inspired production, the *Communist Manifesto*, was lobbed – slow-fused – into world history, and another, Disraeli's *Sybil*, helped to form Victorian Toryism, Carlyle affected those who sought the 'sweetness and light' of Celtic and Anglo-Irish literary cultures, *and* the 'fire and strength' of the Protestant Unionist and the ultramontane Catholic. His eclipse and slow rediscovery, and the complexity of his relationship to social upheaval – part symptom, part diagnosis, part cause – both helps to account for this obscurity and explains why Ireland came out of the 1840s moving socially in a different direction from the rest of Britain, yet managing to influence its social and ideological evolution.

A decade in which industrial and revolutionary themes, active since the 1780s, become synergically intertwined, stressed two cultural factors:

the 'Puritan revolution' and millenarianism.[7] In both, Carlyle was directly concerned, as the biographer of Oliver Cromwell (1845) and the associate of Edward Irving. Yet his personality was not orthodox. The Balliol Scot Home Ruler and radical Edward Caird wrote of his thinking as 'Puritanism idealised, made cosmopolitan, freed from the narrowness which clung to its first expression'.[8] His influence was particularly significant in a decade not only marked by demographic disaster, but by a Catholic Church struggling from doctrinal incoherence and domination by a secular political movement into its own identity.

In this chapter, I first want to frame Carlyle's relevance in the context of the fate of the *ancien régime*, the impact of technology, and Ireland's 'slave role' in British industrialisation. Then I want to show how Carlyle anticipated the impact of the transport-based stage of industrialisation, and the emerging counter-thesis of the 'mechanisation' of human responses and the loss of social equilibrium. At this point – roughly the time of Carlyle's *Latter-Day Pamphlets* (1850) – his own interests moved on from Ireland, but ideologies influenced by him led to a reorientation of social thought in two inimical directions. A Protestant Carlyle evolved on the mainland, and in northern Ireland. A Catholic Carlyle evolved in the south. But the workings-out of these ideologies in the early twentieth century were to share many common factors and milieus, not least the British Empire itself.

Technophilia Hibernica

To Linda Colley mainland unity was an accomplished fact by 1837, but a decade later there were good Protestant reasons – the Disruption, the Treason of the Blue Books – for Scots and Welsh *not* to feel British.[9] Ireland, which in 1841 also had many 'developmental' ingredients, was diverted by the 'famine years' to a completely different terminus. By 1900 this was what Conor Cruise O'Brien complained of: a nationalism racy of the soil, religious and sacrificially heroic but notably deficient in civic, or even urban, leaven.[10]

In 1850 the economic success of northern England, South Wales, central Scotland and the Lagan valley stood in contrast to the failure of the Scottish highlands, rural Wales and most of Ireland: success defined a 'progressive' nationality in which ethnicity was acceptably civic. Realising the gospel of integrity through work depended on steam-powered industry. The engineer and the navvy, much more than the intellectual, the politician and the soldier (after the death of Wellington in 1852 at any rate) personified the epoch which Patrick Geddes and Lewis Mumford christened 'paleotechnic'.[11]

Did nationalism and clericalism alone reduce Irish technology to the navvy level? In fact, the technical ingenuity of the Victorian Irish would have been notable in a *thriving* economy.[12] To cite only a maritime sequence: Robert Fulton, whose parents were Scots-Irish from Kilkenny, pioneered commercial steam navigation with his *Clermont* on the Hudson in 1808. Captain Alexander Blakely, of Sligo, invented the 'built-up' long-range gun in the 1855, only to have it pirated by Sir William Armstrong.[13] William Dargan dredged Belfast Lough to create the modern port, as well as building most of the Irish railway system and financing the Dublin Exhibition of 1857. In 1887, the Clareman and Fenian John Patrick Holland patented the first modern submarine (combining internal-combustion power, while on the surface, with batteries to operate electric motors while submerged). The British Admiralty bought up his rights, but had to face Sir Charles Parsons of Birr in his equally threatening *Turbinia* steam yacht.[14]

The century saw an Irish discourse of frustrated modernisation, as Joe Lee has remarked. Visible in John Mitchel's *Jail Journal* (1854) in which our hero is shown the British empire like the captive of some Jules Verne technocrat, this was typified in fiction by Charles Lever's nationalist talker Joe Atlee in *Lord Kilgobbin* (1872), whose outlook on Irish politics, derived from Thomas Davis and Robert Kane, anticipates not only Shaw's engineer Larry Doyle in *John Bull's Other Island* (1904), but James Joyce's technology-fixated Leopold Bloom:

> 'Great Ireland – no first flower of the north or gun of the sea humbug – but Ireland great in prosperity, her harbours full of ships, the woollen trade, her ancient staple, revived: all that vast unused water power, greater than all the steam of Manchester and Birmingham tenfold, at full work; the linen manufacture developed and promoted – '
> 'And the Union repealed?'
> 'Of course; that should be first of all. Not that I object to the Union, as many do, on the grounds of English ignorance as to Ireland. My dislike is, that, for the sake of carrying through certain measures necessary to Irish interests, I must sit and discuss questions which have no possible concern for me.'[15]

Though Atlee gets nowhere, and his lady runs off with a Fenian, Charles Stewart Parnell shared this line, contemporaries noting that his froideur only dissolved when discussing rural railways or mineral schemes for his Roundwood estate.[16] Technophilia, of a curdled crazy form, surfaces in *Ulysses* (1922): the near-paranoia of 'the Citizen', the bar-room boasts of 'Skin-the-Goat' as well as Bloom himself and his innumerable schemes for tramways, electric launches and hydro power.[17] If engineering is a sub-plot of *John Bull's Other Island*, Doyle's 'endless, crazy dreaming' was shared by the Trieste emigré, patriot and long-distance pioneer of Irish cinema, and George Russell (AE), practical apostle of agricultural co-operation when not, almost literally, away with the fairies. Patrick Geddes, a shrewd judge under his somewhat cloudy rhetoric, did not get things utterly wrong when he beheld Dublin in 1913 as the 'geotechnic' city of the future.[18]

'Creative Chaos'

1848 was a *Zeitbruch*, culturally as well as socially. In Europe it refor-mulated nationalism as Tom Nairn's 'modern Janus': appraising consensual economic development and constructing histories of ancient wrong, something aggravated by the waves of migration which broke over the industrial areas. Ireland was donor, not recipient.[19] The Famine meant that the industrialism and federalism that Young Ireland had preached bifur-cated almost savagely. The gainers were the poet–priest–peasant conduits of O'Brien's Catholic-nationalist imperialism; other Catholic Irish had to emigrate and settle alongside a planter majority already sensitised to ethnic threat.[20] It would be unsurprising if the terminus were not the Committee Room of Joyce's 'centre of paralysis', or Fluther Good's 'terrible state of chassis' interpreted as 'stasis' rather than 'chaos'.[21]

Stasis was rooted in the way the post-Famine economy evolved. In Britain the 1840s 'railway revolution' accelerated regional industrial specialisation and through speculation – gambling by another name – reconciled aristocracy, London finance and local entrepreneurs. The specialisation alloted the Irish, facing starvation, was that of the *Gastarbeiter*: essential but unprivileged.[22] This two-Ireland identity lasted over a century, with low growth-rates stemming from agrarian conservatism and later republican austerity in the South seemingly endorsing emigration and Protestant industrialisation in Ulster.[23]

The Ricardian economists' notion of 'unequal development' still presupposed that all development runs in the same direction.[24] But Europe as a 'world region' shows that one region's decline could be a condition of another's advance. The 'unsuccessful' became necessary servitors – Braudel's *fabriques d'hommes a l'usage d'autrui* – to 'devel-oped' areas which inflicted economic defeat, and appropriated the booty of raw material and low-skill, low-wage labour.[25] In the mid-nineteenth century, peasant misery and alcoholism in the Carpathians, pogroms in Russia, and criminality in south Italy, extruded hard-working emigrants to the Ruhr, the Borinage, Lombardy, in just the same way as starvation drove thousands from Ireland to Britain.[26]

Ireland abutted on a key area of furious, contradictory economic development: the 'creative chaos' – to use Joseph Schumpeter's phrase – of the Irish Sea.[27] This resembled until the mid-1700s Braudel's Mediterranean in its instability: smuggling on a huge scale, illegal distilling, the itinerant commercial culture of Scots pedlars and drovers and Irish harvesters and fisherfolk.[28] Even when 'legitimised' it was predatory: an economy dominated by the slave trade out of Liverpool, and slave-harvested sugar, tobacco and later cotton as inward cargoes to the Clyde. Success also sanctioned dealing in drugs in Jardine-Matheson's Hong Kong and – in the American Civil War – blockade-runners and commerce-raiders. The 'motherland' of the wider Empire, this inland sea replicated the polity of the Mediterranean, but under the fitful control of grand territorial noblemen: the Dukes of Argyll, Atholl, the Marquesses of Londonderry and Bute. With properties scattered round the *littoral* and few scruples about how they got their money, these carried on a version of the old Scottish 'territorial jurisdictions', a power of pit and gallows transmitted to their overmighty capitalist successors: the Peels and Gladstones, the Coatses, Guinnesses, Pirries, Kylsants and Beardmores – and even, through transatlantic connections, to such dollar imperialists as Carnegie and J. P. Morgan.

This maritime 'world' managed, between 1845 and 1865, to move from textile- to transport-based industry *and* gain civic 'legitimacy'. Lancashire – 'Manchesterthum' – was the harbinger: the world centre of cotton, but no longer its prisoner. In Scotland, linen and cotton gave way to a dominance in engineering and heavy industry. Wales made the transition from minerals and iron to tinplate and steam coal export on a tremendous scale. All of this was not just national but world-dominant: socialised and calibrated by an evolving capitalist culture and an intelligentsia which amalgamated Gramsci's 'organic' and 'traditional' types, and found itself spiritually at home in the Lake District of Wordsworth, Coleridge, Southey and Thomas Arnold. But Ireland, after the disaster of the Famine, served the 'economic miracle' – although a damned close-run one – with cheap and docile labour. 'Uneven development' around the Irish Sea did not mean variations on a common advance but the winners taking all.

The railway: the infrastructure that undermined

In this regional perspective Ireland's nationalism was less reactionary than realistic: the choice was either to manoeuvre against the flow of British 'policy', or reject a competitive structure that was loaded. That comforting parallels with eighteenth-century Scotland did not work was evident in the case of the railways. Starting from behind (Ireland had fewer miles of railway in 1845 than Britain had two decades earlier) by 1855 it had a thousand miles, when Sweden had not an inch. In Britain the 'Railway Mania' bought off the doom predicted by Marx and Engels, helping to create a new capital-goods based economy.[29] Six hundred miles of Irish track were built by Dargan, a pupil of Thomas Telford, and resembling Brassey and Brunel rolled into one.[30] His financial collapse in the slump of 1866, through the failure of his textile businesses, was a national disaster.[31] But though he and his contemporaries had put in place the infrastructure – railways, steamers, docks and telegraphs – and made efficient the large markets of Dublin and Belfast, these opened Ireland to imports. Industry was almost confined to Ulster. Elsewhere it was thin and got thinner – 22.8 per cent of the workforce in 1851 and 16.0 per cent in 1881.[32]

The railway as economic generator, the German economist Friedrich List realised in his *National System of Political Economy* (1841), required protection as well as state-sponsored construction, opinions which echoed the protectionism of the Grattan parliament. Matthew Carey, its leading advocate, went to the United States where, refined by his son Henry as *The Principles of Political Economy* (1839), his ideas influenced List, Count Szechenyi and Ferenc Deák in Hungary. Parnell's protectionism had American ancestry, and List's economics returned to Ireland in Arthur Griffith's *The Resurrection of Hungary* (1904). But by then the Irish economy had crawled for half-a-century.

Thus Ireland's largest 'industrial' investment obeyed Ricardo's law, to produce pastoral agriculture and emigrant labour which would remit cash home, and keep an agrarian–clerical elite in power. Had Irish capitalism ridden out the 1860s, it would still have been disadvantaged, even before improved transport brought in cheap foodstuffs from North America and East Europe to turn an agrarian economy into crisis. John Stuart Mill's remark in 1866 that Ireland's peasantry was a 'European' phenomenon became reality after 1873.[33] Britain's transportation specialisation further detached north-east Ulster, essentially an outlier of the Clyde, while the south shared the Europe wide move towards a defensive agrarian nationalism, led by a clerico-ethnic intelligentsia.[34] Joe Atlee's or Leopold Bloom's progressivism became self-parodic when confronted with this.

Ireland and the critique of industrialisation

A consequence of this was the inflected 'modernism' of Ireland. In *Lord Kilgobbin* Atlee remarks that 'Scotland has no national absurdities: she asks neither for a flag nor a parliament. She demands only what will pay.'[35] The centrality of nation, land and Church to Ireland, had however, consequences which were neither absurd nor remote from British intellectual concerns. The Irish were close enough to the English critical tradition to share its doubts about a 'progress' that did not work for them; while the general sense of dislocation in the 1860s was endorsed by 'Celtic culture' as seen by Ernest Renan and Matthew Arnold. Market-driven 'improvement' was challenged by democratic agitation and financial crisis, an ecological critique, and a series of horrendous, technologically-driven wars. To Arnold and Renan as 'revisionist' 1848ers, regional tributaries to the central culture could help combat materialism and socialism.[36] This blended with print capitalism – the Macmillans, Arnold's and later Yeats' publishers, were Scottish Celts turned 'Christian Socialists' who scooped the university market – and with a growing appreciation of the unconscious and habitual.

So much Irish literary history consists of the projection-back of the literary renaissance of the early twentieth century, its world reputation and its controversies, that IreLit has evicted earlier, more awkward loyalties, as firmly as EngLit stamped out Teutonic philology during World War I.[37] Conor Cruise O'Brien registers chapbook patriots, addresses from the scaffold, street ballads and prison journals. But would these really propel? Scotland excelled Ireland in print-capitalist nationalism – Scott-and-Burns Jacobitism, a long and articulate period of independence, religious and land grievances, some quite up-to-date martyrs – but its people did not move.[38] To look at the reading matter of the youthful Davis and Duffy, Charles Kickham, Michael Collins, Eamon de Valera, is to see activism kindled by the friction between nationalism and British print capitalism.[39]

The continuing effect of this dialogue is patent in Bernard Shaw's clever retrospect of it in *John Bull's Other Island*. Evidently influenced by Lever, Shaw has his Irish progressive Larry Doyle aim at an essentially Scots future.[40] But Doyle appreciates – and is paralysed by – the madness of Father Keegan, who embodies both the 'ideal' of Ireland and the critique of industrialism. This makes English Tom Broadbent compare him to Carlyle and Ruskin, yet he is also 'Keegan furioso': dislocated and perceptive in a European, poetic sense which goes back to Ariosto and Dante, and in Ireland even earlier, to the madness of King Sweeney. Keegan's encounter with an oriental whose indifference to Western values, theological as well as material, has subverted both Christianity and positivism, has set him running in the woods, in search of values alien to the economism of Broadbent and Doyle.

Shaw wrote after the religious-habitual subconscious hypothesised by Arnold and Renan had been explored in the 1890s by Robertson Smith and J. G. Frazer, and later by Freud and Jung, Durkheim and Weber, Eliot and Joyce.[41] Keegan combines practicality and mysticism in the way that denoted AE, cooperator and spiritualist, the Yeats who mastered double-entry bookkeeping, Patrick Geddes and even Shaw himself. This was the anti-positivist 'cultural recuperation' project within modernism, and Shaw's stress on its Celtic roots anticipates, say, J. L. Hammond's interpretation of Gladstone's commitment to Home Rule – in defiance of the intellectual establishment, the Tyndalls, Huxleys and Sidgwicks – as a turn of mind which was theological rather than scientific, and Celtic rather than Saxon. Gladstone was of both lowland and highland ancestry.[42]

This epical interpretation of the Irish experience was also carried on by Standish James O'Grady – a direct Carlyleian – and his Celtic researches, and figures in Yeats' ritual anathematisation of the world of Huxley–Shaw–Bastien–Lepage 'mechanism' in *Autobiographies* (1913). It figures, albeit more politely, in T. S. Eliot's *Notes Towards a Definition of Culture* (1948). This was one end of the scale; at the other was Pearse's call for the reification of the Irish mind through the overthrow of the 'murder machine' of English-language education, not least by the agency of poetic self-sacrifice. The drive towards this had accumulated Ossianic as well as Arnoldian accents, but much of the fire imagery that Pearse conjured up at Bodenstown in 1914 is pure Carlyle.[43]

Machines and heroes

It was the fusion of academic Philocelticism with the English critical tradition which produced an 'other' fearsome enough to evict earlier enthusiasm for railways and steamers. Thomas Hardy, whose rural craftsman background was more frequently encountered in Ireland than in England, matured as a writer during this period and can be reckoned at least a quasi-Celt through his Cornish connections. In *Tess of the D'Urbervilles* (1891), Tess and her fellow harvesters are forced to work to the rythym of the steam-thresher. Its engineer appears so alien from the 'human soul' as to be literally diabolic:

> By the engine stood a dark, motionless being, a sooty and grimy embodiment of tallness, in a sort of trance, with a heap of coals by his side: it was the engine-man. ... What he looked he felt. He was in the agricultural world, but not of it. He served fire and smoke; these denizens of the fields served vegetation, weather, frost and sun ...

> His fire was waiting incandescent, his steam was at high pressure, in a few seconds he could make the long strap move at an invisible velocity. Beyond its extent the environment might be corn, straw or chaos; it was all the same to him. If any of the autochthonous idlers asked him what he called himself, he replied shortly, 'an engineer.'[44]

This alienated being could be a phantom of Empire; he certainly seems to relate directly back to Thomas Carlyle at the end of his notorious passage on the Irish in *Chartism* (1839):

> The Giant Steamengine in a giant English Nation will here create violent demand for labour, and will there annihilate demand. But, alas, the great proportion of labour is not skilled, the millions are and must be skilless, where strength alone is wanted; menials of the Steamengine, only the chief menials and immediate body-servants of which require skill.[45]

One way of comprehending this assault was naturalism, recording the surrender of man before the inexorable pressure of heredity and environmental conditioning. Epitomised by Zola's *Rougon-Macquart* sequence (1871–93), this influenced Ireland through the Dublin–Paris conduit and became patent not only in the Anglo-Irish career of Zola's closest English-language disciple, George Moore, but in the autodidactic 'proletarian realism' of 'Robert Tressell' (Robert Noonan) and Patrick MacGill.[46]

The other Irish reaction was the heroic. Though the Carlyle of *Chartism* could be seen as anti-Irish, and his Anglo-Saxonism was one reason for his influence on the British literary–political elite in the mid nineteenth century, there was was also the man who enquired:

> The Sanspotato is of the selfsame stuff as the superfinest Lord Lieutenant. Not an individual sanspotato human scarecrow but had a life given him out of Heaven, with Eternities depending on it; for once and no second time. With immensities in him, over him and around him; with feelings which a Shakespeare's speech would not utter; with desires as illimitable as the Autocrat's of all the Russias.[47]

His 1841 lectures, *On Heroes, Hero-Worship and the Heroic in History*, acted on Young Ireland – the Catholic Gavan Duffy and the Protestants Thomas Davis and John Mitchel in particular – moving them to postulate a revolutionary Celtic hero, able to take on Luther and Cromwell. Owen Dudley Edwards sees this tradition propelling militant nationalism up to the period of Pearse and Griffith.[48] The heroic was strengthened as the market became less attractive – not least through the analysis of the conservative Catholic sociology of Fréderic Le Play, David Urquhart and Robert Monteith, and its concentration on culture, authority and locality.[49]

Carlyle: positivist–Protestant

Irish *ressentiments* were plainly latent, waiting to be concentrated by the Catholic Church and Cullen's 'devotional revolution', when 'the old passivity and timidity in the face of British power was generally replaced by confidence and even, in many cases, by truculence.'[50] Like Carlyle, this responded to puritan and millenarial concerns – we will discuss later Carlyle's ideas about mechanism and *Past and Present* – but behind both, and the spirit of 'ninety-eight', was the social thought of the Scottish Enlightenment. Carlyle encountered Adam Ferguson's *Essay on the History of Civil Society* (1767), both directly and via Ferguson's influence on German writers, Schiller and Goethe in particular.[51] Secondly he, as well as the Catholic social thinkers, was influenced by the French sociologist Henri de Saint-Simon (1760–1825) and his concept of social evolution through the alternation of periods of 'organic' stability and 'critical' change. Such a *Zeitbruch* Carlyle saw in his *French Revolution* (1837). In this, for good or ill, the entire old order is volcanically blown apart, with no possibility, save that provided by some sort of spiritual rebirth, of it being pieced together again.[52]

The concentration of Saint-Simon and his disciple Auguste Comte on social characteristics attracted British empiricists, yet the British Comtists, or positivists – Richard Congreve, Frederic Harrison and Professor E. S. Beesly – became known as 'secular Catholics'. The positivists were sympathetic to Irish nationalism, and included John Kells Ingram, author of 'Who fears to speak of Ninety-Eight?', and for a time Patrick Geddes.[53] Carlyle's historical dialectic resembled theirs in having the 'hero' as charismatic figure – both actual and as a metaphor of individual possibilities – who could secure a new organic settlement.[54] This ideal: 'bold, modern and all-surrounding and kosmical' – Whitman's term – influenced America through Emerson and the transcendentalists as early as the 1830s. Through Whitman himself it later returned to Ireland via his Irish disciples, Thomas Sigerson, Standish James O'Grady, George Russell (AE) and Shaw himself.[55] The epical Carlyle was 'read' in this way by Young Ireland. But the interpretations of him were different in Britain and Ulster.

Thomas Babington Macaulay, Carlyle's junior by five years, played his part in this. His *Lays of Ancient Rome* (1842) appeared only a year after *Heroes, Hero-Worship and the Heroic in History*. Macaulay was from a Lewis family, and claimed his *Lays* as part of an international demotic *epos* shared by, *inter alios*, the Celts.[56] Yet its heroic tropes accompanied the successive parts of his *History of England*, published between 1849 and 1855. This, coming after his critique of Southey (1830), championed Graeco-Roman-Protestant rationality against Tuscan-Milesian superstition and deference.[57] This Protestant history, with Carlyle hovering about it, was ingested into Unionism. The conservative individualism of Andrew Bonar Law and Rudyard Kipling's and Ulster's interpretation of technological good fortune as ethnic superiority was built on the Cromwellian dogma of the Anglo-Saxonist 'Captain/Soldier of Industry' paradigm.[58]

'Protestant' Carlyleian heroes applying themselves to empirical improvement inhabited the 'industrial biography' of Samuel Smiles (1812–1904), Scot, radical doctor-turned-railway company secretary, whose eloge of George Stephenson in 1857 led him to a biographical history of the Industrial Revolution. *Lives of the Engineers* in 1862 apotheosised the Anglo-Saxon artisan turned technocrat through application rather than theory.[59] In the year that his *Self-Help* appeared, 1859, Smiles became an enthusiastic member of the Volunteer corps of amateur soldiers, raised in mainland Britain to counter a threat of French invasion. Ireland was excluded from this, though an unofficial movement evolved, directed at defending the pope as an Italian ruler, and opposed to British enthusiasm in Britain for Italian secular liberalism. Volunteers were Protestant – although Fenians infiltrated corps in Liverpool – and particularly strong in Scotland; their peak was during the Fenian emergency of 1867.[60] Yet their pedigree and their future cast back to the Ireland of the 1780s and forward to Ireland after 1910, while Smiles' son, as proprietor of the Belfast Ropework, became a prominent businessman-Unionist.[61]

Carlyle: Celtic–Catholic

Seamus Deane has argued that Irish literary nationalism took its cue from Burke on Marie Antoinette: 'traditional sanctity and loveliness' subjected to sexual, democratic, mechanistic (what is the guillotine if not a machine?) assault. But the 'plain people' applauded 'Godless France', and indeed developed the organisational 'machines' of religion and politics. In fact, Deane almost provides an Irish version of Martin Wiener's English *Culture and the Decline of the Industrial Spirit 1850–1980*, in which ideas of chivalry and gentry throttle Irish market society.[62] But Carlyle was quite remote from this 'gentleman heresy', regarding landlords as 'a selfish, ferocious, famishing, unprincipled set of hyenas, from whom at no time and in no way has the country derived any benefit whatsoever'.[63] Carlyle was a hero to the Fenian John O'Leary, as he would be later (along with another Fenian, Michael Davitt) to the young David Lloyd George. He appealed to both because he demanded liberation from landlordism as well as from conventional religion.[64]

He could also be interpreted favourably by Catholic-tending Churchmen. Newman at one time 'hoped he might have come round right' and regretted he 'settled the wrong way'.[65] And he would later appeal more directly to Irish Catholics through the neo-medievalism of Abbot Samson of Bury St Edmunds in *Past and Present* (1843). Mitchel, the most Carlyleian of nationalists, was Protestant, but Gavan Duffy, reared in an environment almost as Scottish as Ecclefechan, became a central supporter of Cullen's 'devotional revolution', while remaining a continuing Irish friend.[66] Carlyle was directly influential on the Catholic fiction of Father Patrick Sheehan, and close reading of sermons and clerical memoirs (a forbidding enterprise) would detect consistent echoes, as in Don Byrne's 1930s' memoir of Maynooth:

> To see the oak stalls in the College Chapel, darkening a little with the years, is to think of all who have been students there, before my time and since. With no effort I can slip from the moorings of Past and Present, and see in this moment all rolled in one. The slowly-moving line of priests down through the Chapel is never-ending; it goes into the four provinces of Ireland; it crosses the seas into England and Scotland, and the greater seas into the Americas and Australia and Africa and China; it covers the whole earth ...[67]

Whatever this is, it is not Burkeian conservative. Indeed, in *The French Revolution* there is but one reference to Burke, intriguingly framed:

> Great Burke has raised his great voice long ago; eloquently demonstrating that the end of an Epoch has come, to all appearance the end of Civilised Time. Him many answer: Camille Desmoulins, Clootz Speaker of Mankind, Paine the rebellious Needleman, and honourable Gaelic Vindicators in that country and in this: but the great Burke remains unanswerable; 'the Age of Chivalry is gone,' and could not but go, having now produced the still more indomitable Age of Hunger. Altars enough, of the Dubois–Rohan sort, changing to the Gobel-and-Talleyrand sort, are faring by rapid transmutations to – shall we say, the right Proprietor of them? French Game and French Game-Preservers did alight on the Cliffs of Dover, with cries of distress. Who will say that the end of much is not come?[68]

Forget the plumage, in other words: wise up to the resilience of landlords and great houses. The message is hammered home in the closing pages, where the heart of Carlyle's matter stops being France and becomes the Irish peasant:

> But what if History somewhere on this Planet were to hear of a Nation, the third soul of whom had not, for thirty weeks each year, as many third-rate potatoes as would sustain him? History, in that case, feels bound to consider that starvation is starvation; that starvation from age to age presupposes much; History ventures to assert that the French Sansculotte of Ninety-three, who, roused from long death-sleep, could rush at once to the frontiers, and die fighting for an immortal Hope and Faith of Deliverance for him and his, was but the second-miserablest of men! The Irish Sans-Potato, had he not senses

then, nay a soul? In his frozen darkness, it was bitter for him to die
famishing; bitter to see his children famish. It was bitter for him to be
a beggar, a liar and a knave. Nay, if that dreary Greenland-wind of
benighted Want, perennial from sire to son, had frozen him into a
kind of torpor and numb callosity, so that he saw not, felt not, – was
this, for a creature with a soul in it, some assuagement or the cruellest
wretchedness of all?[69]

Carlyle found the Jacobins and their *Zeitbruch* unavoidable. The revolution had killed the past stone dead. Burke may have created English
Toryism, but Ireland became European – and as such, potentially
menaced by Jacobinism.

For all his Anglo-Saxonism, Carlyle implied that the simultaneous
crises of Church and people favoured the former. Not only does *Past and
Present* confront the cash nexus with medieval Catholicism, but its
climax is an extraordinary passage in which the fate of the papacy is literally combined with Carlyle's theme of the menace of mechanisation.
Carlyle describes how Pope Gregory XVI, being elderly, was made into
'an automaton':

> The old Pope of Rome, finding it laborious to kneel so long while they
> cart him through the streets to bless the people on Corpus Christi day,
> complains of rheumatism; whereupon his cardinals consult; –
> construct him, after some study, a stuffed, cloaked figure, of iron and
> wood, with wool or baked hair; and place it in a kneeling posture.
> Stuffed figure, or rump of a figure; to this stuffed rump he, sitting at
> his ease on a lower level, joins, by the aid of cloaks and drapery, his
> living head and outspread hands; the rump with its cloaks kneels, the
> Pope looks, and holds his hands spread; and so the two in concert bless
> the Roman population on Corpus Christi day, as well as they can.[70]

This may suggest Carlyle at his most Luther-like, but he counters this by
citing the heroism of Jesuits battling cholera, and claims that the situation
of the puppet-Pope is that of post-revolutionary Europe:

> This poor Pope, – who knows what is good in him? In a time other-
> wise prone to forget, he keeps up the mournfulest ghastly memorial
> of the Highest, Blessedest, which once was; which, in new forms,
> will have to be again.[71]

> ... He will ask you, What other? Under this my Gregorian chant, and
> beautiful wax-light Phantasmagory, kindly hidden from you is an
> Abyss of Black Doubt, Scepticism, nay Sansculottic Jacobinism; an
> Orcus that has no bottom. Think of that.[72]

With this Carlyle combined his machine metaphor with his fundamental
pessimism about what the fusion of technology, market society and

wealth would imply. In a world in which the 'Steamengine' was 'changing his shape like a very Proteus; and infallibly, at every change of shape, oversetting whole multitudes of workmen ...,'[73] the nation became a flawed, demagogy-prone instrument. Carlyle's collegiate alternative was confounded, however, by the railway mania-driven recovery, and his worked-out remedies in *Latter-Day Pamphlets* were scorned. By 1851 his radicalism was waning as fast as his Irish interests, after their brief kindling in 1849, and he turned back to his study and to the authoritarian enlightenment in the shape of Frederick the Great.[74]

The ultramontane opportunity

Yet Irish Catholicism was able to respond to this challenge. Under Cullen it effectively moved towards the sort of theocratic politics from which Carlyle's own Scotland exited in 1843, after the split in the Kirk destroyed its educational and poor-relief role. But there was a crucial difference. After 1848 the days of the pope as a secular ruler were numbered. He had to change from would-be Italian unifier to benevolent religious despot. After famine and diaspora, the 1851 'Papal aggression' agitation, disputes over Italian unification and the Garibaldi riots of 1864, the Irish found in ultramontanism a form of semi-independent identity.

Rome, on the other hand, faced with anti-clerical regimes in Germany and France, instability in Iberia, and clerical subordination in Austria, recognised in Ireland a key investment for the future.[75] Its bishops were a tenth of the Vatican Council of 1869, but because of their American and imperial connections – by 1910 every seventh Canadian, every fifth Australian was Catholic – Ireland grew in importance within the Catholic world, even winning the praise of Froude:

> Roman Catholicism, which grew sick and stagnant in power and prosperity, has in Ireland been braced in vigour by calamity. Like the myth Monster, it has been in contact with the hard soil of fact, and has gathered fresh life from it.[76]

We are now sceptical of the link between modernisation and secularisation. Irish Catholicism did not decline, any more than Presbyterianism did in Scotland. Instead it thrust the 'devotional revolution' into the 'industrial revolution'.[77] The Synod of Thurles in 1852 started to remake a shattered country into an exclusivist yet 'modernising' society comparable to, but more centralised than, rural, Presbyterian Scotland. If Cullen was not a 'captain of industry' he could actually behave more like Carlyle's ideal of one, as could a military commander like Moltke or an authoritarian statesman like Bismarck, while Lancashire millowners were

fatally subject to market forces. Not only were Church and army similarly
authoritarian, but both reacted to Carlyle's 'Abyss of Black Doubt,
Scepticism, nay Sansculottic Jacobinism' with their own, market-insu-
lated, conservative mechanisms.

Cullen, though Anglophobe, was liberal in comparison with the
Vatican; he won over the most formidable rebel from the English clerisy
– John Henry Newman – and although the Catholic University was a
misfire, Newman's own brand of liberalism scorched Anglican muscular
Christianity in the 1860s. Cullen also echoed Carlyle on Empire, emigration, and 'the organisation of labour'. The spirit of Abbot Sampson
seemed present in the Jacobin management of the Christian Brothers' and
Jesuit Colleges, which resembled a regiment, or a ship and its crew, with
authority uncontested.[78] Such Foucaultian 'total' institutions dominated
the industrial society of the 'second' or 'transport-oriented' phase of
industrialisation; in which collegiate forms of control organised workers'
lives *outside* small houses, school, in male workplaces, male pubs and
male sports. In a civic order corporate rather than democratic, English
'establishments' – themselves residues of older electoral hegemonies –
were confronted by local hierarchies who reinforced parish organisations
with the Ancient Order of Hibernians or the St Vincent de Paul Society,
Glasgow Celtic Football Club or the Gaelic Athletic Association.[79]

The 'devotional revolution', with its stress on ceremonial, parochial
organisation and missionary self-sacrifice, furthered the 'capitalist'
virtues of centralisation, promotion by merit, 'mission statements',
education, building investment (overwhelmingly in 'English gothic'
churches) and attention to the consumer qua parishioner. This was
coupled with the 'fire and strength' of missionary effort, *particularly* in
the Empire, where the hierarchies were of Irish origin.[80] Catholicism
could outbid the Protestants on heroism and sacrifice, though sometimes
making common cause. Lee writes that Cullen

> constantly objected to conventional official calumnies concerning the
> nature of poverty, censuring the managers of the Poor Law who 'treat
> poverty as a crime to be dealt with more severely than murder'.[81]

The salience of the 'welfare mission' may help to explain something
common to Britain and Ireland: the absence of radical anticlericalism.
The Church aligned itself with two other post-Carlyleians: Mill, who
stressed distribution as the keynote for the next phase of political
economy, and T. H. Green, whose 'Liberal Legislation and Freedom of
Contract' lecture of 1881 gave a philosophic rationale not only for the
Irish Land Act but for the later Anglo-Catholic *Lux Mundi* movement.[82]
The Gladstonian 'Union of Hearts' gained the sort of resilience that over-
came the vicious but overdriven Unionist assault on Home Rule.[83]

In fact, the Home Rule division within Protestantism allowed a British Catholic 'heroism' to emerge, evident in Cardinal Manning's mediation on the London dock strike in 1889, Robert Louis Stevenson's *Father Damien* tract in 1890 and the obsequies for Newman and Manning in 1890 and 1892. That the monumental *Cambridge Modern History* was trusted to a Catholic Home Ruler in 1895, though Lord Acton was neither Irish nor orthodox, was as significant as Edward Elgar's inauguration of the English musical renaissance in 1899 with his setting of Newman's *The Dream of Gerontius* – or for that matter Conan Doyle's Sherlock Holmes personification of the detective as patriot. Protestant prejudice became passé in England, ironically, just when clericalism provoked the 'revolt of the intellectuals' in France, during the Dreyfus Affair. Yet by 1906 anti-Dreyfusard Catholics like Belloc and Chesterton were taken as paracletes for 'the people of England, who have not spoken yet'. By 1914 a crusade could be mounted against Prussianism (unquestionably Protestant) on behalf of Catholic Belgium, and even in one sensitive region Tom Devine writes that 'any doubts about the loyalty of the Irish in Scotland to the British State were conclusively removed'.[84]

Where were the hero-sisters?

But if this reconciliation left Protestant Ulster to one side, with an identity created by fear of 'the other', the society of Catholic Ireland still had a quality remote from that of other UK provinces: the exaggerated absence from its debates of the womenfolk of the majority religion. Catholic Irishwomen were either subordinate or symbolic in such a way that they presented few parallels with an increasingly feminised mainland politics. Here, too, the Carlyleian shadow lay long. On the mainland women had been indirect beneficiaries of the 'heroic' in the theoretical or practical instances of George Eliot or Florence Nightingale. An early history of the suffrage movement like Ray Strachey's *The Cause* (1928) is typical in its personalisation of political action. But Irish Catholic women were not just non-political but, until the 1960s, almost unknown to history.

Carlyle's advancement of symbol over system, much criticised by contemporaries, was particularly pronounced when he handled gender.[85] While the masterpiece of his own hero, Goethe's *Faust*, ends with the ringing line, 'Das ewig Weibliche zieht uns hinan'. (The eternal female leads us on) – and woman in *Faust* is flesh and blood, Eros as well as Agape – the Carlyleian woman is as abstract as her Catholic sister. The only female to appear in the whole of *Past and Present* is Irish and crucial: the widow who, denied alms in Edinburgh, succumbs to exhaustion and typhus, infecting and so killing another seventeen people:

> Nothing is left but that she prove her sisterhood by dying, and infecting you with typhus. Seventeen of you lying dead will not deny such proof that she was flesh of your flesh; and perhaps some of the living may lay it to heart.[86]

The Irish widow negates materialism, just as the Irish peasant of *The French Revolution* negates Burke. Yeats may have followed Burke in transmuting Marie Antoinette into the anti-modern symbol of Cathleen ni Houlihan, but Carlyle's juxtaposition is both more brutal and more ambiguous.

Protesting against their designation as drudges, pampered but constrained passengers, or remittance-collectors, Englishwomen took up social work or literary protest.[87] In *fin de siècle* continental nationalism, feminism identified with social democracy. This was intensified in the British seaboard cities, where women took leading roles in voluntary and educational organisations. The educationalist Blanche Clough and the welfare campaigner Eleanor Rathbone were both from Liverpool, the Potter sisters were Lancashire, the Pankhursts' Women's Social and Political Union was born in Manchester. But in Ireland until the Gaelic revival Catholic women were either silenced, made into reifying images of the Madonna or Cathleen ni Houlihan, or were completely overshadowed by rebellious Protestant sisters.[88]

What had disappeared was sex. Carlyle's last, unpublishable, *Latter-Day Pamphlet* was 'The Phallus and the Money-Bag', an attack on the moral decadence of utilitarianism and the sensuality of such as George Sand, the title of which has a visual symbolism which would have intrigued Freud.[89] Carlyle had already painted a far different Marie Antoinette from Burke's – 'within the royal tapestries, in bright boudoirs, baths, peignoirs, and the Grand and Little Toilette': exquisite, erotic, parasitic.[90] Her ineptness compromises the throne in the 'Diamond Necklace' affair; her image might, intriguingly, be that of Boucher's toothsome Miss O'Murphy.[91] Sublimating the latter – and Limerick's Lola Montez (the only woman who caused a revolution in 1848 (in Munich) albeit a conservative clericalist one) – ensured that the salience of Carlyleian-Catholic women would be slight. They appear seldom even in recent histories of Ireland, the Irish abroad, and the Catholic Church itself. In imaginative writing they are passive in Boucicault or Trollope; even Shaw failed to create a female lead in *John Bull's Other Island*, flawing perhaps his most serious play. Joyce's female *Dubliners* are uniformly frustrated; Molly Bloom was as unhelpful a role model as Somerville and Ross's psychopathic Charlotte Mullen; while O'Casey's heroines – who *are* the power-and-feelings people of his plays – all end as tragic.

The clergy had decided that Catholic female destiny was vocation, home-making and, a poor third, career: something reinforced by an institutional religion which (substituting gender for *ethnie*) oddly paralleled Irish subordination to Britain. Despite population decline, the number of nuns rose from 120 in 1800 to 1,500 in 1851 and 8,000 in 1901.[92] 'Convents are really small, self-contained totalitarian states where life is lived according to a rigid schedule', the writer Mary Colum remembered, while Katherine Tynan found an archaic but cultivated existence.[93] Such *Past and Present*-like examples advertised celibacy to the wives, widows and daughters who sustained their (ageing) husbands, sons and brothers: a difficult burden to shift.[94]

The feminist reaction, in the shape of Lady Gregory, Edith Somerville and Martin Ross, Alice Stopford Green, and on the far fringe Maude Gonne and the Gore-Booth sisters, was firmly post-Protestant. Authoritarian male dominance produced several important female rebellions. One of the greatest Mazzinian novels, with a European reputation, in which nationalism is seen as the road out of Catholic tyranny, was *The Gadfly* (1892) by Ethel Voynich, the daughter of the Cork mathematician George Boole. A similar stance was taken in the Trollopian novels of Mary Laffan Hartley, a convert to Protestantism.

In part this isolation was because Catholicism grafted class constraints on to its own authoritarianism. Irish nuns found themselves subject to the English class system and ended as lay sisters rather than choir nuns.[95] It was the 1960s – Edna O'Brien's era – before the others escaped, and thereafter tales emerged – of the Laundries, or the orphanages run by the Poor Sisters of Nazareth – whose horrors almost outbid *Maria Monk*.[96] As Carlyle would say, think about that.

A hybrid intelligentsia?

Infallibility and Immaculate Conception – in rapid development between the visions at Lourdes (1858) and Knock (1879) – impelled the dogmas of the post-1848 Church while, with collapsing agricultural prices, the political dynamism induced by the land issue per se was in retreat. So, while the post-1870 agitation revived anti-landlordism of a very Carlyleian sort (his venom against them is totally lacking, for instance, in a Fenian like Charles Kickham) it also gave the priests an organisational role, while they in turn fetishised quasi-religious symbols of the nation.

Irish agriculture 'modernised' better than post-high-farming Britain, though less effectively than Denmark (which had also gone through a clerical-modernising process under Bishop Nicholas Grundtvig, 1783–1872).[97] Yeats's 'dream of the noble and the beggar-man' – and the nationalism of ascendancy types from Yeats and Douglas Hyde to Maude Gonne and Constance Markiewicz – was an Irish variation on the power of the 'traditional intelligentsia' which in its British form puzzled Gramsci.[98] But it did little for manufacturing, depressed after the 1870s, and dependent on strong farmers, auctioneers and the clergy as well as British demand. In *John Bull's Other Island* the bullying Father Dempsey backs the Englishman Broadbent; operating his religious machine, he would have been quite at home in the France of Balzac or Stendhal.[99]

With 25 per cent of the national intelligentsia in orders by 1925 (less than 10 per cent elsewhere in the archipelago) and 39 per cent by 1939, the Church laid its shadow across the country: semi-imperial and stiflingly conservative. Contrast George Boyce on the Cullenite Church – 'the fixed point of nationalist identity in a changing world, and indeed the guardian of a complete, satisfying and noble faith' – and Joe Lee on its later career:

> Rarely has the Catholic Church as an institution flourished, by mate-
> rial criteria, in the Free State. And rarely has it contributed so little,
> as an institution, to the finer qualities of the Christian spirit.'[100]

Shaw and most 'modernisers' argued that Ireland could only escape this stasis if it included Ulster, where a Scottish enlightenment-inspired 'Drennanite' liberalism, like that of the 1790s, could be revived, just as Arthur Griffith saw a Belfast-built Irish merchant marine as a unifier along with his dual monarchy. Shaw assured the Protestants that they would soon run the whole show and, given Lord Pirrie's support for Home Rule and the 'reformed' Unionist episode of 1906–10, this was not utterly forlorn.[101] But it was damaged by the extremism of the Tory party in 1910–14 and destroyed by its co-option into the wartime coalition. Subsequently, partition meant that the twenty-six counties stayed a conservative component of the UK economy, with an agrarian economy and clerical control. A depressed Ulster economy no longer attracted, while Free State industrialisation was unable to take off, despite the Ardnacrusha power scheme in the 1920s or de Valera's 'industrialisation through protection' after 1932.[102] Only the Whitaker Report of 1958 – two years after Suez, one year after the Treaty of Rome (but patently conscious of both) – broke the spell.[103]

If we think of the Condition of Ireland in the nineteenth century being framed by two concentric 'worlds' – the Irish sea, encircled by the Atlantic – Catholic nationalism fits into a new context. As focus for a people who became more complex and multifarious as they expanded – perforce – into new environments, nationalism was confronted by the symbol of the 'machine'. This was both Ireland's 'eternal nay' and an effective metaphor for the ganglions of the diaspora. In the larger world their own technical machine failed: the catastrophe of the 1840s meant that Irish industry never went from experiment to process, except in the Hong Kong-like Lagan Valley. But Irish human resources – and the 'bitter wisdom' derived from the country's experience – helped others to succeed. The Irish political machine triumphed in America and contributed notably to the British Labour Party. The great success of the 1924 Labour government was Monaghan-born John Wheatley as Minister of Health and his creation of state housing policy, while Robert Tressell's *The Ragged Trousered Philanthropists*, which 'won the 1945 election for Labour', would provide an icon for activists often from an Irish background whose loyalty to Moscow often paralleled the way the religious machine had buttressed the ultramontane papacy.[104] It was a Carlyleian outcome: the 'mechanical age' transfixed the Irish, while the Catholic nation became an insistent but ever-changing *fata Morgana*. Offering a means not just of catching up but of unifying these experiences, it hovered until the 1960s in one shape or another – enticingly, but always out of reach – before the Irish people.

8

Remembering and forgetting: The French Revolution and the baptism of Clovis

MALCOLM ANDERSON

Parallels may be drawn between the commemoration of 1998 and the great celebrations in France of the Revolution and Clovis because all raise questions about founding myths of the modern nation. The French example is also a fertile source of reflections about the significance of commemorating and how this activity evolves in changing political and social circumstances. In addition, there is a French dimension to '98 because the Revolution was one of the factors behind the uprising and the French attempted a military intervention in Ireland to support the rebellion and use it to their own advantage. These general parallels form a background to this chapter, the main focus of which, however, is what these commemorations signified within France.

French people now live in an age of commemorations. In the last two decades of the twentieth century, one commemoration followed another. To take as an example the last five years of the 1980s, there was the 300th anniversary of the revocation of the Edict of Nantes (1985), the fiftieth anniversary of the Popular Front (1986), the millennium of the installation of the Capetian dynasty, the twentieth anniversary of May 1968, the bicentenary of the French Revolution, the centenary of the birth of General de Gaulle (1990), and the fiftieth anniversary of the appeal of 18 June 1940. In the 1990s, the series continued with the 1500th celebration of the baptism of Clovis (1996), celebrated like the reign of Hugues Capet as the birth of the French nation, and the 400th anniversary of the promulgation of the Edict of Nantes (1998). These are only the most important because the number of commemorations, above all of writers, painters, musicians, artists, every year is now a major activity, supported by a service in the Ministry of Culture for national celebrations and by a national association for these celebrations. This chapter seeks to identify some of the major aspects of these two commemorations and poses the question – what does all this commemoration mean?

The scale of the commemorations

The commemorations of the Revolution and Clovis were on a different scale. The former, in 1989, was *the* commemoration of the end of the twentieth century, carrying an inspirational yet burdensome historical legacy. It was a year-long event, the high point of which was a spectacular parade on 14 July imagined by adman-designer-artist Jean-Paul Goude. This national day coincided with a G7 meeting in Paris (badly viewed by some as symbolising the *aristos* of the north against the *sans culottes* of the south), which was attended by thirty-three heads of state or government. The commemoration attracted wide international attention, including some tart remarks from Margaret Thatcher and sarcasm in the British press, always alert to an opportunity to provoke Anglo-French discord. It took three presidents of the bicentennial Mission to complete the preparations for it (two of whom – Michel Baroin and Edgar Faure – died before it happened; the third was Jean-Noël Jeanneney).

Celebrations of the Revolution took place all over France; all political parties, social movements, trades unions and newspapers had views about it.[1] By contrast, the commemoration of the baptism of Clovis was a much less extravagant affair. Although it had official patronage and a relatively generous budget, there was only one spectacular occasion associated with it (the visit of the pope) and it did not engage the government and political parties in the same way. The baptism was not regarded as a world historical event and, indeed, the world outside France took very little notice of it. But this commemoration also divided the French, sometimes bitterly. The two commemorations were part of a lengthy self-interrogation of national identity in France.

Historiography of the events commemorated

Both commemorations encouraged scholarly activity. That of Clovis was on a more modest scale for a variety of reasons. The activity preceding and during the bicentenary of the Revolution was very intensive. Hundreds of historians gathered in Paris for a conference in July 1989 on the theme of The Image of the Revolution,[2] which among other things noted the flourishing of research and scholarly publication. This was subsequently surveyed in a volume under the direction of Michel Vovelle and edited by Antoine de Baecque.[3] Historical work was commissioned on the bicentennial itself, concentrated in the *Institut d'histoire du temps présent*, with large numbers of graduate students producing specialised monographs. The archives of the Mission[4] and other administrations were placed at its disposal. The ambition is to produce a detailed history of the context of the bicentenary and to use the bicentennial moment to analyse the problems of end of twentieth-century France.

In this they were following the lead of Jean-Noël Jeanneney in his report to the President of the Republic when the commemoration was over:

> Without over-emphasising the mirror effect, it cannot be doubted that the way in which the bicentenary was prepared and the way in which it unfolded will give precious insight in future to the state of French society, politics and culture at the end of the 20th century.[5]

But those who defended the revolutionary tradition did not have a particularly comfortable bicentenary partly because of the efforts of the distinguished revisionist historian, François Furet, who commanded wide public attention. He was backed by a more rumbustious performance from Pierre Chaunu, a historian of the golden age of Spain and a Protestant. The latter wrote a polemic to coincide with the commemoration, 'Le grand déclassement', in which he argued that the Revolution brought death and destruction to the neighbours of France.[6] He further argued that the Revolution retarded the development of the country towards a modern society and one which could have out distanced England. Instead the Revolution resulted in inflation, a return to a subsistence economy, the growth of illiteracy, an atrocious religious persecution, massacres, particularly in the Vendée, and a war of aggression resulting in losses comparatively greater than those of the First World War. These themes, produced by a historian who proclaimed attachment to Republican values, were close to the counter-revolutionary critiques of right-wing Catholics, some Gaullists, particularly Phillipe de Villiers, the leader of the National Front, Jean-Marie Le Pen, and sundry proto-fascists.

A range of books was produced for the commemoration of the baptism of Clovis[7] but virtually no serious works of scholarship despite the presence of distinguished historians on the official organising committee – Hélène Carrère d'Encausse, Pierre Chaunu, Georges Duby, François Furet, Jacques Le Goff. Laurent Theis produced an informative work showing the paucity of contemporary sources about Clovis, what Gregory of Tours had said about him, and how later chroniclers had embellished the story.[8] Chaunu published another book[9] which was a long interview given to a young colleague and which gave credence to the myth of Clovis as the founder of France because, unlike Charlemagne,

Clovis belonged to France alone and this myth was at the centre of French exceptionalism, defined as precocious national identity, a sacralised monarchy, a Church with a high degree of independence of the papacy, which eventually resulted in the passage from a Gallican Church to a secular state. Above all, Chaunu defended the dubious continuity of French history over a millennium and a half in a curious mixture of erudition, intuition, convictions and provocations.

Couteaux saw the contemporary significance of Clovis in these terms:[10] the baptism at Reims was the foundation of legitimate political authority in France; the broken vase of Soissons (which Clovis intended to return to the Church) was the abandonment of the spoils system and the foundation of the State as guarantor of justice: the victory of Tolbiac against the Alamans marked the invention of the nation as the alternative to, and the enemy, of empires; the affirmation of the monarchy as independent of religion was the beginning of the independence of the secular power; France was born by the choice of Paris as capital; and Clovis marked the beginnings of the idea of sovereignty. This is what Lévi-Strauss in *La pensée sauvage* called 'histoire mythique'[11] By this he meant the stubborn fidelity to a past conceived as an intemporal model, expressing a commitment to values adopted consciously or unconsciously. The relevance of the model to the contemporary world is assumed to be proven – the ancestors have taught us eternal truths. Mythical history is paradoxically connected and disconnected to the present; disconnected because the ancestors had a different nature to ourselves; connected because since the time of the ancestors nothing fundamental has changed.

This kind of mythical history called forth a spirited response to the effect that it was all nonsense. Pierre Bergé called Clovis a kinglet, without much significance who was a sinister character, murderer of members of his family and his rivals, a pillager, traitorous and incestuous, and whose date of baptism was quite uncertain.[12] Supporters of the commemoration, according to this view, were engaged in a re-reading of history which represented a spurious attempt to gather the whole nation in a sort of communion around an event which was of interest to only one of the great religions practised in France. The vast majority who supported the separation of the churches and the state; this separation was compromised because the Catholic hierarchy was officially associated with it and subsidised religious ceremonies.

Notable characteristics of the commemorations

There was the preliminary debate between those who opposed the commemorations as such (or the form that they might take) and those who thought that commemorating sustained a collective memory, essential for a healthy and cohesive society. The former thought that commemorating the Revolution was an enormous waste of money, and the latter that insufficient resources were being devoted to it. What particularly annoyed those who opposed the whole business of commemoration was what Chaunu called 'managed memory'[13] – the manipulation for political purposes of remembering and forgetting. This position attracted strange bedfellows – the Communists who feared that a centrist celebration would omit the struggle for social justice culminating in Year II, some Catholics and conservatives who wanted the whole truth in order to highlight the violence, intolerance and persecution by the Revolutionaries. Both wanted to use the famous aphorism of Clemenceau 'the Revolution is a bloc', so that they could either claim the heritage for themselves alone, as the Communists attempted, or argue for the rejection of the revolutionary heritage in its entirety (in the words of Léon Daudet for the 150th anniversary, 'the Revolution is a bloc – a bloc of garbage').[14]

Others wanted 'to go shopping', and celebrate acceptable parts of the Revolution – this was true of the Catholic hierarchy, the right-wing government and most of the moderate press. In this way, it was hoped, everyone could have something to celebrate. This was condemned on the right and the left as intellectually dishonest and a spurious quest for consensus. The centrists wondered aloud why some regarded consensus as loathsome and dishonest. Yet it was not the moderate centre which dominated the debate but, in the run up to the commemoration, the counter-revolutionary right. Unexpected events, however, helped to deflect this hostility. During 1989, the momentum of the commemoration owed a good deal to Tiananmen Square and the fall of the Berlin Wall.

The movement of rejection of the legacy of the Revolution had seemed so strong in 1987 (added to continuous criticisms of the arrangements – worshipping the golden calf of the media, extravagance, lack of direction, consensual mush, etc.), after the return of the right to power, that it seemed that the commemoration would be seriously compromised. This rejection was helped by Chaunu and Furet, and by the discredit of Soviet Communism (seen by many on the left as completing the revolution of 1989). It was also helped by a revulsion against political violence – a profound ideological change, according to Alfred Grosser:

> Not long ago, the Terror, symbolised by the guillotine, was explained, excused and even glorified. What would a revolution be that was not bloody, moderates are necessarily latent counter-revolutionaries.[15]

In 1989 bloodshed was a mark of horror and failure. This helped the counter revolutionaries. Phillipe de Villiers mounted a campaign over the 'populicide' of the Vendée, equating Jacobins with the perpetrators of the Holocaust and the Gulag.

The official Church did not join the counter-revolutionary camp but succeeded in alienating virtually everyone with its views about the commemoration. The bishops in 1989 invited Catholics to associate themselves with the commemoration and join in – a reversal of 1889 when the bishops anathematised the Revolution and regarded it as a satanic incarnation. But the bishops would only associate themselves with the commemoration of the Revolution in highly selective and some-what detached ways. Jeanneney, the president of the Mission for the Bicentenary, bullied the bishops in the hope that their participation in the commemoration would complete the reconciliation of the 'two Frances' begun a century previously with the *Ralliement* of the Church to the Republic. The Catholic right was outraged that the bishops could even contemplate drawing a line under the crimes of the Revolution and waxed indignant about the hierarchy's hesitations and reticences. The bishops were in a no win situation and pleased no one.

There was still a chasm between the pro-Revolutionaries and anti-Revolutionaries, but there were also splits within the pro-Revolutionary camp. Some in government and in the press saw these divisions as poten-tially dangerous because the commemoration could revive old battles and re-awaken old passions. A commemoration, in the minds of the official sponsors was supposed to enhance the sense of national unity not to revive a latent civil war. The official celebrations 'toned down' the Revolution by a muted consensual style, preference for Danton over Robespierre, liberty over equality, prominence to the army and to the peoples of the former colonial empire, and focused strongly on the Declaration of the Rights of Man.

On the latter, *Nouvel Observateur* (13–19 July 1989) commented:

> [T]he rights of man has become the choice morsel of the Revolution, the prime piece of the roast – everyone takes seconds of the Rights of Man. Who is against the Rights of Man? Dogs perhaps. In any case, not men. Dictators are almost always in favour of them but have their own conception of them. 115 per cent of advertising executives, 300 per cent of show biz people support them.

This was not entirely true: Le Pen denounced the declaration of the Rights of Man as carrying the germ of totalitarianism – the revolutionary new man led directly to Hitler and Pol Pot. Furet was ironic about the Left having only recently re-discovered the prime importance of the Rights of Man.

The universalism of the human rights theme, however, flattered French pride and served French interests. It irritated Mrs Thatcher who told the French press that

> human rights did not begin with the French Revolution. They go back to the Judaeo-Christian tradition … then came the magna carta of 1215, and the declaration of rights of the 17th century, and our tranquil revolution of 1688 … incidentally we celebrated this event last year but much more discreetly.[16]

She gained very little French sympathy, although Jean François Revel said she did not choose her moment very well but she was, first of all, right – Voltaire wrote the English Letters, not Hume and Locke who wrote the French letters and, second, there were extenuating circumstances – 'for months we have been battering the whole world to death with our claims that France and only France brought liberty to the world'.[17] Jean-Noël Jeanneney and President Mitterrand, in fact, recognised the English contribution.

Political reactions

The commemoration posed difficulties for all political parties because they, with the exception of the Communist Party, were equivocal about the revolutionary heritage. A large part of the Right could no longer execrate the revolution and all its works, because the great majority of its electorate was firmly Republican (Chirac's neo-Gaullist party had adopted the headgear, the Phrygian hat, of the *sans culottes* as its logo), and the Catholic Church had rallied to the Republic a century ago. The Left was equally uncomfortable with the Marxist–Leninist interpretation of the Revolution which had dominated, for the best part of a century; the standard interpretation from the Sorbonne's Institut de l'Histoire de la Révolution Française was no longer acceptable.

For the largest party of the left, the Socialist Party, the commemoration was difficult. The Socialists came to power in 1981 armed with a rhetoric mainly derived from the Revolution – a new taking of the Bastille, rupture with capitalism, émigrés of Koblenz (businessmen who exported their capital), and so on. They became more reticent about Revolutionary references as they learned how difficult it was to govern a modern society whilst espousing the rhetoric of a radical break with capitalism and with the monarch of the *ancien régime* – Giscard d'Estaing. Insecurities about the Revolution were acute among the Socialists because they had needed the idea of unfinished business of the Revolution for self-identity. But this, of necessity, faded in the 1980s.

Reform not revolution became the motto although the left wing of the party continued to hope that it was otherwise. At the beginning of 1989 Michel Charzat on the left of the party returned to the old theme – 'The Left accepts the Revolution *en bloc*. Therefore what distinguishes the left from the right is that the left accepts all the revolution and in particular 1793'.[18] This was evidently not the case, and the range of opinion in the Socialist Party went as far as agreeing with the moderate right that there were aspects of the Revolution which were not admirable. The party tried to submerge the differences in innocuous activities such as planting liberty trees and setting up 'Vive la liberté' committees.

Communists were not in power and were suffering a dramatic decline in electoral support. There was consensus in the party on a passionate commitment to the revolutionary origins of the Republic. Communists saw the commemoration as a good opportunity to mark their difference from the Socialists, by claiming to be the only legitimate guardians of the revolutionary tradition. However, the PCF had become more moderate. In the run up to the 150th anniversary, the party had invited the nation to undertake a new Revolution – an invitation not renewed for the 200th anniversary. Nonetheless, it remained sectarian, claiming that socialist backsliding went as far as to minimise the class element in 1789, which was a betrayal of the masses and a sign of tepidness. They flaunted the terror and went out of their way to spoil 'Mitterrand's celebration'. They claimed (again) that there was a new social crisis and that, in the name of the Revolution, France had to resist integration in the new Europe.

The mainstream right – RPR and UDF – had no coherent strategy, and left it up to individuals how they commemorated; some identified with the nationalist/patriotic and statist/centralist aspect of the Revolution, others excoriated the millions of deaths, lasting hatreds, economic catastrophe and so on. All accused the socialists of hijacking the commemoration. Alain Juppé, then the rising star of the neo-Gaullists, said yes to 1789 ('we are its true heirs') but he and most neo-Gaullists were pessimists of the Revolution.[19] Chirac was ambiguous, supporting the commemoration when in office but, after losing the 1988 elections and returning to the Paris town hall, he became hostile (eventually boycotting the 14 July celebrations, which was widely regarded as a political mistake, and he was vilified for desertion, emigration, and myopia).

The far right had a number of themes. For Le Club de l'Horloge, the Revolution sealed the indivisibility of the nation and created equal rights but the socialists had fractured the nation. This was close to the populist line of Le Pen – accepting the Revolution without enthusiasm as a catalyst of national unity and as a very modest part in a long national history. In a rumbustious article in *Le Figaro* (27 December 1988), he called for a new revolution ('the priests of 1789 have become the merchants of the

Temple'). Discredit of politicians and financial scandals served the interests of the FN very well.

The ceremonial

The celebrations culminated in the 14 July parade which took the form of
the usual military parade but with more women, more helicopters. Some
happenings – outside La Santé leftists demonstrated in favour of the
Action Directe hunger strikers (extreme left-wingers jailed for murder)
chanting, 'Let's not celebrate, let's make a revolution' – more amusingly,
demonstrators against the government's lack of support to creative arts
threw 600 decapitated heads, with strikingly impressive expressions, in
the Seine.
    In the evening there was a remarkable carnival consisting of:

* Italians with painted yellow faces with a display of flag manipulation;
* Chinese students with masks to hide their identity marching to the
  single beat of an enormous drum;
* 300 professional drummers wearing the tricolour sash of the French
  mayors, followed by 1,500 amateur drummers from every part of
  France;
* Mixed corps of more than 1,000 professional and amateur musicians
  from all regions of France and a ballet of some thirty members;
* Jessey Norman, black American opera singer, sang the 'Marseillaise'
  with great verve and emotion to a backdrop of an immense wall of
  water;
* Float of a Senegalese musician Doudou N'Diaye Rose with a vast staircase – surrounded by 292 torchbearers in colonial outfit – top of float
  six African women percussionists in flowing African garb;
* Britain's royal tattoo, British firemen and 150 dancers representing
  London's ethnic mix;
* Soviet troop – thick flow of confetti, plastic ice rink, music linking
  Russia's past to the Soviet future;
* African float – a great Pyramid of 91 Guinean percussionists, ringed by
  about 400 Africans impersonating Senegalese soldiers – bare-breasted
  women drummers;
* More drummers on foot, descendants of railwaymen from Nevers, in
  front of a large locomotive with a Jean Gabin lookalike inspired by Jean
  Renoir's film of Emile Zola's *La Bête humaine*;
* 250 all black marching band from Florida A&M, some imitating
  Michael Jackson walking backwards and accompanied by blonde

cheerleaders and sundry fans, plus Chinese dancers performing a hip-hop dance;
• Spectacular fireworks.

Reactions were overwhelmingly favourable. There was a complete turn about of the previously more sober critics such as *Le Monde*, but the rampant Africanisation and the 'Marseillaise' sung by a black American offered the extreme right a target to attack. The extreme left also disapproved because it was a media event that evaded the realities of the Revolution.

Participation in the commemoration was broadly based – 7,500 events; 5,000 communes supported by 2000 associations; 27 per cent of the population attended, 7 per cent participated directly in organising or acting in an event. Right and left municipalities were active in equal proportions. A vast range of activities was organised; *bals populaires* were more numerous and enthusiastic than usual. Streets were renamed to commemorate the Revolution. In the end, the bicentenary was a popular success and succeeded in capturing the imagination of very large numbers of French people.

The contrast with the commemoration of the baptism of Clovis

The government nominated a national committee to commemorate 'The origins of the Nation: from Gaul to France' on 11 March 1996. This was late in the day. The committee included notable members of the French hierarchy including Mgr Lustiger, Cardinal Archbishop of Paris, the president of the Protestant federation of France, the Revd Jacques Stewart (although the Synod of the Reformed Church at Mazamet was very reserved about the ceremony), a range of distinguished historians mentioned above, but no one who could claim to be an authority on Clovis, and no Moslems. This commemoration could be seen, and was seen, as a response to the bicentenary of the Revolution, celebrating a long national history and a different set of values.

Very quickly committees formed to denounce this anniversary – 'Réseau Voltaire pour la Liberté d'Expression'; 'Clovis n'est pas la France'; 'Collectif d'individus contre la venue du Pape'. The Catholics, for their part, also organised an 'Association pour le Quinzième Centenaire de la France' and other committees to plan activities. Behind the hostile reactions, the memory of commemoration of 1896 was present. In 1896 the Church, having rallied to the Republic in 1892, was determined to show that it had not rallied to lay conceptions of political authority – political activity could only be justified by its conformity to divine will. The origins of France were, according to the almost universal Catholic view in those days, in the religious act of baptism which made France symbolically 'the eldest daughter of the Church', and the French nation was thenceforth essentially Catholic.

This version was bitterly contested by those who regarded the Revolution as the founding of modern France. But the Catholics who were in the forefront of the 1896 commemoration insisted on the apostasy of France, the deviation from its divine mission – the themes of hereditary identity, fidelity to a past transformed into a mythical history, disquiet about contemporary decadence, political rejection of the Republican ethos were all closely intertwined. They called on France to renew at Reims the baptismal promises made by ancient France, to renounce Satan and to swear a new fidelity to Christ – a position adopted even by a liberal Catholic such as Fernand Brunetierre. The Catholic religion was the guardian of French identity, and it was precisely this association that the opponents of the commemoration in 1996 feared and rejected.

This time, however, the Catholics were seriously divided. There were those who said, with the president of the bishops committee Justice and Liberty, that to wish to annex the identity of France is first an illusion and, second, is contrary to the teachings of the Church. Cardinal Lustiger also condemned the idea of a Christian nation as not a Christian concept. Not all Catholics (about 1/3 were against, according to an IPSOS opinion poll) were favourable to the visit of the pope for the celebration, on the grounds that this commemoration was at the place where religion and politics joined in the search for the mythical origins of the French nation; this ran the risk of excluding whole categories of the national community. Progressive Catholics said that they would not go to Reims, although they accepted the idea that Christianity had contributed something essential to French identity, because it officialised the idea of France as the eldest daughter of the Church and therefore the view that the Church had some sort of right over French society.[20] These voices were not strong enough to eclipse a Catholocentric view of French identity among Catholics.

The *Front National* tried to hijack the whole event, using the slogan, 'Clovis – Jeanne d'Arc – Le Pen même combat'. This was very much in line with the FN attempt to take over all the mythic figures of France – more or less successfully in the case of Jeanne d'Arc. The FN put the image of the baptism of Clovis on its membership card. During the whole of 1996 the FN organised meetings of 'amitiés françaises', the high points being the meeting at the Panthéon on 13 April and a torchlight procession to Reims Cathedral on 14 December. The director of cultural affairs of the FN said that the commemoration should make the French remember that 'the spiritual, intellectual, moral and also the biological substance of our country is disappearing' and a 'very effective religious, cultural and moral subversion has dechristianised the country, deformed history, destroyed its memory and annihilated its immune system'. 'Only a national and Christian resistance can save the situation'.[21] These were very much the themes of Action Française from the Dreyfus Affair until the defeat of the Nazis, and indeed, in 1996, the small revived AF present echoed these themes. They were also reflected in the very extensive press of the extreme right – *National Hebdo, Présent, Rivarol, Itinéraires, Libre Journal, Lettres Françaises* and others, as well as in books and pamphlets. The FN's denial of the civic nationalism of the revolutionary tradition in favour of a historical marker of identity – Catholicism – and an ethnic homogeneity clearly had an audience that went beyond its electorate.

The pope himself was welcomed at Reims by an enormous crowd and in his address, after celebrating mass in the open air, he showed great skill in avoiding the pitfalls of mythical history. He called for a new commitment to spiritual values and no allusion was made to the 'apostasy' of France or to the exclusive claim of the Church to the creation of French national identity. For the political mainstream, the event was effectively de-politicised. The President of the Republic, Jacques Chirac, was clearly pleased by the whole occasion but in general the government and the major parliamentary parties kept a discreet distance from the entire commemoration.

Conclusion

It is tempting to regard the whole business of commemoration in France as, first, a public relations exercise on the part of the French state to promote a certain image of France, second, a commercial promotion of books, documentaries, films and other cultural products, and third, a welcome opportunity to engage in political posturing and an attempt to discomfort political opponents and rivals. Commemorations are doubtless all of these things but they do not explain the existence of an audience for such events. It is the audience for commemoration which is difficult to explain rather than the purposes to which commemorations are put.

A complex transition seems to be taking place in France, away from a deep feeling for, and intimate connection with, the past as the source of commitments and political identities, towards something very different. This is history as a national heritage (*patrimoine*) – a stock of artefacts, images and stories that are translated into a rich variety of products to be appreciated and consumed according to taste. History as *patrimoine* means that you do not have to approve what has happened in the past to enjoy it and appreciate it and, in a superficial sense, pay homage to it. This is a complex transition which clearly is not yet complete because, as both the examples show, there are ghosts still to be exorcised – there remains a conflict between those who wish to see the Revolution as the point at which the modern French nation came into being and those who want to see the French nation as originating in the mists of antiquity. However, the beginning of the transition dates from the attendance of President Pompidou at the centenary of the Paris Commune, paying tribute to the dead of 1871 at the *mur des fédérés*. It is impossible to conceive a right-wing president or prime minister doing this before him.

In 1980, the year of the patrimony in France, the understanding of *patrimoine* as the whole of the monuments, artefacts, treasures of the past and their histories became widely disseminated. Previously, the notion of *patrimoine* in France had been understood as a legal term for legacy. This different appreciation of the past is almost certainly connected with recent political history and the social changes making France a more mobile, open, consumerist society. There is nothing in the recent past (since 1940) which can easily be celebrated because all the major political events have been deeply divisive. In order to promote a sense of French nationhood, a celebration of the *patrimoine* seems to be the obvious solution.

9
The centralisation of memorials and memory

NEAL ASCHERSON

I

I was in Omagh on the day of the first commemoration, the coming together of the town's people with a phalanx of Irish and British political and religious figures to mark the moment, exactly a week before, when the car bomb exploded. Since then I have wondered whether those twenty-nine dead men, women and children and the hundreds maimed, blinded or less terribly injured will find a monument. And where, and raised by whom?

In local cemeteries or churches? Perhaps, but in Northern Ireland that means that there can never be a single monument. A plaque, down in Market Street where the bomb went off or in Tyrone Hospital? Perhaps, but I know, somehow, that there will never be a central site of remembrance, inaugurated by solemn state ceremonies in Belfast or Dublin, dedicated to the Omagh victims – or indeed to all the other non-combatants who were killed in the Troubles before them. This is because of their innocence. They did not put on uniform or swear any secret oath to a cause or a nation. They were just shopping or strolling on a Saturday afternoon. They were civilians, and the commemorators, those who centralise memory into metropolitan national monuments, are not much concerned with civilians.

Where is the central monument of non-combatants who perished in the Second World War? Or the victims of the great flu epidemic, which slew so many more than the guns of the First World War? (Or to the dead of the Irish Famine?) The answer is that here and there – in graveyards or on the local sites of tragedy – such memorials do exist, but locally. There is a plaque in the station underpass at Reutlingen to remember the hundreds killed as they sheltered there from Allied bombing – a *Terrorangriff*. There is a plaque in Bethnal Green Tube station, in

London, for the hundreds who died on the staircase in a panic stampede during an air raid. But there is no colossus of sculpture or concrete block of symbolism for the civilians anywhere in the central statue zone of a metropolis.

It has never been otherwise. The Heritage Cult, in its early-modern version, has simply preferred to omit civilians slain either by war or by natural tragedy. When, if ever, did a king command a memorial for them? Nobody immortalised the Black Death victims in stone. Central Europe is full of baroque 'plague pillars', like the famous one in Vienna's Graben, but their purpose is to thank God on behalf of those who escaped, not to remember those who did not.

Central commemoration, in its present familiar form, is in many ways a post-Renaissance pastiche of Roman imperial practice. There is the monument to a victory or conquest, erected on the spot, and there is the metropolitan Arch of Triumph; there is, for instrance, the enormous victory monument to Trajan's conquest of the Dacians at Adamclisi, in the steppe behind Constanta, and there is Trajan's Column in Rome. What is to be remembered is the victor and 'his' battle. The dead among his own soldiers, though they, like the vanquished barbarians, may be carved into the monument, are not subjects of commemoration. During the post-Roman period, central commemoration in Europe survived in its old monumental form only at Constantinople. In Western Europe, the church appropriated and refunctioned the royal wish to commemorate; the swords or hearts of warrior princes were laid in shrines and buried under abbey floors while older relics – standing stones, burial cairns – were regarded by the common people as marking forgotten battlefields or the graves of pagan heroes.

By the start of the nineteenth century, the classical tradition of the battle or conquest monument had long been revived – though usually as a built marker of some kind on the spot of the action. Now it took neo-Roman form, as central commemoration in a capital city: a stele like Nelson's Columns in London and Dublin or the Siegessäule and Angels of Victory in German cities, in the naming of railway stations (Waterloo, Austerlitz) or boulevards and squares. But it was not until the end of the last century that official commemoration at local and central levels began to dedicate itself to 'the fallen' rather than to the hero or to the abstract notion of a triumph or victory. In the wake of the Boer War, this new approach allowed monuments inscribed with the names of the local dead to appear in market towns and provincial cities all over the United Kingdom.

There is one obvious generalisation to be made about this process. The centralisation of memory, usually but not invariably through the action of the state or its agencies, is to do with the rise of popular nationalism. In the high nation-state era, now coming towards its end, the state managed and administered the imaginative concept of unity. The state claimed to incarnate the Nation, and appointed itself curator of the national memory. At first it was a matter of imposing a more or less teleological version of history, in which selected hero-figures were declared to be the common 'ancestors' of all members of the nation and to be in some sense pioneers of modernity. But the establishment of a lay religion of the nation, with its pantheon and martyrs, could not satisfy the expectations aroused as modern nationalism mobilised millions of ordinary people and drove them for the first time into the political process – not always the democratic process, of course. The public monument, for the last century, has been required to become collective as well as individual in its human references. It has to proclaim in some way that the masses of the nation were also actors in the drama of national emancipation, glory or self-defence. As the part allotted to those millions was usually that of cannon fodder, monuments of commemoration in the twentieth century were mostly concerned with the war dead, for which a special state language was devised. This represented death in war as an act of national integration, for the luckless individual and for the bereaved community: 'the supreme sacrifice', or – this found on many post-1918 German war memorials – *Heiliges Vaterland, Dir zuliebe ist keiner zuviel gefallen.*

Each nation-state developed central metropolitan war memorials and shrines. This has had at least two consequences. One is the slow devaluing of local commemoration in favour of central ceremonies, honouring 'the fallen' as symbols of national integration and cohesion rather than the actual men and women of a given community who lost their lives and often still survive as individuals in living memory. The second is the development of an ossified, formal ritual for state visitors, who are required to visit the central shrines and pay tribute. A capital city without such a site is now almost unthinkable, at least in Europe or North America. Here is the key to the painful contorted row in Germany about the plan for an enormous Holocaust memorial in Berlin. Critics of this plan are well aware that foreign statesmen cannot be expected to offer bows and flowers to the *German* war dead of the last world war (see the public relations disaster when President Reagan visited the Bitburg war cemetery in 1985). These critics suggest that the new capital of united Germany is cynically using the Jewish victims of National Socialism in order to establish an acceptable national memorial site for Great and Good visitors from abroad. A particularly nasty phrase describes the planned memorial as a *zentrale Kranzabwurfstelle* – a central wreath-disposal point.

Memorial, Novorossisk, 1943.'The Front Line of the Small Land was Here'
(Sculptor N. Bozhenenko; Architect I. Nikitin)

Memorial, Novorossisk, 1943. 'Defence Line'
(Sculptor V. Tsigal; Architects Ya. Belopolsky, V. Kananin, V. Khavin)

Memorial to the heroic Black Sea sailors 'Torpedo Cutter'
(Architect N. Nikitin)

Memorial 'The Small Earth' in the memorial complex 'Heroes of the Civil War and the Great Patriotic War
1941–1945' (Sculptor V. Tsigal; Architects Y. Belopolski, R. Kananin, V. Havin)

Memorial 'Border Defence'
(Sculptor V. Tsigal; Architects Y. Belopolski, R. Kananin, V. Havin)

II

Let me now give a few other national examples and variants of this process. In the later Soviet Union and in Russia, there has been a clear progression from the local and often touching memorial to the dead of the Great Patriotic War towards centralised monuments. These new structures, which began to appear in the Brezhnev period – some 35 to 40 years after the war – were planned on a gigantic, megalomaniac scale. Most of them departed from the commemoration of individuals, and even from the idealised but more or less life-sized representations of Soviet soldiers. The biggest of them, like the Motherland colossi at Volgograd or Kiev, overshadow cities. Almost all adopted a coarse form of symbolism; some incorporated not just preserved tanks but whole naval vessels or jet aircraft.

The city of Novorossisk, for example, on the Black Sea coast, became in the 1980s an urban sculpture gallery dedicated to the heroic deeds of Leonid Brezhnev, who allegedly provided leadership and political inspiration during the desperate battles at Malaya Zemlya, on the outskirts.

In the post-war decades, Poland went through a similar commemoration to the centralised national monument, from the small memorial dedicated to named human beings to increasingly vast and portentous structures erected as the memory of war and occupation grew more distant. As in the Soviet Union, the driving motive here was the attempt to integrate individual loss and suffering into a Party- and state-led ideology of unity and social cohesion.

At first, Warsaw was itself a spectacle of commemoration. Almost entirely ruined, with every remaining vertical surface pockmarked with bullet holes or shrapnel scars, the city needed no explicit monument to what had taken place. Gradually, the hundreds of sites on the central streets where mass executions had taken place were marked with small stone plaques recording the individual atrocity and at least the numbers of those shot there, adorned with a small lamp and a vase usually filled with fresh flowers. It was only in the 1960s, as the regime turned increasingly towards invocations of traditional patriotism in order to maintain its credibility, that a generation of larger, more thematic and centralised monuments made its appearance: the Ghetto Fighters monument before which Willy Brandt knelt in 1970, the first of many monuments to the Warsaw Rising of 1944, or the memorial to the defenders of Westerplatte – a giant bayonet-shaft driven defiantly deep into Polish earth. One has to remember that at the time that the first Warsaw Rising monument was built, open discussion of what really took place during the rising and the role of Stalin in allowing the Germans to crush it was forbidden.

But the state-led centralisation of memory was suddenly challenged in 1980, during the Solidarity upheaval. The shipyard workers of Gdansk had for years been demanding that a monument should be raised to their dead comrades shot down by army and police during the strikes of 1970. Those who went each year to the spot, bringing symbolic building materials and tools, were regularly arrested, beaten up and imprisoned; the electrician Lech Walesa was among them. In 1980, at last, the shipyard workers were able to put up their monument, and they built in the yard the colossal triple mast crowned with anchors and inscribed with defiant poetry, which still stands outside the gate.

At that moment the state's monopoly of memory was directly challenged. But the concept of using commemoration of the dead as an engine of imaginative national integration was the same. All Poles were meant to look towards this monument and to feel a surge of proud anger at the humiliations, injustices and lies imposed on this 'Catholic nation' by Soviet imperialism and its local lackeys. It was a commandment to remember, to refuse to forget what the official custodians of memory had tried to obliterate from the nation's memory. As such, the Gdansk monument was entirely successful; it was too big to be pulled down, its outlines appeared even during the ensuing martial law period on everything from T-shirts to wall graffiti, and weddings in Gdansk took to going straight to it after the church ceremony to lay the bridal flowers at its foot.

Now, in free-enterprise Poland, the commemoration industry has taken a new turn. Large and small patriotic monuments continue to appear, but they have a curiously schmalzy, commercialised look. The tiny boy-soldier from the Rising, his Disney-sweet features almost lost under an adult steel helmet, is a favourite camera target for foreign tourists. Even the new memorial to the eastern Deportees, the millions removed to death or slavery by Stalin in 1940, is blowsy with sentiment, 'appealing' rather than appalling.

Here, I think, we are looking at one aspect of the decentralisation of the commemoration. The pendulum swing is now gradually moving away from the central control of memory, back towards a multitude of different ways in which individuals, groups or communities are struggling to regain power over what they commemorate and how. The Polish example is a sort of privatisation, even though the new monuments

are not set up for profit by entrepreneurs but by decentralised private
bodies – survivors' associations, small nationalist parties, lay Catholic
societies – who raise their own funds.

III

I want to end with an example from the Scottish past which is about
commemoration without centralisation. The events took place between
1660 and 1688; the commemorations and raising of memorials continued
into the middle of nineteenth century, and in a few places into the 1920s.
I am talking about the Covenanters and their graves, and the key source
here – a quite amazing work of research and imagination – is Thorbjoern
Campbell's *Standing Witnesses*, published by the Saltire Society in 1996.

The events and the martyrs commemorated belong to the violent
politico-religious upheavals of the Scottish seventeenth century. They
concern the fifty-year struggle of Presbyterian fundamentalism to restore
a form of Calvinist theocracy to Scotland, and to resist the reintroduction
of episcopacy in general and the Roman Catholic faith in particular. The
fundamentalists (afterwards known broadly as 'Covenanters' or, after one
particular insurgent, as 'Cameronians') had inherited an almost literal
view of 'Christ the King' which diminished the power of a monarch to
that of a godly prince whose duty was to enforce the correct Church order
and discipline and to defend 'the saints ' (God's elect upon earth) against
their foes. A monarch who did not fulfil those functions had no claim on
the obedience of the lieges or subjects. The society envisaged by the
Covenanter leaders was a highly decentralised one; while a godly prince
might be expected to rule from Edinburgh, real moral authority would be
dispersed to the synods and kirk sessions at local level.

The struggle essentially began in 1646, when the fundamentalists
rejected the 'Engagement' compromise with the king and episcopacy. At
this point, the movement split away from the landowners and magnates
who had previously given leadership to the ultra-Presbyterian cause but
now abandoned it for the 'Engagement'. One result of this was to leave
the movement a plebeian assemblage of small farmers, almost all of them
based in the south-west of Scotland, with a new leadership composed of
charismatic preachers and of local peasants who sometimes showed
remarkable ability as guerrilla fighters.

The story of the Covenanters, however, was a half century of military
and political failure. In 1648, the 'Whigamore Raid' rode out of the west
and briefly occupied Edinburgh, in a vain hope to instal a Calvinist
theocracy. After the 1660 restoration of the monarchy in England and
Scotland, attempts by Charles II and then James VII to engineer a return

to episcopal authority and ritual, and later to steer both kingdoms back towards Catholicism, provoked the fundamentalists of the west into fresh insurrection. Another attempt to capture Edinburgh was defeated at the battle of Rullion Green, in 1666. A final Covenanting uprising was launched in 1679, when the insurgents won a battle at Drumclog but were soon after decisively defeated by royal troops at Bothwell Brig. Some years later, the attempt by James VII to re-establish his authority over the Church through a compulsory oath led to further resistance, and then to a ferocious counter-offensive of government repression. Refusal to take the oath was punished by execution on the spot, usually by shooting, and usually inflicted by small squads of dragoons who hunted down 'the saints' in the hills of Galloway and Ayrshire. The so-called 'Killing Time' lasted from about 1684 to the 1688 'Revolution' which dethroned James VII and assured Scotland and England a Protestant succession. The death toll between 1679 and 1688, counting battle casualties and some 200 prisoners from Bothwell Brig drowned when their prison ship sank on the way to America, was probably under 2,000. But the mythology and iconography of the struggle were to prove powerful and durable in popular imagination.[1]

The key image of the Covenanters has remained the lonely hillside, where a horseman watches for the dragoons while the faithful 'savoury remnant' listen to their minister in an open-air conventicle. The commemoration of the martyrs is highly decentralised, often in places now so empty and remote that access to them is not easy, even for experienced hillwalkers. The only approach to a 'central' or 'national' shrine is the Martyrs' Memorial, erected soon after the end of the Killing Time, which stood in the Greyfriars churchyard at Edinburgh and honoured some of the ninety-five Covenanters and their leaders who were executed in the capital. The Nithsdale Cross at Glengarnock, put up in the 1920s, is also a regional memorial. Apart from those two, the monuments are scattered in local churchyards or on hillsides, often on the spot where execution was said to have been carried out. Indeed, 'scatteredness' and loneliness are the chosen qualities of this commemoration, taken as allusions to the loneliness of the helpless children of God, the faithful who preferred to die rather than renounce their beliefs with an oath.

The process of commemoration falls into three phases, and perhaps three uses of language. The first, beginning in 1701, was the decision by the so-called 'Society People' (the survivors of the Covenanting struggle and their allies) to erect graves for the martyrs and to renew and maintain those that already existed. The language of inscriptions was often vengeful and sometimes threatening, as if the holy war was unfinished business even in eighteenth-century Scotland. This is from the gravestone of Robert Grierson at Balmaclellan:

THIS MONUMENT TO PASSENGERS SHALL CRY
THAT GOODLY GRIERSON UNDER IT DOTH LY
BETRAY'D BY KNAVISH WATSON TO HIS FOES
WHICH MADE THIS MARTYRS DAYS BY MURTHER CLOSE
IF YE WOULD KNOU THE NATURE OF HIS CRIME
THEN READ THE STORY OF THAT KILLING TIME
WHEN BABELS BRATS WITH HELLISH PLOTS CONCEAL'D
DESIGND TO MAKE OUR SOUTH THEIR HUNTING FIELD
HERE'S ONE OF FIVE AT ONCE WERE LAID IN DUST
TO GRATIFY ROME'S EXECRABLE LUST
IF CARABINES WITH MOLTEN BULLETS COUD
HAVE REACHED THEIR SOULS THESE MIGHTY NIMRODS
WOUD THEM HAVE CUT OF; FOR THERE COULD NO REQUEST
THREE MINUTES GET TO PRAY FOR FUTER REST.[2]

And this is from Eaglesham, near East Kilbride:

PSA. CXII. & VI. THE RIGHTEOUS
SHALL BE IN EVERLASTING REME-
MBRANCE.
HERE LIE GABRIEL THOMSON
AND ROBERT LOCKHART
WHO WERE KILLED FOR OUNING THE COVEN-
ANTED TESTIMONY BY A PARTY OF HIGH-
LANDMEN AND DRAGOONS UNDER THE
COMMAND OF ARDENCAPLE 1ST MAY 1685.
THESE MEN DID SEARCH THROUGH MOOR AND MOSS
TO FIND OUT ALL THAT HAD NO PASS
THESE FAITHFULL WITNESSES WERE FOUND
AND MURDERED UPON THE GROUND
THEIR BODIES IN THIS GRAVE DO LIE
THEIR BLOOD FOR VENGEANCE YET DOTH CRY
THIS MAY A STANDING WITNESS BE
FOR PRESBYTRY GAINST PRELACY –[3]

Robert Paterson, the original for Walter Scott's *Old Mortality*, belonged to this tradition, an aged Cameronian loyalist who rode about the hills using his skills as a stonemason to renew the graves and their inscriptions. But by the time he died, in 1801, a second language of commemoration was about to appear. The Covenanting tradition was to be appropriated in south and west Scotland by radicals and admirers of the French Revolution, who saw in the levelling, individualist rebellion of the late seventeenth century an antecedent to the Rights of Man. This identification was expressed in an extraordinary commemoration in

1815, when the weavers of Strathaven marched out to celebrate the anniversary of the battle of Drumclog in 1679, and made a clear association between revolutionary radicalism and the Covenanting past. (Some of the same men were to take part in the ill-fated 'Radical War' two years later, the uprising led by weavers which gathered in Glasgow and was crushed in the Bonnyrigg skirmish in 1821).[4]

The same spirit, much more cautiously expressed, can be recognised in the plaque put up on a former school building at Drumclog in 1839, by the original school committee:

> On the battlefield of Drumclog, this Seminary of Education was erected, in memory of those Christian Heroes, who, on Sabbath the Ist of June 1679, nobly fought, in defence of Civil and Religious Liberty, Dieu et mon Droit.

From red Radicals, the Covenanters had become constitutionalist Whigs. But all this was the work only of a politicised minority. Throughout the nineteenth century, the individual gravestones continued to be re-cut and renewed in the older 'Society People' manner, work often carried out by local craftsmen if not by the family descendants of the dead. The language, where new wording had to be composed, adopted deliberate archaisms: a pious pastiche of seventeenth-century Scots (well exemplified in Wodrow's 'Analecta').

A third phase, less clearly defined, seems to have opened in the early twentieth century. A new impulse to commemorate the Covenanting martyrs appeared in western and south-western Scotland in the 1920s. No central government or Scottish Office initiative, no historical quango or even local authority seems to have played a part. Instead, the evidence is that local groups of working people undertook commemoration work. An instance quoted in *Standing Witnesses* is the erection of a new monument to the martyr James Smith near Galston in 1926, by 'a group of miners'.[5] Was this the initiative of a local Orange lodge, or of a miners' trade union branch which sensed – as the Strathaven weavers had sensed – some kinship between the old struggle and the new, between the fight for religious purity and the battle for a new socialist world order? It would be good to know more.

It may be that yet another reinvention is imminent, guising the martyrs as proto-nationalists fallen in an early independence struggle. This would be poor history. Scottishness to the Presbyterian fundamentalists of the 1680s was to some extent defined by spiritual and moral criteria. The inscriptions carry no references to national independence, but do almost invariably refer to the 'Covenanted work of Scotland's Reformation'. Calvinism in one country, perhaps. But national identity or self-assertion is not primarily perceived in terms of sovereignty. Presbyterian rhetoric in

Scotland, apt to identify the faithful nation with the chosen Children of
Israel, located the collective identity in steadfast holiness and piety. The
dragoon who cut off a pious victim's head and then played football with it
is reproached on one memorial as 'By Birth a Tyger, rather than a Scot'.[6]

Above all, the military and political failure of the Covenanters,
coupled with the distant, 'expeditionary' nature of their persecution,
meant that they never became a central phenomenon to be centrally
commemorated. Much more than the Jacobites, they were perceived as a
peripheral, localised menace whose conquest of power at Edinburgh
would have threatened all existing orders and institutions. Their strain of
intolerant ruralism must suggest in our own times that a Covenanter
theocracy might have turned into an anti-urban, anti-intellectual reign of
terror prefiguring aspects of the Pol Pot regime in Cambodia. Their
graves remain scattered across some of the most beautiful and empty
landscapes of Scotland. Will the day ever come when a grand
metropolitan monument to the Covenanters is raised in Glasgow or
Edinburgh? The omens remain against it.

10
A question of covenants: poetry as commemoration

GERALD DAWE

I

Commemoration, according to my dictionary, means a 'call to remembrance', a 'calling to mind' on behalf of the 'remembrancer'. The poet is that 'remembrancer', even in today's fickle tally of fashion. I would imagine too that, at some level of consciousness, people throughout these islands, from the most damaged and deprived parts to the more detached and affluent, have a residual notion of that cultural gene. Poetry is the custodian of the past – whether that be through the written, spoken or sung word.

There is a colloquial underpinning of this practice which I should mention because it touches upon a key point in what I have to say and illustrate in this brief chapter.

In the North of Ireland, particularly in what used to be called 'the country' – which for a Belfast boy like myself literally meant everywhere but Belfast! – there was a phrasing which roughly goes as follows: 'Do you mind?' – which means do you remember? A further resonance runs, 'Mind that for me'. In other words, keep an eye on, 'mind', protect, be careful, look out. Memory and vigilance, the past and protection, go hand in hand and are united by codes of intimacy and, if only by assumption, loyalty.

One would hardly ask the question or make the appeal to a total stranger, except in truly exceptional circumstances. This is not a pedantic prologue. My point is fairly basic and it is this: that poetry in the cultural configuration in which I grew up and continue to function in – if at a slightly more distant remove – poetry set in this background is assumed to be commemorative in both of these colloquial ways: a summons to memory ('Do you mind?') and a custodianship ('minding') of historical and cultural belonging. That word 'belonging' has a double-edged quality, too, of which I am mindful in what follows: as loyalty to a place and people, but also of things inherited, intuitively handed down and owned as cultural possessions, terms now assumed under the notion of 'my' community.

It strikes me now that the society I grew up in was obsessed with commemoration, and throughout the 1950s and '60s northern (and indeed southern) Irish society accepted the rules of this commemoration without too much turbulence. From the late '60s and early '70s to the present, these rules have been pitched into bloody turmoil as the divided memory banks and customs (such as the memorial service at Enniskillen) turned inside out. Those who had previously assumed their acts of commemoration to be valid have been forced to justify them. In the northern Unionist psyche this cultural act of self-definition is interpreted as an apology, a sign of weakness and demeaning compromise. So we are faced with a very strange irony here: that while poetry can be seen as a commemorative art-form, in Northern Ireland the poet has faced a cultural condition which has been – and continues to be – not so much troubled by the rites and passages of commemoration, but whose very civic and social spaces are *defined* – physically and morally – by such preoccupations, from parades, flags and emblems to gable-end murals, songs and culture-speak. *Remembering* is an act of cultural possessiveness; *minding* an act of cultural defence.

Poetry is therefore implicated in this widespread cultural tension: ballads sung in praise of nationalist or republican soldiers are matched with loyalist and unionist hymns to empire and resistance. While the musical scores might be merely an echo of one another, the poem as ballad was firmly grounded in either a lament for loss of prestige and cultural power, and a summons to try again, or a victory march and praise for the stalwart defenders. Symbolically, if you like, the poem as commemorative ballad – selectively revisiting the past – has meant that poetry in Ireland has generally had to keep its feet on the ground. The role of landscape, place names, the predominant use of the vernacular, what Patrick Kavanagh called in 'Inniskeen Road; July Evening' 'the half-talk code of mysteries / And the wink-and-elbow language of delight',[1] not to mention the profound populist suspicion of artistic *experiment*, all these literary characteristics have been deeply influenced by the popular Irish cultural customs and expectations, which in turn are predicated upon the sentiment surrounding commemoration. Writers who have genuinely broken free have generally lived in splendid isolation from both audience and general recognition. But to reiterate: in a society such as Northern Ireland's, where commemoration has suffused every pore of cultural life, a poet can be pulled in two directions – by revoking the popular and inherited customs of 'minding' and protecting, he or she might seek inspiration elsewhere or, and this has been my own experience, poetry can develop into a way of discovering a different and more complex form of commemoration. By which I mean that poetry actually dramatises and objectifies the commemoration process itself and probes the commemorated civic landscape.

In this sense, a poem turns accepted, dominant reality – formulated history – into an imagined parallel universe, a critical reality in which the reader can see what has become of the past, of all that minding and remembering. Shorn of traditional consolations, the poem implicitly asks the reader to inhabit an open ground, a civic space: 'Is this just?', 'Have we sufficiently understood this or that honouring/historical moment/belief?'and so on: Poetry in the wars,[2] as Edna Longley memorably has it.

II

The best way for me to illustrate what I mean is by tracing the lines of three of my own poems. Two come from my second collection, *The Lundys Letter,*[3] which was published in 1985. It had taken me almost seven years to unshackle myself from the confusions of the 1970s which were gathered throughout the early years of 'The Troubles' into a very dark and constrained first volume called *Sheltering Places*[4] which appeared in 1978. The seven years, I realise now, were all about relocating and seeing, quite literally, where and what I had come from – in a nutshell, a typically Belfast Protestant hybrid of refugee and planter stock, with profound stability and instability masked under the surface of generations of adapting to and ordering northern society. When I wrote this following poem,'Secrets',[5] sometime in or around 1980, it was as if a door opened and I could see something for the very first time. I was commemorating a way of life: a codified landscape of home, family and the martial statues of an imperial past which were literally dotted all around the streetscapes and imaginative rooms of my childhood and youth

Secrets

I was coming-of-age in a sparse
attic overlooking the sluggish tide.

Down the last flight of stairs
a grandfather clock struck

its restless metronome to those
who went about their business

with a minimum of fuss. My
puritan fathers, for instance,

stumbled from separate beds
and found their place

under the staunch gaze
of monumental heroes, frozen

stiff in the act of sacrifice;
they had always been

tightlipped about God-
knows-what secrets.

Then, in or around the same time, I read A. T. Q. Stewart's *The Ulster Crisis*,[6] the story of northern Unionist resistance to Home Rule, told through a masterful narrative and eye on iconography. As one of the leading Belfast businessmen of the time remarked: 'You couldn't do better than take the old Scotch Covenant [1580]. It is a fine old document, full of grand phrases. and thoroughly characteristic of the Ulster tone of mind at this day.'[7] Near-on half a million people signed the Covenant, even in Edinburgh where it was signed on the Covenantors' Stone in the old Greyfriars churchyard. In particular, the following passage struck me like a thunderbolt:

> The climax of Covenant Day came when Carson left the Ulster Club to go on board the Liverpool steamer. The docks were only a few minutes' walk away, but it took an hour for the wagonette, drawn not by horses but by men, to reach its destination. More than 70,000 people had managed to jam themselves into Castle Place, all of them intent upon getting near enough to shake Carson's hand, and at the quayside they would not let him go. 'Don't leave us,' they shouted. 'You mustn't leave us.' When at last he got on board the steamer, aptly named the *Patriotic*, they called for yet another speech from him as he stood in the beam of a searchlight at the rail of the upper deck. He left them with the message they never tired of hearing, and promised to come back, if necessary to fight. Then as the steamer cast off he heard the vast crowd in the darkness begin to sing 'Rule Britannia' and 'Auld Lang Syne', and then 'God Save the King'; and as she moved into the channel rockets burst in red, white, and blue sparks above her, and bonfires sprang up on either shore of the Lough.[8]

Within a year or so, out of reading this passage I wrote, or maybe transcribed is a better word, the following poem, 'A Question of Covenants'.[9]

A Question of Covenants

28 September 1912

The *Patriotic* turns to face
an invisible sea. From Castle Place
thousands swarm through side-streets
and along the unprotected quays just
to glimpse Carson, gaunt as usual,
who watches the surge of people
call, 'Don't leave us. You mustn't leave us',
and in the searchlight's beam,
his figure arched across the upper deck,
he shouts he will come back
and, if necessary, fight this time.

It is what they came to hear
in the dark September night,
As the *Patriotic* sails out
Union colours burst in rockets
and bonfires scar the hills
he departs from, a stranger to both sides
of the lough's widening mouth
and the crowd's distant sinnging,
'Auld Lang Syne' and 'God Save the King'.

The question I wanted the poem to dramatise, or simply pose, concerns the contract and oath entered into in 1912 and how that sense of understanding has been interpreted since then in exclusively negative terms, as masking prejudice, bigotry, triumphalism. All of which is true, but it is not the complete picture. Those hundreds of thousands of northern Protestants and Unionists were also demonstrating (commemorating, if you prefer) a distinctive kind of identity. This is the Covenant they signed:

> Being convinced in our consciences that Home Rule would be disastrous to the material well-being of Ulster as well as the whole of Ireland, subversive of our civil and religious freedom, destructive of our citizenship, and perilous to the unity of the Empire, we, whose names are underwritten, men of Ulster, loyal subjects of His Gracious Majesty King George V, humbly relying on the God whom our fathers in days of stress and trial confidently trusted, do hereby pledge ourselves in solenm Covenant throughout this our time of threatened calamity to stand by one another in defending for ourselves and our children our cherished position of equal citizenship in the United Kingdom, and in using all means which may be found necessary to defeat the present conspiracy to set up a Home Rule

Parliament in Ireland. And in the event of such a Parliament being forced upon us we further solemnly and mutually pledge ourselves to refuse to recognize its authority. In sure confidence that God will defend the right we hereto subscribe our names. And further, we individually declare that we have not already signed this Covenant. God save the King.'[10]

In two years' time, in 1914, this rhetoric would of course lead millions to their deaths. By 1998, it had become an atrophied and hollow parody played out on the fields of Drumcree and the streets of lower Ormeau.

III

The significance of these two poems as a test case of their relationship between poetry and commemoration is simply that I know the outcome! Written almost twenty years ago, I discovered through writing these poems that commemoration is only really the start of a process of cultural knowledge, not the end product. From 'Secrets' and 'A Question of Covenants' I realise now, looking back, that I unearthed part of my own cultural legacy as a northern Protestant, a legacy which had been repressed and pitilessly caricatured, demonised, and patronised: a cause of embarrassment in what were once called 'enlightened circles'. The unexposed relations between these various social factors represented an artistic 'poor showing': Protestantism and the literary imagination parodied as an oxymoron, a contradiction in terms. So even though I stood in a severely critical relationship with that culture, and was particularly opposed to the inner history of its prejudices, I needed in some way to write it out of myself and identify its strengths to commemorate. An act that in turn led at the time to various funny and not-so-funny mocking jibes. 'Secrets' is a poem about 'family'; 'A Question of Covenants' is about that tricky word 'community'. What links the two poems together – along with others that came along as the 1980s progressed (if that is the right word) into the early '90s – is an (I trust) *imaginative* engagement with the patriarchal culture of northern authoritarianism and the imperatives of History: Carson as leader, the father figure, my own great grandfather, William Bailey Chartres. As a devout Unionist, he stood on that day eighty-odd years ago (see, commemoration at every turn of phrase) in the Ulster Hall and later on in the City Hall and signed the Covenant. Of emigrant origin, with a young widowed mother and younger brother to look after, and then an intriguing and earthy wife of refugee stock and their two daughters, this man insisted himself upon me and ended up being commemorated in poems by a great grandson with whom he would have had little in common. The impact of writing these and other poems lead me ironically *away* from condemning the world he had known, into understanding, without condoning, it and all its manifest and well-publicised structural and constitutional injustices. As one door shut, another opened, and this is precisely what I mean when I say that all poetry is *in some way* commemorative. Maybe a better way of putting this is to quote Thom Gunn's introduction to the poems of Ben Jonson when he talks of poetry as being 'occasional':

> all poetry is occasional: whether the occasion is an external event like a birthday or a declaration of war, whether it is an occasion of the imagination, or whether it is in some sort of combination of the two. (After all, the external may lead to the internal occasions.) The occasion in all cases – literal or imaginary – is the starting point, only, of a poem, but it should be a starting point to which the poet must in some sense stay true. The truer he is to it, the closer he sticks to what for him is its authenticity, the more he will be able to draw from it in the adventures that it produces, adventures that consist of the experience of writing.[11]

Be that as it may, having started this poetic process of commemoration, another side of the cultural configuration of northern society, held so long in quarantine as unessential and a diversion from the main plot, opened out for me.

Following the strange tales of family names like any genealogical rootsearcher, I discovered that the Huguenot William Bailey Chartres had married a Mary Jane Quartz. Both had met in north Belfast, in a district of mixed religious and racial origins, the kind of district which seemingly did not exist in the north, never mind Belfast. Her story began to take over and demand its own form of commemoration – a subversive, destabilising presence which reverses (or challenges at least) the customised perceptions of the north as a culturally divided province of two traditions.

When I wrote the first poem to her, 'Middle Names', another one came hot on its heels, with which I will finish. The poem 'Quartz', after my great grandmother's maiden name, comes from a collection I'm working on, called *The Morning Train*.[12]

The poem tells a familiar emigrant story, apocryphal in part I have no doubt, but one that moved me from the austerity and masculinity of the patriarchal order which had defined the north for almost two centuries – the kind of moral covenant still at the fulcrum of northern Unionism – to the vulnerable hope of a courageous female. A stereotypical conflict perhaps, but one which I know to be true, having seen it play itself out through the psychic and political battles in so many families of my peers and elders. Without laying too much freight on the slight shoulders of this poem, 'Quartz' summarises for me an imaginative movement away from history to language, from power-play to a yearning to live, to making fiction and imagining a different kind of cultural reality by actually inhabiting none, albeit with that dash of the apocryphal. Maybe from these hidden, uncanonical sources a common culture will emerge or resurface, out of which the next generation can mind diversity of background as a bulwark against deadly and deadening division, and not the other way around.

Quartz

Where did you get a name like that from?

So there is something I want to know
great-grandmother, reclining on whichever
foreign shore or ambrosial meadow,
taking a second look at the old place –

the valiant village, the provincial district,
the back-breaking hill-climb to the apartment,
the quiet evening square in this country town
or that frontier post, down by the coastal resort

of some famous lake, say, with roman baths,
or a minority language – I want to know
who your grand dame was, or *pater familias*,
disembarking in a draughty shed, thinking

Liverpool or Belfast was really New York,
blinking in the greyish light of a noisy dawn,
looking out for rooming houses, a decent hotel,
putting one foot in front of the other,

taking the first right and walking, walking,
past the shipping offices and custom houses,
the rattling trams and carters and mill girls,
the steep factories and squat churches till the hills

converge upon this three-storied terrace
with the curtains drawn, the bell-pull shining,
and you pull the bell-pull and in whatever
English you'd learned you stepped in.

11

Sean O'Casey: history into drama

CHRISTOPHER MURRAY

I

The cultural historian Joep Leerssen says in *Remembrance and Imagination* that one kind of Irish history in the nineteenth century was mythic, as opposed to antiquarian. In the mythic version, 'the actual course of events is rejected as a betrayal of 'what should have happened', as a Wrong Turn; this rejection opposes Myth ... to reality'.[1] This is, of course, because the history was a history of failure. The history, by which I mean the written history in whatever version, antiquarian or mythic, is a denial of realism. Its function, Leerssen continues, was to inspire the present. 'Not only that, but the reviving of history was performed time and again, by writer after writer, each of them telling the old story afresh, like a needle stuck in the groove, in an uncanny, obsessive recycling process of the past, of the old familiar, oft-told story of the past' (p. 156). Apart from the metaphor of the gramaphone needle, nowadays rendered obsolete by the compact disk, Leerssen's analysis seems to me both accurate and helpful. O'Casey, it may be claimed, subverts this pattern. Leerssen speaks of the traditional historical methods being a denial of realism by establishing a myth in place of what actually happened. O'Casey's dramatic mode, for example in *The Plough and the Stars* (1926), was the opposite. He demythologised in order to establish realism. Hence, in a way, the riots which greeted the first production of that play.[2]

Thus O'Casey was anti-historical, or even revisionist. This is a major reason why O'Casey has not endeared himself to contemporary Irish intellectuals any more than he did to intellectuals in 1926. In a letter to Owen Sheehy-Skeffington in 1961, which recalled the public debate on *The Plough* called for by Owen's mother in 1926, O'Casey said: 'I didn't understand that my intense realism countered the romantic conception of 1916 – Roisín Dhú, & all that; and honestly was a little bewildered by the popular outcry.'[3] Accordingly, one may see in O'Casey's drama as going against the accepted mode. What he was doing was not commemorating but denigrating, and yet to do that implied, though it did not exercise, a fresh historical analysis of the 1916 Rising. That is one side of O'Casey's approach. The other comes much later in his career when he wanted to advocate a specific change in Irish society. He then used myth, invoked a mythic version of Irish history, in order to create a new myth of cultural revolution. In effect, he departed from realism in order to provide a myth which would be a dynamic model for social change. The example I shall use is a late play, also controversial though in a completely different way, *The Drums of Father Ned* (1959).

In between those two plays, *The Plough and the Stars* and *The Drums of Father Ned*, one sees a major playwright grasping Irish history and re-moulding it in order to startle, disturb, and possibly energise audiences.

O'Casey was baptised into Irish history, like so many Irish writers of his time, including Joyce, by the fall of Parnell in 1891. In the first volume of his autobiography, indeed, O'Casey actually follows Joyce in depicting the fall of Parnell through the eyes of a child. The topic is intro-duced at his father's funeral, when the boy is six years old, and becomes the grounds of a family argument. Later, young Johnny reflects that his mother had told him Parnell was 'a great Protestant, a great Irishman, and a grand man; and it was a good thing there was someone, anyway, fit to hinder the English from walking over the Irish people.'[4] The young boy is confused:

> – But we're not really Irish, Ma; not really, you know, are we?
> – Not Irish? echoed his mother. Of course we're Irish. What on earth put it into your head that we weren't Irish?
> – One day, an' us playin', Kelly told me that only Catholics were really Irish; an' as we were Protestants, we couldn't be anyway near to the Irish. (pp. 175–76)

Johnny gets his first history lessons out on the Dublin streets, when crowds gather to celebrate (and protest against) Queen Victoria's jubilee, and Johnny witnesses demonstrations against the crown. A tram conductor who sings about Wolfe Tone makes the boy sit up:

> – Who was Wolfe Tone, Ma? whispered Johnny, moved strangely by seeing tears trickling down the cheeks of the conductor as he sang.
> – A Protestant rebel who went over to France nearly a hundhred years ago, an' brought back a great fleet to help the Irish drive the English outa the counthry. But God was guarding us, and He sent a mighty storm that scatthered the ships from Banthry Bay.
> – What happened to poor Wolfe Tone, Ma?

> – He fought on a French warship till it was captured by the British; and then he was put into prison, an' executed there by the English government.
> – Why didn' the Irish save him?
> – Oh, I don't know. It all happened long ago, an' everyone's forgotten all about it.
> – But the conductor hasn't forgotten all about it, Ma.
> – Let's look at the lights, and the banners, said his mother, an' not bother our heads about things that don't matter now. (p. 178)

That day the boy witnesses a riot, as the loyalist students of Trinity College and a group of nationalists fight each other, and the mounted police attack the nationalists with violence.

So began O'Casey's initiation into Irish history and politics. In the years that followed, years of poverty after his father's death in 1886, O'Casey had little formal education, suffered greatly from an eye disease prevalent among the poor in Ireland, and yet had, so to speak, his eyes opened for him to the realities of Irish history. In his early twenties he turned away from the affiliations prescribed by his Protestant identity and became a rabid nationalist and republican. He joined the Gaelic League and learned to speak and write Gaelic fluently. He joined the IRB and steeped himself in the militant republicanism of John Mitchel and James Fintan Lalor. His early writings (*c.*1910–13) reflect all too clearly this naive commitment to patriotism. A verse from one of his early poems gives the flavour:

> God of the Gael! our banner bless,
> And Ireland, dear Ireland.
> And in the battle's tedious stress
> Oh! nerve our arm for Ireland!
> Now Fenian proud, lift high your head,
> 'Twas vows, but now 'tis blows instead,
> For vengeance, for our Martyred Dead,
> For Freedom and for Ireland![5]

But then O'Casey met and was captivated by Jim Larkin, the great trade unionist he was later to call the Irish Prometheus. The Dublin lockout of 1913, the first great display of labour opposition to nineteenth-century capitalist hegemony, diverted O'Casey's militancy into socialist channels. After 1913, having reached the liminal age of thirty-three, O'Casey became a Labour man. But, as C. Desmond Greaves has pointed out, 'he did not describe himself as a socialist', not, that is, until after the death of James Connolly.[6] But he joined and became the first secretary of the Irish Citizen Army in 1914, and later (in 1919) wrote the first history of that body and its part in the 1916 Rising in which he himself did not participate.

The point I would make at the outset is that O'Casey was a chroni-cler/historian rather than an activist. He became a writer by steeping himself in the conventional consciousness of grievance which was the historical attitude at the time. The impulse to memorialise is clearly seen in his booklet *The Sacrifice of Thomas Ashe* (1918). Ashe, whom O'Casey knew, was a key figure in the republican movement. Indeed, Roy Foster regards Collins as Ashe's successor.[7] Sentenced to death for his part in the 1916 Rising, Ashe had his sentence commuted to life imprisonment and was released under the general amnesty of June 1917. He was soon re-arrested, went on hunger-strike, and died in prison as a result of forcible feeding. O'Casey immediately published a poem, 'Lament for Thomas Ashe', with the refrain, 'Thomas Ashe, Thomas Ashe, we are mourning for thee.' It was instantly produced for distribution outside Mountjoy Jail, where Ashe had died and it was incorporated into a prose pamphlet, *The Sacrifice of Thomas Ashe*, published a few months later.[8] It is clear that O'Casey was still wholly committed to the republican cause, though he does make the point at the time that Ashe was 'a firm and convinced advo-cate of the rights of Labour'.[9] Therefore, it would be quite wrong to inter-pret *The Plough and the Stars* as the work of a man with no interest in, or knowledge of, the politics of 1916. On the contrary, O'Casey understood the issues thoroughly and, ten years on, reviewed them in the light of the newly founded Irish Free State. That the result was riots at the Abbey Theatre is not at all to be equated with Synge's *Playboy of the Western World* (1907), which also caused riots, since Synge, according to his apol-ogist Yeats, 'seemed by nature unfitted to think a political thought.'[10] O'Casey, in contrast, was political to the core and in holding the mirror up to the 1916 Rising was doing so with satiric intent.

Thus, having discovered Irish history as a young man, O'Casey first participated in it, then withdrew and reshaped himself to become a partic-ular, poetic kind of historian, ultimately creating in the first four volumes of his autobiography a history of the period 1880–1926 within which the character of Johnny Casside/Sean is dramatised. Having established that link between history and drama, we must immediately make the famous distinction Aristotle made in the *Poetics*: 'Poetry, therefore, is a more philosophical and a higher thing than history: for poetry tends to express the universal, history the particular.'[11] History is a record of characters and events; literature is an imagined creation of characters and events. The difference may lie between the real and the ideal: art takes the real and gives it a shape not found in nature. Art in that sense tells lies, invents things, and yet aims at certain unempirical truths.

If history is a narrative always told from the point of view of the victors, then Irish history is a vacuum, since the Irish were constantly losers. The narrative could only be myth or the construction of what

might have been. For O'Casey's work this conclusion takes two forms:
(1) we see history as a process of emptying out, of debunking or even of
satire; (2) we see history as an idealised representation whereby signs
become mythic and the past points to a new future. I want now to look
briefly at each of these two forms in O'Casey's work.

The first is seen in the three Dublin plays, *The Shadow of a Gunman*
(1923), *Juno and the Paycock* (1924) and *The Plough and the Stars*
(1926). Each of these has a real historical background, although that word
is inadequate to describe O'Casey's new form of realism. For in each of
the plays the background invades and overwhelms the foreground, the
public overtakes the private experience. In that sense the characters are
revealed as inhabiting history and becoming its hieroglyphics. These characters are usually depicted as powerless, as underprivileged and without
the means of changing their circumstances. To such people romantic
republican history is illusory. O'Casey mocks them not because he did not
love them but because through mockery he could show up the absurdity
of trying to organise a revolution from the top down rather than from the
bottom up. For example, he introduces a windbag into each of his three
Dublin plays, and the windbag's analysis serves to throw into relief the
inadequacy of the War of Independence. In *The Shadow of a Gunman*
Tommy Owens, in the mistaken belief that the man he is talking to is an
IRA gunman and not just a poet and a shadow of a gunman, bursts out, the
stage direction says, '*fiercely*': 'I'm bloody well tired o' waitin' – we're
all tired o' waitin'. Why isn't every man in Ireland out with the I.R.A.? Up
with the barricades, up with the barricades; it's now or never, now an' for
ever, as Sarsfield said at the battle o' Vinegar Hill.'[12] Patrick Sarsfield
fought at the siege of Limerick in 1691; the battle of Vinegar Hill came a
hundred years later during the 1798 rebellion. Tommy Owens's uncertain
grasp of history is used to expose a bogus form of patriotism.

A more elaborate and more comic development of this technique may
be seen in *Juno and the Paycock*. In Act I there is a discussion about the
clergy, based solely on the fact that Fr Farrell has sent word of a job
Captain Boyle might secure if he is quick about it. Because he is glori-
ously lazy and irresponsible, and develops pains in his legs as soon as a
job becomes even a faint possiblity, the Captain rationalises his resistance
by reaching into Irish history to condemn the role of the clergy there:

> Didn't they prevent the people in ''47' from seizin' the corn, an' they
> starvin'; didn't they down Parnell; didn't they say that hell wasn't hot
> enough nor eternity long enough to punish the Fenians? We don't
> forget, we don't forget them things, Joxer. If they've taken everything
> else from us, Joxer, they've left us our memory.[13]

And Joxer, the ever-reliable parasite, echoes back obligingly, 'For mem'ry's the only friend that grief can call its own, that grief … can … call … its own!' Joxer's line is from a song in the popular operetta *The Gypsy Baron*. Therefore the serious matter of racial memory is trivialised by its involvement with popular song. But the real subversion comes later. When the Captain comes into money, as he thinks, in Act II he feels himself elevated into a new class. He shares with Joxer his new-found sense of affinity with the clergy:

> *Boyle*. Father Farrell stopped me to-day an' tole me how glad he was I fell in for the money.
> *Joxer*. He'll be stoppin' you ofen enough now; I suppose it was 'Mr.' Boyle with him?
> *Boyle*. He shuk me be the han' …
> Joxer (ironically). I met with Napper Tandy, an' he shuk me be the han'!
> *Boyle*. You're seldom asthray, Joxer, but you're wrong shipped this time. What you're sayin' of Father Farrell is very near to blasfeemey. I don't like any one to talk disrespectful of Father Farrell.[14]

The *volte-face* is staggering. But when Joxer hastily agrees that Fr Farrell is 'a daarlin' man', the Captain resumes his narrative but this time inserts another character, Needle Nugent, who can replace Joxer's anti-clerical voice. "He'll be folleyin' you', says he, 'like a Guardian Angel from this out'– all the time the oul' grin on him, Joxer.' The narrative allows Joxer adeptly to switch sides here and visit his disapproval on Needle Nugent: 'I never seen him yet but he had that oul' grin on him!' Boyle can now proceed, using Needle Nugent as unenlightened man within the recon-structed (and to our ears Bahktinian) dialogue and leading into a revised historical view of the clergy:

> 'Mr.Nugent,' says I, 'Father Farrell is a man o' the people, an', as far as I know the History o' me country, the priests was always in the van of the fight for Irelan's freedom.'

He then puts into Nugent's mouth the self-same critique which Boyle himself had expressed in Act I, only to demolish it here.

> 'Who are you tellin'?' says he. 'Didn't they let down the Fenians, an' didn't they do in Parnell? An' now …' 'You ought to be ashamed o' yourself,' says I, interruptin' him, 'not to know the History o' your country.' An' I left him gawkin' where he was.[15]

Joxer wonders if Nugent had ever read *The Story of Ireland*. 'Be J. L. Sullivan?' asks Boyle. 'Don't you know he didn't.'

Now, the *Story of Ireland* was by A. M. Sullivan; J. L. Sullivan was the Irish-American prize fighter. This book, *The Story of Ireland*, which Joxer immediately calls 'a darlin' buk, a daarlin' buk!', was first published in 1867 and updated in 1909. It was an elementary but highly nationalist history of Ireland from the earliest times, written by a man who was editor of *The Nation* from 1858 to 1874 and a Home Rule MP from 1874. Leerrssen says of Sullivan that he 'brought Davis's ideals into practice' and situated his book 'between myth and history', dovetailing one with the other.[16] We find, indeed, that in his account of 1798 Sullivan lauded the contribution of the priests:

> Fathers John and Michael Murphy, Father Roche, and Father Clinch, are names that should ever be remembered by Irishmen when tempters whisper that the voice of the Catholic pastor, raised in warning or restraint, is the utterance of one who cannot feel for, who would not die for, the flock he desires to save.[17]

What we are given, then, in *Juno and the Paycock* is a debunking of Irish history. With spokesmen like Captain Boyle and Joxer history becomes malleable, a means to bolster up any available prejudice. The fact that Captain Boyle can turn one hundred and eighty degrees on a point of Irish history is comical, even absurd, but it shows that all history is capable of being interpreted according to individual bias or self-interest.

This is the comic side of O'Casey's vision but there was a tragic side also. Minnie Powell is uselessly gunned down in *The Shadow of Gunman*, under the illusion that she is making a worthwhile sacrifice. In *Juno*, Johnny Boyle is a survivor of the 1916 Rising, where he was hit in the hip, and he lost his arm during the Civil War. But when he tries to get out of fighting, out of history, he betrays a comrade and suffers retaliation. There is no exit from the prison-house of history, as O'Casey conceives it at this time – for he was to change his mind later.

And so we come at last to the crux of the matter and to *The Plough and the Stars*. When Hannah Sheehy-Skeffington attacked the play in a public debate she said O'Casey was a man with a grouch:

> He likes to see rather the meanness, the littleness, the squalor, the slum squabbles, the women barging each other, and the little vanities and jealousies of the Irish Citizen Army. He has rather the art of the photographer ... than the art of the dramatist.[18]

Of course, in conceding to O'Casey the art of the photographer Mrs Sheehy-Skeffington was conceding that he told the truth, for the camera cannot show what is not there. Yet she was right, in an interesting way, to say that O'Casey had a 'grouch', because that goes to the root of what she calls his 'anti-Easter week play'. In a letter to the press a week before the debate O'Casey had asked: 'Is the Ireland that is pouring to the picture houses, to the dance halls, to the football matches, remembering with tear-dimmed eyes all that Easter Week stands for?'[19] Her reply then was that these people represent 'the Ireland that forgets – that never knew. It is the Ireland that sits comfortably in the Abbey stalls and applauds Mr. O'Casey's play.'[20] Little did she realise that this is what O'Casey knew only too well. When he had given the Abbey audience a political fantasy entitled *Cathleen Listens In* (1923), which said, in effect, 'a plague on all your houses', the audience sat stonily mute, something O'Casey never forgot. Even in 1949, when he recalled the episode in his autobiography, the insult rankled:

> The audience received the little play in dead silence, in a silence that seemed to have a point of shock in its centre. Not even a cold clap of a hand anywhere. They all got up from their seats and silently filed out of the theatre… What would he do, for he was vexed, and a sense of humiliation discouraged him; what would he do?[21]

What he could do and did do was to write *Juno* and *The Plough* in quick succession. I suggest there was an element of revenge in *The Plough*. O'Casey had a lot of old scores to settle, against the Volunteers, whose members had used the trams during the lockout of 1913, against members of the Irish Citizen Army, who had sold out their flag, the eponymous plough and the stars, and brought disgrace on it. The Covey in the play tells how:

> Because it's a Labour flag, an' was never meant for politics … What does th' design of th' field plough, bearin' on it th' stars of th' heavenly plough, mean, if it's not Communism? It's a flag that should only be used when we're buildin' th' barricades to fight for a Workers' Republic![22]

Therefore, in looking back to 1916, in offering a dramatisation of the events leading up to Easter Week, O'Casey was pouring scorn on his audience. They responded with fury on the fourth night of the first production. They were mostly women, come to defend their menfolk who had made the supreme sacrifice in 1916. What triggered the riots was the scene in Act II where the soldiers bring the tricolour into a public house. In a letter of reply O'Casey said he had seen the tricolour in a public house. 'I have seen it painted on a lavatory in "The Gloucester Diamond"; it has been flown from some of the worst slums in Dublin.'[23] Mrs Sheehy-Skeffington was shocked, as she was meant to be and replied: 'Because indecent and obscene inscriptions are similarly so found one may not exalt them as great literature.'[24] Again, her point is vital. For graffiti are a form of transgression, the point of which is to upset orthodox opinion by obscenity or forbidden sentiments. This, once more, was what O'Casey was about. His play is transgressive on a massive scale. It issues two obscene fingers to romantic idealism. It demythologises Padraic Pearse by quoting from three of his major speeches and showing their incendiary effect. It exposes the fighting men as being 'afraid to say they're afraid'.[25] It shows the story of Ireland as complicit in its own destruction.

This, then, is O'Casey's emptying out of history. The realism he favoured saw the Rising as quixotic. Maud Gonne was at the public debate over *The Plough* and spoke briefly even though she had not seen the play. O'Casey had said he was not trying and never would try to write about heroes. In that case, Maud Gonne replied, 'he had no right to intro-duce a real hero – Padraic Pearse – into his play'.[26] This was bound to hit home: 'no right' indeed! From a woman who had not even seen the play. Of course, as the creator of Yeats's Old Woman in *Cathleen ni Houlihan* (1902), seen by a fellow actress as the embodiment of Ireland itself,[27] what Maud Gonne had to say carried weight. In Yeats's play, her last words were significant. She spoke, or rather chanted, of those who should die on her behalf:

> They shall be remembered for ever,
> They shall be alive for ever,
> They shall be speaking for ever,
> The people shall hear them for ever.[28]

Years later, in reflecting on the night of the riots at the Abbey, O'Casey recycled the myth Yeats had, through Maud Gonne, created:

> For the first time in his life, Sean felt a surge of hatred for Cathleen
> ni Houlihan sweeping over him. He saw now that the one who had
> the walk of a queen could be a bitch at times. She galled the hearts of
> her children who dared to be above the ordinary...[29]

Clearly, so far as O'Casey read the situation in February 1926, it was time to leave Ireland. In the Free State the artist was not free to demythologise. Exile was the lot of those Irish writers who assumed the right Maud Gonne would deny them, the right to show an unheroic Ireland.

Yet it is necessary to emphasise that, in contrast to Synge's *Playboy*, O'Casey's *Plough* was highly popular. Synge's *Playboy* had the effect of driving away from the Abbey many of its nationalist supporters. But the box office returns for O'Casey's *Plough* show clearly that the public supported the play and kept packing in to see it. It has proved to be the most-revived of all Abbey plays. Significantly, it was the first play staged by the new Abbey in 1966, the year of the jubilee commemoration of 1916. It may even be that *The Plough,* by its combination of vigorous populism and passionate rejection of warfare, from 1926 helped to mould a consciousness sceptical of the heroic reading of 1916. Certainly de Valera as Taoiseach, responding to Irish-American hostility to O'Casey, tried in 1934 to forbid the Abbey to take *The Plough and the Stars* as well as Synge's *Playboy* on tour to the USA.[30]

II

But this is not the whole story of O'Casey and his use(s) of history in the theatre. It is, indeed, only one side of the story, the narrative of 'bringin' disgrace', as the Covey puts it. In his later plays O'Casey searched for a counter-history which would provide a true guide to action. I shall touch here on three plays to make this point clear, ending up with the ill-fated and neglected *The Drums of Father Ned* (1958).

The Star Turns Red (1940) is dedicated to 'the men and women who fought through the great Dublin lockout in nineteen hundred and thirteen'.[31] It is thus a history play, a dramatisation of events almost thirty years in the past. Yet in the text O'Casey prescribes the time of the action as 'Tomorrow, or the next day'.[32] Therefore what O'Casey offers here is history as myth or fantasy, history projected forward to engage with issues urgent in the time shared by the audience. In effect, this is a play about Jim Larkin, Red Jim in the text, and his battle for the workers against the might of the Dublin employers joined in alliance. But because it comes by implication up to the year 1939 *The Star Turns Red* is also a play about Fascism and the alliance between church and right-wing power. What O'Casey does, then, is on the one hand to depict the 1913 conflict in terms of Fascist oppression and on the other hand to see the end of the 1930s as a time threatened by forces hostile to freedom of thought and action. He collapses history to make it a two-way process. In a play heavy with symbolism, the major symbol is the star of Bethlehem, for the action takes place on Christmas Eve when a large, silver star adorns the spire of a towering church visible in the background. At the end of the play, as battle lines are joined, this star turns red, thus becoming a communist rather than a Christian symbol. The real point lies in the transformation. O'Casey is arguing for a new dispensation, a different rough beast from the one Yeats had imagined slouching its way towards Bethlehem. Elsewhere, O'Casey contrasts the Russian and the Irish revolutions, and comes down in favour of Russia:

> The terrible beauty had been born there, and not in Ireland. The cause
> of the Easter Rising had been betrayed by the commonplace bour-

geois class, who laid low the concept of the common good and the common task, and were now decorating themselves with the privileges and powers dropped in their flight by those defeated by the dear, dead men.[33]

As a social realist O'Casey believed that history is man-made, but in *The Star Turns Red* he declares that history can also harness the forces of Christian revolution. After all, O'Casey believed that Christ was the first communist.[34]

In *Red Roses for Me* (1943) a similar idea operates but in a less doctrinaire form and in a style more rich and entertaining. This, too, is a history play, set in Dublin in 1911, and is centred on a young labourer drawn into a strike of railway workers which results in his death. The young man is clearly based on O'Casey himself, and there is much else that is autobiographical about this warm and naive play, but inasmuch as O'Casey survived the 1911 strike it is obvious that he intended here to intervene in history in order to rewrite it. Once again this is a mode quite different from that in which *The Plough and the Stars* was created. Once again the form transcends realism. Once again the dramatic process is a transformation. In Act III this idea is given remarkable theatrical power when the Dublin landscape becomes transformed into richly coloured splendour and the hero Ayamonn likewise is enabled to change the vision of the people from abject despair to lively hope. This visionary scene, set on a bridge over the Liffey, marks the artist's victory over reality, as reality becomes myth. The hero – and it is significant that O'Casey can now endorse a hero – invokes examples from Celtic myth to rouse the listless people to the cause. This is *Cathleen ni Houlihan* in a new guise, that of the workman's overalls. O'Casey can now accept Yeats's idea of sacrifice once the cause is right. Ayamonn dies when violence breaks out during the strike and Dublin has a proletarian martyr. Historically this never happened but O'Casey poetically imagines the possibility. When the Inspector comments regarding Ayamonn's martyrdom that 'It wasn't a very noble thing to die for a single shilling', Sheila's reply is clearly what O'Casey wanted his audience to hear: 'Maybe he saw the shilling in th' shape of a new world.'[35]

In O'Casey's later plays, then, one can easily see a turning away from the purposes of his early work towards the construction of a new mythology of emancipation. He does not resort to agitprop methods in pursuit of this aim, for he was always the poet in the theatre and disdained didacticism of the kind exemplified in Clifford Odets's *Awake and Sing!* (1935).[36] By contrast, the play he regarded as his best, *Cock-a-Doodle Dandy* (1949), while bitingly satiric of Irish mores and manners in the 1940s, is as fantastic, as reliant on magic and as colourful as a child's fairy tale. *The Drums of Father Ned* is in that vein also, but here O'Casey uses history once again and, as it happens, for the last time.

He begins the play with what he calls a 'Prerumble', or prologue scene, set in 1920. Here, in an expressionist setting, i.e. distorted so as to underline its dream quality, the Black and Tans re-appear, this time in the countryside, which they are laying waste in retaliation for IRA assaults. They take prisoner two men who are life long enemies. Born in the same year, in the same town, in the same street (on opposite sides of the road), these two went to the same school and worshipped at the same church; yet they would rather die at the hands of the Black and Tans than shake hands. After a few amusing attempts, with bullets, to force reconciliation the 'Tans decide that to let these two men live would do more harm to Ireland than execution would achieve.

The play itself then begins, and it is thirty-five years later, or present time when O'Casey wrote the play. Now the two men, still sworn enemies, are prominent citizens in this small town of Doonavale, pillars of their society, one being Lord Mayor and the other his deputy. As much as they hate each other they do business together and between them they own most of the town. However, the focus is now on the next generation, poised to cast out the authority of the old. The son of one of the men, Binnington, is in love with the daughter of the other, McGilligan. This pair, Michael and Nora, have responded to a new spirit of rebellion fostered by Father Ned, whom O'Casey keeps off-stage all through the play. Father Ned is a quasi-mythic figure, the diametric opposite of all those stereotypical priests, like Fr Domineer or Canon Creehewel, who throng O'Casey's satiric comedies. Father Ned symbolises everything the older generation are frightened of, be that sex, change, or rebellion. He is at present overseeing the young people's entertainments for the *Tóstal*, or carnival. He wants artistic activity everywhere: even the servants are at it, much to the Lord Mayor's distress:

> *Bernadette.* Father Ned says that through music, good books, an' good pictures, we may get to know more about th' mystery of life.
> *Binnington (furiously).* Oh, doesn't this stuff make a body yell! Mysthery of life! There's no mysthery in it, girl. There's nothin' more in it than gettin' all you can, holdin' what you have, doin' justice to your religious duties, and actin' decent to a neighbour.[37]

Among the activities for the *Tóstal* is a play-within-the play about the 1798 Rising, and as they take over Binnington's drawing-room for rehearsal, the Man of the Pike is heard to say, 'get outa th' way! We have to get on with th' work of resuscitatin' Ireland' (p. 32). Here O'Casey is being mischievous, and yet there is a serious intent when a visitor from Northern Ireland asks what the *Tóstal* might be and if it might not be some kind of battle, we have this exchange:

> *Bernadette*. Ay, it is so, th' time when we skelped th' English outa th'
> towns of Wexford.
> *Skerighan (with amused mockery)*. Aw, lass, ye con do a gay lot in
> your dhreamin'.
> *Bernadette*. We have our history, misther. (p. 56)

It is a dignified reply, 'We have our history'. Whereas the pageant of the
history play has its own attractions, just as Boucicault's melodramas do,[38]
it is also set up as a critique of the freedom attained by the likes of
Binnington and McGilligan in 1922, when they took opposite sides on
the Treaty question. The text of the pageant centres on liberty: 'the liberty
we must have to live!', as the rebels put it (p. 35). Young Michael
Binnington faces down the English Captain with the assertion that might
just as well be directed against Binnington Senior:

> We are young, and God has given us strength and courage and
> counsel. May He give us the victory! ... It is high time for a change.
> ... Your peace, Captain, within the life we live, is but quiet decay.
> (pp. 35–6)

'Defend yourself, you traitor!' is the obvious response, and a melodra-
matic sword fight is rehearsed.

Inevitably, given the comic vigour of the play, victory goes to Father
Ned and to the young generation which sees him as guru. For the enemies
incapable as Montague and Capulet of mending a feud that never had a
rational or historical basis, the final blow comes when their attempt to
forbid the relationship between Michael and Nora meets this response:

> *Michael (laughingly)*. A bit late now to give th' ordher.
> *Binnington (angrily)*. How's it too late?
> *Nora*. Well, we studied at the same College.
> *Michael*. An' lived in the same flat.
> *Nora*. An' slept in th' same bed o' Sundays. (p. 99)

The drums of Father Ned which sound in the background soon after this
revelation mark the onset of a new campaign in Ireland.

Of course, this is fantasy. And yet O'Casey, by framing the play with
the prehistory of the War of Independence and by making the *Tóstal* the
pretext for the cultural revolution led by a new-age priest, manages to
construct a myth that was full of possiblities. It is necessary to explain
that the *Tóstal* was a government-sponsored annual festival initiated in
1953 with the purpose of encouraging tourism. In 1957 it spawned the
Dublin Theatre Festival, and it was for this venue that O'Casey was

invited to write a play. Therefore, *The Drums of Father Ned* may be seen as cleverly negotiating and recirculating the energies released by this new cultural revival in Ireland. Alas, the gods were determined to have the last laugh. A fierce row developed over the decision to include a play by O'Casey in the 1958 Dublin Theatre Festival. The Archbishop of Dublin let his disapproval be known; O'Casey withdrew his play in high dudgeon and in retaliation forbade the professional production of any of his plays thereafter. The whole controversy provides an ironic comment on *The Drums of Father Ned* itself, but it also soured O'Casey's last days and confirmed him in his view of priest-ridden Ireland.

In fact, O'Casey had here written very positively of Ireland. *The Drums of Father Ned* is a version of pastoral to counteract the outworn ideals of peasant Ireland and Victorian values. In a sonnet published as preface to the play O'Casey said it was an attempt:

> To snatch from Erin's back the sable shawl,
> And clothe her as she was before her fall;
> In cloak of green as bright as spring's young call.

(p. x)

He does not say, 'before the fall' but 'before her fall'. This must be before the establishment of the repressive regime often associated with Éamon de Valera and the 1937 Constitution.

III

Thus, whereas *The Plough and the Stars* presents in tragic form the fruits of the ideology that led to the 1916 Rising and its misdirected assault on subjugation, as O'Casey saw it, *The Drums of Father Ned* presents in comic form the fruits of an ideology that had reintroduced subjugation at another level. Both plays use history and in that sense are invitations to reconsider the past in view of the present. But O'Casey, in characteristic fashion, put the cart before the horse when it came to the conventional view of Irish history. Instead of celebrating heroic failure he deconstructed it. Instead of seeing history as unalterable and the memory of it ritualistic, O'Casey the socialist saw history as process, man-made and alterable, and the memory of it likewise malleable. His own development was not continuous but open to revision, and his later plays reverse the relationship between realism and myth that his early plays establish. He who began by demythologising the old Ireland of the aristocratic ideal ends up creating a myth for a new democratic Ireland.

But everything that O'Casey wrote early and late was impressed by his humanity and generosity of spirit, together with that outspokenness he admired in his father, 'famed by all as one who spat out his thoughts into the middle of a body's face.'[39] That quality is what unifies his work, be it tragic or comic. I suppose that is what is meant by integrity. It certainly is what makes the autobiographies so illuminating as reminiscences and the plays so arresting as imaginative dramatisations of Irish history.

12
Telling the time:
theatre and commemoration

Era-provincial self-regard
Finds us, as ever, unprepared
For the odd shifts of emphasis
Time regularly throws up to us

Derek Mahon.[1]

I

In the early days of computer technology, programers discovered that significant amounts of memory could be saved by shortening basic coded commands. Consequently, dates were commonly entered and processed as two digits instead of the traditional four. Thus 1973 became 73, and so on. The turn of the century must have seemed a long way away. As the clock got closer to ticking over into 2000, some experts predicted that computers would only recognise the 00 and read it as 1900, if at all. The *fin de siècle* fear was that 00, as the signifier of an unknown time, might wreak inestimable commercial and civil havoc on a computer-dependent global economy. The apocalyptic possibilities of this vision were manifold. More resonant in cultural terms, perhaps, was the irony of an enthusiastically anticipated hi-tech millennium that could not tell its own time. By failing, in Seamus Heaney's phrase, to find symbols adequate to our predicament,[2] technology was in danger of losing memory instead of saving it.

Linked with the discourse on the new millennium (soon to be better known by its designer label, Y2K), commemoration, in which time and memory merged, became a catchword of political and cultural debate. In Ireland alone, the last decade of the twentieth century saw the commemorations of the Famine, the 75th anniversary of the 1916 Rising and the bicentenary of the 1798 rebellion. The calls to remember the past persist.

How best to remember the dead of Bloody Sunday: memorial or tribunal? How to commemorate the deeds of 1916 – with pride or embarrassment and, critically, to what end? The way we commemorate an event from the past reflects not just that event, but unavoidably tells us about the present and how we envision the future. In the Irish paradigm, we need only compare the exuberant commemoration of the Easter Rising in 1966 with the embarrassed silence which characterised government and media response to the 75th anniversary in 1991 to understand that the collective memory of a society is no less malleable than that of Freud's individual. Although we may 'like to think we endure around truths immemorially posited'[3] what, and how, we remember is always disputable.

Although the combination of a future of European integration and a past marked consistently by attempts to emerge from colonial control is particularly Irish, questions of how we commemorate can not be confined to a post-colonial ghetto. In the former West Germany, Holocaust commemoration became and remains characterised by ritual repentance and mourning. In the East German account, on the other hand, the geno-cide of the Jews became simply a part of the greater narrative of the Nazi suppression of communism in general. The complex problem of commemoration was compounded when the newly unified Germany attempted to remember as one nation. Today, many monuments in the former East Berlin have been literally re-inscribed to remember *all* the war dead and not simply those who died at the hands of the Nazis in defence of communism. The most obvious example is a monument in the grounds of the Olympic Stadium erected during the Nazi regime as a symbol of the inexorable rise of the party. Today it has been partly destroyed: its swastikas are broken and a new dedication to Holocaust victims obscures its original inscription. In the face of this most trans-parent palimpsest, it is impossible to regard memory as fixed.

The representation of remembrance in the form of commemoration is, nonetheless, the point at which late twentieth-century concerns about the past and the future converge. The great gap between experience and remembrance is both temporal and imaginative as remembrance itself becomes constitutive of the experience. Theorised as such, it is precisely this great gap that provides a liminal space for cultural enquiry and artistic creativity. Above all forms of artistic representation, theatre embraces that space to play out remembrance and experience in a coinci-dence of time, action and place. Tried and tested as they are, Aristotle's unities have repeatedly provided the apparatus for Irish investigations of memory and commemoration. Thomas Kilroy articulates the difference between theatre and other forms of writing as

> this curious desire to move about actual living bodies, to give them voice and the mantle of character in a conspiracy of play ... It is also

this element which makes the place of Drama in Literature so prob-
lematical.[4]

While theatre in Ireland retains its firm association with the word, criticism that reads the work of McGuinness or Friel as literature alone, turns
a blind eye to the complexity of the play as performance. This is particularly true of Friel's *The Freedom of the City* and *Making History*, and
McGuinness's *Observe the Sons of Ulster Marching Towards the Somme*,
which function as explorations of the interface between public and
private remembrance. 'Words are signals, counters ...'[5] and as such, are
part of a wide theatrical vocabulary. Recognition of the performative
nature of these plays or, in other words, recognition that they are, above
all, made for performance, is fundamental to understanding how Irish
theatre continues to find ways of telling our time.

II

Observe the Sons of Ulster Marching Towards the Somme is one of the
more complicated theatrical explorations of memory and remembrance.
Helen Lojek has commented on the complexity of McGuinness's under-
taking; 'The play's concern with what makes men march is paralleled by
an examination of ways the past shapes the men who shape the myths
which shape the past.'[6] It is appropriate that eight characters should be
employed in the exploration of the multiple layers of history, myth and
fiction that shroud and compose the Battle of the Somme and, by implication, the symbology of the larger Unionist movement. Dramatically,
these layers are facilitated by the intricate interweaving of text and
performance, action and rhetoric and, indeed, by the large cast.

The dramatic action is initiated by the elderly Pyper's monologue
spoken in the setting of contemporary Ulster. His opening lines give
immediate resonance to the action to follow:

> Again. As always, again. Why does this persist? What more do we
> have to tell each other? I remember nothing today. Absolutely
> nothing. (p. 97)

The organisational device of repetition is foregrounded in these first
words as Pyper articulates the repetition and repeatability of the past and
the consequent circularity of present loyalist experience. He establishes
simultaneously his deep reluctance to remember and the inevitability of
that remembrance. Pyper's inability to choose his memories and his
unwillingness and his compulsion to remember the horrors of war are
closely linked with the notion that talk of the horror creates a coherence

and a fictionality that diminishes the terrible suffering of battle; 'they invent as freely as they wish ... Invention gives that slaughter shape.'[7] Yet despite that recognition, Pyper's memory becomes a space where the eight soldiers act out their roles in war, preceding the Battle of the Somme. However obstinate, Pyper's past in history refuses to remain unremembered and in the necessary re-playing creates a shape and a coherence of its own. Thus the ghosts of his past become the characters of the present of the play and endure – parading in his memory until the action of the Somme is repeated and the skies above them have turned salmon pink.

Observe the Sons of Ulster Marching Towards the Somme is thus a memory play, where Pyper's memory functions as a sort of proscenium frame for the action. Friel's historian Lombard, in *Making History*, asserts the primacy of action over remembrance and says that, 'History has to be made before it is remade.'[8] Here, however, an audience sees both processes unfold at once. The complexity of the theatrical device which allows Pyper to be at once a character and a spectator finds its formal co-relative in the fractured action of playing within the play. Like McGuinness's *Carthaginians*, this incorporates the convention of the play within the play as the soldiers play out the Battle of Scarva on the eve of the Battle of the Somme. McGuinness's deceptive realism sets a scene where the lads, nervous and jittery in the anticipation of battle, welcome the distraction of football foolery and playacting. Roulston suggests praying, and there is a profound moment of peace and wholeness as Millen and McIlwaine join him in singing a hymn. McIlwaine's comic creative storytelling of the 1916 Rising and Pearse 'the boy who took over a post office because he was short of a few stamps' (p. 175), and Crawford's 'Is there time for a quick match?' similarly divert attention from the increasingly inevitable advance to battle. Crawford refers to the artful banter which directly precedes the playing of Scarva:

> Crawford: Yous two are pretty sharp.
> McIlwaine: Lethal, son, lethal.
> Anderson: We practise in the dark.
> Crawford: Did yous ever think of taking it up full time?
> Anderson: Good idea.
> McIlwaine: What would we do?
> Anderson: Any suggestions?
> Pyper: Something sad.
> Anderson: Damn sadness. Something to make the blood boil.
> McIlwaine: Battle of the Boyne? (p. 181)

The soldiers organise themselves into the characters of the Catholic King James and the Protestant King Billy with an amount of comic squabbling.

Millen's protest at being given the part of King James, while loaded with traditional allegiance has, on the surface at least, more to do with the knowledge that he must lose. Millen concludes 'This is not a fair fight'. displeased as Anderson reminds him of the narrative foreclosure of the play: 'And remember King James, we know the result, you know the result, keep to the result' (p. 182).

Anderson's further commentary on the progress of the battle is replete with the descriptive clichés of loyalist symbology; 'glorious religion', 'the traitor James', 'minion of Rome', and humourous in his unwilling concession to the players' unprofessional interruptions 'will the trusty steed shut his mouth when I'm in the middle of the story?' The boister-ousness of the action is silenced abruptly when, as the battle reaches its expected climax, Pyper and Crawford as King Billy and his white steed come crashing to the ground turning the traditional myth on its head.

The failure of the replay to yield the 'true' result unsettles the men and is identified by Millen as a bad omen, 'not the best of signs', then dismissed brusquely by the others: 'It was only a game'. But for the loyalist soldiers, fighting for England in a demonstration of true alle-giance and loyalty, the subversion of their myth of origin even in a game, is profoundly debilitating. The re-enactment of the Battle of Scarva in commemoration of the Battle of the Boyne is an essential part of the symbology of Ulster loyalism and is indeed contingent on the knowledge that year after year the outcome of the battle is the same – 'we know the result' – signifying victory, authority and rightful existence. By the changed outcome of this ostensible replay, the rules of its performance are broken, being not a re-enactment but an alternative version, perhaps even a token of the arbitrariness of victory. Thus the performance of the lads, and its changed script, signals the unreliability of myth and the falli-bility of historical fact as a justification for present action. Its occurrence on the eve of another loyal battle casts the anticipated action in doubt, challenging – from within – that very loyal tradition of commemoration and veneration. Indeed, the destabilising effect of their mock Scarva is compounded by the staunch loyalty of the actors who, despite their deep belief that they are 'God's chosen', are powerless to rectify the performed defeat of their play battle. Their crisis is that despite the hint that myth may not really provide an adequate justification for their present course of action, they are trapped within a tradition that does not allow them to take cognizance of alternative versions.

McGuinness's juxtaposition of the Battle of Scarva with the Battle of the Somme draws attention to the replay of action on the stage in another commemoration. By replaying the Battle of the Boyne, (in the mediated version of the Battle of Scarva), in the new context of the Battle of the Somme, the soldiers establish a narrative of continuity which connects the discrete battles in the homogeneous project of Ulster loyalism. 'Again, as always again', says Pyper, acknowledging the continuous present of the past in commemoration. The ghosts of the past refuse to be still, repeating endlessly their own action of remembrance, employing the myth of the sacrifice of the Boyne as a direct precursor of their sacrifice at the Somme. (This is perhaps a literal application of Conor Cruise O'Brien's observation that the Irish are commemorating themselves to death although his comment was intended to castigate proponents of the 'other' tradition of Republicanism.) Thus, despite the intimation that historical myth may not be the inherited force of legitimate action, in the unexpected result of Scarva, the desire to repeat the past, to incorporate the images of past glory into the present, 'to keep to the result' ensures that confinement in, and perpetuation of, tradition is inevitable. Significantly, McIlwaine's comic retelling and rewriting of the historical facts of the 1916 Rising shows not simply the willingness to alter the historical facts of the Nationalist rebellion and the insistence on the inalterability of their own historical myth as argued by Lojek but, more crucially, demonstrates McIlwaine's perception of the subversive power of iconoclasm. Fully cognizant of its significances he attacks and undermines the foundational event of the 'other side' in order to discredit the legitimacy of the whole movement.

On their return to Ulster on leave, Anderson and McIlwaine make a private pilgrimage to 'The Field. The holiest spot in Ulster'. There, alone but for their props of a bottle of Bushmills and a lambeg drum, their attempts to celebrate the Twelfth of July after the day itself has passed are in vain:

> It's no good here on your own. No good without the speakers. No good without the bands, no good without the banners. Without the chaps. No good on your own. Why did we come here to be jeered at? Why did we come here, Anderson? (p. 148)

McIlwaine's sense of loss derives from the perception that the meaning of the celebration is no longer immanent. Without the pomp and ceremony of the annual march the day is unrecognisable. Consequently, a celebration of the day without the trappings of the traditional celebration in the midst of marching men yields no euphoria of belonging. The other soldiers, who also return on leave after the celebrations of the Twelfth, have refused to march with the Belfast men. 'And why? Because it wasn't the Twelfth of July.' There is then a fundamental understanding that tradition deems certain action appropriate at certain times. Convention gains authority by force of repetition and gradually assumes the unquestioned status of a natural inevitability. Thus it is conventional, traditional and right that men should march on the twelfth day of July every year, but an aberration that

McIlwaine and Anderson should try to appropriate this action for their own celebration. Such an understanding of tradition reveals fundamental similarities with the notion of theatrical performance. The concept of the suspension of disbelief allows theatre the licence to perform outside the rules of normal daily life; this convention is accepted as soon as the spectator sits in the darkened theatre and waits for the action to begin. Even the most outlandish is made possible and acceptable by the setting of the theatre. Similarly, the parading and beating of war drums, the mass movement of men through the streets of Belfast is sanctioned by the time and place deemed appropriate and right by tradition. The time and context are missing for Anderson and McIlwaine and consequently their celebration lacks authority and authenticity.

The profound theatricality of the rituals of commemoration is nowhere more tangible than when McIlwaine stands on the empty stage in the burgeoning realisation of the emptiness of the holiest spot in Ulster. Even the symbol of the lambeg drum, loaded with connotation, does not signify what it signifies in the context of the traditional rituals and he kicks it in disgust. The intuition of the hollowness of the attempted celebration is inseparable from McIlwaine's doubts about the loyalist part in the war.

> Every nail we hammered into the Titanic, we'll die in the same amount in this cursed war … It's good for nothing. A waste of time. We won't survive. (p. 154)

His frenzied tirade culminates in the assertion that the proud men of Ulster are not making a sacrifice to prove loyalty to Britain: 'Jesus, you've seen this war. We are the sacrifice.' (p. 156)

The helplessness of McIlwaine's situation is that despite his realisation of the futility of their deaths, he is unable to deviate from the advancing historically charged tradition which locks the lads into a narrative of continuity, compelling them to celebrate Scarva and the holiest spot in Ulster even though both commemorations are failures. His recourse to the images of the past thus implicates him, as it does the other lads, in a present and future of replication and imitation where the action of all tenses is articulated in 'Again. As always, again'. Correspondingly McIlwaine embraces the rhetoric of loyalism and the fierce beating of the drum to obliterate the incompatibilities of the commemorated past with the present: 'Drown me out will you? Give me noise…Stop me hearing myself. Stop me!'(p. 157) Strapped into the drum, by Anderson, McIlwaine is 'raised up by what he buckles under'.[9] Heaney's lines provide an appropriate metaphor for the workings of tradition; as his hands bleed satisfactorily, the sense of well-being conferred on McIlwaine brings him home to his sense of self and belonging. The misgivings about the war do not disappear but they are located in a system that will silence them and confer meaning on the lads through participation.

Following the same pattern, Pyper, who by sexual unorthodoxy and class difference is initially an outsider, becomes one of the lads by learning the common commemorative language of the group. Dramatically, this development is foregrounded in the contrast between his mock heroic speechifying in the first section of the play when he, in feigned military style, lists the reasons why Millen has enlisted, and his real subscription to the values of the Ulstermen evidenced in his final speech. Pyper's speech becomes identifiable as the language of loyal Ulster as the play moves towards his final prayer. At the same time, his language becomes increasingly self-conscious, straining to incorporate the motifs of home and homecoming in the anticipation of death. Pyper's identification of the smell of the Somme with 'a river at home' works itself into a rhetorical claim that:

> It's bringing us home. We're not in France. We're home. We're on our own territory. We're fighting for home. This river is ours. This land is ours. We've come home ... The Somme, it's not what we think it is. It's the Lagan, the Foyle, the Bann. (p. 188)

Pyper's language is weighed down by the highly literary activity in which it is engaged. His words are burdened in the attempt to find home in away and to identify the familiar in the foreign. Indeed, his effort to make the experience congruent with the landscape of shared experience causes him to speak an inflated rhetoric that his words cannot sustain. Craig's admonition that he is 'trying too hard' refers directly to Pyper's own need to articulate and believe the justification for their part in the war. The other soldiers have no need of Pyper's reminders. But Craig's remark is also an acknowledgment that the long standing beliefs of loyalism are adequate justification of their involvement: 'We know where we are. We know what we've to do. And we knew before we enlisted.' (p. 188)

Pyper's literary construction of parallels and recurring motifs is therefore superfluous as the soldiers come to the realisation that 'There is nothing imaginary about this ... This is the last battle. We're going out to die.' But Pyper's composition and delivery illustrate the constructedness of rhetoric and, although not assimilated into the shared imagery of the Ulstermen in this instance, the rivers and placenames of home are movingly invoked in his final prayer. The exchange of sashes that precedes it is a token of consolidated friendships, but this ritual is initiated only after Anderson's gesture of acceptance and assimilation in offering Pyper an Orange sash to wear, 'So we'll recognize you as one of our own. Your own' (p. 193). It is in this capacity that Pyper is sanctioned to pray in the name of all the lads, deriving his faith and hope from the collective notion of identity of which he is now a part. The authority that is lacking in his earlier self-conscious speech is restored here by his fellowship in discourse as he declares his love for the lives of the sons of Ulster. In his articulation of the common inspiration for enlistment, he recites the homeplaces of the men in a personal and collective tribute:

> Let this day at the Somme be as glorious in the memory of Ulster as that day at the Boyne when you scattered our enemies. Lead us back from this exile. To Derry, to the Foyle. To Belfast and the Lagan. To Armagh. To Tyrone. To the Bann and its banks. To Erne and its islands ... Lord look down on us. Spare us. I love –. Observe the Sons of Ulster marching towards the Somme. I love their lives. I love my own life. I love my home. I love my Ulster. (p. 196)

In the chant that follows, Ulster is invoked eight times, once for every soldier, and as the chant becomes a battle cry the eight voices become one.

There is then a sense of the inevitability of historical confinement as Pyper moves from outside the group to inside. In the end, he, like the others, cannot survive alone outside the shared symbology of commemoration which in the present is called tradition. The process by which he moves to that assimilation is reluctant, but his movement is nonetheless illustrative of the general condition of the lads who are unable to remain untouched by the hands of their 'ancestors, interfering' (p. 163).

However politically inevitable, Pyper's progress from the periphery to the centre is nonetheless theatrically subversive. By speaking a long opening monologue and by virtue of his heightened eccentricity, he becomes the closest thing to a main character in McGuinness's ensemble piece. The notion of a main character is, however, destabilised by his ambiguities; he does not provide a centre, being himself on the edge of the consensual; he is both spectator and character in the action of the play and yet does not control the action in either of these roles; his homosexuality makes him different from the others and yet he is the only man who talks about women in the play.

McGuinness continues to undermine theatrical conventions of representation in the third part of the play, entitled 'Pairing'. As the title suggests, the lads return home in pairs to sites central to their myths. But despite McGuinness's employment of the familiar duo, stereotypical polarities are resisted; each couple breaks down to reveal multiple parts, rendering the model of dichotomy obsolete. Crawford and Roulston find themselves within a church which becomes the site of confessions by both men. The revelations that Crawford is half Catholic and that the preacher Roulston has lost his faith is disconcertingly precipitated by a brawl in the church. Anderson and McIlwaine go to the Field where, as earlier detailed, their hard men Belfast manner gives way to profound doubts about their allegiance. Millen and Moore reverse their roles in attempting to overcome fear of death and Millen asks, 'Was it you or I lost their nerve? Who crossed that bridge?' Finally, Craig and Pyper subvert the traditional representation of all duos in Irish theatre by their overtly homosexual relationship. Critics have commented on the implications of homosexuality as an instrument of challenge and questioning in the play, claiming even that that the condition of homosexuality in the eighties could be used as a metaphor for national consciousness '– division, introversion.'[10] Whatever about the national connotations, homosexuality as an alternative to dominant sexual orthodoxy perpetually challenges inherited tenets of belief and social order. This is as true for questions of social analysis as for issues of dramatic representation. McGuinness's imperative to observe the sons of Ulster invites us then to observe the discrete personalities of the lads who collectively make up the 36th Battalion. In his rejection of the binary opposition, and in his subversion of the notion of main character, McGuinness facilitates the dramatic representation of the traditionally uniform face of Ulster Unionism as a multiplicity of diverse individuals. Edna Longley writes:

> The image of the web is female, feminist, connective – as contrasted with male polarisation. So is the ability to inhabit a range of relations rather than a single allegiance. The great advantage of living in Northern Ireland is that you can live in three places at once.[11]

Structurally, then, the play complements McGuinness's thematic claim that the characters discover the feminine side of themselves. This is not to say that the male characters of *Observe the Sons of Ulster Marching Towards the Somme* consider Ulster anything other than their Ulster, let alone three political areas. Nor does Longley's approach approximate political strategy. But her idea complements McGuinness's exposition of the plurality of elements in Ulster Unionism. The traditional modes of male polarisation are rejected and instead a diversity of representation is facilitated. This heterogeneity is served by giving the typically one dimensional Ulster Unionist movement the geographical and personal specifics with which the characters make Ulster truly diverse and truly their own. Pyper's prayer not only re-echoes the rituals of introduction in the opening scenes where each character is immediately associated with place but locates the play in a discourse of geography and placenames generally associated with the idealisations of the rural South, or at least the Gaelic tradition of *logainmneacha*. Coleraine is associated with red skies unlike the pink skies of France. Eniskillen reappears periodically in song. The Belfast boys so thoroughly adhere to the stereotype that they are identified even before they appear on stage. If McGuinness's play is without precedent, it is because of the manner in which the monolithic face of Ulster Unionism is portrayed as various and multifaceted and susceptible to similar badges of identification as nationalist rhetoric.

Furthermore, the device which creates the dramatic space for multiplicity concurrently facilitates simultaneity. The pairing section of the play not only deconstructs binary opposition. In further subversion of male sequential narrative, the scenes take place simultaneously and emphasise the characters' development of individuality together. In her seminal essay on feminine morphology, Cixous writes that 'woman unthinks the unifying, regulating history that homogenizes and channels forces, herding contradictions into a new field'.[12] This could well be a description of McGuinness's writing which, in its investigation of the accretion of myth, history and fiction, deconstructs the notion of history as a continuous linear narrative. The play's organisational device of repetition is also a function of the lives of its characters who, in embracing the concept of linear inheritance, lock themselves into a cycle of simulation and replication. Traditional causality, as well as traditional mimetic order, is questioned in this way as commemoration (in myth) becomes an authorising force, sanctioning action in the present. To round off the comparison, the transgressive feminist act of rewriting history is analogous to the ominous slippage of the script in the Battle of Scarva.

Holocaust scholar James Young suggests that once we have assigned monumental form to memory, we have somehow divested ourselves of the obligation to remember.[13] If, in shouldering the memory work, monuments have actually relieved viewers of their memory burden, theatre as a medium has the potential to interrogate the meaning of the shifting monumental memory of those stones in Berlin. But the complex nature of commemoration might be better served if, instead of setting remembering and forgetting against each other as either/or, we listen to what our writers have long suggested and embrace the 'not… ignoble condition'[14] of both/and.[15]

Notes

NOTES TO FOREWORD

1. See Daniel Mulhall, 'Review: *The Scottish Nation*', in *Scottish Affairs*, 34, winter 2001, pp. 34–8.
2. Dr Martin Mansergh (Special Advisor to the Taoiseach), 'The Irish Peace Process and its Impact on Ireland's Wider Relationships', lecture delivered at the University of Aberdeen, 12 November 1999.
3. Colm Tóibín, 'Lady Gregory's Toothbrush', in *The New York Review of Books*, XLVIII, 13, p. 41.
4. T. M. Devine, *The Scottish Nation, 1700–2000*, London: Allen Lane, 1999, pp. 486–7.

NOTES TO INTRODUCTION

1. Among the more important works on 1798 are: Thomas Bartlett, David Dickson, Dáire Keogh and Kevin Whelan (eds), *The 1798 Rebellion: a Bicentennial Perspective*, Dublin: Four Courts Press, 2001; Allan Blackstock, *An Ascendancy Army: the Irish Yeomanry 1796–1834*, Dublin: Four Courts Press, 1998; Mary Cullen (ed.), *1798: 200 Years of Resonance*, Boston: Irish Reporter, 1998; Nancy J. Curtin, *The United Irishmen: Popular Politics in Ulster and Dublin, 1791–1798*, Oxford: Clarendon Press, 1998; Michael Durey, *Andrew Bryson's Ordeal: an Epilogue to the 1798 Rebellion*, Cork: Cork University Press, 1998; Nicholas Furlong, *Fr. John Murphy of Boolavogue (sic) 1753–1798*, Dublin: Geography Publications, 1998; Daniel J. Gahan, *The People's Rising*, Dublin: Gill & Macmillan, 1995; D. J. Gahan, *Rebellion!: Ireland in 1798*, Dublin: The O'Brien Press, 1998; Michael Kenny, *The 1798 Rebellion*, Dublin: Town House and Country House, 1996; Dáire Keogh and Nicholas Furlong (eds), *The Mighty Wave: The 1798 Rebellion in Wexford*, Dublin: Four Courts Press, 1996; Dáire Keogh and Thomas Bartlett, *1798*, Dublin: Gill & Macmillan, 1998; John Killen (ed.), *The Decade of the United Irishmen: Contemporary Accounts, 1791–1801*, Belfast: Blackstaff, 1997; Mary McNeill, *The Life and Times of Mary Ann McCracken 1770–1866*, Belfast: Blackstaff Press, 1997; William A. Maguire (ed.), *Up in Arms!: The 1798 Rebellion in Ireland*, Belfast: Ulster Museum, 1998; John Newsinger (ed.), *United Irishman: The Autobiography of James Hope*, London: Merlin, 2001; R. O'Donnell, *1798 Diary*, Dublin: The Irish Times, 1998; Patrick O'Farrell (ed.), *The '98 Reader: An Anthology of Song, Prose and Poetry*, Dublin: Lilliput Press, 1998; Norman Porter (ed.), *The Republican Ideal: Current Perspectives*, Belfast: Blackstaff Press, 1998; Kieran Sheedy, *'The Tellicherry Five': The Transportation of Michael Dwyer and the Wicklow Rebels*, Dublin: The Woodfield Press, 1997; Jim Smyth (ed.), *Revolution, Counter-Revolution and Union: Ireland in the 1790s*, Cambridge University Press, 2001; Kevin Whelan, *The Tree of Liberty: Radicalism, Catholicism and the Construction of Irish Identity*, Cork: Cork University Press, 1996; Kevin Whelan, *The Fellowship of Freedom*, Cork: Cork University Press, 1998; Kevin Wheelan and Matthew Stout, *The United Irishmen and the 1798 Rebellion*, Cork: Cork University Press, 1998.
2. Tony Allan, *The Irish Famine*, London: Heinemann, 1998; Susan Campbell Bartoletti, *Black Potatoes: The Story of the Great Irish Famine*, Boston: Houghton Mifflin, 2001; L. A. Clarkson, E. M. Crawford, Paul S. Ell and Liam Kennedy (eds), *The Great Irish Famine*, Dublin: Four Courts Press, 1999; Leslie Clarkson and Margaret Crawford, *Feast and Famine*, Oxford University Press, 2001; Mary E. Daly, *The Famine of Ireland*, Dundalk: Dundalgan Press, 1986; James S. Donnelly Jr., *The Great Irish Potato Famine*, London: Sutton, 2001; Peter Gray, *Famine, Land and Politics*, Dublin: Irish Academic Press, 1998; Kieran A. Kennedy (ed.), *From Famine to Feast*, Dublin: Institute of Public Administration, 1998; John Killen, *The Famine Decade*, Belfast: Blackstaff, 1995; Christine Kinealy, *This Great Calamity*, Dublin: Gill & Macmillan, 1994; Christine Kinealy, *A Death-Dealing Famine*, London: Pluto, 1996; Christine Kinealy, *The Great Irish Famine*, Basingstoke: Palgrave, 2001; Carla King, *Famine, Land and Culture in Ireland*, Dublin: University College Dublin Press, 2000; Noel Kissane (ed.), *The Irish Famine: A Documentary History*, Dublin: National Library of Ireland, 1996; Helen Litton, *The Irish Famine: An Illustrated History*, Dublin: Wolfhound, 1994; Donald MacRaild, *The Great*

Famine and Beyond, Dublin: Irish Academic Press, 1999; Christopher Morash, *Writing the Irish Famine*, Oxford: Clarendon, 1995; Christopher Morash and Richard Hayes (eds), *Fearful Realities: New Perspectives on the Famine*, Dublin: Irish Academic Press, 1995; Frank Neal, *Black '47*, Basingstoke: Palgrave, 1997; Asenath Nicholson and Maureen Murphy (eds), *Annals of the Famine in Ireland*, Dublin: Lilliput Press, 1998; Brendan Ó Cathaoir, *Famine Diary*, Dublin: Irish Academic Press, 1997; Cormac Ó Gráda, *The Great Irish Famine*, Cambridge University Press, 1995; Cormac Ó Gráda (ed.), *Famine 150: Commemorative Lecture Series*, Dublin: Teagasc, 1997; Cormac Ó Gráda, *Black '47 and Beyond: The Great Irish Famine in History, Economy, and Memory*, Princeton, NJ: Princeton University Press, 1999; Patrick O'Sullivan (ed.), *The Meaing of the Famine*, London: Leicester University Press, 2000; John Percival and Ian Gibson, *The Great Famine*, London: BBC, 1995; Cathal Póirtéir (ed.), *The Great Irish Famine: 1845–1852*, Cork: Mercier Press, 1995; Edward Purdon, *The Irish Famine, 1845–52*, Cork: Mercier Press, 2000; Robert James Scally, *The End of Hidden Ireland: Rebellion, Famine and Emigration*, New York: Oxford University Press, 1996; Colm Tóibín and Diarmaid Ferriter, *The Irish Famine: A Documentary*, London: Profile Books, 2001; Kevin Whelan, *Interpreting the Famine*, Cork: Cork University Press, 1996.

3. Liam Chambers, *Rebellion in Kildare*, Dublin: Four Courts Press, 1998; William Farrell, *Voice of Rebellion: Carlow in 1798*, Dublin: Wolfhound Press, 1998; Liam Kelly, *A Flame Now Quenched: Rebels and Frenchmen in Ireland, 1793–1798*, Dublin: Lilliput Press, 1998; Ruan O'Donnell, *The Rebellion in Wicklow 1798*, Dublin: Irish Academic Press, 1997; A. T. Q. Stewart, *The Summer Soldiers: The 1798 Rebellion in Antrim and Down*, Belfast: Blackstaff Press, 1995; Bill Wilsdon, *The Sites of the 1798 Rising in Antrim and Down*, Belfast: Blackstaff Press, 1997.

4. One of the most important publications of 1998 was undoubtedly Dáire Keogh and Nicholas Furlong (eds), *The Women of 1798*, Dublin: Four Courts Press, 1998. See also John D. Beatty (ed.), *Women's Narratives of the Irish Rebellion of 1798*, Dublin: Four Courts Press, 2001.

5. Tom Hayden (ed.), *Irish Hunger: Personal Reflections on the Legacy of the Famine*, Boulder, Co: Roberts Rinehart, 1998; Cathal Póirtéir (ed.), *Family Echoes*, Dublin: Gill & Macmillan, 1995; Alexander Somerville and Keith Snell (eds), *Letters from Ireland during the Famine of 1847*, Dublin: Irish Academic Press, 1994.

6. Christine Kinealy and Trevor Parkhill (eds), *Famine in Ulster*, Belfast: Ulster Historical Foundation, 1997; Christine Kinealy and Gerard MacAtasney, *The Hidden Famine: Hunger, Poverty and Sectarianism in Belfast, 1840–50*, London: Pluto, 2000; Ned McHugh, *Drogheda before the Famine*, Dublin: Irish Academic Press, 1998; Ignatius Murphy, *Before the Famine Struck: Life in West Clare*, Dublin: Irish Academic Press, 1996; Ignatius Murphy, *People Starved: Life and Death in West Clare*, Dublin: Irish Academic Press, 1996; Seamus O'Brien, *Famine and Community in Mullingar Poor Law Union, 1845–1849*, Dublin: Irish Academic Press, 1999; Tim Robinson (ed.), *Connemara after the Famine*, Dublin: Lilliput Press, 1995.

7. Margaret Crawford (ed.), *The Hungry Stream: Essays on Famine and Emigration*, Belfast: Institute of Irish Studies, 1997; David Fitzpatrick (ed.), *Oceans of Consolation: Personal Accounts of Irish Migration to Australia*, Cork University Press, 1995; Arthur Gribben (ed.), *The Great Famine and the Irish Diaspora in America*, Amherst: University of Massachusetts Press, 1999; Edward Laxton, *The Famine Ships: The Irish Exodus to America, 1846–51*, London: Bloomsbury, 1997.

8. See David Cairns and Shaun Richards, *Writing Ireland: Colonialism, Nationalism and Culture*, Manchester: Manchester University Press, 1988; Adele M. Dalsimer (ed.), *Visualizing Ireland: National Identity and the Pictorial Tradition*, Boston and London: Faber and Faber, 1993; Declan Kiberd, *Inventing Ireland: The Literature of the Modern Nation*, London: Jonathan Cape, 1995.

9. Adele M. Dalsimer and Vera Kreilkamp, 'Introduction', in Dalsimer (ed.), *Visualizing Ireland*, p. 3.

10. Walter Forde, letter to the editor, *The Irish Times*, 11 May 1998.

11. An exemplary study of how communities tried to come to terms with the devastating effects of the First World War through a 'culture of commemoration' in the UK, in Germany and France is Jay Winter's *Sites of Memory, Sites of Mourning: The Great War in European Cultural History*, Cambridge: Cambridge University Press, 1995; for the pre-First World War period, see Matthew Campbell, Jacqueline M. Labbe and Sally Shuttleworth (eds), *Memory and Memorials, 1789–1914*, London: Routledge, 2000; a more specific look at how national memory has been constructed in France is offered in Avner Ben-Amos, *Funerals, Politics, and Memory in Modern*

France, 1789–1996, Oxford University Press, 2000; the relationship between personal and public remembrance is addressed in Elisabeth Hallam and Jenny Hockey, *Death, Memory and Mementos*, Oxford: Berg, 2000.
12. Michael Billig, *Banal Nationalism*, London: Sage, 1995.
12. See Patrick Comerford's overview of books published to mark the commemorations of the 1798 rising, 'All that delirium of the brave', *The Irish Times*, 13 June 1998.
13. See Dan Ben-Amos and Liliane Weissberg (eds), *Cultural Memory and the Construction of Identity*, Wayne State University Press, 1999.
14. See Benedict Anderson, *Imagined Communities: Reflections on the Origin and Spread of Nationalism*, London: Verso, rev. edn, 1996.
15. Anthony Smith, *The Ethnic Origins of Nations*, Oxford: Blackwell, 1986, p. 208.
16. Anthony Cohen, *The Symbolic Construction of Community*, London: Routledge, 1985, p. 118.
17. C. Beveridge and R. Turnbull, *The Eclipse of Scottish Culture: Inferiorism and the Intellectuals*, Edinburgh: Polygon, 1989, p. 16.
18. David McCrone, *Understanding Scotland: The Sociology of a Nation*, London: Routledge, 2nd edn, 2001, p. 3.
19. See Michael J. Horgan (ed.), *Hiroshima in History and Memory*, Cambridge: Cambridge University Press, 1996.
20. John Bodnar, *Remaking America: Public Memory, Commemoration, and Patriotism in the Twentieth Century*, Princeton, NJ: Princeton University Press, 1994.
21. Joseph Ruane and Jennifer Todd, '"Why can't you get along with each other?", Culture, Structure and the Northern Ireland Conflict', in Eamonn Hughes (ed.), *Culture and Politics in Northern Ireland, 1960–1990*, Milton Keynes: Open University Press, 1991, pp. 29–30.
22. See Michael S. Roth, *The Ironist's Cage: Memory, Trauma, and the Construction of History*, New York: Columbia University Press, 1995.
23. As Conor Cruise O'Brien wrote of 1966: 'a great commemorative year, a year in which ghosts were bound to walk.' O'Brien, *States of Ireland*, London: Panther, 1974, p. 143.
24. Tom Dunne, *The Irish Times*, 24 March 1998.
25. *The Irish Times*, 6 May 1998.
26. George Schöpflin, *Nations, Identity, Power: The New Politics of Europe*, London: Hurst, 2000, p. 74.
27. Ibid., p. 76.
28. Ibid., p. 77.
29. Ibid.
30. The never-ending series of commemorative events ranged from 'The Walking Gallows' in Athy (commemorating Lieut. Edward Hepenstall of the Wicklow Militia, who perfected the technique of 'half-hanging') and the restaging of the Battle of Ballinamuck, Co. Longford, involving 400 soldiers and 40,000 spectators, to the re-enactment of the Wexford Senate in the grounds of Johnstown Castle, Co. Wexford, as well as in Brisbane, Australia, and the opening of visitors' centres like the National 1798 Visitors' Centre in Enniscorthy – not to forget a string of summer schools devoted to the commemoration of '98 (e.g. Goldsmith, Byrne-Perry, Bram Stoker, George Moore, John Hewitt, William Carleton, Parnell, General Humbert and others).
31. See Tom Garvin, *1922: The Birth of Irish Democracy*, Dublin: Gill & Macmillan, 1996.
32. 'The complexity and pain of history need explanations, not apologies', is Roy Foster's position: 'Sorry is not enough', *Independent on Sunday*, 18 July 1999. The historian Gerard DeGroot contended: 'Apologising for the past is terribly easy. Meaningless acts are always simple. The angst suffered by Mr Blair when he apologised to the Irish would not fill a sheet on a psychiatrist's pad.' And Magnus Linklater, feeling 'advanced apology fatigue', chimed in: '… it demeans the whole act of forgiveness and atonement. The idea that by simply issuing a public apology you can, as it were, wipe the slate of history clean undermines the genuine act of contrition.' 'There's really no need to apolgise', *Scotland on Sunday*, 1 October 2000.
33. See Patrick M. Geoghegan, *The Irish Act of Union: A Study in High Politics, 1798–1801*, New York: St Martin's Press, 2000; also Dáire Keogh and Kevin Whelan (eds), *Acts of Union*, Dublin: Four Courts Press, 2000.
34. See Julian Jackson, *France: The Dark Years, 1940–1944*, Oxford: Oxford University Press, 2001; see also Henry Rousso, *The Vichy Regime Syndrome: History and Memory in France Since 1914*, Cambridge, MA: Harvard University Press, 1991.
35. Christian Graf von Krockow called the 1848 revolution in Germany 'the forgotten revolution', 'Die vergessene Revolution', *Die Woche*, 17 April 1998; Robert Taylor contended that no one

commenmorates 1848 because it was a failure and 'cast forward a dark shadow', 'Springtime for Hitler', *Prospect*, March 1998.

36. The controversy about the Holocaust monument in Berlin is well covered in two books: Michael S. Cullen (ed.), *Das Holocaust-Mahnmal: Dokumentation einer Debatte*, Zurich: Pendo, 1999; Michael Jeismann (ed.), *Mahnmal Mitte: Eine Kontroverse*, Cologne: DuMont, 1999.
37. For a general background, see James E. Young, 'The Art of Memory: Holocaust Memorials in History', in J. E. Young (ed.), *Holocaust Memorials in History: The Art of Memory*, New York: Prestel, 1994; see also Nancy Wood, *Vectors of Memory: Legacies of Trauma in Postwar Europe*, New York: New York University Press, 1999.
38. Salomon Korn, *Geteilte Erinnerungen: Beiträge zur deutsch-jüdischen Gegenwart*, Berlin: Philo Verlag, 1999.
39. Kristin Ann Hass, *Carried to the Wall: American Memory and the Vietnam Veterans Memorial*, Berkeley: University of California Press, 1998.
40. Lyn Spillman, *Nation and Commemoration*, Cambridge: Cambridge University Press, 1997.
41. For a wider comparative context, see John R. Gillis (ed.), *Commemorations: The Politics of National Identity*, Princeton, NJ: Princeton University Press, 1997.
42. See also Keith Jeffery, *Ireland and the Great War*, Cambridge: Cambridge University Press, 2000.
43. Fintan O'Toole, 'At the heart of Drumcree is a walk down memory lane', *The Irish Times*, 7 July 2001.
44. The nexus of commemoration and reconciliation in an African context is addressed by Wole Soyinka in *The Burden of Memory, the Muse of Forgiveness*, New York: Oxford University Press, 1998. The question of criminal trials as a way of healing societies riven by atrocities is explored in Mark Osiel, *Mass Atrocity, Collective Memory, and the Law*, New Brunswick, NJ: Transaction, 1999. How South Africa is dealing with its past is examined in Sarah Nuttall and Carli Coetzee (eds), *Negotiating the Past: The Making of Memory in South Africa*, Oxford: Oxford University Press, 1998; see also Ifi Amadiume and Abdullahi A. An-Na'im (eds), *The Politics of Memory*, London: Zed Books, 2000. Desmond Tutu persuasively argues for the possibility of reconciliation in *No Future Without Forgiveness*, London: Rider, 2000.
45. Fintan O'Toole, 'They Fear To Speak of '98', *The Irish Times*, 9 December 1997.
46. The best introduction to the subject of commemoration in France is still Pierre Nora's concluding chapter, 'The Era of Commemoration', in P. Nora (ed.), *Realms of Memory: The Construction of the French Past: Vol. 3, Symbols*, Columbia University Press, 1998.
47. Talking cures are not a panacea, they can also go horribly wrong and produce anything but a healing effect, as Daragh Carville shows in his play *Language Roulette* (1996).
48. Fintan O'Toole, 'Introduction: On the Frontier', in Dermot Bolger, *A Dublin Quartet*, London: Penguin, 1992, pp. 1–6; p. 2.
49. *The Irish Times*, 12 April 2000.
50. *The Irish Times*, 10 April 2000.
51. Brian Friel, *Translations*, London: Faber and Faber, 1981, p. 67.
52. Ibid.
53. Seamus Heaney, *The Cure at Troy*, London: Faber and Faber, 1990, p. 77.
54. Patsy McGarry, 'Where past holds living just as earth holds dead', *The Irish Times*, 4 July 1998.
55. See Michael's memory, in Friel's *Dancing at Lughnasa* (1990), which 'owes nothing to fact'. B. Friel, *Dancing at Lughnasa*, London: Faber and Faber, 1990, p. 71. The Scottish poet and novelist (*The Fanatic*, 2000) James Robertson explains: 'The facts of history do not alter very much, although the emphasis we give them shifts. What changes is the truth we take from these facts. Ironically, that is what, ultimately the pack of lies called a novel tries to capture.' 'History Repeating', *Scotland on Sunday*, 30 April 2000.
56. See Paul Ricoeur, *Das Rätsel der Vergangenheit: Erinnern-Vergessen-Verzeihen*, Göttingen: Wallstein, 2000, pp. 140–1.
57. Ibid., p. 145.; see also n.32 above for the debate on public apologies.
58. Milan Kundera, *The Book of Laughter and Forgetting*, quoted in Ivan Klíma, 'Literature and Memory', in I. Klíma, *The Spirit of Prague and other Essays*, London: Granta 1994, pp. 36–7.
59. Ibid., p. 37.
60. C. C. O'Brien, *States of Ireland*, London: Panther, 1974, p. 252.

NOTES TO CHAPTER 1: WHO FEARS TO SPEAK OF '98?

1. Kevin Whelan, *The Tree of Liberty*, Cork: 1996, p. 133. See the chapter "98 after '98' for an excellent discussion of the disputed legacy of the United Irishmen in the nineteenth century.
2. Quoted in Whelan, *Tree of Liberty*, p.150.
3. Ibid.
4. Ibid., p. 151.
5. Quoted in Kevin Whelan, *Fellowship of Freedom: The United Irishmen and 1798*, Cork: 1998, p. 125.
6. There are many extant versions. This is one from a MS version in Trinity College Dublin, reproduced in *Up in Arms: The 1798 Rebellion in Ireland*, record of an exhibition at the Ulster Museum, Belfast, 1998, p. 300.
7. Miles Byrne's *Memoirs* were republished for the '98 bicentenary (Enniscorthy: Duffy Press, 1998) with a new introduction by Kevin Whelan and an afterword by Thomas Bartlett.
8. John Turpin, 'Oliver Sheppard's 1798 Memorials', *Irish Arts Review* (1991), p. 71.
9. Whelan, *Fellowship of Freedom*, 1998, p. 169.
10. Ibid., p. 171.
11. Quoted in: Thomas Bartlett, Kevin Dawson and Dáire Keogh, *The 1798 Rebellion: An Illustrated History*, Boulder, CO: Roberts Rinehart Publishers, 1998, p. 47.
12. A very good description of the events of 'Wolfe Tone Day' is contained in Gary Owens, 'Nationalist Monuments in Ireland, c.1870–1914: Symbolism and Ritual', in Brian P. Kennedy and Raymond Gillespie (eds), *Ireland: Art into History*, Dublin, 1994, pp. 103–17.
13. *Wexford Independent*, 2 November 1898.
14. For a complete survey of the centenary monuments, the following are worth looking at: Gary Owens, 'Nationalists Movements', John Turpin, 'Oliver Sheppard', and Nuala C. Johnson, 'Sculpting Heroic Histories: Celebrating the Centenary of the 1798 Rebellion in Ireland', *Trans. Inst. Brit. Geog.*, xix (1994), pp. 117–93.
15. Maud Gonne, *A Servant of the Queen*, Dublin: 1938, pp. 271–2.
16. For a comprehensive account of this subject see Lawrence W. McBride, 'Historical Imagery in Irish Political Illustrations, 1880–1910', in *New Hibernia Review*, II, Spring 1998, pp. 9–25.
17. Published as an historical facsimile, with a new introduction by Kevin Whelan, by the United Irish Commemoration Society, Belfast: 1998.
18. W. G. Lyttle, *Betsy Grey, or, the Hearts of Down*, Bangor: 1888.
19. *Down Recorder*, 16 July 1898, quoted in Jack McCoy, *Ulster's Joan of Arc, An Examination of the Betsy Gray Story*, pp. 33–4.
20. David Dickson, Dáire Keogh and Kevin Whelan (eds), *The United Irishmen: Radicalism, Republicanism and Rebellion*, Dublin: 1993.

NOTES TO CHAPTER 2: HISTORY À LA CARTE?

1. Ciaran Brady '"Constructive and Instrumental": The dilemma of Ireland's First "New Historians"', in Ciaran Brady (ed.), *Interpreting Irish History: The Debate on Historical Revisionism 1938–1994*, Dublin: Irish Academic Press, 1994, p. 8. *The Bloody Bridge, and Other Papers Relating to the Insurrection of 1641*, Dublin: 1903. Mary Agnes Hickson, *Ireland in the Seventeenth Century, or: The Irish Massacres of 1641–2, Their Cause and Results*, London: Longman, Green & Co, 1884.
2. This was marked by a formal meeting in the Mansion House, where the first Dáil met in January 1919, which was attended by President de Valera, by veterans of the first Dáil and their descendants. *Irish Times*, 21–22 January 1969.
3. Seamus Deane, 'Wherever Green is Red', in Máirín Ní Dhonnchadha and Theo Dorgan (eds), *Revising the Rising*, Derry: Field Day, 1991, p. 91.
4. On the official commemoration of the French Revolution see Steven Laurence Kaplan, *Farewell Revolution. Disputed Legacies 1789–1989*, Ithaca and London: Cornell University Press, 1995. See also Malcolm Anderson's chapter in this volume.
5. Irish emigration is invariably associated with the Great Famine, however in recent years there have been considerable efforts to link the 1798 rising with the Irish diaspora. This is most apparent in the 1798 Museum at Enniscorthy, where a section of the exhibition is devoted to this theme.

6. My thanks to Alice Kearney of the Commemoration Office, Department of the Taoiseach for providing me with copies of press releases relating to these and other commemorative events.
7. In August 1847 responsibility for all relief passed to the newly-established Irish Poor Law Commission. No further funds were provided from Whitehall. Thomas P. O'Neill, 'The Organisation and Administration of Relief, 1947–52', in R. D. Edwards and T. D. Williams (eds), *The Great Famine*, Dublin: Irish Committee of Historical Sciences, 1956, p. 246.
8. John A. Murphy (ed.), *The French are in the Bay: the Expedition to Bantry Bay,* Cork: Mercier Press, 1997, is the proceedings of a commemorative conference that was held in Bantry in 1996.
9. Roger McHugh, 'The Famine in Irish Oral Tradition', in Edwards and Williams (eds), *The Great Famine*, pp. 391–436; Cathal Pórtéir, *Famine Echoes*, Cork: Mercier Press, 1995, p. 15. Carmel Quinlan, '"A Punishment from God": the Famine in the Centenary folklore Questionnaire', *Irish Review*, 19, 1996, pp. 68–86; Cormac Ó Gráda, '"Making History" in Ireland in the 1940s and 1950s: the Saga of The Great Famine', *Irish Review*, 12, 1992, pp. 87–107. Mary E. Daly, 'The Great Famine and the 1940s', *Sunday Tribune*, 15 January 1995.
10. The formal commemoration of the centenary of the death of Daniel O'Connell lasted for five days. They began with a meeting in the Mansion House in Dublin which was attended by the Taoiseach Éamon de Valera, Richard Mulcahy, the leader of Fine Gael, and many other dignitaries including the Catholic archbishop of Dublin. This meeting also launched the 'Save Derrynane [O' Connell's house in Co. Kerry] campaign'. This was followed by four days of events in Co. Kerry, beginning with a solemn high mass and a Euracharistic procession, and ending with an *aeriodhacht* [an open-air festival of Irish music, dancing, verse, etc.] at Carhen, O'Connell's birthplace. *The Irish Times*, 15–17 May 1947.
11. The ceremonies marking the anniversary of 1798 included a visit by President Sean T. O'Kelly and Taoiseach Éamon de Valera to Arklow to view formal processions and to unveil a commemorative plaque, and more elaborate events in Killala, Co. Mayo to commemorate the French landing. This was attended by the French minister in Ireland; the President, Taoiseach and several bishops. University College Cork announced a projected William Smith O'Brien memorial library as its way of marking the centenary of 1848. *The Irish Times*, 14 June 1948; 16 June 1948; 2 August 1948.
12. *The Irish Times*, 16 May 1997.
13. Maurice Hartigan, 'The Eucharistic Congress Dublin 1932', MA thesis, University College Dublin 1979.
14. Margaret O'Callaghan, 'Language, Nationality and Cultural Identity in the Irish Free State, 1922–7: the *Irish Statesman* and the *Catholic Bulletin* Reappraised', *Irish Historical Studies*, 94 1984.
15. Speech by Minister of State, Avril Doyle TD at the launch of the Friends of Comóradh '98, Johnstown Castle, Wexford, 24 November 1995.
16. Thomas Davis, *Essays and Poems with a Centenary Memoir,* Dublin: M. H. Gill and Son, 1945, p. 2. The author of this memoir is not given. The volume also contains a brief introduction by Éamon de Valera. In the paragraph quoted there are echoes of de Valera's famous 'frugal comfort' speech, which was broadcast on St Patrick's Day 1943. For details of the Davis centenary see Mary E. Daly, 'The Great Famine and the 1940s', *Sunday Tribune*, 15 January 1995.
17. See Appendix, last paragraph in E, and F, pp. 54–5.
18. See Appendix.
19. Niall Ó Ciosáin, 'Was there "Silence" about the Famine?' *Irish Studies Review*, 13, Winter 1995–6.
20. Examples are too numerous to mention. However in 1925 a year of food scarcity in the west was described as the worst since 1847; National Archives, Department of the Taoiseach, S 278 A. .When Seán Lemass was attempting to make Cabinet colleagues aware of the serious nature of the economic crisis in November 1932, he told them bluntly that 'It cannot be denied that we are facing a crisis as grave as that of 1847 (S 6222), and in 1947, when de Valera spoke to county engineers to impress on them the urgent need to produce more turf, he referred to a fuel famine and noted that 'famine is not a nice word to Irish ears', quoted in Mary E. Daly, *The Buffer State: The Historical Roots of the Department of the Environment*, Dublin: Institute of Public Administration, 1997, p. 269.
21. *The Irish Times*, 22 August 1994.
22. *The Irish Times*, 16 May 1994.
23. Margaret Kelleher, *The Feminization of Famine: Expressions of the Inexpressible?,* Cork: Cork University Press, 1997 chapter 4 and postscript. For a further discussion of these points see Mary

E. Daly, 'Historians and the Famine: a beleaguered species?', *Irish Historical Studies*, xxx, 120 (Nov. 1997), pp. 591–601.

24. On the eve of the Famine the standard of living in Ireland 'lay somewhere between those of Ethiopia and of Somalia a few years ago, though closer to Somalia's'. In the 1840s Britain had a standard of living similar to modern Egypt or Ethiopia. Cormac Ó Gráda, 'The Great Famine and other Famines', in Cormac Ó Gráda (ed.), *Famine 150*, Dublin: Teagasc and University College Dublin: 1997, pp. 132, 141–2. Moreover, at the time of the Famine the population of Ireland was approximately half that of England and Wales.
25. This is changing; a recent television series on the Irish in the United States has attracted considerable interest.
26. Frank Neal, 'Liverpool and the Famine Irish', in E. Margaret Crawford (ed.), *The Hungry Stream: Essays on Famine and Emigration*, Belfast: Institute of Irish Studies, Queen's University Belfast, 1997, pp. 123–36.
27. For estimates of pre-Famine emigration see Kerby A. Miller, *Emigrants and Exiles*, New York: Oxford University Press, 1985, p. 193.
28. Ibid.
29. *Grosse Île: Report on the Public Consultation Program*, Parks Canada 1994; Marianna O'Gallagher and Rose Masson Dompierre, *Eyewitness Gross Isle 1847* , Sainte Foy, Quebec: Livres Carraig, 1995.
30. John Mitchel, *The Last Conquest of Ireland (Perhaps)*, Dublin: Irishman's Office, 1861; Canon John O'Rourke, *The History of the Great Irish Famine and notes of earlier famines*, Dublin: James Duffy & Co., 1876.
31. *The Great Irish Famine*. Submitted to the New Jersey Commission on Holocaust Education on 11 January 1996, for inclusion in the Holocaust and Genocide Curriculum at secondary level. Prepared by the Irish Famine Curriculum Committee. My thanks to Roy Foster for sending me a copy of this document.
32. Conor O'Clery, *The Greening of the White House*, Dublin: Gill & Macmillan, 1996.
33. Mary P. Corcoran, *Irish Illegals. Transients between Two Societies*, Westport, CT: Greenwood Press, 1993.
34. Photographs of the travelling community are regularly shown on giant screens during formal dinners of the Ireland Fund held in leading American hotels such as New York's Waldorf Astoria Hotel.
35. The *Dunbrody* was completed in 2001 at a cost of €6m. excluding the cost of Fás trainee workers. It was originally planned that the Dunbrody would sail from New Ross to Boston, retracing the path allegedly taken by Patrick Kennedy, the paternal ancestor of the American political dynasty, who left Ireland before the Famine, but the boat lacks modern steel sailing features. The *Jeanie Johnston* is a modern replica of a ship that carried emigrants to the United States in famine times. It is invariably described as a 'good coffin ship' – a very paradoxical term – because is it claimed that none of its passengers ever perished at sea. By February 2002 the cost of the *Jeanie Johnston* had reached €15.8m. excluding the cost of Fás trainee workers. In 2003 it sailed to America.
36. Christine Kinealy has suggested that non-historians and historians from outside Ireland have proved much more willing to argue the case for British culpability. Christine Kinealy, *A Death-Dealing Famine*, London: Pluto Press, 1997, pp. 10–11.
37. Gerard MacAtasney cites a statement by me to support this argument; I never made such a remark. Gerard MacAtasney, *'This Dreadful Visitation': The Famine in Lurgan/Portadown*, Belfast: Beyond the Pale Publications, 1997, p. xv.
38. Blair's statement was read out at a Famine Concert in Millstreet, Co. Cork, held over the June holiday weekend in 1997. The event was attended by the US Ambassador Jean Kennedy-Smith and the British Ambassador Veronica Sutherland. US President Bill Clinton spoke to the assembled crowd by a video-link. The concert received a £10,000 subsidy from the Irish Government's Commemoration Fund, but it attracted relatively small crowds and ultimately lost money. AFri, the Third World charity, accused the organisers of this event of 'dancing on the graves of the Famine dead'. *The Irish Times*, 2 June 1997; 22 May 1997.
39. Des Cowman and Donald Brady (eds), *Teacht na bPrátaí Dubha: The Famine in Waterford*, Dublin: Geography Publications, 1995, and the series of articles that appeared in the *Tipperary Historical Journal* during the years 1995–97.
40. This remark reflects my experience in attending local seminars which presented the findings of a government-funded research project that examined the Famine in detail in a number of poor

law unions: Enniskillen, Co. Fermanagh; Dublin North; Parsonstown (Birr), Co. Offaly; Castlebar, Co. Mayo; Ennistymon, Co. Clare.

41. Joel Mokyr, *Why Ireland Starved,* London: Allen & Unwin, 1983, p. 292; James S. Donnelly Jr., 'The Administration of Relief, 1847–51', in W. E. Vaughan (ed.), *A New History of Ireland, V. Ireland under the Union 1, 1801–70,* Oxford: Clarendon Press, 1989, p. 329.
42. Mitchel, *The Last Conquest*; Austin Bourke, 'The Irish Grain Trade, 1839–48', *Irish Historical Studies,* xx, 1976, pp. 156–69; Peter Solar, 'The Great Famine was no Ordinary Subsistence Crisis', in E.M. Crawford (ed.), *Famine: the Irish Experience, 900–1900,* Edinburgh: John Donald, 1989, p. 123; James Donnelly, 'The Construction of the Memory of the Famine in Ireland and the Irish Diaspora, 1850–1900', *Eire/Ireland* xxxi, 1 and 2, 1996, pp. 26–62, notes that the export of food was the most commonly cited argument on this question during the nineteenth century. Kinealy gives a rather confusing account of the export of food, which fails to refer to Solar's work and appears designed to allow readers to take comfort in Mitchel's version. Kinealy, *A Death-Dealing Famine,* pp. 60, 79–80.
43. Frank Geary, 'The Act of Union, British-Irish Trade and pre-Famine deindustrialization', *Economic History Review,* xlviii, 1, February 1995, pp. 68–88.
44. These conclusions are based to a considerable extent on, as yet unpublished research relating to Enniskillen Poor Law Union that was carried out by Dr Desmond McCabe, under the direction of Professor David Fitzpatrick, as part of a government-funded research programme.
45. On Ulster see MacAtasney; also Christine Kinealy and Trevor Parkhill (eds), *The Famine in Ulster,* Belfast: Ulster Historical Foundation, 1997; Flann Campbell, *The Dissenting Voice: Protestant Democracy in Ulster from Plantation to Partition,* Belfast: Blackstaff, 1991, pp. 181, 456; Daly, 'Historians and the Famine'.
46. See, for example, Frank Gallagher, *This Indivisible Island: The History of Partition,* London: Victor Gollancz, 1956.
47. Dáire Keogh and Nicholas Furlong (eds), *The Women of 1798,* Dublin: Four Courts Press, 1998; women seem to have had a better prospect of surviving the famine than men, see David Fitzpatrick, 'Women and the Great Famine' in Margaret Kelleher and James H. Murphy (eds), *Gender Perspectives in Nineteenth-Century Ireland: Public and Private Spheres,* Dublin: Irish Academic Press, 1997, pp. 50–69.
48. Brendan Bradshaw, 'Nationalism and Historical Scholarship in modern Ireland', in Brady (ed.), *Interpreting Irish History,* p. 204.
49. Chris Morash, 'Literature, Memory, Atrocity', in Chris Morash and Richard Hayes (eds), *'Fearful Realities': New Perspectives on the Famine,* Dublin: Irish Academic Press, 1996, pp. 110–18.
50. Roy Foster, 'History and the Irish Question', as reproduced in Brady (ed.), *Interpreting Irish History,* p. 143.
51. Gerald Keegan, *Famine Diary: Journal to a New World,* Dublin: Wolfhound Press, 1991; Jim Jackson 'The Making of a Best Sellar' [sic], *The Irish Review,* 11, Winter 1991, pp. 1–8.

NOTES TO CHAPTER 3: THE POPPY MY FATHER WORE

1. Brian Feeney, 'Spineless decision sets us back three decades', *Irish News,* 16 October 1997.
2. Seamus McKinney, 'College bins "culture policy"', *Irish News,* 16 October 1997.
3. Brian Girven and Geoffrey Roberts, 'The Forgotten Volunteers of World War II', *History Ireland,* Spring 1998.
4. Keith Jeffery, 'The Great War in Modern Irish Memory', in T. G. Fraser and Keith Jeffery (eds), *Men, Women and War (Historical Studies XVIII)* Dublin: Lilliput Press, 1992.
5. John Bruton, 'It is fitting to honour all who gave their lives', *Irish News,* 4 November 1997.
6. Paddy Harte, 'It's time to honour the South's forgotten heroes', *Irish News,* 13 March 1997.
7. John Robb, 'Failures have left the poppy a mark of division', *Irish News,* 10 November 1997.
8. Paddy Harte, quoted in Liam Reid, 'The seeds of hatred', *Sunday Tribune,* 9 November 1997.
9. Eamon McCann, 'A sacrifice forced upon young men out of greed', *Irish News,* 3 November 1997.
10. Robin Percival, 'Who remembers what when poppy wearing?', *Irish News,* 8 November 1997.
11. Kate Fearon, 'Are victims of violence ready for truth?', *Irish News,* 5 August 1998.
12. Nell McCafferty, 'The seeds of hatred', *Sunday Tribune,* 9 November 1997.
13. Paddy Hayes, quoted in Nell McCafferty, 'Seeds of hatred'.

14. See Fintan O'Toole, 'How the Orange Order has mocked its past', *Irish Times*, 19 July 1996.
15. Quoted in Michael Farrell, *Northern Ireland: The Orange State*, London: Pluto Press, 1992, p. 90.
16. Brian Girven and Geoffrey Roberts, 'Forgotten Volunteers'.
17. See George Fleming, 'Magennis VC: The Story of Northern Ireland's Only Winner of the Victoria Cross', *History Ireland*, 1998.
18. Robin Percival, 'Who remembers'.
19. James Kane, 'VC', *New Ulster*, November 1995.
20. Gordon Lucy, 'The Battle of the Somme', *Ulster Review*, summer 1996; see also F. P. Crozier, *Brass Hat in No-Man's-Land*, Butler and Tanner, 1937.
21. King's regulations 1912, para. 451; Christopher Hunt, Imperial War Museum, to G. Fleming, 26 August 1997.
22. Among the papers to carry the advertisement was the *Sunday Life*, 5 July 1998.
23. See 'Veteran's disgust at loyalist propaganda', *Irish News*, 15 November 1997.
24. See Steven McCaffery, 'Cenotaph probe into UVF wreath', *Irish News*, 13 November 1997.
25. Advertisement in the *Irish Times*, 3 July 1998.

NOTES TO CHAPTER 4: MEMORY, FORGIVENESS AND CONFLICT

An earlier version of this chapter appeared under the title 'Trust-Building in Northern Ireland: The Role of Memory', in Lorraine Waterhouse and Halla Beloff (eds), *Trust in Public Life*, Edinburgh: Hume Papers on Public Policy, 7, 3, 1999, We are grateful to the editor of the Hume Papers, Brian G. M. Main, for the permission to re-publish.

1. Penelope Fitzgerald, 'Nuthouse Al', *London Review of Books*, 18 February 1999, p. 12.
2. Ivanov in Arthur Koestler, *Darkness at Noon*, Harmondsworth: Penguin Books, 1966, p. 125.
3. Ian Buruma, 'The Joys and Perils of Victimhood', *The New York Review of Books*, XLVI, 6, 8 April 1999, p. 8.
4. Priscilla B. Hayner, 'Fifteen Truth Commissions – 1974 to 1994: A Comparative Study', in Neil J Kritz (ed.), *Transitional Justice: How Emerging Democracies Reckon With Former Regimes*, 1, Washington, DC: United States Institute of Peace, 1995, pp. 225–61; p. 225.
5. Kader Asmal, *Victims, Survivors, and Citizens: Human Rights, Reparation and Reconciliation*, Capetown: University of Western Cape, 1992, p. 11.
6. Belfast Agreement [1998], (*Agreement Reached in the Multi-Party Negotiations*), n.p., n.d. [p. 21].
7. Roger Errera, 'Memory, History and Justice in Divided Societies: The Unfinished Dialogue between Mnemosyne and Clio', Paper presented at a conference on Constitution-making, Conflict and Transition in Divided Societies, Bellagio, Italy, February 1999, p. 16.
8. Ibid., pp. 5–6.
9. See Gary Wills, 'Augustine's Magical Decade', in *The New York Review of Books*, XLVI, 8, 6 May 1999, p. 31.
10. Jacques Le Goff, Cited in Errera 1999, p. 8.
11. Seán Ó Tuama and Thomas Kinsella, *An Duanaire, 1600–1900: Poems of the Dispossessed*, Dublin: Dolmen Press, 1981.
12. See Helen Meany, 'Embracing the Challenge', *The Irish Times*, 9 June 1998. For the role of television drama, see Jennifer C. Cornell, 'Recontextualising the Conflict: Northern Ireland, Television Drama, and the Politics of Validation', Oregon State University paper, n.d., which argues for 'a model of practice for writers which seeks not to make peace or induce reconciliation, but rather to encourage the conditions necessary for their spontaneous generation' (p. 17).
13. J. J. Lee, *Ireland 1912–1985: Politics and Society*, Cambridge: Cambridge University Press, 1989, p. 375.
14. Katrina Goldstone, 'Thanks for the Memory', *The Irish Times*, 21 January 1998. She wonders whether 'the contemporary rush to commemorate the past' is 'a necessary rite of passage or an inability to confront the future'.
15. Neil Jarman, *Material Conflicts: Parades and Visual Displays in Northern Ireland*, Oxford: Berg, 1997, pp. 124, 118, 152, 107, 256.
16. Ibid., p. 7.
17. Ibid., p. 67.

18. Michel-Rolph Trouillot, *Silencing The Past: Power and the Production of History*, Boston: Beacon Press, 1995, p. 48.
19. Ibid., pp. 26–7.
20. Ibid., p. 106. This is simply a practical matter. In her book, *The Silent Woman*, Janet Malcolm makes the startlingly obvious point: 'Each [writer] faces not a blank page but his own vastly overfilled mind. The problem is to clear out most of what is in it ... the goal is to make a space where a few ideas and images and feelings may be so arranged that a reader will want to linger awhile among them, rather than to flee ...' Cited in Joyce Carol Oates, 'The Case of the Canned Lawyer', *The New York Review of Books*, XLVI, 6, 8 April 1999.
21. Charles Townshend, *Political Violence in Ireland: Government and Resistance since 1848*, Oxford: Clarendon Press, 1983, p. 83.
22. Amartya Sen, cited in Colm Tóibín, 'Erasures', *London Review of Books*, 30 July 1998, p. 00.
23. Terry Eagleton, cited in Tóibín, 'Erasures'.
24. Ibid.
25. Suzanne Breen, 'Families left with no grave to cry at wait for word', *Irish Times*, 3 April 1999.
26. Edith Wyschogrod, *Spirit in Ashes: Hegel, Heidegger and Man-Made Mass Death*, New Haven, CT: Yale University Press, 1983, p. 126.
27. Ian Buruma, 'Joys and Perils', p. 4.
28. Ibid.
29. Ibid.
30. Ibid., p. 9.
31. Ibid.
32. Ibid.
33. Marie Smyth, 'Remembering in Northern Ireland: Victims, Perpetrators and Hierarchies of Pain and Responsibility', in Brandon Hamber (ed.), *Past Imperfect: Dealing with the Past in Northern Ireland and Societies in Transition*, Derry: INCORE, 1998, p. 32.
34. Ibid., pp. 44, 48.
35. Idith Zertal, 'From the People's Hall to the Wailing Wall: A Study of Memory, Mass Hysteria and War, 1960–1967', unpublished paper read at the United States Institute of Peace, Washington DC, 25 June 1998, pp. 9–10.
36. Ibid., *passim*.
37. Ibid., p.5.
38. Ibid.
39. Smyth, 'Remembering', pp. 47–8.
40. Hannah Arendt, *The Human Condition*, Chicago: University of Chicago Press, 1958, pp. 237, 243. Arendt notes that the discoverer of the role of forgiveness is Jesus of Nazareth, but the fact that it is articulated in a religious sense 'is no reason to take it any less seriously in a strictly secular sense.' In that respect it is worth noting that the political dimension is beginning to be recognised within Irish religious circles in recent years. cf. Michael Hurley (ed.), *Reconciliation in Religion and Society*, Belfast: Institute of Irish Studies, 1994, *passim*; and *Remembrance and Forgetting: Building a Future in Northern Ireland*, Belfast: The Faith and Politics Group, 1998, *passim*.
41. Byron Bland, *Marching and Rising: The Ritual of Small Differences and Great Violence in Northern Ireland*, Stanford University: Center for International Relations and Arms Control, 1996, p. 13.
42. Lawrence Weschler, *A Miracle, A Universe: Settling Accounts with Torturers*, Harmondsworth: Penguin Books, 1990, p. 4.
43. Padraig O'Malley, *Biting at the Grave: The Irish Hunger Strikes and the Politics of Despair*, Belfast: Blackstaff, 1990, p. 9.
44. There are examples of good practice in other transitional states – the testimony of the 55,000 victims of political violence in Guatemala was conceived as a cathartic experience of remembering which might help to restore unity and trust to torn communities. See, too, an interview with Archbishop Desmond Tutu for a passionate appraisal of the South African Truth and Reconciliation Commission, in Frank Ferrari, 'Forgiving the Unforgivable', *Commonweal* (New York, 12 September 1997), pp. 13–18. For a more dispassionate account see two articles by Timothy Garton Ash, 'True Confessions', and 'The Curse and Blessing of South Africa', *The New York Review of Books*, XLIV, 12, 17 July 1997, and XLIV, 13, 14 August 1997.
45. One example would be the official opening of the Peace Park at Messines in Flanders in November 1998. See 'Remembering Ireland's Dead', *Irish Times*, 11 November 1998; and Andy Pollack, 'Solemn ceremony inaugurates peace park', *Irish Times*, 12 November 1998.

NOTES TO CHAPTER 5: THE RIVERS TO DRUMCREE

My deepest thanks are due to the long-suffering Eberhard Bort for his patience and encouragement in the birth of this essay. My gratitude is also as deep as any of the rivers under discussion to Ms Margaret MacPherson for so nobly and appreciatively preparing my antediluvian copy for press. As always, my obligations are endless to the National Library of Scotland and to Edinburgh University Library.

1. The self-assurance of this editorial voice implies authorship by either the novelist Charles Lever (1806–72) or the poet John Francis Waller (1809–94) who succeeded him in the *DUM* editorial chair in 1845, but in stylistic and topographical authority the probability lies with Lever. The *Wellesley Index to Victorian Periodicals*, to whose ascriptions I am in general most indebted, is silent on this point. The quotation suggests long editorial gestation, and preceding matter asserts the journal's Irishness and complains of its want of Irish topography incompatably with the courtesies of immediate inheritance. The preface disclaims any 'idea of encroaching on the tourist's province, or of anticipating any lady or gentleman who desires to shine in a full-blown octavo, having "Ireland in 1845" on its title-page and Daniel O'Connell for its frontispiece.' That has a Lever Unionist bravura. It promised not to lose sight of the antiquarian, the historical, the biographical, the legendary, or the picturesque, or the use of the rivers in verse or prose from 'the homes of genius near at hand', as well as 'graver themes' from 'times too many, when those pure streams were polluted with kindred blood; when brother met brother in terrible antagonism; when hearts which should have grown together in love throbbed wildly in the bosoms of foemen, and Religion herself, the handmaid of heaven, was invoked as the Nemesis of contending armies' (ibid., 315–17). The series ran on and off for ten years.
2. T. W. Rolleston, *Myths and Legends of the Celtic Race* (1911), p. 129, and n., basing himself on the version in Kuno Meyer and Alfred Nutt, *The Voyage of Bran* (1895), I, p. 219. The preface is much concerned with the need for 'the people inhabiting the British Islands' to realise they are not 'Anglo-Saxon' but 'Anglo-Celtic'. ('There is nothing to justify this singling out of two Low-German tribes when we wish to indicate the race-character of the British people.') Rolleston's preoccupation, prevalent in his time, had difficulty in surviving the 'Anglo-Irish' war of 1919–21.
3. Alan Bruford, 'The Twins of Macha', in Glenys Davies (ed.), *Polytheistic Systems (Cosmos – The Traditional Yearbook of the Cosmology Society*, V, Edinburgh University Press, 1989), pp. 125–41, discusses the linkage of early Irish legends and is in itself concerned with the horse-goddess aspect of Macha (who in human female form cursed the Ulstermen that under duress they would suffer pains of pregnancy for having forced her to race against horses while on the verge of childbirth); but notes Macha is sister to Boand, the river-goddess of Boyne, mother to Oengus (or Aonghus) Óg, and his cross-references to Welsh ('Rhiannon') and Gaulish ('Epona') horse-goddesses may also be paralleled among water-goddesses, notably in what Bruford identifies as the worldwide legend of 'the man who acquires a supernatural wife and loses her by breaking a tabu of some sort that she has imposed'. The legend of Oisin/Ossian's transportation to and from Tír na n Óg across the sea to reign as consort for 300 years with Niamh Chinn Óir whom he then loses by falling off his magic horse while back in Ireland, combines both horse and water, while in more generic form the Welsh legend of the lady of Llyn y Fantoch or Fan Foch supplies it for a lake-goddess. The child of such a water-goddess is often protected by water (e.g. Aonghus, when courting a swan-maiden or, for that matter, Achilles dipped by Thetis, his water-nymph mother, into the Styx save for his heel). The opening of Bruford's last sentence is inspirational: 'at any rate it has been fun for me…'.
4. The main Anna Livia passage (or current) is conveniently extracted in Harry Levin (ed.), *The Essential James Joyce* [1948] (London: Grafton Books, 1977), pp. 502–3 (–18).
5. Thomas Babbington Macaulay, 'Horatius', verses lxix, lxxii, *Lays of Ancient Rome and Miscellaneius Essays and Poems* (London: Dent, 1945). I discuss the *Lays* with some remarks on Macaulay's Celtic inheritances in my *Macaulay*, 1988, chapter 2. The versifiers of the Young Ireland weekly the *Nation* owed much to Macaulay, but were repelled by his passionate Unionism (the *Nation*, 1 April 1843, quoted in Malcolm Brown, *The Politics of Irish Literature*, 1972, p. 5 – an invaluable if inaccurate work).
6. Thomas Moore, 'Epistle VII. To Thomas Hume, esq., M.D. from the City of Washington', *Poetical Works* (London: John Dicks, 1873), p. 151, in which he notices the importance of American classical rebaptism of rivers: 'And what was Goose Creek once is Tiber now!'

7. Thomas Moore, 'Irish Melodies', *Poetical Works*, p. 200. Joyce on Parnell may be conveniently studied in 'Ivy Day in the Committee Room' (*Dubliners*, 1914, in Levin, *Joyce*, pp. 96–110), and more notably in the Christmas dinner episode of *A Portrait of the Artist as a Young Man*, 1916 (Levin, *Joyce*, pp. 192–202). For Parnell's sentimentalism see Katharine O'Shea, *Charles Stewart Parnell: His Love Story and Political Life* (1914) – without undue reliance.

8. Edmund Spenser, *The Faerie Queene*, A. C. Hamilton (ed.) (Harlow: Longman, 1977), p. 516. Alastair Fowler, *Spenser and the Numbers of Time* (London: Routledge, 1964), pp. 174–5, 191. P. W. Joyce, *The Wonders of Ireland and Other Papers on Irish Subjects* (London and New York, 1911), pp. 75–9. Patricia Coughlan (ed.), *Spenser and Ireland: An Interdisciplinary Perspective* (Cork: Cork University Press, 1985), p. 55; see also Richard McCabe, 'The Fate of Irena', in Coughlan, *Spenser*, p. 119: 'His was a Cromwellian dream a century before Cromwell'; Andrew Hadfield, *Edmund Spenser's Irish Experience* (Oxford: Clarendon, 1997), pp. 144–5. Roland M. Smith, 'Spenser's Irish River Stories', *PMLA* (December 1935), pp. 1047–56. Rivers in order of appearance are: Liffey, Slaney, Aubrian [possibly the Tolka where in 1014 Toirdhealach Ó Briain, grandson of Brian Bóramha, was drowned killing a Norseman during his grandfather's victory at Clontarf, whence Abha Uí Bhriain, the river of the descendant of Brian – not an identification made elsewhere], Shannon, Boyne, Bann, Blackwater, Foyle, Drowis [whose Lough Melvin supposedly erupted from the grave of a king at his burial, drowning most of his people], Allo, Awbeg, Suir, Nore, Barrow, Kenmare, Bandon, Lee, Avonbeg [thus becoming another progenitor of the Parnell epiphany at Avoca 250 years later]. Smith gives Spenser credit for the collection of many Gaelic legends, and he clearly had good linguistic and folklore informants. I remain sceptical about Blomius: Irish mountains have fairly rational names as a rule.

9. The bifurcation of the Protestant pagan theme against Roman Catholics neatly coincides with the *Dublin University Magazine* of the 1840s where its crusade against paganism rapidly became one to conserve paganism (or what was left of it in records of folklore, superstition, stories, etc.), the notable instance being its expert on the Boyne, Sir William Wilde (1815–76), who revised his *DUM* work for book publication, notably in his *Irish Superstitions* (Dublin, 1849) and *The Beauties of the Boyne and the Blackwater* [i.e. the third, or Meath, Blackwater] (1849). J. R. O'Flanagan, *Historical and Picturesque Guide to the River Blackwater*, 1844, is the alternative title to his *Blackwater in Munster* (London, 1844), above text pages.

10. Patrick S. Dinneen and Tadhg O'Donoghue (eds), *Dánta Aodhagáin Uí Rathaille* (London: David Nutt (Irish Texts Society), 1911), lv, pp. 72–91 [where almost the entire poem is uttered by the banshee Clíodhna herself, including a genealogy for the deceased Donnchadh Ó Cheallachán going back to Adam – she was indeed incessant]; the O'Callaghan in question was from a family originally in Clonmeen, near Kanturk. P. W. Joyce, *The Origin and History of Irish Names and Places*, 1870, p. 188: 'Cleena [*sic*] has her palace in the heart of a great rock, situated about 5 miles SSW from Mallow...' For James Stephens's 'The Wave of Cliona' see his *Collected Poems* (1954) or his *Reincarnations* (1918).

11. For Boulton and Somervell see Percy A. Scholes, *The Oxford Companion to Music*, where each has a note. Boulton's publications are fugitive, many not in the British Library. He may well have composed/edited 'The Castle of Dromore' in the early 1880s soon after his days at Balliol College, Oxford (BA 1881, MA 1884); it seems to have been in an early volume, *Songs of the Four Nations*, and was in *Songs Sung and Unsung*, 1894. His *Slumber Songs and Carols*, 1927, pp. 36–7, includes Hyde's translation as well as Boulton's English text (and a fine silhouette of spirits). For Boulton less happily grappling with Blackwater hauntings see his *The Huntress Hag of the Blackwater* (London, 1926), e.g. p. 12:

   Eager the summons to obey
   I hear my guardian angel say
   'Beware!, Love-philtres apt for you
   In witch's cauldron she doth brew.'

   See also Boulton's entry in *Catholic Who's Who*.

12. *Dublin University Magazine*, 26, October 1845, pp. 444–5. The text is identical with O'Flanagan once the story begins.

13. 'La Mère Bauche' was originally published as one of Trollope's *Tales of All Countries, First Series* (1861), but was ready in 1859 and hence dates from his Irish years. It reads like an Irish plot worked into a story of the Pyrenees. His first non-Irish novel, *La Vendée*, may have had such an origin, as indeed did the beginnings of the Barsetshire series.

14. *Arms and the Man* (premiered in 1894) was the first of Shaw's 'Pleasant' plays, published in his *Plays Pleasant and Unpleasant* (1898).

15. Joan Lindsay, *Picnic at Hanging Rock* (1967) differs from its film version in some particulars: it may imply more of a human agency for the disappearances, and its hint of possible reality behind the story (set in 1900) accords with it. In the case of the McAuliffe disappearance it might be Clíodhna's re-enactment of her own removal by aquatic forces from her lover.

16. Charlotte Grace O'Brien, *Lyrics* (London, 1886), p. 32. See also pp.33–4 for 'A Death on the Shannon' and 'The Shannon – A Change of the Weather', both written in 1885. For 'The River' see John Cooke (ed.), *The Dublin Book of Irish Verse, 1728–1909,* 1909, pp. 684–5. 'Many are the lovely places in Ireland of which the tourist knows nothing, and of them the wider-spreading, far-reaching, blue-glancing Shannon are the most worthy of loving praise; or, at least, I thought so, for the fates of my life made me a true lover of the Shannon before I well had sense to know my right hand from my left.' (Charlotte Grace O'Brien, 'The Making of Our Home', in Stephen Gwynn, *Charlotte Grace O'Brien: Selections from Her Writings and Correspondence with a Memoir* (Dublin: Maunsel & Co., 1909), p. 219. Her sonnet 'Gladstone 1881–2' is to me as good a famine poem as any inspired by the Great Famine thirty-odd years previously.

17. David Trimble (comp.), *The Orange Lark amd other songs of the Orange Tradition* (Lurgan: Ulster society, 1987), pp. 86–8, 50–1. Whether Mr Trimble is in fact merely a patron or an actual editor is unclear, but his preface has a paternal pride. The selection shows a historical and ethnological intelligence consistent with what is otherwise known of him.

18. Cooke, *Dublin Book,* pp. 50–2, may be eclectic enough to rebuke subsequent Irish anthologists, acting with six advisers including a Jesuit, a Protestant Nationalist MP, a future firing-squad victim of 1916, and 'AE' aka George Russell, first thanks going to the Protestant Primate of All Ireland for the use of his and his deceased wife's poetry (William and Cecil Alexander), but the Revd Stephen J. Brown, SJ, *Poetry of Irish History* (1927), pp. 193–5 (following his female predecessor editor M. J. Brown, when the book was entitled *Historical Ballad Poetry of Ireland* (1912)), was as elated: he hailed her as the author of 'two vigorous Orange songs' in his *Ireland in Fiction,* 1919, pp. 99–100, while listing her Irish novels *The Rockite* (1829) as 'the Tithe War (c.1820) from Protestant standpoint' and her *Derry* (1833) as 'Story of the Siege, written from ultra-Protestant standpoint. The proceeeds of the sale of the book are to be devoted to teaching the Protestant religion "in their own tongue to the Irish-speaking aborigines of the land" – (Pref.). The Author says elsewhere that "Popery is the curse of God upon a land." And the expression of similar views is very frequent in the book.' 'Charlotte Elizabeth' (as she signed her books from 1824, when she began her thirty-odd volumes in the same year as her rupture with Captain Phelan, until her death, notwithstanding her marriage to Lewis Hippolytus Joseph Tonna (1812–57)) might have wondered about such recognition from a Jesuit and, had she followed her normal custom, would have had hopes of his conversion to Protestantism. She hated Catholicism but wrote with eager affection of Catholics and seems to have married two of them, the second being apparently an anti-clerical Spaniard twenty-two years her junior ousted from diplomatic status by Spanish power vagaries. D. J. O'Donoghue (1866–1917), multi-biographer of Irish poets, called 'The Maiden City' and 'No Surrender' 'quite the best Orange songs that have been written' (*DNB*). 'Charlotte Elizabeth' (née Brown, daughter of a canon of Norwich Cathedral) won international celebrity, her works gaining an introduction in the New York edition (1844) by Harriet Beecher Stowe (1811–96), then in an anti-Catholic mood before she went on to anti-slavery and *Uncle Tom's Cabin*; but Stowe noted the attack on British child labour in *Helen Fleetwood* (1841). The date of 'The Maiden City' is problematic, but for Brown's denunciation of the Irish Municipal Reform Act see her preface to the fourth edition of *The Rockite* (London: James Nisbet, 1846):

> The old municipal charters of Protestantism, so dearly purchased by former genera-
> tions, and secured to their posterity by the most solemn pledges that a united throne and
> senate could give, were rent to fragments and scattered upon the winds. (vi).

But she bitterly denounced Protestant class prejudice against the native population:

> [W]e are too proud, too obstinately prejudiced to opinion, to sit down among the Irish
> race, and address them in a tongue that sounds of home and kindred, and every
> endearing sympathy to which their hearts can vibrate.

The use of Jane Austen conveys an origin of her ironies: her second novel was called *Perseverance* and her fourth *Consistency.*

19. James Carty, *Class-Book,* Book III (1930), p. 58; see also pp. 60–1, and (for Macaulay's text) p. 64, introduced by Carty:

> The following passage by a famous English historian tells how the three ships, the
> *Phoenix*, the *Dartmouth,* and the *Mountjoy,* came up the Foyle to relieve Derry, and

how the brave captain of the *Mountjoy* gave his life for his native town.
20. John Cook (ed.), *The Dublin Book of Irish Verse, 1728–1909* (Dublin, 1909).
21. Jefferson to Adams, 4 September 1823, Lester J. Cappon (ed.), *The Adams-Jefferson Letters: The Complete Correspondence Between Thomas Jefferson and Abigail and John Adams*, II (Chapel Hill, NC: University of North Carolina Press, 1988), p. 596.
22. Originally published in *Knight's Quarterly Magazine* (January 1824), and frequently reprinted with his *Lays of Ancient Rome* (1842), whence its considerable influence on Young Ireland, on the *Dublin University Magazine*, and on various other hotbeds of verse.
23. 'Boulavogue' originally appeared in the *Irish Weekly Independent*, 18 June 1898, when the paper was run by the faithful supporters of the dead Parnell (which put them under Roman Catholic priestly condemnation), in alliance with Fenians headed by Fred Allan (d. 1937), Secretary of the Supreme Council of the Irish Republican Brotherhood and organiser of the centenary celebrations of the United Irishmen. The poem, no doubt to remind readers of former clerical identification with extreme nationalism, was then entitled 'Father Murphy of the County Wexford'. The earlier versions both feature Father Murphy prominently but, like McCall's, retire him from most of the action. (Zimmermann, *Songs of Irish Rebellion: Political Street Ballads and Rebel Songs, 1780–1900* (Dublin, 1967), pp. 290–1, 144–8). Blacker's poem was apparently inspired by the dissolution of the Orange Order (officially) on 14 April 1836 – it was dissolved by its Grand Master, Ernest Augustus, Duke of Cumberland and next in succession to Victoria at whose accession in 1837 he became King of Hanover); Cumberland (1771–1851) actually acted to frustrate government action against the Order. Blacker was careful to make no mention of Cromwell in the poem, which would certainly have been unwelcome to Cumberland. For the full text, see Cooke, *Dublin Book*, pp. 29–32. Charlotte Elizabeth gave her qualified support in *Letters from Ireland 1837* (London, 1838), p. 285. As good a crypto-Orangeman as any, she died on the Twelfth of July, as her husband Tonna noted with pride.
24. From the third verse of 'Kelly the Boy from Killane', a popular '98 ballad. Unlike the Father Murphy songs, it also salutes the nominal leader, Beauchamp Bagenal Harvey (1762–98), a Protestant (deposed after the repulse from New Ross), although its chief icon is the seven-foot-odd eponymous hero. It is also highly internationalist in explaining why he fought:
    Glory O, Glory O to the heroes who died
    In the cause of long-downtrodden Man!
Ironically, Blacker's final verse has almost the exactly similar aims with the insurgents he denounces:
    For 'happy homes', for 'altars free', we grasp the ready sword –
    For freedom, truth, and for our God's unmutilated word.
25. For the text of 'Róisín Dubh' see Seán Ó Tuama and Thomas Kinsella (eds), *An Duanaire 1600–1900: Poems of the Dispossessed* (Montrath: Dolmen Press, 1981), pp. 308–11. The translation differs slightly from mine. For the Mangan version, see Cooke, *Dublin Book*, pp. 134–6.
26. Rory Fitzpatrick, *God's Frontiersmen: The Scots-Irish Epic* (London: Weidenfeld & Nicolson, 1989), p. 24.
27. 'And he that will not take this toast, may he be damned, crammed and jammed down the great gun of Athlone, and the gun fired in the Pope's belly, and the Pope fired in the Devil's belly, and the Devil into Hell, and the door locked, and the key in the pocket of a good stout Orangeman. [*Pause, and Drinking*] And here's a fart for the Bishop of Cork!' This, or its variants, dates from the early eighteenth century. The Bishop of Cork was of course the Church of Ireland bishop, the Roman Catholic one being officially excluded with mortal danger to him if discovered. The allusion is to Peter Browne (1666–1735), Fellow (1692) and Provost (1699) of Trinity College Dublin whence he obtained his bishopric (1710). He denounced toasts in memory of the dead, apparently because of the presumed derivation from the Roman Catholic practice of praying for souls in purgatory, and in 1713 published *Drinking in Remembrance of the Dead* which particularly attacked the toast of the Glorious Memory of William. The fart is helpful in dating the toast, both for its recipient and for its necessitous delivery in nether garments less constricting than the eighteenth century later preferred.
28. Risteárd Ó Foghludha eag., *Seán Clárach, 1691–1754: a shaothar fileata agus scéal a bheathadh* (Baile Átha Cliath: Foillseacháin Rialtais, 1934), p. 46, the poem title 'Bimse Buan ar Buairt gach Ló' eponymous with the first verse. Other likenesses are asserted with Conor ('the famous') son of Neasa ('of the glories'), and Fergus ('the fair, the generous') – whom Conor supplanted as king in Ulster thanks to Neasa's wiles, but Seán Clárach Mac Domhnaill mentions that not at all.

29. Sullivan's brother Alexander Martin included it in his popular history (*sic*) *The Story of Ireland* (1870), coupled with doubts

> suggested to my mind by the facts of authentic history as to whether King Conor Mac Nessa was likely to have played the foul part attributed to him in this celebrated [story of Deirdre and Conor's treacherous murder of her lover] … All that can be said is that no other incident recorded of him would warrant such an estimate of his character; and it is certain that he was a man of many brave and noble parts.

Quoted with poem in Browne, *Poetry of Irish History*, p. 9. *The Story of Ireland* (Dublin: Talbot Press, 1927) is said to have converted Winston Churchill to Home Rule; he, of course, had comparable doubts about the darker passages in the reputation of his heroic collateral ancestor John Churchill, first Duke of Marlborough. Marlborough's existence is more certain than Conor's; but then the Sullivans did not claim even collateral descent from Conor Mac Nessa.

30. Wilde, *Beauties of the Boyne*, p. 187. In its original version, 'Irish Rivers – No.V The Boyne – Third Article – Conclusion', *DUM*, 30 (December 1847), p. 728, cites 'a vellum autograph copy of the "History of the Cemeteries"' (Wilde cited John O'Donovan's translation in George Petrie, 'The Round Towers of Ireland' (1833) in his *The Ecclesiastical Architecture of Ireland*, 1845). The next passage quoted above is only partly included in Wilde's book-text and comes from the *DUM*.

31. Wilde conducted Macaulay round the Boyne a few years later to supply him with the necessary topographical background to the battle of the Boyne, already discussed in his own book, and dedicated its next edition to him. See also Wilde, *Lough Corrib, its Shores and Islands* (1867 – the year Wilde took the British Medical Association round the Boyne Valley).

32. Míchél Ó Cléirigh, *Genealogiae regum et sanctorum Hiberniae, by the Four Masters*, Dublin: Gill, 1918; *Annala Rioghachta Eireann: Annals of the Kingdom of Ireland, by the Four Masters, from the earliest period to the year 1916*, ed. by John O'Donovan, New York: AMS Press, 1966. Partly quoted by Wilde, *Beauties of the Boyne*, pp. 116–17.

33. Richard Geoffrey Keating, *Foras Feasa ar Éirinn*, Book 1, section XLVI, Dublin, 1811. For a more modern translation see that produced by the Irish Texts Society, Patrick S. Dinneen (ed.), *The History of Ireland by Geoffrey Keating*, London: Irish Texts Society, 1902–14 (vol.III, 1908), II, 344–49, the passages in question being at 347, 349, with the original Gaelic on 346, 348. Dinneen's final sentence is a little more poetic: 'They mourned for him there; and his grave was made; and he was buried at Ross na Riogh.' But Samuel Ferguson only knew O'Mahony's version, which more definitely separates the mourners from the original funeral party, making a conjecture which Ferguson worked into shepherds.

34. Keating, trans. Dinneen, II, pp. 346–7, Exodus, xxxii.

35. For an example, see [William Carleton], 'The Death of a Devotee', *Christian Examiner* (October 1829), pp. 267–83, reprinted in *Tales of Ireland* (London: Garland, 1834), pp. 1–40, and later in William Trevor (ed.), *The Oxford Book of Irish Short Stories* (Oxford: Oxford University Press, 1989).

36. Magh Sleacht, meaning literally 'the plain of slaughter' or 'the plain of injury', was identified by John O'Donovan (1809–61) as near Ballymacgouran, Co. Cavan. *Magh Nuadhad*, the Gaelic for Maynooth, means the plain of Noudons, the ancient Celtic God – says Father Dinneen, *Foclóir Gaedhilge agus Béarla* (London: Irish Texts Society, 1927), p. 801. Priests in celebration of Mass at some public function would wear red vestments. The maledictive stones, popularly known as 'cursing-stones', were noted by Ferguson and subsequent editors in Inishmurray, off Sligo, to which may be added Tory Island, off Donegal (Cooke, *Dublin Book*, pp. 766–7, text pp. 203–7). In Tory, the cursing-stone was variously taken as having been given to the islanders by St Columba/Columcille, or alternatively as having had its use forbidden to them by him. (Personal knowledge).

37. I am obliged to Conor Cruise O'Brien, *States of Ireland* (1973), who made some epigraphic use of Ferguson's lines with reference to Northern Ireland and the twenty-six counties: he had divined purpose in Ferguson (he told me) with contemporary intent. As always, his instincts are a kindly light leading me on. His father, Francis Cruise O'Brien, had republished the long-forgotten final section of the first edition of Lecky on clerical influence in 1911 (the book *Leaders of Public Opinion in Ireland* progressed through several editions without it).

38. Trevor, *Oxford Book*, pp. 52–72.

39. This attempt at violation of a decendant's wishes in fact recalls Carleton's sequel to 'The Death of a Devotee' in which a priest who has repudiated his Catholicism and embraced Protestant evangelicalism is after his death made the battleground of rival faiths: 'The Priest's Funeral',

Christian Examiner (January/February 1830); *Tales of Ireland*, pp. 43–109. One suggestive line is: '… the coffin was taken upon the shoulders of four able Priests…' (p. 108). But if Carleton's story (and he, like Ferguson, was an intimate of the Wildes) was in Ferguson's mind or at his elbow when writing, he certainly intended his pall-bearers to be more highly respected than Carleton intended for his mercenary priests. 'What though a dying man should rave…', however, has echoes of: '…were we to observe the capricious wishes of a feeble-minded old man, on the verge of the grave – childish by age and illness – we would require many messengers.' (p. 62)

40. De Vere was probably consciously producing a Catholic version in reply to Ferguson but, apart from its poetic inferiority, it seems to turn Cormac and Boyne into a necropolitical union:

> But on his bier the great dead King
>   Forgot not so his kingly oath:
> And from sea-marge to mountain spring
>   Boyne heard their coming, and was wroth

(de Vere, 'King Cormac's Choice', reprinted in *The Legends of Saint Patrick*, 1895, pp. 397–9): composition seems unlikely before 1872. De Vere expressed special pleasure to Ferguson on his 'Burial of King Cormac' when it appeared, and – apart (a huge apart) from religious sectarian difference – retained his admiration, as indeed the similarity of his own effort suggests (Mary Catherine Lady Ferguson, *Sir Samuel Ferguson in the Ireland of His Day*, London: Cassell, 1896, II, pp. 262–3).

41. Máire Mac ant Saoi, Introduction to Robert O'Driscoll, *An Ascendancy of the Heart: Ferguson and the Beginnings of Modern Irish Literature in English* (Dublin: Dolmen Press, 1976).

42. Samuel Ferguson, *Poems* (Dublin, 1880).

43. C. S. Lewis (1896–1963), *Out of the Silent Planet* (1938), *Perelandra* (1943), the latter reprinted as *Voyage to Venus*. Lewis rediscovered Ireland in part through Yeats, and may have had some thought of Aonghus in Maleldil. Ferguson's poem seems to have been written about 1863–64 (Ferguson, *Ferguson*, II, pp. 256, 258). He had spent his honeymoon in the Boyne valley, visiting Slane, Brugh and Rosnaree (ibid., I, pp. 185–6).

44. It is a pleasing thought that the only major Irish politician who rendered the name of Haughey with any natural beauty was Ian Paisley, who gave it the aspirate 'c' of its Gaelic origin: 'Hauchy'.

45. Langford Read's *The Complete Limerick Book* has a weak specimen about a young lady from Drogheda as a result of whose conduct when something annoyed 'er, nobody afterwards employed 'er. Langford Read, *The Complete Limerick Book: The Origin, History and Achievements of the Limerick, with about three hundred and fifty Selected Examples*, New York: Gale, 1974.

46. Patrick J. Corish, *The Catholic Community in the Seventeenth and Eighteenth Centuries* (Dublin: Helicon, 1981), pp. 53–9, 67–9, 144–5, and works therein cited. Its cover has a fine portrait of Plunket[t?].

47. That is the only point when the priest holds God's place, although many have assumed its more general application.

48. Thomas Babington Macaulay, [Warren Hastings], *Edinburgh Review*, October 1841. Editions of his *Critical and Historical Essays* are numerous enough to make citation worthless, but the passage is roughly at the end of the essay's first third.

49. De Vere, 'Archbishop Plunket', Brown, *Poetry of Irish History*, pp. 191–3. J. P. Kenyon, *The Popish Plot* (Harmondsworth: Penguin, 1974 [1972]), pp. 233–4, largely confirms de Vere's judgment: 'Plunket was only an Irishman, anyway. … [Charles] agreed quite happily that Plunket was innocent, but "his enemies were waiting for him to make a false step", and the moment was not propitious for a counter-attack.' But the Revd Professor P. J. Corish, the greatest Irish Roman Catholic historian in holy orders of our time, notes the ugly role of two of Plunket's fellow-clerics in bringing about his martyrdom (*Catholic Community*, p. 69).

50. Corish noted (ibid., p. 145) that 'Despite its curious arrangement and faults of omission,' Patrick Francis Cardinal Moran, *Memoir of Oliver Plunket* (1861) 'has not been completely superseded.' Moran was Archbishop of Sydney, New South Wales, but failed in his hopes of succession (at one remove) to his uncle Paul Cardinal Cullen in Dublin, the history of whose Catholic Archbishops he had published in 1864. His turn to Plunket may reveal some investment in the see of Armagh, but that failed in its turn (1885, 1887 respectively). Moran (1830–1911) ruled Sydney from 1884. Cullen had ruled Armagh 1849–52 before transfer to Dublin.

51. My sister Ruth Dudley Edwards's *The Faithful Tribe*, is useful and enjoyable in describing

Scarva – the book in general is full of first-rate insights on commemoration. Edwards, *The Faithful Tribe: An Intimate Portrait of the Loyalist Institutions*, London: HarperCollins, 1999, pp. 15–18, 109–10.

52. Anon., 'The Battle of the Boyne' [collated from two old versions of the ballad], Alfred Percival Graves (ed.), *The Book of Irish Poetry*, Dublin: Talbot Press, 1907, pp. 161–2. The first verse sets the tone:

> July the first of a morning fair
> In sixteen ninety famous,
> King William did his men prepare
> To fight with false King Shamus.
> King James he pitched his tents between
> The lines for to retire;
> But King William threw his bomb-balls in
> And set them all on fire.

With the maximum of allowance for Graves (1846–1931), whose artistry was no more blunted by fidelity to his originals than would be that of his son Robert, the poem's dating of the first of July suggests pre mid eighteenth-century origins. So too does the easy use of Gaelic 'Seamus' for 'James'.

53. On King James's Irish Parliament: Macaulay, *History of England*, London: Dent, 1966, chapter XII.

54. Ferguson, *Poems*.

55. Frank McGuinness (b.1953), writing from a Donegal Catholic inheritance, has captured the meaning of this better than anyone else in his profoundly empathetic play *Observe the Sons of Ulster Marching Towards the Somme* (1985) – even the title is a masterpiece of delicacy, being a prayer uttered to God on the eve of the sacrifice, the imperative catching the blend of local government officialdom and petty formality implicit in a populist religion yet conscious of a need of ritual in its anti-ritualism. The one weakness seems the failure to distinguish between varieties of Protestantism, excellent though it is as to the varieties of anti-Catholicism: Catholics have difficulty grasping the intensity of feeling between Presbyterians against Church of Ireland, Presbyterians against Unitarians, Church of Ireland against Methodists, and so on. Maurice Healy, in *The Old Munster Circuit* (1939), p. 51, recalls an inquiry made of an Ulster barrister whom his Catholic colleagues asked to distinguish between a Calvinistic Presbyterian and a Presbyterian *tout court*:

> 'I'll tall ye,' said John [Bartley]. 'A Calvinistic Prasb'tayrian believes all you Papishes wull be domned because ye're predastined to be domned; but we or'nary Prasb'tayrians b'lieve all you Papishes wull be domned on yer mer'ts.' The English alphabet does not quite do justice to John's incisive northern accent.

Carson's and Craig's use of the different Ulster sects is noteworthy, the Ulster Covenant being signed by the Moderator of the General Assembly and by the Bishop of Connor immediately after Carson and the Marquess of Londonderry. It was very much in keeping with the use of Roman Catholic clergy by their Home Rule exemplar Charles Stewart Parnell, whose local League branches were well staffed with priests as treasurers. But Carson and Craig ran no risk of the Protestant clergy pulling them down.

56. Cooke, *Dublin Book*, pp. 25–6. John Hewitt, *Rhyming Weavers and Other Country Poets of Antrim and Down*, 1974. Orr as a rekindling of Burns for Irish purposes may be seen, for instance, in 'To the Potatoe', *Poems* (1804), reprinted in Hewitt, *Rhyming Weavers*, pp. 107–8. (The spelling suggests that Vice-President Danforth Quayle might have retrieved his fortunes by claiming sympathy as a disadvantaged Ultonian. There is, however, no reason to believe that Orr tried to humiliate small children by publicly reproving their supposed deficiencies in orthography.)

57. Jane Francesca Lady Wilde, 'Our Ancient Capital' [1859?], in *Ancient Legends of Ireland*, New York: Sterling, 1996, p. 299: 'But the Irish race remains distinct from all others, as Jew or Zincali.' She did not include herself in it, and on p. 326 noted Dublin as populated by 'Danes, Normans, Saxon settlers, and mongrel Irish'. Michael Collins, *The Path to Freedom* (1922), takes its logic on the same principle, without much concern about Dublin. These ideas were probably basic to much of formal Irish nationalism among Catholics. Ulster Protestant racial theory frequently expresses itself on the same principle, e.g. Lord Ernest Hamilton, *The Soul of Ulster* (1917). Nevertheless, there were many mongrels.

58. Dudley Edwards, *Faithful Tribe*, p. 292; and see following pages where Portadown is described

as 'the Orange Vatican' and mention made of the commemorative Orange banners of which Revd Brian Mac Cuarta SJ notes his 'Introduction' to *Ulster 1641 – Aspects of the Rising*, edited by him:

> While William on his horse, together with the half-closed gates of Derry, have provided the staple of loyalist iconography, it is striking that very few Orange banners depict an episode from 1641. Out of sight, in this case, is not out of mind.

The book reproduces a banner from Loyal Orange Lodge 273, Portadown No.1 District, which depicted bearded, armed, soberly-garbed, Catholic men (bearing a startling resemblance to James VI and I, in the foremost figure), striding through the Bann with spears against naked Protestant women who guard their breasts with their hair, with at least one small child alongside. Ruth Dudley Edwards notes the tradition that the Portadown Orange organisation in the late eighteeenth century derived from folk fears of a repetition of 1641. Brian Mac Cuarta (ed.), *Ulster 1641 – Aspects of the Rising*, Belfast: Institute of Irish Studies, 1993.

59. See Macaulay, *History of England*, chapter XV.
60. Thomas Carlyle (ed.), *Oliver Cromwell's Letters and Speeches*, London, 1846, Part V. Campaign in Ireland 1649. (If any commemoration of Cromwell persisted in nineteenth-century Protestant Ulster, it would have been by ownership of Carlyle's *Cromwell*, whose documents are exceptionally faithful for the time and whose commentary is exceptionally frivolous for it).

> Not long after my last to you before Waterford, – by reason of the tempestuousness of the weather, we thought fit, and it was agreed, to march away to Winter-quarters, to refresh our men until God shall please to give farther opportunity for action. We marched off, the 2d of this instant; it being so terrible a day as ever I marched in all my life. (Cromwell to Speaker William Lenthall, 19 December 1649, II, p. 195).

61. Wexford seems to have been a mistake. Cromwell's army got out of hand and started a massacre while Cromwell was still in negotiation with the garrison. Naturally, Cromwell could not report to Speaker Lenthall that he had proved unable to manage his own troops, so both he and his enemies acquiesced in the furtherance of the black legend.
62. Oscar Wilde, *The Importance of Being Earnest* (produced 1895), Act I.
63. *A Sermon Preach'd to the Protestants of Ireland now in London*, Edinburgh: Robert Brown, 1714. Ramsay was obliged to make the Jacobite claimant both a vengeful Stuart and an impostor, and straddled his contradictions manfully:

> We must be blindly infatuated, should we ever take any Steps that would send us back again to *Egypt*, or pave the way for a *Popish* Impostor, nurs'd up in this bloody *Popery*, both in all the Maxims of Tyranny who being attainted and abjured by the Nation, will not come with the favourable prepossessions of a legal Successor, but the angry Resentments of an injured Exile, against the Dethroners of his pretended Father.

Egypt was cited as the residence of the degraded Jews under a hostile Pharaoh before they were rescued by Moses (Exodus).
64. For a review of the Bloody Bridge controversy, see especially Jacqueline Hill, '1641 and the quest for Catholic Emancipation, 1691–1829', and Toby Barnard, '1641: a bibliographical essay', in Mac Cuarta, *Ulster 1641*, pp. 159–87, 218–28. Among the many other excellent qualities of this book is its homage to my late dear friend Walter Love, supreme historiographer of the event and its mythology, whose notes are preserved at Trinity College Dublin. He is dead for a third of a century but eternally living for me. For the quotation, Carlyle, *Cromwell*, II, p. 206 (added after the first edition).
65. Mitchel was replying to J. A. Froude, *The English in Ireland in the Eighteenth Century, Reviews of Froude's Work*, Dublin, 1873, I, pp. 72–155. *1641: Reply to the Falsification of History*, by James Anthony Froude, entitled 'The English in Ireland', published Glasgow: Cameron and Ferguson [1875?], National Library of Scotland, not in British Library. For Mitchel in his high polemic, see his *The Last Conquest of Ireland (Perhaps)* (1876), p. 116: 'The Almighty, indeed, sent the potato blight, but the English created the Famine.' See also the invaluable if inaccurate Malcolm Brown, *The Politics of Irish Literature* (1972).
66. Froude, *English in Ireland*, II, p. 117. In fairness to Froude, his absurdities do seem to have delighted Parnell and Wilde. Parnell quoted him to the United States Congress as evidence for Parnell's recruitment of American public opinion against English landlordism. Oscar Wilde (his father now being dead) reviewed his novel, *The Two Chiefs of Dunboy* as 'Mr Froude's Blue Book'.
67. G. K. Chesterton, *The Victorian Age in Literature*, London: Williams & Norgate, 1925, pp. 60–1.
68. Stopford A. Brooke and T. W. Rolleston, *A Treasury of Irish Poetry in the English Tongue*

(1900), pp. 134–7. The slaughtered kin haunt Islandmagee, of which Dr Raymond Gillespie remarks:

> Some violence was simply the result of giving men arms in a situation in which controls of their actions were weak. The attack on the Magees of Islandmagee in early January 1642 by a troop of Scots from Ballymoney is one example of such gratuitous violence as was the drowning of the settlers at Portadown by Toole McCann in November 1641. All sides agreed that such violence was unacceptable.

('Destabilizing Ulster, 1641–2', Mac Cuarta, *Ulster 1641*, p. 113).

69. Mac Cuarta has pointed out that Lord Ernest's *The Irish Rebellion of 1641* (1920) was in fact the last book treatment for the next seventy-odd years (*Ulster 1641*, p. 1). The book was timeous, as Lord Ernest's war work during the Anglo-Irish or Black and Tan hostilities: it was intended, evidently, to underwrite auxiliary vigilante groups recruited by the state to keep Catholic subversives under firm control, a precaution sometimes taken to excess.

70. A.M. Sullivan, *A Story of Ireland; or, A Narrative of Irish History from the Early ages to the Present Time. Written for the Youth of Ireland*, Dublin, 1867, pp. 58–9. Sullivan declared that 'the puritanical executive' in Dublin invented the 1641 Catholic massacre: 'To be sure, they knew there had been no massacre – quite the contrary, but this made little matter.' Sibbert, *On the Shining Bann: Records of an Ulster Manor: A Book for All Touring in Northern Ireland*, Belfast, 1928, pp. 61, 58.

71. Deposition quoted in Thomas Fitzpatrick, *The Bloody Bridge, and Other Papers Relating to the Insurrection of 1641*, Dublin, 1903, p. 195. Mary Agnes Hickson, *Ireland in the Seventeenth Century, or: The Irish Massacres of 1641–2, their cause and results*, London: Longman, Green & Co, 1884, pp. 136–7:

> The supposed spectre, which appeared there a few evenings later, may well have been a poor, forlorn, bereaved woman, who stole from the woods or mountains (where she had been hiding since her children or friends were drowned), to wail over their corpses, sunk in the river or washed down in its currents to the ocean. In the dark winter evening this distracted and solitary mourner holding that mournful 'Wake of the Absent' … would have appeared to poor Mrs Price and to others in that superstitious age and wasted and troubled land a visitor from another world. … At the present day numbers of the Irish people believe in the existence of ghosts and fairies and in apparitions like that alleged to have been seen at Knock in Connaught, a few years ago.

And the British today often believe in horoscopes written by drunken journalists. Hickson convinced herself that 'not less than 25,000 people could have been murdered' which dwarfs all other totals and thus accounts for her refutation of the ghost by an imaginary lunatic. But, in 1873, Patrick Francis Moran of archiepiscopal emulatitive talents dismissed the depositions of survivors as 'little more than a series of contradictory statements and exaggerated hearsay reports'. Hilary Simms ably juxtaposes these depressing illustrations of history to the historian's taste ('Violence in County Armagh', in Mac Cuarta, *Ulster 1641*, p. 137).

72. Padraic Colum, *The King of Ireland's Son*, London: Harrap, 1916 [Sixth Book] 'The House of Crom Duv', beginning.

73. Dublin in Gaelic is *Baile Átha Cliath*, i.e. 'the town of the ford of the spear', a reasonable description for a Viking base. Donegal's name was originally Tír Chonaill, 'Conall's country', matching Tyrone, 'Owen's country'. Donegal itself derives from *Dún na nGall*, 'the fortress of the foreigners'. Dublin (*Dubh linn*) would be best translated as 'Blackpool'.

74. Charles Kingsley, *The Water-Babies* (Edinburgh: Nimmo).

75. I am uneasily conscious of omitting the Lagan, provider of Ireland's only real Industrial Revolution – whose immigration in the nineteenth century supplied much of the muscle and force of the modern Ulster Protestant population. I am all the more conscious of it since, alone of Irish rivers, it has inspired a first-class analysis, *The Lagan Valley, 1800–50* (1949), by a great local son and another dear friend now dead, Edward Rodney Richey Green, whose Quaker origins enabled him to delight in the cultures of all sides of the sectarian divide.

NOTES TO CHAPTER 68: IN THE SHADOW OF CALTON HILL

1. For a useful and specifically Scottish study of the 'spatial contingency of social action' see Catriona M. M. MacDonald, 'The Vanduaria of Ptolemy: Place and the Past', in D. Broun, et al., *Image and Identity: The Making and Re-making of Scotland Through the Ages*, Edinburgh: John

Donald, 1998, pp. 177–94; the works of J. A. Agnew, D. Harvey, E. W. Soja, E. Relph and D. Massey cited therein provide wider discussion of the issues and implications for historical study.

2. For the full text of the Address see E. W. McFarland, *Ireland and Scotland in the Age of Revolution: Planting the Green Bough*, Edinburgh: Edinburgh University Press, 1994.

3. For two influential classics from a voluminous literature see Thomas Johnston, *The History of the Working Classes in Scotland*, Wakefield: EP Publishing, 1974 (reprint of 4th edition, Glasgow: Unity Publishing, 1946), specially ch. IX. 'The Political Democracy', pp. 211–64; E. P. Thompson, *The Making of the English Working Class*, Harmondsworth: Penguin, (revised edition) 1968.

4. See E. W. McFarland, *Ireland and Scotland*; J. D. Brims, 'The Scottish "Jacobins", Scottish Nationalism and the British Union' in R. Mason (ed.), *Scotland and England: 1288–1815*, Edinburgh: John Donald, 1987, pp. 247–65.

5. A useful study of popular protest in England (which also touches on Gerrald's trial) is J. A. Epstein, *Radical Expression, Political Language, Ritual, and Symbol in England, 1790–1850*, Oxford: Oxford University Press, 1994.

6. Henry Cockburn, *Memorials of his Time*, Edinburgh: A. & C. Black, 1856, p. 250.

7. Peter MacKenzie, *Reminiscences of Glasgow and the West of Scotland*, J. Tweed, Glasgow 1875, (2 vols), II, pp. 388–9.

8. For fuller details of Hume's long career see V. Chancellor, *The political life of Joseph Hume, 1777–1855 the Scot who was for over 30 years a radical leader in the British House of Commons*, London: V. Chancellor, 1986; R. K. Huch and P. R. Ziegler, *Joseph Hume, the people's M.P.*, Philadelphia: American Philosophical Society, 1985.

9. Peter MacKenzie, *The Life of Thomas Muir*, Glasgow: W. R. M'Phun, 1831.

10. J. Hume to P. MacKenzie, 14 June 1831 in P. MacKenzie, *Reminiscences*, II, pp. 387–8.

11. Ibid.

12. Daniel O'Connell, Henry Grattan and Richard Shiel were amongst the Irish representatives present. See P. MacKenzie, *Reminiscences* II, pp. 388–9.

13. The list of subscribers gave its own defining profile. Headed by Hume they included: the Duke of Norfolk; the Duke of Bedford; the Earl of Essex; Lord Worsley; Lord Brougham; Mr Coke of Norfolk (Earl of Leinster); Lord Hollan; Sir John Easthope; Admiral Sir John Codrington; the Rt. Hon. Edward Ellice; the Rt. Hon. Cutlar Ferguson and some forty plus MPs. ibid., p. 389.

14. J. Hume to W. Tait, 4 January 1842, Edinburgh Central Library, Edinburgh Room [ECL/ER].

15. J. Hume to W. Tait, 14 September 1838, ECL/ER; Minutes of the Proceedings, Committee for Erecting Monuments to the Political Martyrs 1793/4, 23 February 1839, ECL/ER. The design proposed by Edinburgh must have been different from that proposed by London. In 1837 Hume asked Tait what Edinburgh's thoughts were regarding 'the kind of monument', adding: 'It is supposed that an Obelisk of the size of the Obelisk of Cleopatra, would answer well, and I send you a plan of two Obelisks that have been suggested', J. Hume to Tait, 22 April 1837. Hume enclosed plans for two obelisks, one square, the other a pentagon 'to allow a side for the name of each of the Martyrs', Plan of Obelisk, 22 April 1837, ECL/ER.

16. Amongst several of Braxfield's comments which entered popular memory was his audible whispered exhortation from the bench to one of the jurors, 'Come awa', Maister Horner, come awa', and help us to hang ane o' thae damned scoondrels!', cited in T. Johnston, *History of the Working Classes*, p. 220. Peter MacKenzie also noted the use of Scots during the trial by the Senior Macer when asked to control the spectators, a scene which MacKenzie related in suitable subaltern style with English 'translations' parenthesised: 'My Lords, they are aw (all) cheering and stamping with their feet, and clapping their hauns (hands); so you see my Lords, it's perfectly impossible for me to tak (take) them aw into custody.' Cited in Mackenzie, *Reminiscences*, II, p. 45.

17. For full details of the meeting and the resolutions passed see Cockburn, *Memorials*, pp. 247–8.

18. Ibid., p. 248.

19. Ibid., p. 248. Thomas Muir Moffat's father had been a close friend of Thomas Muir, deeply involved in events and recipient of Muir's only surviving letter from Botany Bay. See C. Bewley, *Muir of Huntershill*, Oxford: Oxford University Press, 1981. William Muir was also related.

20. Ibid. p. 249.

21. The dates of erection of these other monuments were: David Hume; 1777; William Playfair 1825–6; Robert Burns 1830; Dugald Stewart 1831; See M. Turnbull, *Monuments and Statues of Edinburgh*, Edinburgh: Chambers, 1989, pp. 4–29.

22. The Nelson Monument had been erected in 1807 to commemorate the victory of Trafalgar. Every year on 'Trafalgar Day', 21 October, it was emblazoned with signal flags proclaiming across the Edinburgh landscape the famous message: 'England expects every man to do his duty.' Turnbull, *Monuments*, pp. 20–1.
23. Cockburn, *Memorials*, p. 249.
24. Ibid.
25. See the two lead front page advertisements in *The Scotsman*, 21 August 1844.
26. Ibid.
27. Ibid.
28. *The Scotsman*, 24 August 1844
29. Ibid.
30. Cockburn, *Memorials*, pp. 250–1.
31. *The Scotsman*, 24 August 1844.
32. Ibid.
33. Turnbull, *Monuments*, pp. 14–15, 71.
34. *The Scotsman*, 24 August 1844.
35. Ibid.
36. At Muir's trial the Lord Advocate referred to the United Irishmen as 'wretches'. This was challenged in Edinburgh by Hamilton Rowan of the United Irishmen. He was honoured at a subsequent dinner in Belfast where one of the toasts was to 'The Scotch Convention, Mr Muir, the swine of England, the rabble of Scotland and the swine of Ireland'. H. W. Meikle, *Scotland and the French Revolution*, Edinburgh: James Maclehose and Sons, 1912, p. 140, 1n.
37. *The Scotsman*, 24 August 1844.
38. Ibid.
39. Ibid.
40. Ibid.
41. Ibid.
42. Ibid.
43. The same phraseology was also used by Watson, an exile Scot in Paris, when he published an 'Address to the People of Great Britain' inviting them to welcome the French. Watson asked the Patriots of Scotland whether Wallace had died, Buchanan and Fletcher had written and Ossian sung in vain? And he warned: 'Think of Ireland bleeding before you and be assured that the same fetters are being forged for you'. See Meikle, *Scotland and the French Revolution*, pp. 171–2.
44. *The Scotsman*, 24 August 1844.
45. Ibid.
46. Cockburn, *Memorials*, p. 251.
47. Ibid.
48. Quoted in MacKenzie, *Reminiscences*, II, p. 396.
49. Ibid.
50. Quoted in MacKenzie, *Reminiscences*, II, p. 390.
51. *The Scotsman*, 1 October 1845.
52. Cockburn, *Memories*, p. 252.
53. Ibid.
54. Cockburn, *Memories*, p. 252.
55. *The Scotsman*, 21 June 1848.
56. *The Scotsman*, 24 August 1844.
57. L. W. Wright, *The Chartist Movement in Scotland*, Manchester: Manchester University Press, 1970, p. 222.
58. Ibid. pp. 223–6.
59. Ibid.
60. Ibid. pp. 230–1.
61. Rankine also talked of the French being superior to the English in inventive genius, but he hoped that if matters were pushed to such an extremity, the English would improve upon the noble example set them by the French Republic. *The Scotsman*, 14 June 1848.
62. Ibid.
63. *The Scotsman*, 21 June 1848.
64. *The Scotsman*, 26 July 1848. *The North British Weekly Express* was committed to the Charter, the 'Rights of Labour' and also the 'Repeal of the Union'. The paper was the property of the leading Edinburgh Chartists.

65. Ibid.
66. Ibid. The same issue also carried reports from Ireland of proclaimed districts, 'rebel councils' and Clubs.
67. According to Rankine, the Gerrald, Muir, Washington, Wallace, Baird and Hardie, Emmett and Faugh a' Ballagh Clubs were already in operation. See National Archives of Scotland, AD2/19.
68. *The Scotsman*, 8 August 1848.
69. National Archives of Scotland, AD2/19.
70. National Archives of Scotland AD2/19. Indictments of John Grant, printer, Henry Rankine, late editor *North British Express*, Robert Hamilton, tailor, for conspiracy and sedition, March–July 1848; indictment of James Cumming for conspiracy and sedition, April–July 1848.
71. *The Scotsman*, 8 November 1848.
72. Henry Cockburn, *Journal of Henry Cockburn; being a continuation of the Memorials of his time. 1831–1854,* Edinburgh: Edmonston and Douglas, 1874, II, p. 235.
73. Elizabeth M. Mein, *Through Four Reigns: The story of the Old Waverley Hotel and its founder (Robert Cranston)*, privately printed, Edinburgh: 1948, p. 4.
74. *The Scotsman*, 29 July 1848.
75. Ibid.
76. *The Scotsman*, 31 July 1848.
77. Connolly's poem 'THE LEGACY. *The Dying Socialist to His Son*' first appeared in an American journal and was reprinted in *Irish Worker*, 23 May 1914. It is reprinted in *James Connolly Selected Writings* (ed. P. Beresford-Ellis), Penguin: Harmondsworth, 1973, pp. 298–302.
78. See C. Desmond Greaves, *The Life and Times of James Connolly*, London: Lawrence & Wishart, 1961, pp. 85–6.
79. Ray Burnett, 'Edinburgh and the Roots of Scottish Socialism', *History Workshop Conference* 24, Glasgow, 17–18 November, 1990.
80. Victor G. Kiernan, 'Gramsci and Marxism' in R. Milliband and J. Saville (eds), *The Socialist Register 1972*, London: The Merlin Press, 1972, p. 3.
81. *Shan Van Vocht*, January 1897, reprinted in P. Beresford-Ellis (ed.), *James Connolly: Selected Writings*, p. 121.
82. See Greaves, *Life and Times*, pp. 88–91. A 'Scotto-Hibernian' was a contemporary Dublin newspaper's depiction of Connolly, cited by Greaves, p. 80.
83. *Shan Van Vocht*, January 1897, reprinted in Beresford-Ellis, *Life and Times*, p. 121.
84. *Workers' Republic*, 20 August 1898, reprinted in Aindrias Ó Cathasaigh (ed.), *The Lost Writings, James Connolly*, London: Pluto Press, 1997, p.18.
85. *Workers Republic*, 13 August 1898.
86. For John Leslie see James D. Young, 'John Leslie, 1856–1921: A Scottish-Irishman as Internationalist', *Saothar*, 18 (1993), pp. 55–61. According to H. W. Lee, the historian of the SDF, Leslie had been involved with the Fenian movement in his Edinburgh youth. See H. W. Lee and E. Archbold, *Social Democracy in Britain. Fifty Years of the Socialist Movement*, part I. Part I by H. W. Lee / Part II by E.Archbold, edited (with an introduction) by Herbert Tracey, London: Social-Democratic Federation, 1935.
87. John Leslie, *The Irish Question*, Cork, London, 1894 (Cork: Cork Workers Club, 1974, Historical Reprint no. 7), p. 5. Leslie's pamphlet first appeared in serial form in the SDF's *Justice*, to which Leslie was the regular Edinburgh contributor. As he was born in 1856, it would seem reasonable to assume that Leslie's initial interest in the writings of Lalor was most likely sparked by the retained memory of Lalor's writings and the *Irish Felon* in the Old Town.
88. Greaves, *Life and Times*, p. 65.
89. *Workers' Republic*, 13 August 1898, cited in Greaves, *Life and Times*, p. 109.
90. *Edinburgh Evening News [EEN]*, 5 June 1968.
91. Ibid. The two nieces were Mrs C. MacKay and Mrs G. Richards.
92. Ibid.
93. *EEN*, 10 June 1968.
94. Personal conversation with John Hendry, 1985.
95. *EEN*, 13 June 1968.
96. Ibid.
97. *EEN*, 19 June 1968.

98. *EEN*, 10 June 1968
99. Ibid.
100. The lecture was delivered at Liberty Hall, Dublin, 10 May 1968. The footnote reference occurs in the published edition of the lecture, Owen Dudley Edwards, *The Mind of an Activist – James Connolly*, Dublin: Gill and Macmillan, 1971, pp. 130–1, 16n.
101. The best source for tracing Connolly's itinerary remains Greaves, *Life and Times*, See pp. 229–73. Rogers would have been 15 years old in 1913. Connolly's time in Edinburgh prior to October 1913 was equally brief. In 1911 he made his only other visit subsequent to his return from the USA in 1910, the occasion on which he told John Leslie he was thinking of leaving Ireland once more and settling in England. See Greaves, *Life and Times*, p. 208.
102. *Freeman's Journal*, 14 November 1913, cited in Emmet Larkin, *James Larkin*, London: New English Library, 1968 edn, p. 129.
103. Family tradition and personal conversations with older Edinburgh Old Town residents, 1968–1969.
104. *EEN*, 24 March 1968; 1 April 1968.
105. *Sun* (Scottish edition), 10 September 1990.
106. *EEN*, 15 March 1993.
107. *EEN*, 18 January 1993.
108. *EEN*, 12 March 1993; 15 March 1993; 29 April 1993; 18–19 May 1993; 2 June 1993; *Scotsman*, 19 May 1993.
109. *EEN*, 21 September 1994.
110. *EEN*, 3 October 1994.
111. Ibid.; *Scotsman*, 3 October 1994. Cllr. Sean McKnight was the Sinn Féin speaker.
112. *EEN*, 15 June 1996..
113. Personal conversation with James Slaven, James Connolly Society.
114. *Glasgow Herald*, 31 May 1991.
115. The statement decrying the popular will for the Parliament to be sited on Calton Hill was attributed to Brian Wilson MP.
116. ECL/ER, 'Commemoration Programme 30 August 1968'; *Scottish Vanguard*, 2, 8/9 (Aug/Sep 1968). The marginal note to the programme indicates that both Naomi Mitchison and Douglas Young were present and spoke as late additions. There had been a smaller commemoration the previous Saturday in Glasgow to mark the anniversary of Thomas Muir's birth in the High Street, Glasgow.
117. *Scottish Vanguard*, 2, 8/9 (Aug/Sep 1968). The report in *Scottish Vanguard* implies that Jack Kane spoke from the platform but the programme lists him as sending greetings.
118. Ibid.
119. Ibid. See Elizabeth M. Mein, *Through Four Regions*.
120. Ibid.

NOTES TO CHAPTER 7: CONTRARY HEROES

1. Quoted in Dan H. Laurence (ed.), *Bernard Shaw: Collected Letters, 1874–1897*, London: Max Reinhardt, 1965, p. 691.
2. To cite two metropolitan accounts of the subject matter of this essay, in Anthony D. Smith's *National Identity*, Harmondsworth: Penguin, 1991, the treatment of Irish nationalism is brief and 'pre-revisionist'; in Owen Chadwick's *The Secularisation of the European Mind in the Nineteenth Century*, 1975, Cambridge University Press, 1991. Ireland (surely the great exception to Chadwick's thesis) does not appear at all.
3. Conor Cruise O'Brien, *Ancestral Voices*, Dublin: Poolbeg Press, 1994.
4. There is no reference in Ciaran Brady, *Interpreting Irish History*, Dublin: Irish Academic Press, 1994; a nanosecond sighting in *Ireland's Field Day*, London: Hutchinson, 1985, in Declan Kiberd', 'Anglo-Irish Attitudes', p. 86, and in Seamus Deane, *Celtic Revivals*, London: Faber, 1985, p. 30.
5. See, for example, Malcolm Brown, *The Politics of Irish Literature*, London: Allen and Unwin, 1972, pp. 117–9, which follows the 'Anglo-Saxonist' line.
6. Owen Dudley Edwards, 'Irish Nationalism', in Owen Dudley Edwards (ed.), *Celtic Nationalism*, London: Routledge, 1968, pp. 123ff.; for Carlyle's influence on the literary intelligentsia see Christopher Harvie, *The Centre of Things,* London: Unwin Hyman, 1991, pp. 18–21.

7. See Sheridan Gilley, 'Edward Irving: Prophet of the Millennium, and Raphael Samuel, 'The Discovery of Puritanism, 1820–1914', in Jane Garnett and Colin Matthew (eds), *Revival and Religion since 1700*, London: Hambledon Press, 1993, esp. pp. 95–105 and 204–24.
8. Edward Caird, 'The Genius of Carlyle', in *Essays on Literature and Philosophy*, I, Glasgow: Maclehose, 1892, p. 234.
9. Linda Colley, *Britons: Forging the Nation, 1707–1837*, London: Yale University Press, 1992; see my review in *The Welsh History Review* (1997).
10. See Deane, *Celtic Revivals*, p. 18.
11. Patrick Geddes, *Cities in Evolution*, London: Williams and Norgate, 1915, chapters 3 and 4; and see Helen Meller, *Patrick Geddes: Social Evolutionist and City Planner*, London: Routledge, 1990. By this they meant the technological period in which carbon energy was utilised without being fully understood or incorporated into a tolerable ecology.
12. I go into the Irish technology issue in greater detail in 'Larry Doyle and Captain MacWhirr: the Engineer's Story', paper presented at the 'Stories of Ireland' conference, Belfast, July 1997.
13. *The Times*, 22 February 1997.
14. See article 'Ship' in *Encyclopaedia Britannica*, 24, New York, 1911, pp. 918ff. Roy Johnston, 'Society and Technology in Celtic Nation-Building', in Cathal Ó Luain (ed.), *For a Celtic Future*, Dublin: Celtic League, 1983, pp. 201–16; and John de Courcy Ireland, 'John Philip Holland, Pioneer in Submarine Navigation', *The North Munster Antiquarian Journal*, 10, 2, 1967, pp. 206–12.
15. John Mitchel, *Jail Journal*, Glasgow: 1876; Charles Lever, *Lord Kilgobbin*, London: Downey, pp. 100–1; and see Robert Kane, *Industrial Resources of Ireland*, 1844. Knighted at 37, Kane went on to become President of 'godless' Queen's College, Cork.
16. James Bryce, 'Charles Stewart Parnell', in *Studies in Contemporary Biography*, London: Macmillan, 1906, p. 213.
17. *Ulysses*, 1922, London: John Lane, 1947, pp. 310, 609, 679ff.
18. See Catherine Nash, 'Visionary Geographies: Designs for Developing Ireland', *History Workshop Journal*, 45, spring 1998, pp. 49–78.
19. Nairn, 'On Studying Nationalism', in *Faces of Nationalism: Janus Revisited*, London: Verso, 1997, pp. 1–20. See W. J. McCormack, *Ascendancy and Tradition in Anglo-Irish Literary History, from 1789 to 1939*, Oxford: Clarendon Press, 1985, chapter 5. Oliver MacDonagh contributes fruitfully to this theme in 'Ambiguity in Nationalism: the Case of Ireland' (1980), reprinted in Brady, *Interpreting Irish History*, pp. 105–21.
20. Charles Gavan Duffy, *Short Life of Thomas Davis*, London: Unwin, 1895, pp. 180ff.; Edwards, 'Irish Nationalism', p. 123.
21. See James Joyce, 'Ivy Day in the Committee Room', in *Dubliners*, 1913, London: Cape, 1967, pp. 132–52; Sean O'Casey, *Juno and the Paycock*, 1924, London: St Martin's Press, 1960, last lines of Act 3.
22. David Fitzpatrick, 'A Peculiar Tramping People: the Irish in Britain, 1801–70', in W. J. Vaughan (ed.), *A New History of Ireland*, V: *Ireland under the Union, 1801–70*, Oxford: Oxford University Press, 1989, pp. 623–60.
23. Norman Vance, *Irish Literature: a Social History*, Oxford: Blackwell, 1990, p. 140, writes of mid-Victorian Ireland being 'subjected unevenly to the industrialising process', but in net terms Ireland was deindustrialised. If the Lagan Valley were removed from the statistics, the fall would be even steeper. For the twentieth century see David Johnston, *The Inter-War Economy in Ireland*, Dublin: Institute of Economic and Social History, 1985, p. 43.
24. Cormac Ó Gráda, *Ireland: A New Economic History, 1780–1939*, Oxford: Clarendon Press, 1994, pp. 347–8.
25. Fernand Braudel, *La Mediterranée et le monde méditerranéen à l'époque de Philippe II*, Paris: 1966, p. 46. I-Feng Hsui, *Regions in the Development of Historic Capitalism, a Comparison of Scotland, Baden-Württemberg and Taiwan*, Tübingen Ph.D., 1999, stresses the deliberate quality of 'unequal development'; agricultural crises, for example, were instrumentalised to provide labour for industry elsewhere.
26. W. L. Langer, *Political and Social Upheaval*, New York: Harper, 1969, pp. 10ff.
27. T. M. Devine, *The Scottish Nation, 1700–2000*, London: Allen Lane, 1999, pp. 56–7, 486–9.
28. See Angus Calder, *Revolutionary Empire*, London: Cape, 1981, p. 629.
29. Eric Hobsbawm, *Industry and Empire*, 1968, Harmondsworth: Penguin, 1969, pp. 109ff.
30. See William Thomas Dargan (1799–1867) in the *Dictionary of National Biography*; another

Telford pupil was the Highland Railway's engineer Joseph Mitchell.
31. Dargan, obituary in *The Times*, 8 February 1867.
32. H. D. Gribbon, 'Economy and Industry', in W. J. Vaughan (ed.), *The New History of Ireland*, VI, Oxford: Clarendon, 1992, pp. 333ff.
33. John Stuart Mill, *England and Ireland*, London: Longmans, 1867, p. 26.
34. Tom Garvin, 'Great Hatred, Little Room: Social Background and Political Sentiment among Revolutionary Activists in Ireland, 1890–1922', in D. G. Boyce (ed.), *The Revolution in Ireland, 1879–1923*, London: Macmillan, 1988, pp. 91–114.
35. Lever, *Lord Kilgobbin*, 2, p. 18.
36. McCormack, *Ascendancy*, pp. 219ff.
37. Ibid., p. 250; Chris Baldick, *The Social Mission of English Criticism*, Oxford: Oxford University Press, 1989, chapter 4.
38. McCormack ascribes this to the effectiveness of the Clearances (*Ascendancy*, p. 246) neglecting the considerable cultural output covered by William Donaldson, *Popular Literature in Victorian Scotland: Language, Fiction and the Press*, Aberdeen: Aberdeen University Press, 1986.
39. See Thomas Flanagan in Vaughan, *New History*, pp. 490ff. Owen Dudley Edwards, *Eamon de Valera*, Cardiff: GPC Books, 1997, p. 32. De Valera read Macaulay and Goldsmith as well as Kickham, and considered himself a monarchist, only becoming interested in the Gaelic literary movement on his marriage. Richard Ellmann, *James Joyce*, Oxford: Oxford University Press, 1983, pp. 31, 45, notes Lamb, Tennyson, Meredith and Hardy among his reading. According to Bernard Aspinwall, Patrick MacGill, 'the first self-conscious, Catholic, working-class writer', read no Irish writers at all. ('Patrick MacGill, 1890–1963: an Alternative Vision', *Studies in Church History*, 28, p. 499.)
40. See Shaw, *John Bull's Other Island*, London: Constable, 1907, p. vii.
41. Ibid., Act III; in his interesting discussion of the play in 'Myth and Motherland' (in *Ireland's Field Day*, pp. 61–82), Richard Kearney puzzlingly leaves Keegan out. See Robertson Smith's *Religion of the Semites* (1889) and J. G. Frazer's *Golden Bough* (1890); and see Stuart Hughes, *Consciousness and Society*, 1958, London: Paladin, 1974, pp. 33–67.
42. J. L. Hammond, *Gladstone and the Irish Nation*, London: Longmans, 1938, pp. 523–52.
43. Edwards, 'Irish Nationalism', p. 123; and see the quote from Pearse's Bodenstown speech, starting with a quote from Ruskin, and climaxing with fire imagery which might be from the end of Carlyle's *The French Revolution*, in Deane, *Celtic Revivals*, p. 72. See also Priscilla Metscher, 'Patrick Pearse and the Irish Cultural Revolution: the Significance of Pearse as an Irish Educator', in Heinz Kosok (ed.), *Studies in Anglo-Irish Literature*, Bonn: Bouvier, 1982, pp. 137–46.
44. Thomas Hardy, *Tess of the D'Urbervilles*, London: Osgood; McIlvaine,1891, pp. 67–8, and see Francis Klingender, *Art and the Industrial Revolution* (1948).
45. Thomas Carlyle, *Chartism*, London: Chapman and Hall, pp. 27–33.
46. See Robert Tressell's *The Ragged Trousered Philanthropists* (1911) and Patrick McGill's *Children of the Dead End* (1919) and Bernard Aspinwall, 'Patrick MacGill, 1890–1963: An Alternative Vision', *Studies in Church History*, 28: The Church and the Arts.
47. Carlyle, *Chartism*, p. 22.
48. Edwards, 'Irish Nationalism', p. 123.
49. Bernard Aspinwall, 'David Urquhart, Robert Monteith and the Catholic Church: A Search for Justice and Peace', *The Innes Review* (1982), p. 72.
50. Oliver MacDonagh in Vaughan (ed.), *New History of Ireland*, pp. 237ff.
51. Ralph Jessop, in *Carlyle and Scottish Thought*, London: Macmillan, 1997, stresses Carlyle's debt to Reid and the common-sense school but does not mention the connection with Ferguson. Fania Oz-Salzberger, *Translating the Enlightenment*, Oxford: Oxford University Press, 1995, shows the influence of Ferguson on German thought, which would return via Carlyle to Thomas Davis. See Eileen Sullivan, *Thomas Davis*, Lewisburg: Bucknell University Press, 1974, p. 49.
52. Thomas Carlyle, *The French Revolution*, 1837, London: Chapman and Hall, 1895, Part III, Book VII, Chapter VIII, 'Finis'. The key Saint-Simonian work was his *Nouveau Christianisme* of 1825.
53. G. K. Peatling, 'Who fears to speak of politics?: John Kells Ingram and hypothetical nationalism', *Irish Historical Studies*, xxxi (November 1998), pp. 202–21; and see T. R. Wright, *The Religion of Humanity: the Impact of Comteian Positivism on Victorian Britain*, Cambridge, 1886.

54. See Hill Shine, *Carlyle and the Saint-Simonians: the Concept of Historical Periodicity*, 1941, New York: Octagon Books, 1981.

55. Walt Whitman, *Democratic Vistas*, 1871, London: Nonesuch, 1938, pp. 708–9; for the Irish Whitmanites see Thomas Flanagan, 'Literature in English' in Vaughan (ed.), *New History of Ireland*, p. 484.

56. Thomas Babington Macaulay, 'Introduction' to *Lays of Ancient Rome*, 1842, Leipzig: Tauchnitz, 1851, p. 8.

57. Sullivan, *Thomas Davis*, pp. 51ff.

58. For Bonar Law see Robert Blake, *The Unknown Prime Minister*, London: Eyre and Spottiswoode, 1955, chapter 1; and for Kipling see Charles Carrington, *Rudyard Kipling*, 1955, Harmondsworth: Penguin, 1970, pp. 69, 74.

59. See Asa Briggs, 'Samuel Smiles and the Gospel of Work', in *Victorian People*, 1955, Harmondsworth: Pelican, 1965, pp. 124–57.

60. Hugh Cunningham, *The Volunteer Movement, 1859–1908*, London: Croom Helm, 1975, pp. 81–2.

61. Jonathan Bardon, *A History of Ulster*, Belfast: Blackstaff Press, 1992, pp. 345–7.

62. Martin Wiener, *Culture and the Decline of the Industrial Spirit*, Cambridge: Cambridge University Press, 1981, p. 38.

63. Cited by Tom Johnston in *Our Scots Noble Families*, Glasgow: Forward Publishing, 1909.

64. John O'Leary, *Recollections of Fenians and Fenianism*, 1896, Shannon: Irish University Press, 1969, p. 47.

65. Newman to Mrs J. Mozley, 25 February 1840, in *Letters and Correspondence*, London: Longmans, 1891, p. 299.

66. Sir Charles Gavan Duffy, *My Life in Two Hemispheres*, 1898, Shannon: Irish University Press, 1969, pp. 9, 52.

67. See Terence Brown, 'Canon Sheehan and the Catholic Intellectual', in *Ireland's Literature*, Mullingar: Lilliput Press, 1988, pp. 65–74; quote from Donn Byrne, *I Remember Maynooth*, London: Longmans Green, 1937, pp. 28–9.

68. Carlyle, *French Revolution*, p. 62

69. Ibid., p. 368.

70. Carlyle, *Past and Present*, p. 132.

71. Ibid., p. 133.

72. Ibid., p. 134.

73. Carlyle, *Chartism*, p. 33.

74. See Morse Peckham, 'Frederick the Great', in K. J. Fielding and Rodger L. Tarr, *Carlyle Past and Present*, London: Vision, 1976, pp. 198–215.

75. Desmond Bowen, *Paul Cardinal Cullen and the Shaping of Modern Irish Catholicism*, Dublin: Gill and Macmillan, 1983, pp. 204–10. For overseas activity see Kenneth Scott Latourette, *Christianity in a Revolutionary Age*, III: *The Nineteenth Century Outside Europe*, London: Eyre and Spottiswoode, 1961, p. 58.

76. J. A. Froude, 'Romanism and the Irish Race in the United States', in *The North American Review*, 129, 1879, cited by Owen Dudley Edwards in 'The Irish Priest in North America', in W. J. Sheils and Diana Wood (eds), *The Churches, Ireland and the Irish*, Ecclesiastical History Society and Blackwell, 1989, pp. 311–24.

77. J. J. Lee, *The Modernisation of Irish Society*, Dublin: Gill and Macmillan, 1973, pp. 42ff.

78. Lee, *Modernisation*, p. 47.

79. Ibid., p. 45.

80. Gilley, 'Edward Irving', p. 241.

81. Lee, *Modernisation*, p. 45.

82. John Stuart Mill, *Principles of Political Economy*, London: Longmans, 1992, chapter VII; Melvin Richter, *The Politics of Conscience: T. H. Green and his Age*, London: Weidenfeld and Nicholson, 1964, chapter 4.

83. Harvie, *The Lights of Liberalism: University Liberals and the Challenge of Democracy*, London: Allen Lane, pp. 235ff.

84. Devine, *Scottish Nation*, p. 496.

85. For example, by W. R. Greg in *Literary and Social Judgements*, London: Trübner, 1877, I, pp. 143–83.

86. Carlyle, *Past and Present*, p. 144. This incident was taken from Dr W. P. Alison's *Observations of the Management of the Poor in Scotland* (Edinburgh: Blackwood, 1840).

87. See Bonnie S. Anderson and Judith P. Zinsser, *A History of their Own*, 1988, Harmondsworth: Penguin, 1990, II, pp. 167–96.
88. As far as I can see, there is not a single reference to an Irishwoman, of any religion or none, in the index of Anderson and Zinsser.
89. See Fred Kaplan, *Thomas Carlyle*, Cambridge, Cambridge University Press, 1979, p. 322–3.
90. Carlyle, *French Revolution*, I, p. 27.
91. Ibid., p. 46.
92. See Catriona Clear, *Nuns in Nineteenth-Century Ireland*, Dublin: 1987.
93. Mary Glum, *Life and the Dream*, 1947, cited in Mary Luddy (ed.), *Women in Ireland, 1800–1818: a Documentary History*, Cork: Cork University Press, 1995, p. 116.
94. J. J. Lee, 'Women and the Church since the Famine', in Mary MacCurtain and Donncha Ó Corrain (eds), *Women in Irish Society*, 1978, Dublin: Arlen House/Women's Press, 1984, pp. 37–45.
95. Susan O'Brien, 'Lay Sisters and Good Mothers: Working-Class Women in English Convents, 1840–1910', in Sheils and Wood, *Church*, p. 460.
96. See Gemma Hussey, *Ireland Today: Anatomy of a Changing State*, 1993, Harmondsworth: Penguin, 1995, chapter 18.
97. Ó Gráda, *New Economic History*, p. 255.
98. Antonio Gramsci, 'The Intellectuals', in *Prison Notebooks*, trans. Quintin Hoare and Geoffrey Nowell-Smith, London: Lawrence and Wishart, 1971, pp. 18–20.
99. Ó Gráda, p. 255; *New Economic History*, Shaw, *John Bull*, Act. III.
100. Liam O'Dowd, 'Intellectuals and Irish Nationalism', in Graham Day and Gareth Rees (eds), *Regions, Nations and European Integration: Remaking the Celtic Periphery*, Cardiff: University of Wales Press, 1991, p. 127; Boyce, 'Culture and Counter-Revolution', in *Revolution*, p. 118, and J. J. Lee, *Ireland, 1912–1985*, Cambridge: Cambridge University Press, 1989, p. 159; and see Terence Brown, *Ireland: A Social and Cultural History, 1922–79*, London: Fontana, 1981, chapters 1 and 2.
101. Patrick Colum, *Arthur Griffith*, Dublin: Browne and Nolan, 1959, pp. 87ff.; Shaw, *John Bull*, 'Preface of 1929'.
102. Lee, *Ireland*, chapter 8.
103. Brown, pp. 213–4.
104. See Ian S. Wood, *John Wheatley*, Manchester: Manchester University Press, 1990, and Alan Sillitoe's introduction to the Panther edition of Tressell's book, 1965, p. 7.

NOTES TO CHAPTER 8: REMEMBERING AND FORGETTING

1. See C. Blondel, *La Presse Nationale Française et le bicentenaire de la Révolution à travers une étude de trois journaux: le Figaro, le Monde, et l'Humanité*, IEP Paris DEA, 1992.
2. Michel Vovelle (ed.), *L'Image de la Révolution française: communications présentées lors du Congrès mondial pour le bicentenaire de la Révolution Française*, Sorbonne 6–12 July 1989, 4 vols., Paris: Pergamon Press, 1990.
3. Antoine de Baecque, *Recherches sur la Révolution: un bilan des travaux scientifiques du Bicentenaire*, Paris: La Découverte – Institut d'Histoire de la Révolution française, 1991.
4. Mission du Bicentenaire de la Révolution française et de la Déclaration des droits de l'homme et du citoyen: *Un Evénement intellectuel, le bicentenaire et la Révolution française: dossier*, Paris: Mission, 1989.
5. Mission du Bicentenaire, *Le Bicentenaire de la Révolution: Rapport au Président de la République*, 5 March 1990.
6. Pierre Chaunu, *Le Grand déclassement: à propos d'une commémoration*, Paris: Laffont, 1989.
7. See, for example: M. Rouche, *Clovis*, Paris: Fayard, 1996; M. Mussot-Goulard, *Le Baptême qui a fait la France: de Blandine à Clovis*, Paris: Perrin, 1996; Georges Tessier, *Le Baptême de Clovis, 25 décembre 496?*, Paris: Gallimard, 1996.
8. Laurent Theis, *Clovis: de l'histoire au mythe*, Bruxelles: Editions Complexe, 1996.
9. Pierre Chaunu, E. Mension-Rigou, *Baptême de Clovis, baptême de la France. De la religion d'Etat à la laïcité d'Etat*, Paris: Balland, 1996.
10. Paul-Marie Coûteaux, *Clovis, une histoire de France: Cinq leçons de politique française*, Paris: Lattès, 1996.
11. Claude Lévi-Strauss, *La pensée sauvage*, Paris: Agora Pocket, 1990, p. 313, *passim*.

12. Pierre Bergé, *L'Affaire Clovis*, Paris: Plon, 1996, pp. 33–47.
13. Chaunu, *Le Grand déclassement*, p. 00.
14. R. L. Kaplan, *Farewell Revolution. Disputed Legacies, France, 1789–1989*, Ithaca: Cornell University Press, 1995, p. 10.
15. A. Grosser in *Le Monde*, 18–19 December 1989.
16. *Le Monde*, 13 July 1989.
17. *Le Débat*, November–December 1989, pp. 63–4.
18. M. L. Netter, *La Révolution n'est pas terminée*, Paris: Presses Universitaires Françaises, 1989.
19. *Le Monde*, 8 July 1989.
20. B. Ginisty, *Témoignage Chrétien*, 13 September 1996.
21. *Le Monde*, 14 April 1989.

NOTES TO CHAPTER 9: CENTRALISATION OF MEMORY

1. William Aiton, *A History of the Rencounter at Drumlog and Battle at Bothwell Bridge ... and Reflections on Political Subjects*, Hamilton: W. P. Borthwick & Co., 1821, pp. 7–8; 98–131.
2. Thorbjoern Campbell, *Standing Witnesses*, Edinburgh: Saltire Society, 1996, p. 40.
3. Ibid., p. 88.
4. See Peter Berresford Ellis and Seumas Mac a' Ghobhainn, *The Scottish Insurrection of 1820*, London: Pluto Press, 1989.
5. Campbell, *Standing Witnesses*, p. 104.
6. Ibid., p.96.

NOTES TO CHAPTER 10: A QUESTION OF COVENANTS

1. Patrick Kavanagh, *Selected Poems*, ed. Antoinette Quinn, London: Penguin, 1996, p. 6.
2. Edna Longley, *Poetry in the Wars*, Newcastle-upon-Tyne: Bloodaxe, 1986.
3. Gerald Dawe, *The Lundys Letter*, Oldcastle: Gallery Press, 1985.
4. Gerald Dawe, *Sheltering Places*, Belfast: Blackstaff Press, 1978.
5. Dawe, *Lundys Letter*, p. 10.
6. A. T. Q. Stewart, *The Ulster Crisis: Resistance to Home Rule 1912–1914*, London: Faber and Faber, 1979.
7. Ibid., p. 61.
8. Ibid., p. 66.
9. Dawe, *Lundys Letter*, p. 13.
10. Stewart, *Ulster Crisis*, p. 62.
11. Thom Gunn, 'Introduction', *Ben Jonson*, Harmondsworth: Penguin, 1974, reprinted in Thom Gunn, *The Occasions of Poetry: Essays in Criticism and Autobiography*, London, Faber and Faber, 1982, pp. 106–7.
12. Gerald Dawe, *The Morning Train*, Oldcastle: Gallery Press, 1999.

NOTES TO CHAPTER 11: SEAN O'CASEY: HISTORY INTO DRAMA

1. Joep Leerssen, *Remembrance and Imagination*, Cork: Cork University Press/Field Day, 1996, p. 11.
2. See Robert G. Lowery (ed.), *A Whirlwind in Dublin: 'The Plough and the Stars' Riots*, Westport, CT: Greenwood Press, 1984.
3. *The Letters of Sean O'Casey, 1959–1964*, IV, ed. David Krause, Washington, DC: Catholic University of America Press, 1992, p. 234.
4. Sean O'Casey, *I Knock at the Door*, London: Pan Books, 1971, p. 87. Subsequent references will be given in the text in parentheses.
5. *Feathers from the Green Crow: Sean O'Casey, 1905–1925*, ed. Robert Hogan, Columbia: University of Missouri Press, 1962, p. 20.
6. C. Desmond Greaves, 'Seán O'Casey and Socialism', *The O'Casey Enigma*, ed. Micheál Ó hAodha, Dublin and Cork: Mercier Press, 1980, p. 65.
7. R. F. Foster, *Modern Ireland 1600–1972*, Harmondsworth: Penguin/Allen Lane, 1988, p. 489.

8. See Ronald Ayling and Michael J. Durkan, *Sean O'Casey: A Bibliography*, London and Basingstoke: Macmillan, 1978, p. 5. *The Sacrifice* was a revised edition of *The Story of Thomas Ashe*, published November 1917. See Ayling and Durkan, pp.7–8.

9. A letter, which is in effect an obituary notice, to *Dublin Saturday Post*, 6 October 1917, in *The Letters of Sean O'Casey 1910–1941*, I, ed. David Krause, London: Cassell, 1975, p. 64.

10. W. B. Yeats, *Essays and Introductions*, London: Macmillan, 1961, p. 319.

11. S. H. Butcher, *Aristotle's Theory of Poetry and Fine Art*, 4th edn, New York: Dover Publications, 1951, IX.3, p. 35.

12. Sean O'Casey, *Collected Plays*, I, London: Macmillan; New York: St Martin's Press, 1963, p.113.

13. Ibid., p. 25.

14. Ibid., pp. 37–8.

15. Ibid., p. 38.

16. Leerssen, *Remembrance and Imagination*, pp. 151–2.

17. A. M. Sullivan, *The Story of Ireland; Or, A Narrative of Irish History, from the Earliest Ages to the Present Time*, Dublin: M. H. Gill, 1909, p. 519.

18. Krause, *The Letters of Sean O'Casey*, I, p. 178.

19. Ibid., pp. 170–1.

20. Ibid., p. 172.

21. Sean O'Casey, *Inishfallen, Fare Thee Well*, London: Pan Books, 1972, p. 169.

22. O'Casey, *Collected Plays*, I, p. 181.

23. Krause, *The Letters of Sean O'Casey*, I, p. 169.

24. Ibid., p.171.

25. O'Casey, *The Collected Plays*, I, p. 221.

26. *Joseph Holloway's Abbey Theatre: A Selection from his Unpublished Journal Impressions of a Dublin Playgoer*, eds Robert Hogan and Michael J. O'Neill, Carbondale and Edwardsville: Southern Illinois University Press, 1967, p. 266.

27. Máire Nic Shiubhlaigh, *The Splendid Years*, Dublin: James Duffy, 1955, p. 19.

28. *The Variorum Edition of the Plays of W. B. Yeats*, ed. Russell K. Alpach, London and Basingstoke: Macmillan, 1966, p. 229.

29. O'Casey, *Inishfallen, Fare Thee Well*, p. 176.

30. Hugh Hunt, *The Abbey: Ireland's National Theatre 1904–1979*, Dublin: Gill and Macmillan, 1979, p. 146.

31. Sean O'Casey, *Collected Plays*, 2, London: Macmillan, 1949, p. 239.

32. Ibid., p.240.

33. O'Casey, *Inishfallen, Fare Thee Well*, pp. 162–3.

34. *The Letters of Sean O'Casey*, I, p. 637.

35. Sean O'Casey, *Three More Plays*, London and Basingstoke: Macmillan, 1965, p. 310. Note that this text of *Red Roses for Me* is O'Casey's final, approved version. See Ayling and Durkan, *Sean O'Casey*, p. 134.

36. *The Letters of Sean O'Casey*, I, p. 639.

37. Sean O'Casey, *The Drums of Father Ned: A Microcosm of Ireland*, London: Macmillan, 1960, p. 19. Subsequent references will be give in the text in parentheses.

38. Robert Hogan calls this play-within-the-play an 'extended parody ... of a patriotic melodrama à la Boucicault – or, more properly, à la J. W. Whitbread, Ira Allen or P. J. Bourke, *Since O'Casey and Other Essays in Irish Drama*, Gerrards Cross: Colin Smythe; Totowa, NJ: Barnes and Noble, 1983, p. 166, 4n.

39. O'Casey, *I Knock at the Door*, p. 34.

NOTES TO CHAPTER 12: TELLING THE TIME

1. Derek Mahon, *Selected Poems*, London: Penguin, 1993, p. 164.

2. Seamus Heaney, *Preoccupations*, London: Faber, 1980, p. 56.

3. Brian Friel, *Selected Plays*, London: Faber, 1984, p. 418.

4. Thomas Kilroy, 'Theatrical Text and Literary Text', in Alan J. Peacock (ed.), *The Achievement of Brian Friel*, Gerrards Cross: Colin Smythe, 1992, p. 91.

5. Friel, *Selected Plays*, p. 419.

6. Helen Lojek, 'Myth and Bonding in Frank McGuinness's *Observe the Sons of Ulster Marching*

Towards the Somme', *Canadian Journal of Irish Studies*, XIV (1988), pp. 45–53.

7. Frank McGuinness, *Plays*, London: Faber, 1996, p. 97. Henceforth all page numbers will refer to this edition and will be cited within the text.
8. Brian Friel, *Making History*, London: Faber, 1989, p. 9.
9. Seamus Heaney, 'Orange Drums, Tyrone, 1966', *North*, p. 62.
10. O'Toole, 'Island of Saints and Silicon', Michael Kenneally (ed.), *Cultural Contexts and Literary Idioms in Contemporary Irish Culture*, Gerrards Cross, Colin Smythe, 1988, p. 20.
11. Edna Longley, *The Living Stream*, Belfast: Bloodaxe Books, 1994, p. 183.
12. Helene Cixous, 'The Laugh of the Medusa', in P. Bizell and B. Herzberg (eds), *The Rhetorical Tradition*, Boston: Bedford, 1990, p. 1237.
13. James Young, *The Art of Memory: Holocaust Memorials in History*, New York: Thames & Hudson, 1994.
14. Brian Friel, *Selected Plays*, London: Faber, 1994, p. 446.
15. Richard Kearney, *The Irish Mind: Exploring Intellectual Traditions*, Dublin: Wolfhound Press, 1985, p. 9.

Notes on Contributors

Malcolm Anderson	Emeritus Professor of Politics, University of Edinburgh
Paul Arthur	Professor of Politics, University of Ulster, Jordanstown
Neal Ascherson	Journalist and author; columnist with the *Independent on Sunday*, London (1990–98)
Eberhard Bort	Academic Co-ordinator of The Institute of Governance and Lecturer in Politics, University of Edinburgh
Ray Burnett	Dicúil Foundation, Benbecula
Tony Canavan	Editorial Board, *History Ireland*, Dublin
Peter Collins	Lecturer in History, The University of Ulster; *Cultural Traditions Group*, Belfast
Mary Daly	Professor of Modern Irish History, University College, Dublin
Gerald Dawe	Poet and Professor of English Literature, Trinity College, Dublin
Owen Dudley Edwards	Reader in History, University of Edinburgh
Christopher Harvie	Professor of British and Irish Studies, University of Tübingen, Germany
Aideen Howard	Dramaturg, The National Theatre Society of Ireland (Abbey and Peacock Theatres)
Daniel Mulhall	Irish Consul General, Edinburgh (1998–2002); since 2002 Irish Ambassador in Kuala Lumpur
Christopher Murray	Professor of Anglo-Irish Literature, University College, Dublin

Index

Cardiovascular Molecular Morphogenesis

Books in the Series